THE FORM OF LEGISLATION AND THE RULE OF LAW

What does the rule of law mean, in practical terms, for the way that legislation is prepared, drafted and presented? It is a cornerstone of the UK legal order and requires certain things from the legal system, such as that the law must be intelligible, predictable and accessible. This book examines what those requirements mean for the form that legislation must take.

Using the rule of law as the starting point, the author uses deductive reasoning to determine what flows from this in terms of the form of legislation. Each element of the rule of law is analysed to establish principles about the form that legislation ought to take, and the book examines how each principle can be given concrete effect.

The originality lies in the nexus between the rule of law and the form of legislation. Much has been written about the nature and content of the rule of law, but relatively little has been devoted to legisprudence, the theory and practice of legislation. This book now draws these two subjects together in a detailed and innovative way.

The Form of Legislation and the Rule of Law

Ronan Cormacain

•HART•
OXFORD • LONDON • NEW YORK • NEW DELHI • SYDNEY

HART PUBLISHING

Bloomsbury Publishing Plc

Kemp House, Chawley Park, Cumnor Hill, Oxford, OX2 9PH, UK

1385 Broadway, New York, NY 10018, USA

29 Earlsfort Terrace, Dublin 2, Ireland

First published in Great Britain 2022

A catalogue record for this book is available from the British Library.

A catalogue record for this book is available from the Library of Congress.

Library of Congress Control Number: 2022948378

ISBN: HB: 978-1-50993-805-6
ePDF: 978-1-50993-807-0
ePub: 978-1-50993-806-3

Typeset by Compuscript Ltd, Shannon

Le grá chuig Pól Ó Cormacáin agus Máire Uí Cormacáin

FOREWORD

'Why is legislation so hard to understand? Why is it so complex? And why on earth is there so much of it?' The first lines of Dr Ronan Cormacain's book are as intriguing as the rest of his analysis.

Dr Cormacain places the Rule of Law at the core of his analysis on legislative quality. This has not been done before, at least not systematically. The Rule of Law is at the heart of scrutiny and debate as to the substantive content of the legislation. But not as to its form. And here lies the originality and brilliance of the concept.

The book links drafting techniques to the Rule of Law, and harvests those traditional and modern drafting conventions that derive from and nurture that link. This is an expert way of distinguishing which techniques must be used as a sine qua non of legislative quality. They can and must form the heart of legislative drafting conventions within the UK and beyond.

Methodologically the analysis is sound, and well evidenced. The relevant elements of the rule of law addressed in the book are accessibility of legislation; prospectivity of legislation; predictability of legislation; intelligibility of legislation; constraints on discretion in legislation; and equality before the law in legislation.

The book concludes that the rule of law requires the following clusters of legislative principles:

- availability; navigability; and inclusivity;
- Janus-faced legislation taxonomy and time period to which law applies; effective use of transitional and savings provisions; and use of substantive criteria to justify Janus-faced legislation;
- determinacy; stability; clear commencement; consistency; application in the real world; and implementability;
- focus on characteristics of the user; intelligibility of legislation as amended, and amending legislation; avoiding/dealing with excessive interconnectedness; use of examples; 'Good writing' techniques; 'Plain language' techniques; and easification;
- clear demarcation between law and discretion; different dimensions in which discretion can be constrained; rejecting ouster clauses; curtailing the power to create exemptions from law; use of purpose clauses; rejecting super-enabling clauses; curtailing framework legislation; and rejecting Henry VIII clauses;

- gender neutral and gender silent drafting; gender and equality impact assessments; removing special exemptions and procedures for the Crown; treating armed forces in the same way as other citizens; and vindicability.

Conclusions are dense. And so is the analysis and the bibliography.

So this is not an easy book. It is a book worth reading, again and again, until all its nooks and crannies are understood and analysed. It is of interest to public law academics and practitioners, to users of legislation and to all those who have the misfortune of working with legislation drafted without the benefit of Dr Cormacain's recommendations.

Professor Helen Xanthaki
June 2022

ACKNOWLEDGEMENTS

It would have been impossible for me to complete this book without support, encouragement and assistance from many people, some of whom I would like to thank here.

The foundations for my interest in legislation were laid by my training as a legislative counsel in the Office of the Legislative Counsel in Northern Ireland. I am indebted to all my former colleagues there, in particular George Gray, Alan Esdale, Brenda King, Sharon Murdock and Kenneth Jones. Their hours of patient training raised me from terrible to below-average as a legislative drafter, although, like Luke Skywalker, I left with my training incomplete. As a pedantic drafter, I am obliged to state that this does not imply that any of them are Darth Vader.

The original inspiration for this book came from Tom Bingham, someone who I never had the pleasure of meeting, but whose wonderful book planted the seed in my mind that grew into the idea that legislation ought to promote the Rule of Law. This idea was nurtured by my PhD supervisors Helen Xanthaki and Constantin Stefanou, to whom I am very grateful.

I would like to thank the many people who have read and offered comments on various drafts of this book. In particular I would like to thank Alan Esdale, Ruth Silverman, Paul Silverman, Aoife Sheehy, Ittai Bar-Siman-Tov, Richard Mckenzie-Gray Scott, Oliver Garner, Katie Lines, Jack Simson Caird, Tom West and Mazhar Ilahi. The usual caveat applies, the mistakes remain entirely my own. Although enforcement procedures will apply if they seek to take credit for any successes. I would also like to thank Kate Whetter and Rosie Mearns at Hart, and apologise for all my missed deadlines.

I am also grateful to my colleagues in the Bingham Centre for the Rule of Law, and especially to Murray Hunt. I have learnt a great deal from them on how best to frame a Rule of Law argument when it comes to seeking to persuade parliamentarians.

At a personal level, I wouldn't be where I am now without the warmth and dedication of my parents. They (very subtly) steered me away from a degree in Byzantine studies and towards law and proudly celebrated every small achievement I managed along the way. Go raibh maith agaibh. Ruth, Naomi and Rosa have put up with me being an absent husband and father, squirreled away in my lonely garret instead of spending time with them. I can only hope that they find more time with me a blessing rather than a chore. Thank you to them.

CONTENTS

1

Introduction

1.1. The Problem with Legislation

Why is legislation so hard to understand? Why is it so complex? And why on earth is there so much of it?

These are the questions any sensible non-lawyer would pose upon being faced by the UK statute book. In fact, it isn't just non-lawyers who scratch their heads at these questions; plenty of lawyers, even those involved in the legislative process, would likewise be puzzled. Even legislators, those who actually vote on and enact this legislation, would struggle to both answer the questions, and to come up with solutions to the problems implicit within them. Many years ago, as a consultant legislative drafter, I drafted a long and detailed piece of legislation for a particular jurisdiction. I prided myself on a job well done in achieving the complex policy aims and delivering a well-crafted and legally accurate statute. After delivering a barn-storming exposition of it to the legislators who were to enact it, the chair of the committee thanked me. In a voice conveying long-standing low expectations of lawyers and legislation, she remarked 'It sounds great, but I wonder what that all means?'

Quality in legislation is not in the eye of the drafter who prepares it, nor even in the eye of the legislator who enacts it. Beauty is in the eye of the beholder – in the person who will actually be subject to that legislation, who will use it and be bound by it. This book is an attempt to remedy the problem of legislation that is too hard to understand, too complex and too voluminous. For me, the essence of the solution is to be found in the Rule of Law. The Rule of Law is the cornerstone of the UK legal system. Put simply, the Rule of Law means that everyone is subject to the law. Applying Rule of Law principles to legislation will improve that legislation.

1.2. Giving Effect to the Rule of Law in the Form of Legislation

The purpose of this book is to provide a theoretical underpinning of the relationship between the Rule of Law and the form of legislation, and to provide concrete suggestions on how the application of Rule of Law principles can improve the quality of legislation. Or more simply, to explain why legislation is sometimes so hard to figure out, and what can be done to make it better.

The Rule of Law is a cornerstone of the constitutional structure of the UK and states that we are all subject to the law, and that no-one is above the law. The Rule of Law has been developed over the centuries into a set of principles around accessibility, certainty, predictability and many other ideals that ought to form part of our legal system. This book relies upon that analytical work as providing a sound and justified basis for the nature and content of the Rule of Law.

Given that the Rule of Law contains particular principles, how can the form of legislation give effect to them? This book sets out form of legislation principles to give effect to the Rule of Law. The methodology is deductive reasoning – if X is our principle, what flows from X in terms of how we construct a piece of law? Many of these concrete suggestions will be familiar to those who have delved into the minutiae of legisprudence in the past. For instance, the need for intelligibility and clarity in legislation are common tropes for those who have studied that field. What is hopefully new is that, first, these have a philosophical underpinning rooted in the Rule of Law, second, that they set out a coherent and holistic set of principles for the enactment of legislation, and third that there are also novel principles for improving the quality of law.

The end goal of this book is legislation that is better quality, easier to understand and that vindicates the values of the Rule of Law. Although there may be quibbles around the precise content of the Rule of Law, there is unanimous support for it from all political parties and all those involved in the legislative process in the UK. Our statute book expressly proclaims the importance of the Rule of Law.[1]

It is not just the UK, but the international community, by means of international treaties and declarations, that has highlighted the importance of the Rule of Law.[2] The General Assembly of the United Nations has affirmed the importance of the Rule of Law a number of times[3] as has the Secretary General.[4] One of the Millennium Development Goals is to 'strengthen respect for the rule of law in international as in national affairs'.[5] The Organisation for Security and Co-operation in Europe (OSCE) in its 1990 Copenhagen Document welcomed the commitment of all participating states to build democratic societies based upon the rule of law.[6] The Organisation for Economic Co-operation and Development (OECD) has attempted to define it.[7] Given this support, it is hard to argue that the form of legislation should not reflect Rule of Law values.

[1] Part 1, Constitutional Reform Act 2005.

[2] See Universal Declaration of Human Rights 1948, European Convention on Human Rights, Statute of the Council of Europe, Consolidated Version of the Treaty of the European Union, which all mention the Rule of Law.

[3] A/RES/61/39, A/RES/62/70, A/RES/63/128.

[4] A/61/636.

[5] A/RES/55/2, Para 9.

[6] Preamble to Copenhagen Document (1990), OSCE.

[7] Equal Access to Justice and the Rule of Law, OECD Development Assistance Committee (DAC) Mainstreaming Conflict Prevention (2005).

This book is the first systematic attempt to link the form of legislation with the Rule of Law. Much has been written about the Rule of Law already. I do not attempt to offer a fresh definition of the Rule of Law or justify its existence. Instead, I accept that there is such a thing as the Rule of Law and that it is a good thing. By comparison, not much has been written about the form of legislation, and in particular, on the drafting and enactment of legislation. The focus in the literature is on the nature of legislative drafting and the meaning of quality legislation. Although it is possible to find statements that the form of legislation must be in accordance with the Rule of Law, there has been no systematic effort to delve deeper. I do something different by focusing on the nexus of the form of legislation and the Rule of Law.

1.3. Methodology

The methodology of this book is straightforward. In each chapter, I examine an element of the commonly held and agreed upon components of the Rule of Law. This is done in Part 1 of each chapter, where a Rule of Law element is my starting premise. From each element I derive principles that give effect to it. This is done in Part 2 of each Chapter.

With such compendious amount of writing on the Rule of Law, it has been necessary to make some subjective decisions on what to accept as the content of the Rule of Law. There is a remarkable degree of overlap between key writers such as Tom Bingham, Lon Fuller and Joseph Raz on the content of the Rule of Law. Rather than engage in a fruitless debate on which is the 'best' definition, I simply say that I prefer Bingham's approach. Therefore, I adopt Bingham's definition as the framework upon which to hang my analysis.[8] However, in each chapter I supplement his analysis with that of other key writers in order demonstrate a universally accepted criteria for the content of the Rule of Law.

This book is about the form of legislation, not its content. It is about the structure, the process, the procedure for making law, not about the eventual substance of that legislation. Although there is an element of fuzziness in the line separating form and content, the focus is not on *what* we put into the legislation, but *how* we put it into the legislation. It is not the policy of the legislation, but how we express that policy in the legislation.

1.3.1. Elements of the Rule of Law that Relate More to the Form of Legislation

My focus has been only on those elements of the Rule of Law that have a bearing upon the form of legislation. I fully accept that the elements I have chosen may

[8] T Bingham, *The Rule of Law* (London, Penguin UK, 2011).

sometimes stray into content not form of law, and equally that some elements I have not chosen may sometimes relate to form and not content. However, I have had to draw the line somewhere, and the elements chosen for analysis tend much more towards form than substance of legislation.

The elements of the Rule of Law which I have chosen are:

- Accessibility of legislation (chapter two)
- Prospectivity of legislation (chapter three)
- Predictability of legislation (chapter four)
- Intelligibility of legislation (chapter five)
- Constraints on discretion in legislation (chapter six)
- Equality before the law in legislation (chapter seven)

1.3.2. The Principles for Enacting Legislation in Accordance with the Rule of Law

For readers who want the answer in advance, I set out below the summary findings of the principles that ought to be followed in order for the form of legislation to give effect to the Rule of Law. Each of these principles are explained in the corresponding chapters:

- Availability (chapter two)
- Navigability (chapter two)
- Inclusivity (chapter two)
- Janus-faced legislation taxonomy and time period to which law applies (chapter three)
- Effective use of transitional and savings provisions (chapter three)
- Use of substantive criteria to justify Janus-faced legislation (chapter three)
- Determinacy (chapter four)
- Stability (chapter four)
- Clear commencement (chapter four)
- Consistency (chapter four)
- Application in the real world (chapter four)
- Implementability (chapter four)
- Focus on characteristics of the user (chapter five)
- Intelligibility of legislation as amended, and amending legislation (chapter five)
- Avoiding/dealing with excessive interconnectedness (chapter five)
- Use of examples (chapter five)

- 'Good writing' techniques (chapter five)
- 'Plain language' techniques (chapter five)
- Easification (chapter five)
- Clear demarcation between law and discretion (chapter six)
- Different dimensions in which discretion can be constrained (chapter six)
- Rejecting ouster clauses (chapter six)
- Curtailing the power to create exemptions from law (chapter six)
- Use of purpose clauses (chapter six)
- Rejecting super-enabling clauses (chapter six)
- Curtailing framework legislation (chapter six)
- Rejecting Henry VIII clauses (chapter six)
- Gender neutral and gender silent drafting (chapter seven)
- Gender and Equality Impact Assessments (chapter seven)
- Removing special exemptions and procedures for the Crown (chapter seven)
- Treating armed forces in the same way as other citizens (chapter seven)
- Vindicability (chapter seven)

1.4. The Rule of Law

This section explains and expands upon the Rule of Law by reference to the established corpus of knowledge on the subject. For readers who are already familiar with the content of the Rule of Law, feel free to skip this section.

In my view, there is a duality to the Rule of Law.[9] At one level, the Rule of Law is the basic principle that we are all subject to the law. At another level, the Rule of Law comprises the ideal of the values that a legal system ought to possess.

1.4.1. Rule of Law as a Principle

At its very simplest, the Rule of Law is the principle that everyone, both state and citizen, is bound by the law. I can only but agree with the definition given by Tom Bingham:

> All persons and authorities within the state, whether public or private, should be bound by and entitled to the benefit of laws publicly made, taking effect (generally) in the future and publicly administered in the courts.[10]

[9] See further R Cormacain, 'Legislation, Legislative Drafting and the Rule of Law' (2017) 5 *The Theory and Practice of Legislation* 115.

[10] Bingham (n 8) 8.

This section comprises a whistle-stop tour of the main Rule of Law theorists. It expands upon this basic definition, and shows how it has been developed and justified.

Turning first to the Government, the Government makes the rules and is expected to follow the rules. The state is not itself above the law. Bingham describes this as the 'duty to govern in accordance with law'.[11] This means for example that the executive doesn't have an untrammelled power to lock people up,[12] and that police do not have a right to enter property without express authorisation by statute.[13] As the Supreme Court reiterated, 'If the Rule of Law is to mean anything, decisions as to what is necessary or expedient in this context cannot be left to the uncontrolled judgment of the executive'.[14] More prosaically, if the government has made lockdown rules on coronavirus, government advisers cannot simply ignore those lockdown rules.[15]

Turning second to the citizen, the basic principle includes an obligation upon the citizen to obey the law. There may be several reasons for this: the law is morally good and ought to be obeyed for this reason, the law is backed up by sanctions and citizens will be penalised if they fail to obey, and pragmatically, society works better if everyone follows the rules. For those of a religious inclination, the Bible advances a further argument for obeying the rules, that they contain sound advice on how best to live your life: 'your statutes are my delight, they are my counsellors'.[16] Much of this Psalm is in praise of laws, a welcome change after having read Shakespeare's encouragement to, first of all, kill all the lawyers.[17]

AV Dicey is usually regarded as the first theorist to coin the phrase 'the Rule of Law' in 1885.[18] For Dicey, the second component of the Rule of Law was that all persons are subject to the ordinary laws and the ordinary courts. Using Bingham's colourful example, if you maltreat a penguin in London Zoo, it doesn't matter if you are the Archbishop of Canterbury, you will still be prosecuted.[19] Dicey also developed the theory of sovereignty of Parliament – the idea that Parliament was the supreme power in the land and could make any law on any subject without any constraint. Although this is a fundamental tenet of English constitutional law, it does not sit well with the Rule of Law notion that there are limits to what legislation can do. If Parliamentary sovereignty means that Parliament can pass any law it wishes then, as

[11] T Bingham, 'The Case of Liversidge v Anderson: The Rule of Law Amid the Clash of Arms' (2009) 43 *The International Lawyer* 33, 38.

[12] *Liversidge v Anderson* [1942] AC 206, although this was the dissenting judgment in this case.

[13] *Morris v Beardmore* [1980] 3 WLR 283.

[14] *Ahmet and others v HM Treasury* [2010] UKSC 2 at para 45.

[15] UKCLA, 'R Cormacain: Instinct or Rules: Making Moral Decisions in the Cummings Scandal' (*UK Constitutional Law Association*, 28 May 2020) <https://ukconstitutionallaw.org/2020/05/28/ronan-cormacain-instinct-or-rules-making-moral-decisions-in-the-cummings-scandal/>.

[16] Psalm 119, Verse 24. Most of Psalm 119 is a paean to statutes, uplifting reading for depressed drafters!

[17] Shakespeare, Henry VI.

[18] AV Dicey, *An Introduction to the Study of the Law of the Constitution* (1885).

[19] Bingham (n 8) 4.

Lane asks, 'if the Rule of Law is the foundation of the State, then how can Parliament claim a power not bound by any legal restrictions'?[20] It is my argument that sovereignty of Parliament should be seen as co-equal with the Rule of Law, meaning that they ought to balance each other out, not that one should trump the other.[21]

Theories of the Rule of Law were further developed by Hayek, who saw laws as pieces of functional or instrumental machinery that give certainty and stability rather than directing individuals towards a particular course of action.[22] For Cass, the core concept of the Rule of Law is a government of laws.[23] Joseph Raz argues simply that people should be ruled by the law and obey it.[24] Jeremy Waldron argues that the Rule of Law means that law stands above every other authority in the land.[25] It can be said that, at the level of the basic principle, every major theorist is in agreement, the Rule of Law means that everyone is bound by the law.

This may have been sufficient at one point in time, or where there are checks and balances built into constitutions. Magna Carta, the 1215 motherlode of our notions of the Rule of Law, states that no-one could be imprisoned, save by the law of the land.[26] The law (or legislation) was the bulwark against the seizure of liberty. The King couldn't simply arrest whoever he wanted, it had to be first authorised by law. In modern constitutional theory, this translates into the Executive being constrained by the Legislature, which must first pass the law authorising the Executive, that law being enforced through, and interpreted by, the Courts. But what happens when the legislature and the executive start to merge (as they do in the UK)? Then one isn't constraining the other.

In my view, there is an unanswerable case that the Rule of Law, at its core, means that we are all subject to the law, and that no-one is above the law. There is a huge weight of authority behind this proposition and there has been no realistic attempt to argue against it. If the Rule of Law is limited to the principle that everyone is subject to the law, then it is impossible for legislation to be against the Rule of Law, because if the legislation authorised it, then it is done in accordance with the law. Therefore, there must be more to the Rule of Law than the basic principle that everyone is subject to the law. If this singular principle is all that it amounts to, then it doesn't really do very much, and is undeserving of its central status in our legal systems. The question is then, what other values are contained within the Rule of Law?

[20] JE Lane, *Constitutions and Political Theory* (Manchester, Manchester University Press, 1996) 44.

[21] R Cormacain, 'Blue-Eyed Babies, Amnesties, Sovereignty of Parliament and the Rule of Law: The Northern Ireland Legacy Proposals' (*UK Constitutional Law Association*, 25 November 2021) <https://ukconstitutionallaw.org/>.

[22] F Hayek, *The Road to Serfdom* (London, Routledge, 1944) 75.

[23] RA Cass, *The Rule of Law in America* (Baltimore, JHU Press, 2003).

[24] J Raz, 'The Rule of Law and Its Virtue', in *The Authority of Law: Essays on Law and Morality* (Oxford, Oxford University Press, 1979).

[25] J Waldron, *The Rule of Law and the Measure of Property* (Cambridge, Cambridge University Press, 2012).

[26] Art 39 states 'No Freeman shall be taken or imprisoned, or be disseised of his Freehold, or Liberties, or free Customs, or be outlawed, or exiled, or any other wise destroyed; nor will We not pass upon him, nor condemn him, but by lawful judgment of his Peers, or by the Law of the Land.'

1.4.2. The Rule of Law as an Ideal

It is my contention that the Rule of Law also comprises other values within it. These are the ideal values that a legal system ought to possess. Once again, I accept Tom Bingham's analysis of the values contained within the Rule of Law. For him, there are eight elements:

1. Law should be accessible, intelligible, clear and predictable.
2. Questions of legal right and liability to be resolved by law, not by exercise of discretion.
3. Law should apply equally to all.
4. Government should exercise powers in good faith.
5. Law must protect fundamental human rights.
6. Courts must be able to resolve legal disputes.
7. Adjudicative procedure of the state must be fair.
8. States must comply with international legal obligations as well as domestic ones.

Many argue that their particular version of the Rule of Law is derived from the basic principle, but each writer who extrapolates from the principle to the ideal derives a slightly different set of values that the legal system ought to possess. For instance, Raz doesn't include human rights within the ideal of the Rule of Law,[27] whereas for Allan, it does include the principal civil liberties.[28] Other writers don't even seek to derive the ideal from the principle, but rather decide that a particular legal value is 'good' and that it ought therefore to form part of the concept of the Rule of Law. Waldron calls this 'constellation theory' as it confuses the individual stars (Rule of Law, justice, democracy etc) with the overall constellation of a good legal system.[29] Echoing this, Drinóczi includes the Rule of Law in a list of other general principles of European states, including democracy, participation, legal hierarchy, legislative competence and constitutional review of legal norms.[30] The risk is that we put lots of subjective common goods into a box and tie it up with a bow labelled 'Rule of Law'.

The indeterminacy of the Rule of Law as an ideal has led many to question whether it has any value at all as a concept.[31] Although Waldron doesn't agree with this argument, he does perceive a sense in which the Rule of Law simply means 'hooray for our side'.[32] In the same vein, Tamanaha argues that everyone is

[27] Raz (n 24).

[28] TRS Allan, 'The Rule of Law as the Rule of Reasons: Consent and Constitutionalism' (1999) 115 *Law Quarterly Review* 221.

[29] Waldron (n 25).

[30] T Drinóczi, 'Legislative Process', in *Legislation in Europe: A Comprehensive Guide for Scholars and Practitioners* (Oxford, Hart Publishing, 2017) 35.

[31] P Burgess, 'Why We Need to Abandon "The Rule of Law"' (*IACL-IADC Blog*, 21 September 2021) <https://blog-iacl-aidc.org/2021-posts/2021/9/21/why-we-need-to-abandon-the-rule-of-law>.

[32] J Waldron, 'Is the Rule of Law an Essentially Contested Concept (in Florida)?' in R Bellamy (ed), *The Rule of Law and Separation of Powers* (Farnham, Ashgate, 2005).

for the Rule of Law, but no-one knows exactly what it is.[33] For Shklar, the concept is simply a self-congratulatory device, ruling class chatter.[34] In a similar vein, Finnis has argued that the Rule of Law simply means that a legal system is in good shape.[35] With respect to all these esteemed writers, I disagree for two reasons. First, I accept Bingham's argument that the ubiquity of an obligation to respect the Rule of Law in domestic and international legal instruments, case law, legal history and political pronouncements means that it cannot simply be ignored.[36] Second, even though there may be soritical vagueness at the outer edges of the definition of the Rule of Law, there is a surprising amount of agreement about both the basic principle of the Rule of Law and many of the elements that make up the ideal of the Rule of Law.

Lon Fuller wrote about what he termed the morality of the law rather than the Rule of Law.[37] However, the substance of the morality of the law is what I have termed the ideal of a good legal system under the Rule of Law. He began by distinguishing between the morality of duty (a minimum standard that all must adhere to) and the morality of aspiration (an ideal standard to which all must aspire). He set out eight ways in which a system of law could fail – 'a total failure in any of these eight directions does not simply result in a bad system of law; it results in something that is not properly called a legal system at all'.[38] This conforms to his morality of duty. He then set out eight desiderata, things which legal systems are exhorted to possess. This conforms to his morality of aspiration.

Fuller did not derive his eight desiderata from the basic principle that everyone is subject to the law. Instead he made a normative judgement about what was good and bad about a system of law. His rationale is a practical one – what would the populace think of as elements of a good legal system. Although the content of his eight desiderata is sound, they can be criticised for not flowing from a single logical source. His desiderata primarily concern the form of the law rather than its content. They are as follows.

1. There should be general laws by which society is regulated.
2. Laws should be promulgated.
3. Laws should generally not be retroactive
4. Laws should be clear.
5. Laws should not contradict themselves.
6. Laws should not require the impossible.
7. Laws should be relatively constant over time.
8. There must be congruence between official actions and declared rules.

[33] B Tamanaha, *On The Rule of Law* (Cambridge, Cambridge University Press, 2004) 3.

[34] J Shklar, 'Political Theory and the Rule of Law' in A Hutchinson and P Monahan (eds), *The Rule of Law: Ideal or Ideology* (Toronto, Carswell, 1987) 1.

[35] J Finnis, *Natural Law and Natural Rights* (Oxford, Oxford University Press, 1980) 270.

[36] Bingham (n 8) 6–8.

[37] LL Fuller, *The Morality of Law: Revised Edition* (Revised, New Haven, Yale University Press, 1969).

[38] ibid 39.

For Raz, the basic idea of the Rule of Law is that 'people should obey the law and be ruled by it' and that 'government shall be ruled by the law and subject to it'.[39] The rationale behind this is that law is capable of guiding human decisions. The strength of Raz's analysis is in his logical derivation of principles from this basic idea of the Rule of Law. These principles are similar in many ways to Fuller's desiderata, in fact Raz acknowledges the merit of many of Fuller's desiderata. His principles are:

1. Laws should be prospective, open and clear.
2. Laws should be relatively stable.
3. Making of laws should be guided by open, stable, clear and general rules.
4. Independent judiciary.
5. Observe principles of natural justice in judicial process.
6. Courts can review implementation of these principles
7. Courts should be accessible
8. Independence of police and prosecutors

The content of the Rule of Law set out in this section underpins the form of legislation principles set out in the other chapters of this book.

1.5. The Form of Legislation

1.5.1. The Nature of Legislation

Legislation is one type, arguably the most important type, of law. Primary legislation is law debated, scrutinised and enacted by the legislature. In the UK it can be an Act of (the Westminster) Parliament, an Act of the Northern Ireland Assembly, an Act of the Scottish Parliament or an Act of Senedd Cymru, as well as other primary legislation passed by the predecessors of these legislative assemblies. Legislation can also be secondary legislation, that is, legislation made under the authority of primary legislation, but made by the Executive (a department or minister) or some other person or body authorised by primary legislation. Secondary legislation will generally (but not always) have some form of parliamentary scrutiny or approval process. Depending upon its source, secondary legislation can be referred to as delegated legislation, executive legislation, statutory instruments, statutory rules, regulations or orders in council. Legislation as a broad category is to be distinguished from the common law, which is law made by the courts.

[39] Raz (n 24) 212. Although there is a suggestion in Raz's later work that 'the Rule of Law respects those civil rights which are part of the backbone of the legal culture, part of its fundamental traditions': J Raz, *Ethics in the Public Domain, Essays on the Morality of Law and Politics* (Oxford, Clarendon Press, 1994) 376.

Legislation is law, and to legislate is to make law. To put this in another way, legislation contains the rules by which society is to be regulated. It is not suggestion nor guidance, nor peer pressure nor a common undertaking to do things in a certain way, it is hard and fast rules. While sometimes politicians may conflate law and guidance,[40] the key differences are that legislation is mandatory, authoritative and the product of a dedicated process for making law.

Other perspectives do of course exist, for example Rubin sees legislation as a government-implementation mechanism.[41] Westermann characterises legislation as goal-prescribing where it sets out the goals at a high level and leaves the detail of those goals to be implemented in a variety of ways at lower levels.[42] But both these approaches still regard legislation as having legal effect. This is one of the key aspects of legislation – that it has legal effect. So if a Prime Minister makes a statement in Parliament that 'smoking is bad and you ought not to do it', it isn't legislation, it is opinion, rhetoric or at most guidance. But when this statement gets converted into the Health Act 2006, this is legislation because Part 1 of that Act legally prohibits smoking in certain premises. It changed the law by setting out rights and duties with legal consequences flowing from a breach of those duties.

It is my contention that legislation must contain law, that is to say, it must contain provisions that have legal effect. This conception of legislation as 'containing law' is under threat, because sometimes what purports to be legislation does not actually contain any law. Legislatures are sometimes prone to pass legislation which does not actually have legal effect, but which is rhetorical, hortatory or aspirational. Greenberg calls this 'nonsense legislation', that is legislation without a legal proposition.[43] Bartole calls this legislation which has a 'mere political relevance'.[44] Seidman terms it symbolic law, as it is law that does not actually do anything,[45] although Adigun sees some benefits in symbolic law.[46] Wyn-Jones criticises what he regards as legislation that is non-committal, containing no rights that can be

[40] See for example the following reports from the Bingham Centre for the Rule of Law, K Lines, 'Government Messaging on Exercising during Lockdown – A Rule of Law Analysis' (Bingham Centre for the Rule of Law) <https://binghamcentre.biicl.org/publications/government-messaging-on-exercising-during-lockdown-a-rule-of-law-analysis>; R Cormacain, 'Coronavirus, Face Coverings on Public Transport Regulations: A Rule of Law Analysis' (Bingham Centre for the Rule of Law) <https://binghamcentre.biicl.org/publications/coronavirus-face-coverings-on-public-transport-regulations-a-rule-of-law-analysis>; R Cormacain, 'Coronavirus Bill: A Rule of Law Analysis (Supplementary Report – House of Lords)' (Bingham Centre for the Rule of Law) <https://binghamcentre.biicl.org/publications/coronavirus-bill-a-rule-of-law-analysis-supplementary-report-house-of-lords>.

[41] EL Rubin, 'Law and Legislation in the Administrative State' (1989) 89 *Columbia Law Review* 369.

[42] P Westerman, 'The Emergence of New Types of Norms' (Social Science Research Network 2006) SSRN Scholarly Paper ID 1609565 <https://papers.ssrn.com/sol3/papers.cfm?abstract_id=1609565>.

[43] D Greenberg, 'Nothing Will Come of Nothing' (2010) 160 *New Law Journal* 1084.

[44] S Bartole, 'Law-Making Principles under the Rule of Law' (2012) <www.venice.coe.int/WebForms/documents/?pdf=CDL%282013%29016-e>.

[45] R Seidman, 'Drafting for the Rule of Law: Maintaining Legality in Developing Countries' (1987) 12 *Yale Journal of International Law* 84.

[46] Muyiwa Adigun and others, 'Symbolic Legislation and the Regulation of Stroke Biobanking and Genomics Research in Sub-Saharan Africa' (2021) 9 *The Theory and Practice of Legislation* 404.

vindicated in a court, and which is vague.[47] Finally, Feldman characterises it as legislation which is non-law-bearing, and he divides it into four types: promissory, declaratory, aspirational and statements of political support.[48]

1.5.2. The Importance of Legislation

Under UK constitutional theory, legislation is the highest form of law. Case law is subservient to it. In terms of scope of subject matter covered, legislation regulates much more than common law regulates.[49] In the modern era, judges are much more likely to apply legislation to the facts of a case than they are to develop the common law themselves. Constitutional supremacy and scope of subject matter are two reasons for the hegemonic nature of legislation.

Seeley was correct (increasingly so) that we live in a 'legislation state'.[50] It is thought that all social wrongs can be righted by legislation. Waldron shares this view, 'every day another demand emerges for new legislation to deal with some difficulty or to reorganize some aspect of social affairs'.[51] As Turner said 'the belief is widely held, that there is no human situation so bad but that legislation properly designed will effectively be able to cure it', although he astutely notes that failure to legislate is normally a charge levied by the opposition parties rather than by the government.[52] The Office of Parliamentary Counsel is aware of this too, stating that 'Legislation is perceived as a sign of action and therefore it is a powerful communication tool'.[53]

Throughout this book I will be referring to legislative examples to illustrate the points I am trying to make. In his book, Tom Bingham humbly apologised for referring to cases he himself had decided – it wasn't ego, it was simply that these were the cases he was most familiar with. Although falling far beneath his standards, as a practicing legislative drafter, I will be referring to legislation that I am most familiar with, which will generally be legislation I have had a hand in drafting. In order to spare the feelings of other drafters, where I criticise a piece of legislation as being an example of bad practice, I try to present one of my own bad examples first.

[47] R Wyn-Jones, 'Let's All Play Welsh Legislation Bingo!' (*Institute of Welsh Affairs*, 31 March 2015) <www.iwa.wales/agenda/2015/03/lets-all-play-welsh-legislation-bingo/>.

[48] D Feldman, 'Legislation as Aspiration: Statutory Expression of Policy Goals' (Institute of Advanced Legal Studies, 16 March 2015).

[49] H Xanthaki, 'Legislative Drafting: A New Sub-Discipline of Law Is Born' (2013) 1 *IALS Student Law Review* 57.

[50] JR Seeley, *Introduction to Political Science: Two Series of Lectures* (London, Macmillan and Co, 1911) 146.

[51] J Waldron, *The Dignity of Legislation* (Cambridge, Cambridge University Press, 1999) 7.

[52] A Turner, 'Steering the Ship of State – Functions of Parliament' (1980) 10 *Victoria University of Wellington Law Review* 209, 209.

[53] Office of the Parliamentary Counsel, 'When Laws Become Too Complex – Inside Government' (March 2013) <www.gov.uk/government/publications/when-laws-become-too-complex/when-laws-become-too-complex>.

1.5.3. The Form of Legislation

The phrase 'form of legislation' simply means the way legislation is structured, organised and expressed. This begins at the micro level of individual sentences, through to individual statutes, and right up to the macro level of the organisation of the statute book as a whole. Structure means how legislation is divided into different components: sections and subsections, chapters and parts, with preambles or enacting words at the start and schedules at the end. Organisation means the way these different components are arranged and placed in a particular order, and the interaction between these different components. Expression means the actual words used in legislative provisions, and how they are chosen in order to give particular meaning. The form of legislation is therefore about how the policy intent behind legislation is conveyed and structured in order to give it legal effect.

1.5.4. Legislative Drafting and the Form of Legislation

The legislative drafter writes down the words that, upon being enacted by the legislature, become the law. Although legislation represents the will of the legislature, it is the drafter who gives that will form and shape. Legislative drafting therefore plays a key role in determining the form of legislation.

Legislative drafting involves taking the policy ideas of another and turning them into law fit for the statute book. Drafters are the translators of policy into legislation. Jamieson speaks of the 'transcendental endeavour to translate policy into law' as the essence of drafting legislation.[54] Ismail makes the same point saying that drafters must express their clients' meaning.[55] Daintith and Page say that the drafter's skill lies in 'translating the government's intentions into legislative form'.[56] Carter says that drafters 'translate the Government's policy into legislation'.[57] Bowman drilled deeper into this when he said that 'the drafter's main and most valuable function is to subject policy ideas to a rigorous intellectual analysis'.[58] For Bowman, before translating the policy into law, it is necessary to first properly analyse the policy. Lord Thring, the very first First Parliamentary Counsel in the UK, took the same view over 100 years ago. His advice was that the minister should decide on what the principles of the Act were, and then instruct the drafter to prepare the Bill in accordance with those principles.[59]

[54] N Jamieson, 'Would a Parliamentary Counsel by Any Other Name Be More of a Law Draftsman' [1982] *Statute Law Review* 13, 20.

[55] NH Ismail, 'Legislative Drafters: Lawyers or Not?' (2013) 39 *Commonwealth Law Bulletin* 455, 456.

[56] T Daintith and A Page, *The Executive in the Constitution: Structure, Autonomy and Internal Control* (Oxford, Oxford University Press, 1999) 254.

[57] R Carter, '"High Quality" Legislation – (How) Can Legislative Counsel Facilitate It?' [2011] *The Loophole* 41, 51.

[58] G Bowman, 'Why Is There a Parliamentary Counsel Office?' (2005) 26 *Statute Law Review* 69, 70.

[59] H Thring, *Practical Legislation: The Composition and Language of Acts of Parliament* (London, HMSO, 1877) 4, 5.

1.6. Principles for the Form of Legislation as Contained in Legislative Drafting Principles

One of the only sources of guidance for how legislation ought to be structured are contained in the principles of legislative drafting. These drafting principles are what Zamboni has called the internal quality of legislation, its technical or drafting qualities.[60] Duprat calls these instead 'formal legistics' although he sees these as being the same as drafting techniques.[61] For Xanthaki they are the rules of regulation.[62] Although principles have not been derived from the Rule of Law before, there do exist drafting principles from other sources. That is the context in which this book is placed.

As with the Rule of Law, there are many different taxonomies as to what constitute the principles of sound legislative drafting. As with the Rule of Law, there is no true consensus on what the principles are. As with the Rule of Law, there is a remarkable degree of overlap between the principles put forward by different writers. However, unlike with the Rule of Law, there has been little academic discourse on the principles of legislative drafting. Situated within the general subject heading of legisprudence, legislative drafting is seen more as a technical skill rather than something that deserves academic investigation. One side goal of this book is to remedy this inattention and to provide evidence for Xanthaki's assertion that we are participating in the birth of legislative drafting as a new academic sub-discipline.[63]

Most of the principles set out below are practical and pragmatic rather than being reasoned out from an underlying rationale. The principles have been put forward by drafters themselves based upon their own experiences. The exception to this is Xanthaki whose principles are all derived from the functional rationale that legislation exists to effect social change.

The use of the phrase 'principles of legislative drafting' rather than 'rules of legislative drafting' is deliberate. Principles represent suggestions or guidance. They are values or concepts that ought to be borne in mind, but not something that requires dogmatic adherence to. Rules are something absolute that must not be broken. Drafting has more of the creative than the technical to it. Being straitjacketed into rules tends to stymie drafting and retard its development.

For a profession whose role it is to write rules, drafters in the UK are surprisingly anarchic when it comes to rules for their own profession. For a long time, there were no drafting manuals in the UK.[64] However, the Parliamentary Counsel

[60] M Zamboni, 'Goals and Measures of Legislation', in *Legislation in Europe: A Comprehensive Guide for Scholars and Practitioners* (Oxford, Hart Publishing, 2017) 97.

[61] JP Duprat and H Xanthaki, 'Legislative Drafting Techniques/Formal Legistics', in *Legislation in Europe: A Comprehensive Guide for Scholars and Practitioners* (Oxford, Hart Publishing, 2017) 109.

[62] H Xanthaki, *Drafting Legislation: Art and Technology of Rules for Regulation* 1st edn (Oxford, Hart Publishing, 2014).

[63] Xanthaki (n 49).

[64] G Bowman, 'The Art of Legislative Drafting' (2005) 7 *European Journal of Law Reform* 3, 15.

Office has recently produced what it calls Drafting Guidance.[65] According to Greenberg, 'the only drafting matter on which it is wise to be dogmatic is that it is unwise to be dogmatic on any drafting matter',[66] although this advice is normally shortened to a statement that the first rule of legislative drafting is that there are no rules of legislative drafting. Even though Thring framed 'rules' for drafting, he said that each rule had so many exceptions that the rules should instead be seen as something that assists drafters rather than absolute requirements.[67]

1.6.1. Bentham

Jeremy Bentham was someone intensely concerned with the proper form for legislation. In Ogden's introduction to Bentham's Theory of Legislation he states that uniform and scientific methods for drafting were inspired by Bentham.[68] In his letter to James Madison, Bentham himself wrote that when it comes to the form of law, the goal was cognoscibility – the quality of being understandable.[69] He delved deeper and produced a sound rationale for his guiding principle of cognoscibility. This is the fundamental rationale of maximising adherence to the law, or as he put it 'producing, to the greatest extent possible, in respect of number of observances compared with the number of non-observances'.[70] This is a pragmatic approach – if we want the law to be obeyed then we must make it understandable.

In a letter of 1817,[71] Bentham derives some principles from his first starting point of cognoscibility. He cites the following properties that are desirable in a body of laws:

1. Notoriety.
2. Conciseness (in terms of bulk).
3. Clearness of language.
4. Compactness (of form).
5. Completeness/comprehensiveness.
6. Intrinsic usefulness
7. Justifiedness/manifested usefulness.

Bentham uses the word notoriety in the sense that the law must be well-known 'only in so far as it is present to the mind, can any idea be productive of any effect'.[72]

[65] Office of the Parliamentary Counsel, 'Drafting Guidance' (Office of the Parliamentary Counsel, UK, 2020).

[66] D Greenberg, *Craies on Legislation* 10th edn (London, Sweet & Maxwell, 2012) 387.

[67] Thring (n 59) 40.

[68] J Bentham, *Theory of Legislation* (CK Ogden ed, London, Routledge, 1950).

[69] J Bentham, *Legislator of the World: Writings on Codification, Law, and Education* (Oxford, Clarendon Press; Oxford University Press, 1998) 9, Letter to James Madison, October 1811.

[70] ibid 12.

[71] ibid. Letter to the citizens of several American States, July 1817, Letter II.

[72] ibid 119.

The reference to justifiedness is a reference to his idea that each legislative provision should be accompanied by a statement justifying it.

1.6.2. Xanthaki

Xanthaki sets out a hierarchy of principles (in the form of a pyramid) for quality in legislation.[73] The top of the pyramid is the principle that the law is *efficacious*, by which she means that it must solve the social problem that it aims at. Zamboni[74] and Mousmouti[75] both echo this, seeing effectiveness as a key criterion of quality in legislation, by which they mean the capacity of the legislation to produce the social results desired by the political actors. Efficaciousness as a principle is aimed more at those creating the policy rather than the legislation itself. Those constructing the policy come up with the solution to the problem: the drafter works with whatever solution they have decided upon and puts that solution into legislative form.

The next level of the pyramid down is that the law must be *effective* in that it gives full effect to the intended policy. This is within the bailiwick of the drafter's responsibilities. It flows from the function of the drafter of converting policy into legislation. The next level down contains three entries: the law must be *clear*, *precise* and *unambiguous*. Clear means that citizens can easily understand the law. Precise means that the law is exact rather than vague. Unambiguous means that the law can only admit to one meaning. The bottom level contains two entries. The first is that the law must be written in *gender neutral* terms, that is, that it doesn't refer to any particular gender. The second is that the law is written in accordance with the principles of the *plain language* movement. Each level in Xanthaki's hierarchy is subservient to the level above it. Thus, if there is a clash between using plain language and being precise, then precision wins out.

Xanthaki's analysis has three main strengths. First, like Bentham, there is a rationale underpinning it. She proceeds on the logical basis that the purpose of legislation is to effect social change, 'a good law is simply a law that is capable of

[73] This hierarchy first appeared in H Asgeirsson, 'On Transferability of Legislative Solutions: The Functionality Test' in C Stefanou and H Xanthaki (eds), *Drafting Legislation: A Modern Approach* (Farnham, Ashgate, 2008) and was developed further in H Xanthaki, 'Drafting Manuals and Quality in Legislation: Positive Contribution towards Certainty in the Law or Impediment to the Necessity for Dynamism of Rules?' (2010) 4 *Legisprudence* 111; H Xanthaki, 'Quality of Legislation: An Achievable Universal Concept or an Utopia Pursuit?' in L Mader and Marta Tavares de Almeida (eds), *Quality of Legislation: Principles and Instruments. Proceedings of the Ninth Congress of the International Association of Legislation in Lisbon, June 24–25, 2010* (Baden-Baden, Nomos, 2011); and most recently Xanthaki (n 62).

[74] M Zamboni, 'Legislative Policy and Effectiveness' (Conference: Effective Law and Regulation, Institute of Advanced Legal Studies, 7 July 2017).

[75] M Mousmouti, 'Making Legislative Effectiveness an Operational Concept' (Conference: Effective Law and Regulation, Institute of Advanced Legal Studies, 7 July 2017).

achieving the regulatory reform that it was released to effectuate or support'.[76] She puts this another way saying that

> A good law is one that is capable of leading to efficacy of regulation. There is nothing technical at this level of qualitative functionality: what counts is the ability of the law to achieve the reforms requested by the policy officers.[77]

From this can be derived principles for the form of legislation that make it more likely that social change will be effected. Her principles flow from this initial proposition. This is soundly rooted in both practice and principle. Legislation is not simply window-dressing; it is there to do something, to change something in society. It is eminently sensible to derive principles for evaluating quality legislation from the rationale behind that legislation.

Second, her hierarchy is simple, coherent and comprehensive. It is simple because it is easy to understand. It is coherent as it makes sense as a whole. Subject to what is said below, it is comprehensive as it covers the full spectrum of what amounts to quality in legislation.

Third, the individual elements making up the hierarchy are soundly rooted in what others see as important criteria for quality legislation. Those who have written about quality in legislation in the past will find many of their individual ideas reflected in the hierarchy. For instance, Bennion[78] and Butt[79] both advocated clarity in drafting. The Renton report argued strongly for certainty and precision.[80] Kimble[81] and Thomas[82] were of the opinion that plain language should be used in legislation. Schweikart[83] and Petersson[84] were in favour of gender neutral drafting. Xanthaki summarises and synthesises much of what is already regarded as important in drafting.

However, there is a gap in this approach as there is a lack of an express normative element which is exogenous to legislative drafting. So Xanthaki does see efficaciousness as a moral virtue, but this is an endogenous virtue as it relates to the form of legislation itself. Most of what she says is about the form of laws, without much focus on their content. Carter has a similar view, arguing that a law can still be of a high quality even if it implements a defective policy.[85] I disagree and see this as a criticism that could be levelled generally at any functional approach. A law imposing the death penalty for parking offences may 'work' in

[76] Xanthaki, 'Quality of Legislation: An Achievable Universal Concept or an Utopia Pursuit?' (n 73) 81.
[77] Xanthaki (n 49) 67.
[78] F Bennion, 'The Readership of Legal Texts' (1993) 27 *Clarity* 1.
[79] P Butt, 'Modern Legal Drafting' (2002) 23 *Statute Law Review* 12.
[80] 'Report of the Renton Committee on the Preparation of Legislation' (1975) Cmnd 6053.
[81] J Kimble, 'Answering the Critics of Plain Language' (1994) 5 *The Scribes Journal of Legal Writing* 51.
[82] R Thomas, 'Plain English and the Law' [1985] *Statute Law Review* 139.
[83] D Schweikart, 'Gender Neutral Pronoun Redefined' (1998) 20 *Women's Rights Law Report* 1.
[84] S Petersson, 'Gender Neutral Drafting: Recent Commonwealth Developments' (1990) 20 *Statute Law Review* 35.
[85] Carter (n 57) 49.

the sense that it stops people from parking where they shouldn't park, but its disproportionality makes it morally wrong. Xanthaki's drafting principles do not require, for example, that laws be constitutional, or protect human rights or be in accordance with the Rule of Law (although this could be seen as implicit within the notion of effectiveness). The only normative aspiration is gender equality under gender neutral drafting. It seems odd that drafting should promote gender equality, but not other sorts of equality. The functional approach lacks a moral dimension, it doesn't matter to what purpose the law is directed, only that it is effective in fulfilling that purpose. A knife which is sharp is a good knife, regardless of whether it is used to chop vegetables or stab people. A law which is effective is a good law, regardless of whether it remedies some social ill or is an instrument of oppression.

This normative lacuna is analogous to the 'thin' conception of the rule of law. In my view, both these approaches are missing something as they fail to include a moral dimension within the law.

1.6.3. Legislative Drafting Principles within the UK

It would be wrong to say that there is an agreed single set of principles on the form of legislation to which all UK drafters adhere. Instead, individual drafters (and drafting offices) have on occasion set down some suggestions on how drafters should draft and what qualities legislation should aspire to.

Henry Thring, the first First Parliamentary Counsel in the UK, offered guidance to drafters in his book *Practical Legislation*.[86] As its title suggests, this is a practical rather than a theoretical work. Thring does not set out general principles underlying the concept of drafting, instead he gives concrete advice on how to construct legislation. However, by closely analysing his concrete suggestions, it is possible to derive some more general principles. He says that legislation must be concise,[87] that it must be clear,[88] brief[89] and uniform.[90] He quotes with approval a comment made by Mr Justice Stephen

> it is not enough to attain to a degree of precision which a person reading in good faith can understand; but it is necessary to attain, if possible, to a degree of precision which a person reading in bad faith cannot misunderstand.[91]

[86] Recently republished as H Thring, *Practical Legislation: The Composition and Language of Acts of Parliament* 3rd edn (M MacKenzie ed, London, Luathe Press 2015).

[87] H Thring, *Practical Legislation: The Composition and Language of Acts of Parliament* 2nd edn (London, John Murray, 1902) 11.

[88] ibid 11, 39, 41, 61.

[89] ibid 41.

[90] ibid.

[91] ibid 9 (Thring does not give the source of this quote).

His more specific and concrete advice was:

- Separate provisions declaring the law from administrative provisions.
- Simpler provisions should precede more complex ones.
- Separate principal provisions from subordinate ones.
- Local or temporary provisions should be separated and placed at the end.
- Procedural issues and points of detail should be contained in a schedule.

Thring notes the influence of Coode on his work. Coode's book expresses similar advice on the construction of legislation, without delving much into general principles.[92]

Bowman, a much more recent First Parliamentary Counsel in the UK, set out his approach to drafting.[93] He summed up his drafting philosophy very simply: first decide what you want to say, second, say it. He also was of the opinion that legislation should be precise, clear and simple. He made some general observations: consider the target audience for the legislation, use short sentences, express things in the positive not negative, use active not passive voice etc. However, he was adamant that these were not rules and that their application was a matter of judgement and degree.

The Good Law initiative is an attempt by the Office of the Parliamentary Counsel (OPC) to improve the quality of legislation in the UK. According to its website, good law is law which is necessary, clear, coherent, effective and accessible.[94] In its report on complexity in legislation, the OPC set out additional matters that could be regarded as criteria for quality in legislation, for example that it is in harmony with other legislation, and that it achieves political, social or legal objectives.[95] In Scotland, the First Parliamentary Counsel spoke of the need for the 'logical and principled development of the law'[96] and the 'coherence of the statute book'.[97] He also argued that legislation should be clear, unambiguous and accessible.[98]

There is a clear overlap between these principles espoused by UK drafters. The same principles re-appear: clarity, brevity, accessibility, precision etc. These principles also mirror those espoused by Bentham and Xanthaki.

[92] G Coode, *Legislative Expression* (London, William Benning and Co, 1845) and see also C Ilbert, *Legislative Methods and Forms* (Oxford, Clarendon Press, 1901).
[93] Bowman (n 64).
[94] <www.gov.uk/good-law>.
[95] Office of the Parliamentary Counsel (n 53) 11.
[96] C Wilson, 'Managing Increasing Government Expectations with Respect to Legislation While Maintaining Quality' [2009] *The Loophole* 21, 22.
[97] ibid 22.
[98] ibid.

1.7. To Whom is this Book Addressed?

This book is directed at anyone with an interest in legislation and the Rule of Law. More specifically, it is aimed at the following groups.

- Lawyers interested in constitutional and public law, and in particular, those interested in legisprudence (the theory and practice of legislation).
- Academics whose field of study is in the politics and practice of making law.
- Parliamentarians of all legislative assemblies, meaning those who introduce, scrutinise and then enact primary and secondary legislation.
- The parliamentary staff who help to steer legislation through legislative assemblies and advise on its legitimacy and efficacy. The legislative drafters whose primary function is to write legislation.
- Other government lawyers who advise on the legality and content of draft government legislation.
- Those civil servants working in Bill teams whose job it is to develop the policy which eventually becomes a draft piece of legislation.
- Lobbyists, think-tanks and NGOs who seek to influence the content of legislation as it is being enacted.
- And finally, anyone in the general public who has ever asked 'why is this law so complicated?'.

2

Accessibility of Legislation

Introduction

The Rule of Law requires that legislation must be accessible. Accessibility means the citizen can tangibly 'see' the legislation, can find it, can read it.[1] Accessibility can also be taken to include the ability to understand that which has been accessed, but I consider this under the separate heading of intelligibility, which is covered in chapter five.

In Part 1 of this Chapter, I examine the meaning of accessibility of legislation in the context of the Rule of Law. Part 2 derives principles for the form of legislation from the starting point of a need for accessibility. Three main principles are derived. First, that legislation must be available to users. Second, that legislation must be navigable in the sense that the users can easily find their way around the statute book. Third, that legislation must be inclusive of all important relevant material.

Part 1: The Theory of Accessibility

2.1. Accessibility

Tom Bingham argued that all law (including case law and legislation) must be accessible to citizens.[2] He didn't deconstruct accessibility into its component parts; he simply used it in its ordinary sense of citizens being able to physically see the law. He advanced three reasons why law should be accessible.[3] First, you need to know in advance what the criminal law is in order to avoid being prosecuted for your actions. Second, in the civil field, you cannot claim rights or perform obligations if you don't know what these rights and obligations are. Third, a successful commercial environment is enhanced if there are accessible legal rules governing commercial relations.

[1] See ch 5 of this book; R Carter, *Burrows and Carter: Statute Law in New Zealand* 5th edn (London, LexisNexis, 2015).

[2] T Bingham, *The Rule of Law* (London, Penguin UK, 2011).

[3] ibid 37, 38.

In John Locke's Commonwealth, it is vital that laws are promulgated. By this he meant that they should be officially made, proclaimed and disseminated to citizens. Following on from this, he says that the supreme authority 'cannot assume to itself a power to rule by extemporary arbitrary decrees, but is bound to dispense justice and decide the rights of the subject by promulgated standing laws, and known authorised judges'.[4] He reiterates this point by stating that there must be 'declared laws',[5] 'settled standing laws',[6] 'declared and received laws'[7] and 'established and promulgated laws'.[8] As justification for this he pre-empted Bingham's argument 'that both people may know their duty, and be safe and secure within the limits of the law'.[9]

Although Locke published his thesis in 1689, even then, this principle was not new. Allen stated that 30 years earlier, Thomas Hobbes 'waxed indignant at the difficulties which confronted the layman in ascertaining the law, and he contended that there ought to be as many copies of statutes abroad as the Bible'.[10] Delving into antiquity, Suetonius wrote the following of Caligula's laws

> These taxes being imposed, but the act by which they were levied never submitted to public inspection, great grievances were experienced from the want of sufficient knowledge of the law. At length, on the urgent demands of the Roman people, he published the law, but it was written in a very small hand and posted up in a corner so that no one could make a copy of it.[11]

Desideratum 2 for Lon Fuller is 'a formalized standard of promulgation'[12] of laws. This is the only one of Fuller's desiderata where the morality of duty is the same as the morality of aspiration – that is, the minimum standard is that all laws must be promulgated. Fuller stated that there ought to be a legal duty to publish law in a specified manner in a specified time frame. Fuller was a realist and stated that 'the requirement that laws be published does not rest on any such absurdity as an expectation that the dutiful citizen will sit down and read them all'.[13] Even though most citizens won't read legislation, Fuller argued that those directly affected by, or those who influence public opinion, will read it.

Raz dealt with accessibility very briefly in his principles about the Rule of Law. In principle 1 he stated that 'the law must be open and adequately publicised'.[14]

[4] J Locke, *Locke: Two Treatises of Government* (London, Awnsham Churchill, 1689).

[5] ibid s 136.

[6] ibid.

[7] ibid s 137.

[8] ibid.

[9] ibid.

[10] Sir Carleton Kemp Allen, *Law in the Making* (Oxford, Clarendon Press, 1964). See also S Hockman, 'Free the Law How the Australasian Legal Information Institute (AustLII) Achieved the Free Availability of Legal Information on the Internet' (2000) 1 *Journal of Information, Law and Technology*.

[11] Suetonius, *Lives of the 12 Caesars* (Alexander Thomson trans, 1883) 278.

[12] LL Fuller, *The Morality of Law: Revised Edition* (Revised, New Haven, Yale University Press, 1969).

[13] ibid 51.

[14] J Raz, 'The Rule of Law and Its Virtue', in *The Authority of Law: Essays on Law and Morality* (Oxford, Oxford University Press, 1979).

This is for the rather obvious reason that if the law isn't accessible, it cannot guide human behaviour. The coronavirus pandemic has shown us that if law isn't accessible, we are left to guide ourselves by reference to ministerial press statements.[15]

Roznai has argued that accessibility 'inherently derives from the Rule of Law'.[16] The World Justice Report requires law to be 'clear, publicised, stable and fair'[17] and this is tied directly to assessing how well a country is heeding the Rule of Law. Waldron states that law should be promulgated.[18] For Upham, in order for the law to be effective, people need to be able to understand it and it must be accessible.[19] Stevenson included accessibility as one of the 'vital components of legal systems and of substantive laws for centuries'.[20] In the course of examining European approaches to legislation, Donelan stated that 'for a legal system to be credible, legislation must be accessible'.[21] SIGMA (a joint initiative of the European Union and the OECD on governance) reinforces this point – 'a principal aim of legislation is to enable those affected by it to organise and regulate their activities in accordance with its normative requirements … ready access to that legislation is a necessary concomitant'.[22] Cass argued that if a legal rule was applicable to persons it must be 'reasonably accessible to those persons'.[23] The European Court of Human Rights has held that 'the law must be adequately accessible'.[24]

The Venice Commission on the Rule of Law took the view that in order to attain legal certainty 'the state must make the text of the law easily accessible'.[25] Relating accessibility directly to the Rule of Law, Greenberg stated that 'accessibility is at the heart of the efficacy of the Rule of Law'.[26] Duprat stated that formal legistics 'aims to make legislation more accessible to the public'.[27]

[15] R Hogarth, 'The Government Must Draw a Clear Line between Law and Guidance during the Coronavirus Crisis' (*The Institute for Government*, 1 April 2020) <www.instituteforgovernment.org.uk/blog/government-law-and-guidance-coronavirus-crisis>.

[16] Y Roznai, 'Access to Justice 2.0: Access to Legislation And Beyond' (2015) 3 *Theory and Practice of Legislation* 333, 336.

[17] MD Agrast and JC Botero, *World Justice Report: Rule of Law Index 2012–2013* (World Justice Report 2013).

[18] J Waldron, *The Rule of Law and the Measure of Property* (Cambridge, Cambridge University Press, 2012).

[19] F Upham, *Mythmaking in the Rule of Law Orthodoxy* (Carnegie Endowment for International Peace 2002) <http://carnegieendowment.org/files/wp30.pdf>.

[20] K Stevenson and C Harris, 'Breaking the Thrall of Ambiguity: Simplification (of the Criminal Law) as an Emerging Human Rights Imperative' (2010) 74 *Journal of Criminal Law* 516.

[21] E Donelan, 'European Approaches to Improving Access to and Managing the Stock of Legislation' (2009) 30 *Statute Law Review* 147.

[22] SIGMA, *Law Drafting and Regulatory Management in Central and Eastern Europe* (1997).

[23] RA Cass, *The Rule of Law in America* (Baltimore, JHU Press, 2003).

[24] *Sunday Times v UK* (1979) 2 EHRR 245, 271.

[25] Venice Commission, 'Report on the Rule of Law' (2011).

[26] D Greenberg, 'Gender Neutrality in the House of Lords (and Ladies)' (2014) 35 *Statute Law Review* v.

[27] JP Duprat and H Xanthaki, 'Legislative Drafting Techniques/Formal Legistics', in *Legislation in Europe: A Comprehensive Guide for Scholars and Practitioners* (Oxford, Hart, 2017) 110.

Marsh-Smith, writing as chief legislative drafter in the Isle of Man, stated that 'access to the law is a basic right'[28] – this was in the context of creating a new system for electronic access to legislation. The courts in Canada take the same view 'to bind the citizen by a law, the terms of which he has no means of knowing, would be a mark of tyranny'.[29] Canadian drafter Keyes agrees, 'if the law is to command respect and function as it is intended, it must be adequately promulgated'.[30] Bing also argues in favour of free access to law.[31] In Australia, Lord Justice Brooke called for 'access to all, free of charge, to our case law and statutes'.[32] The New Zealand Law Commission stated that 'one aspect of the Rule of Law is to ensure Acts of Parliament are accessible and available'.[33]

2.2. Accessibility of Legislation in the UK

In the UK there is a 'push-me pull-you' attitude to accessibility of legislation. The push-me pull-you was an animal in Dr Doolittle with heads at either end of its body, making it hard to know which way it was going. On the positive side, certainly in modern times, accessibility is strongly endorsed. For example, secondary legislation must be published immediately after it is made.[34] On the negative side, legislation that is difficult or even impossible to access is still valid. For example, it is a defence to any crime set out in secondary legislation if that legislation has not been issued, unless reasonable steps have been taken to bring the offence to the attention of the person charged with it.[35]

Dealing with the positive side first, in Wales, Hughes and Davies strongly support additional resources being made available in order that the public may have access to up to date versions of Welsh legislation.[36] The head of Legislation Services in the UK government has directly quoted Bingham's element 1 before

[28] L Marsh-Smith and G Wright, 'Information Technology on a Budget: A Giant Leap for the Isle of Man' ('Winds of Change', Commonwealth Association of Legislative Counsel' conference, Cape Town, April 2013).

[29] *Watson v Lee* (1979) 26 ALR 461, 465.

[30] JM Keyes, 'Perils of the Unknown – Fair Notice and the Promulgation of Legislation' (1993) 25 *Ottawa Law Review* 579.

[31] J Bing, 'Let There Be Lite: A Brief History of Legal Information Retrieval' (2010) 1 *European Journal of Law and Technology*.

[32] Lord Justice Brooke, 'Publishing the Courts: Judgements and Public Information on the Internet' (Commonwealth Law Conference, Melbourne, 15 April 2003). Another Australian judge made exactly the same point 'the content of the law must be adequately accessible' M Gleeson, 'Courts and the Rule of Law' (2001) www.hcourt.gov.au/assets/publications/speeches/former-justices/gleesoncj/cj_ruleoflaw.htm.

[33] Law Commission, *Presentation of New Zealand Statute Law* (Law Commission 2008) page iv.

[34] Section 2(1), Statutory Instruments Act 1946.

[35] ibid, Section 3(2).

[36] D Hughes and Huw G Davies, 'Accessible Bilingual Legislation for Wales (Deddfwriaeth Hygyrch a Dwyieithog i Gymru)' (2012) 33 *Statute Law Review* 103.

going on to state that 'the principle of free public access to the law underpins legislation.gov.uk and the work of the Legislation Services team at The National Archives'.[37] The High Court has spoken of the 'constitutional imperative that statute law be made known'.[38] The courts have directly tied this requirement to the Rule of Law: 'the acceptance of the Rule of Law as a constitutional principle requires that a citizen, before committing himself to any course of action, should be able to know in advance what are the legal consequences that will flow from it'.[39] Lord Renton produced the highly influential Report on the Preparation of Legislation in 1975.[40] In Chapter XVI Renton discussed how computers would help and in that context made some recommendations about access to legislation. He was in favour of a searchable database of legislation that contained copies of the law as enacted, and the law as amended.

Greenberg posits that 'it is of enormous importance that laws are made accessible to the public as soon as possible'.[41] The Law Commission considered the importance of access to legislation in its report on post-legislative scrutiny.[42] After discussing the difficulty with reading out of date legislation, particularly subordinate legislation, they made two recommendations. First, that consolidated subordinate legislation be made available rather than requiring users to try to manually piece together amendments themselves.[43] Second, 'that steps should be taken to ensure that the related provisions of primary and secondary legislation should be capable of being accessed in a coherent fashion by a straightforward and freely available electronic search'.[44]

The government's response came in 2008.[45] They saw the benefit of consolidation, but were concerned about the cost. With regards to electronic access, they discussed the Statute Law Database (the forerunner of the system now provided by The National Archives). They went on to say 'the aim has been to present legislation in the most accessible and useable way, whilst maintaining the traditional strengths of immediacy and accuracy'.[46]

Within Parliament, the critical importance of access to legislation has not been gainsaid. The House of Commons Political and Constitutional Reform Committee carried out an inquiry into the quality of legislation in 2013. In the

[37] J Sheridan, 'People, Patterns and Data – the Story of Legislation.Gov.Uk People, Patterns and Data – the Story of Legislation.Gov.Uk' (*Social Tech Guide*, 2014) www.socialtech.org.uk/blog/people-patterns-and-data-the-story-of-legislation-gov-uk/.

[38] *R (Salih) v Secretary of State for Home Department* [2003] EWHC 2273 (Admin).

[39] *Black Clawson v Papierwerke Waldhof* (1975) AC 591, 638.

[40] 'Report of the Renton Committee on the Preparation of Legislation' (1975) Cmnd 6053.

[41] D Greenberg, *Craies on Legislation* 10th edn (London, Sweet & Maxwell, 2012).

[42] Law Commission, 'Post-Legislative Scrutiny' (2006) Law Com No 302.

[43] ibid.

[44] ibid.

[45] Office of the Leader of the House of Commons, 'Post-Legislative Scrutiny – the Government's Approach' (2008) Cm 7320.

[46] ibid.

course of giving evidence to that Committee, Sir David Lloyd Jones (who became a judge in the Supreme Court) stated that 'it is fundamental that legislation, that the law in general, should be accessible and intelligible'.[47] One of the Committee's recommendations was a Draft Code of Legislative Standards.[48] One element of this Code was that legislation should be accessible. Separately, the Leader of the House of Lords has stated that,

> All Acts are published simultaneously on the Internet and in print as soon as possible after Royal Assent. It is important to ensure that an accurate approved text is published and that all users have access at the same time to the same text.[49]

The Select Committee on European Scrutiny, in its Fifteenth Report, welcomed 'access to legislation in a variety of databases' (although this was in terms of European legislation).[50] In a memorandum to the Select Committee on the Constitution, Michael Ryle, former Clerk of Committees and Secretary of the Hansard Society Commission said that the publication of statute law and the Statute Law Database were constitutionally significant.[51]

However, the negative side is highlighted by two rules. The first is that, in the UK, ignorance of the law is no defence. The fact that a citizen does not know the law is not an excuse for failing to observe the law (this principle is common in many jurisdictions). The second is that legislation is valid (and may therefore be binding) as soon as it is made. Therefore a person may be liable under an Act that has not yet been published, an Act that it would be impossible for the citizen to access. The justification for this rather unfair rule is set out by Austin: it is that every citizen is present in Parliament by dint of being represented there by their Member of Parliament. So, the printing of the statute is not telling the notional citizen something new, it merely refreshes the citizen's memory. Thus 'for before an Act is printed, and whether it is printed or not, it is a statute and is legally binding'.[52] The Court of Appeal found itself bound to hold this statement to be true, ruling that 'it is beyond argument that an Act of Parliament takes legal effect on the giving of Royal Assent, irrespective of publication'.[53] Allen 'doubted whether many substantial hardships result from this'.[54] This is because 'most people become acquainted with the elements of the statutory or Common Law which affect them specially in their particular vocation or circumstance'.[55]

[47] Political and Constitutional Reform Committee, 'Ensuring Standards in the Quality of Legislation' (House of Commons Political and Constitutional Reform Committee 2013) HC 85.

[48] ibid.

[49] HL Deb February 10, 2003 cc 464–466, see also the government's general obligation to publish the statute book, discussed in HC Deb June 13, 1991 WA 613–614.

[50] Select Committee on European Scrutiny, 'Fifteenth Report' (2003).

[51] Select Committee on the Constitution, Minutes of Evidence (April, 2004) paras 17–18.

[52] J Austin and S Austin, *The Province of Jurisprudence Determined* (London, J Murray, 1861).

[53] *ZL and VL v Secretary of State* [2003] EWCA Civ 25 [17].

[54] Allen (n 10).

[55] ibid.

Very rarely, substantive provisions in legislation come into operation in advance of publication. By substantive provisions I mean provisions having substantive effect, not provisions such as the short title of an Act. One example is the Nationality, Immigration and Asylum Act 2002. It received Royal Assent on 7 November 2002 and section 115 of that Act came into force immediately. However, it wasn't actually printed until 28 November 2002. The Court of Appeal, with considerable unease, ruled that section 115 applied from the 7 November 2002.[56] Contrast this with the decision by the European Court in *Skoma-Lux sro v Celní ředitelství Olomouc*[57] that EU legislation is only enforceable against individuals if it has been properly published.

Cabinet Office guidance is that an Act must be published online 'immediately after the approved text has been received from the Lords Public Bill Office'.[58] However, 'Where an Act cannot be published before it takes practical effect, the department should seek to disseminate the final text of the relevant sections to those most interested, or their representatives'.[59] Although this makes a gesture towards accessibility, the quality of that access will invariably be poor.

There are two particularly egregious breaches of the principle of accessibility in UK law: coronavirus legislation and prerogative legislation.

2.2.1. Coronavirus Legislation

During the coronavirus pandemic, the requirement for legislation to be published well in advance of its coming into force has been breached many times. There have been constant complaints on the lack of prior publication of statutory instruments regulating lockdown.[60] For example, the All Tiers Regulations were made at 6am and came into force at 7am on 20 December 2020.[61] They weren't even laid before Parliament until the next day. Even worse, the very first set of coronavirus regulations were made at 1pm on 26 March 2020 and came into force at 1pm on 26 March 2020.[62] This does not just relate to legislation at the start of the pandemic. The Health Protection (Coronavirus, International Travel, Operator

[56] *ZL and VL v Secretary of State for the Home Department* [2003] EWCA Civ 25. For an example of legislation that was relied upon even though it was repealed, see *R v Chambers* where the mistake was only caught at the last minute and the court complained that 'there is no comprehensive statute law database with hyperlinks which would enable an intelligent person, by using a search engine, to find out all the legislation on a subject', [2008] EWCA Crim 2467 [28].

[57] ECR 2007, p. I-10841.

[58] Cabinet Office, *Guide to Making Legislation* (2013).

[59] ibid.

[60] M Russell and others, 'The Marginalisation of the House of Commons under Covid Has Been Shocking; a Year on, Parliament's Role Must Urgently Be Restored' (The Constitution Unit 2021) <https://constitution-unit.com/2021/04/21/covid-and-parliament-one-year-on/>.

[61] The Health Protection (Coronavirus, Restrictions) (All Tiers and Obligations of Undertakings) (England) (Amendment) Regulations 2020 SI 2020/1611.

[62] The Health Protection (Coronavirus, Restrictions) (England) Regulations 2020 SI 2020/350.

Liability and Information to Passengers) (Amendment) Regulations (Northern Ireland) 2022 were made on 7 January 2022, sometime around 1 or 2am. Most of the provisions contained within them came into force at 4am of the same day.[63] Virtually every single Report on coronavirus legislation issued by the Bingham Centre for the Rule of Law raised the point of basic unfairness of a law being applied against a citizen when the citizen had no way of knowing what that law was.[64] Reliance on Government press releases is no substitute for the actual legislation being published in advance.

2.2.2. Prerogative Legislation

Prerogative legislation is a very peculiar type of UK legislation made by the Crown (via Ministers) without any recourse to the legislature. I have previously considered accessibility of legislation made under the Royal Prerogative.[65] In investigating UK prerogative legislation relating to British Indian Ocean Territory (BIOT), I concluded that, despite the views set out above on the importance of access, this legislation was not accessible. Tomkins criticised it as 'unaccountable, indeed wholly secret rule-making'.[66]

It could be thought that the lack of official promulgation of BIOT legislation is accidental. However, it is clear that official government policy is to make it inaccessible. For example, the Secretary of State sent a confidential telegram to the Governor of the Seychelles on the subject of some of this legislation. In paragraph 3 he stated 'our concern is that publication of Ordinance and any regulations thereunder should be limited to minimum by law so as to attract as little attention as possible'.[67] The Governor responded 'Ordinance would be published in BIOT Gazette which has only very limited circulation both here and overseas after signature by Commissioner. Publicity will therefore be minimal'.[68] It is inarguable that, in limited cases in the UK, inaccessibility is a deliberate policy.

Even with less controversial prerogative legislation, for example the legislation regulating the civil service in Northern Ireland, it is very difficult to actually find those laws. I speak from personal experience of drafting non-prerogative legislation on this subject, and trying to find out what the prerogative legislation actually contained. There was no easy way to find it.

[63] Reg 1(3), Health Protection (Coronavirus, International Travel, Operator Liability and Information to Passengers) (Amendment) Regulations (Northern Ireland) 2022.

[64] Bingham Centre for the Rule of Law at https://binghamcentre.biicl.org/.

[65] R Cormacain, 'Prerogative Legislation as the Paradigm of Bad Law-Making: The Chagos Islands' (2013) 39 *Commonwealth Law Bulletin* 487.

[66] A Tomkins, 'Magna Carta, Crown and Colonies' [2001] *Public Law* 571, 573.

[67] Telegram of 22/12/1970.

[68] Telegram of 11/1/1971.

2.3. Difficulties with Providing (Electronic) Access to Legislation

2.3.1. Cost

Hicks gave a presentation designed to assist drafting offices from around the world with purchasing electronic legislation systems.[69] The most basic system would cost between US $60,000 and US $120,000 (at 2011 prices) and would not include a website. In his view, a system that included a website and a way of updating legislation on that website would cost between US $120,000 and US $3,000,000. In Northern Ireland, the tender documentation for a system for drafting, printing and amending primary legislation suggested a contract price of £410,000.[70] It is possible to have a cheaper system. According to Marsh-Smith, the Isle of Man developed a system with a target budget of £60,000.[71] Cost-based objections to a new legislation system can be short sighted. In my view, a modern system can provide large financial benefits. These financial benefits ought to quickly recoup the cost of the financial outlay. For instance, time savings for civil servants researching legislation, avoidance of mistakes arising out of inability to find the law and attractiveness of the jurisdiction to businesses and investors.

2.3.2. Volume

There is no irrefutable logic that there must be a large volume of statutes, but in practice the year on year increase in statutes does seem inexorable. Dhavan argued that part of the problem was a prolific Parliament producing too many laws.[72] Margaret Thatcher stated that the opportunities for judges criticising prolix legislation were 'increasingly rare' due to the fulfilment of Renton's recommendations.[73] Regrettably this has turned out to be a Panglossian prediction. The 2011 annual volumes of UK primary legislation run to 2,789 pages. The 2008 volumes of secondary legislation run to 10,818 pages. The House of Commons Library prepared a briefing note entitled 'Acts and Statutory Instruments: the Volume of UK Legislation 1950 to 2012'.[74] The results from this detailed statistical analysis show that the figures cited above are, if anything, below the average annual page

[69] E Hicks, 'Implementing Legislation Systems – Considerations and Options' (CALC, Hyderabad, India, February 2011).

[70] Information contained in the Tenders Electronic Daily, Supplement to the Official Journal of the European Union, <http://ted.europa.eu/udl?uri=TED:NOTICE:244968-2011:TEXT:EN:HTML&tabId=1>.

[71] Marsh-Smith and Wright (n 28).

[72] R Dhavan, 'Legislative Simplicity and Interpretative Complexity – a Comment on the Renton Committee on "the Preparation of Legislation"' (1976) 5 *Anglo-American Law Review* 64.

[73] Renton, 'The Renton Report's Tenth Birthday' (1985) 6 *Statute Law Review* 60.

[74] https://researchbriefings.files.parliament.uk/documents/CBP-7438/CBP-7438.pdf, House of commons library briefing paper, CBP 7438, 4 November 2019, by Chris Watson.

output of the last 10 years. The government's own drafters agree, citing volume as a cause of complexity in legislation.[75] The vast tidal wave of legislation enacted every year makes it difficult to access the specific legislative provision required. Spencer refers to this as 'binge law-making',[76] and for Karpen one goal of legisprudence is to reduce the quantity of legislation.[77]

2.3.3. Interconnectedness

As a former First Parliamentary Counsel put it, we have 'an intricate web of laws'.[78] It is rare to find a statute that exists in a vacuum, unconnected to any other piece of legislation. If a new criminal offence is enacted, it presupposes the existence of a raft of other pieces of legislation. It requires other legislation to set out the powers of arrest, rules of court indicating the manner in which the offence can be prosecuted, evidential rules on what can be relied upon to prove the offence, sentencing guidelines, prison rules, judicial appointment procedures etc. Each of these are a degree removed from the original provision, but they do have some sort of connection to it. The more interconnected legislation is, the harder it is to make it fully accessible.

2.3.4. Dynamic Legislation

There is not one tidal wave of legislation; there are fresh tidal waves every year. New law is constantly changing old law. So a system of accessible laws doesn't simply have to deal with all the laws in force at a particular date, it has to deal with all the new laws as and when they are made.

At the micro level, although there is a single date upon which a statute is enacted, it regularly comes into force on different days. Take for example the Criminal Justice (Northern Ireland) Order 1999:

- Articles 1, 2, 33, 35, 44 to 47, 53 to 56, 57 (partially), 58 (partially), Schedule 5 (partially), Schedule 6 (partially), Schedule 7 (partially) came into force on the 25th of July 1997.[79]

[75] Office of the Parliamentary Counsel, 'When Laws Become Too Complex – Inside Government' (March 2013) <www.gov.uk/government/publications/when-laws-become-too-complex/when-laws-become-too-complex>.

[76] JR Spencer, 'Criminal Justice Legislation That Everyone Can Understand: A Flying Pig or a Realistic Aspiration' (Institute of Advanced Legal Studies, 25 January 2016). See also What the eye says, 'The Shame of Britain's Binge Law Making' [2005] *Private Eye* 24 (with special thanks to *Private Eye* for sending me this article from their archives).

[77] U Karpen and H Xanthaki (eds), *Legislation in Europe: A Comprehensive Guide for Scholars and Practitioners* (Oxford, Hart, 2017) 1.

[78] Office of the Parliamentary Counsel (n 75).

[79] Under the Criminal Justice (1996) Order (Commencement No. 1) Order (Northern Ireland) 1997 No 267.

- Articles 3 to 22, 24 to 32, 34, 36, 37, 48 to 52, Schedules 1, 2, 3 and 4 came into force on the 1st of January 1998.[80]
- Part III came into force on 1 June 1999.[81]

Different commencement dates make it more difficult to meaningfully access legislation.

2.3.5. Authority

Legislation needs to be authentic and authoritative. Historically this has meant that laws must be published in paper form, or even on vellum as described by Bennion.[82] It should be noted that 'paper' is not synonymous with 'authentic'. The use of correction slips to remedy defects in published legislation shows that paper is no guarantee of accuracy. In some ways, a fully auditable electronic system provides more guarantees against interference with the content of legislation. Some jurisdictions have put electronic systems onto a statutory footing. The EU adopted Regulation 216/2013 on electronic publication of the EU Official Journal. Article 1.2 provides that the Official Journal be published electronically and that this electronic publication is authentic and shall produce legal effects. As another example, the long title of the Legislation Publication Ordinance in Hong Kong reads:

> An Ordinance to provide for the establishment of an electronic database of legislation and approval of a website on which the information in the database may be published and accessed; to give legal status to copies of the legislation published on an approved website.

2.3.6. Paper-Based Process

The only thing that Parliament votes upon is the two-dimensional written page before it. This rules out many accessibility improvements that relate to the medium: no hypertext links, no pop-up windows, no 'click here' suggestions. Most of the modern technological tools developed to promote accessibility are not strictly part of the actual statute passed by Parliament. These are editorial additions that, although helpful, have not been authorised by the legislature, and are therefore not technically part of the legislation. If this position was reversed, it would be interesting how Parliament and the law would react – does a broken link mean that a statute is wrong? Despite such theoretical concerns, in a digital age, reliance upon

[80] Under the Criminal Justice (1996) Order (Commencement No 2) Order (Northern Ireland) 1997 No 523.

[81] Under the Criminal Justice (1996) Order (Commencement No 3) Order (Northern Ireland) 1999 No 230.

[82] F Bennion, 'Modern Royal Assent Procedure at Westminster' (1980) 2 *Statute Law Review* 133.

a printed Act of Parliament limits the use of additional digital tools to enhance accessibility.

2.3.7. Bilingualism

There is an additional factor on availability when we consider the UK as a whole – the need for bilingual legislation. Acts of Senedd Cymru are required to be in both English and Welsh, and both texts are to be treated as being of equal standing.[83] Scotland has a Gaelic Language (Scotland) Act 2005, although there is no legislative obligation to have Scottish legislation in Gaelic language as used in Scotland. It has also been a long-standing policy goal of some political parties in Northern Ireland that there be an Irish Language Act that would make similar provision for Northern Ireland in respect of the Irish language. There is now a policy commitment contained in the New Decade, New Approach agreement to bring forward legislation on the Irish language in Northern Ireland.[84]

There are far reaching consequences of a requirement for bilingual legislation. The most obvious one is the practical one of resources – the time and personnel available to enact legislation in two languages. Then there are matters of process, whether to simply translate one language into the other at various points in the legislative process, or whether instead to co-draft (following the Canadian model for French / English legislation). In Ireland, there is an obligation that 'As soon as may be after the enactment of any Act of the Oireachtas, the text thereof shall be printed and published in each of the official languages simultaneously'.[85] Then there are the difficulties arising from words having different shades of meaning in different languages, meaning that a direct translation of an English word into a Welsh (or Irish or Scottish Gaelic) word may not always make sense, or convey the same meaning.[86] For example, if a statute in Northern Ireland was to translate the English word 'field' into Irish, what Irish word would it use: *geamhar* – a field of corn-grass, *tuar* – a field for cattle at night, r*eidhlean* – a field for games or dancing, or any of the other 29 separate words for field in Irish as described by Manchán Magan.[87]

It is beyond the scope of this book to advise on the best way to draft and enact bilingual legislation, see instead the analysis of Watkins.[88] Suffice to say that bilingualism can both improve and cloud access to legislation – more people can potentially now read the law, but preparing it in both languages takes time, and has

[83] Government of Wales Act 2006, s 156.

[84] New Decade, New Approach (January 2020).

[85] Official Languages Act 2003, in Irish the title is Acht na dTeangacha Oifigiúla 2003.

[86] TG Watkin, 'Bilingual Legislation: Awareness, Ambiguity, and Attitudes' (2016) 37 *Statute Law Review* 116.

[87] M Magan, *32 Words for Field: Lost Words of the Irish Landscape* (Dublin, Gill Books, 2020).

[88] TG Watkin, 'Bilingual Legislation and the Law of England and Wales' (2014) 2 *Theory and Practice of Legislation* 229.

the potential to create ambiguity when there are now two competing authoritative versions of the text.

Part 2: Promoting Accessibility in the Form of Legislation

2.4. Availability

The most basic requirement of accessibility is that legislation is physically available to the public in the sense that they can see the actual text, either on screen or on paper, or in another tangible way for those with a visual impairment. The New Zealand Law Commission stated that access to legislation had three meanings: availability to the public, navigability and clarity.[89] Carter described it in this way: 'availability involves provision to the public, and especially to users, of hard copies, or copies available electronically'.[90] Users need to be able to place their hands on the actual paper of the legislation, or be able to read the actual words of the legislation on screen. Availability in this basic or general sense is arguably not a form of legislation principle. However, it is included here for two reasons. First, as it directly touches upon the enactment and production of legislation, it is not unreasonable to expect those doing the enacting to promote availability even if they can't actually physically deliver it. Second, as will be seen below, when the concept of availability is deconstructed, some aspects of it are actually capable of being implemented in the form of legislation.

2.4.1. Electronic or Non-electronic Availability

The primary focus in this chapter is on electronic availability of legislation. Hard copies of legislation remain useful, but electronic availability is more important for several reasons. First, the hard copy can swiftly become out of date as the law is amended. Second, in the information age, information is increasingly consumed not just electronically, but online. Having said this, there is no guarantee that electronic versions are more accurate than hard copies, or will last as long as hard copies.

According to Gee, the top ambition for university law libraries in the UK is to develop and enhance their electronic and digital resources.[91] His research found that the top free website in UK law libraries was the website of the British and Irish

[89] Law Commission, *Presentation of New Zealand Statute Law* (n 33) 13.

[90] J Burrows and R Carter, *Statute Law in New Zealand* 4th edn (London, LexisNexis, 2009) 141.

[91] D Gee, 'Survey of Major Law Libraries around the World' (2013) 41 *International Journal of Legal Information* 108.

Legal Information Institute at www.baili.org and the second most popular was the official government website on legislation at www.legislation.gov.uk.[92] According to Bertlin[93] legislation.gov.uk has two million separate visitors per month, and provides more than 400,000,000 page impressions per year. Oksanen goes even further, arguing not just that electronic legislation must be available for human consumption, but must also be available for machine processing.[94]

Having said this, there are dangers if legislation is only available electronically. There are those who, for economic reasons, may not be able to afford the technology necessary to look up laws online. There will also be those who live in places with limited electronic infrastructure to allow for online access. During Covid lockdowns, those who rely on internet cafes or public libraries for their internet access may find that route cut off. Finally, some people may have a disability that makes electronic access more challenging.

2.4.2. What Must be Available?

I said above that the principle is that legislation must be available – but what is the exact content of this, what is it that must be made available in order to comply with the Rule of Law? In my view, there are six aspects of availability.[95] The first four aspects are what Fuller would call the morality of duty – minimum requirements that must be fulfilled. The final two are morality of aspiration – a summit to aim at, although the legislation will still be valid even if it doesn't crest the summit.

2.4.3. Aspect 1: Availability of Law as Enacted

Legislation must be placed online as soon as it is made. All that is required for this aspect is a snapshot of the law as enacted, not how it changes over time. Drilling down into this, it becomes apparent that there is an important but subtle distinction between the date a statute is made and the date it comes into effect. Although it is important for law to be available as soon as it is made, it is even more important for it to be available before it comes into force.

There is a quantitative aspect to availability. If a specific statute or the official legislation website is online but doesn't appear near the top of search rankings, it is

[92] D Gee, 'SLS/BIALL Academic Law Library Survey 2012/2013' (2014) 14 *Legal Information Management* 215.

[93] A Bertlin, 'What Works Best for the Reader? A Study on Drafting and Presenting Legislation' [2014] *The Loophole* 25.

[94] Arttu Oksanen and others, 'Semantic Finlex: Finnish Legislation and Case Law as a Linked Open Data Service', *International Conference on Law via the Internet* (Joint project between Aalto University, HELDIG – Helsinki Centre for Digital Humanities, the Ministry of Justice, the Ministry of Finance, Edita Publishing Ltd, Tekes and Viestintäalan tutkimussäätiö 2018).

[95] For an earlier version of this analysis, see R Cormacain, 'Have the Renton Committee's Recommendations on Electronic Access to Legislation Been Fulfilled?' (2013) 19 *Web Journal of Current Legal Issues*.

less visible to users. A great website that is little known or doesn't reach the top of search algorithms isn't truly accessible.

This aspect of availability is something that those enacting legislation can facilitate, for example by recommending or requiring that resources are devoted to the publication of legislation. It is also something the legislator can have a direct effect upon by striving to ensure that commencement dates are sufficiently far from the date that legislation is made so that there is time for the law to be published before it comes into effect. This is a bare minimum, and there should also be sufficient time after publication to allow the public to make preparations to comply with the legislation.

2.4.4. Aspect 2: Availability of Law as Amended

A legislative system needs to keep all legislation up to date, what Benedetto refers to as interventions of compilation and consolidation.[96] This is one goal of the New Zealand Public Access to Legislation project.[97] This means that where new legislation amends old legislation, the old legislation on screen should fully reflect all those amendments. The system needs to tell users what the law is today, as well as what it was when it was enacted. This is the key aspect of a successful system. If the system cannot tell the citizen what the law is, it has failed.

There is one specific tool that has been used in this regard in the UK – the Keeling schedule. I deal with the Keeling schedule in chapter five under the heading of intelligibility.

Aspect 2 is complicated by commencement provisions, or more specifically, by the practice of different provisions commencing at different times. In the past, an Act was made and then a reasonably short period afterwards it came into force. Now it is quite common for the commencement of an Act to spread out over a long period of time, with different provisions coming into force at different times. Sometimes the different commencement dates are set out in the legislation itself, sometimes there is a power of a Minister to commence different provisions at different times. This creates an extra level of complexity for users. In addition to tracking what legislation has been enacted over time, they must also track what legislation has been brought into force over time. For a bad example, see the Public Services Ombudsman Act (Northern Ireland) 2016. In section 64 of that Act:

- Subsection (1) sets out provisions coming into force on 1 April 2016;
- subsection (2) sets out provisions coming into force on the day after Royal Assent;

[96] M de Benedetto, 'Maintenance of Rules', in *Legislation in Europe: A Comprehensive Guide for Scholars and Practitioners* (Oxford, Hart Publishing, 2017).

[97] K Anthony, 'Public Access to Legislation Project: Served with Accompaniments' (2008) 16 *Australian Law Librarian* 21. See also G Lawn, 'Improving Public Access to Legislation: The New Zealand Experience so Far' (2004) 6 *UTS Law Review* 49.

- subsection (3) sets out provisions coming into force on 1 October 2016;
- subsection (4) sets out the provisions coming into force on 1 April 2017;
- subsection (5) sets out the provisions coming into force on 1 April 2018; and
- subsection (6) gives the Assembly Commission the power to commence other provisions on different dates.

Each of these subsections is complicated in its own right. How much simpler for the user (and those trying to organise the statute book) if there was a simple statement that 'This Act comes into operation on 1 April 2016'. Practical realities may make this simple solution unfeasible, for example if there is a particular policy reason why commencement dates need to be staggered.

There are several techniques to address the difficulties posed by different commencement dates. First, the legislator can confirm that a proposed legislative provision will actually be used. There is no point in clogging up the statute book with a provision that the government are not sure will ever be brought into force. For example, as the Easter Act 1928 (introduced as a Private Members' Bill) has never been commenced, why was it ever enacted? Second, the legislature can enact a simple commencement provision that commences the entire Act in one fell swoop, rather than having it commenced in fits and starts. Having said this, a complex set of reforms may need to be spread over time. Third, a commencement date can be inserted on the face of the Act. This way the reader will at least know, from reading the Act, when it comes into force. This tool is less necessary as there is now a power to amend legislation to include the actual commencement date on the face of it.[98] Fourth, where the government seeks a power to commence an Act by future subordinate legislation, a limited rather than extensive power can be given. For example, a power to commence the Act, rather than a power to commence different provisions of the Act on different days. Failing this, there ought to be a clear justification given why different provisions need to be commenced at different times, not just for reasons of administrative convenience.

One problematic issue here is where defective legislation is corrected judicially on the principles set out in *Inco Europe v First Choice Distribution*.[99] Although drafting mistakes are obviously to be avoided, it is inevitable that they will occasionally occur. Overt judicial correction of drafting mistakes (or what Bennion calls a rectifying construction)[100] is an established aspect of the UK legal system. The point here is not to question the limits of that power to correct, but to ask what consequences it has for the availability of legislation. Correcting a mistake may do justice in the individual case before a judge, but will not serve the population as

[98] s 104 Deregulation Act 2015.

[99] [2001] 1 WLR 568 HL.

[100] O Jones, *Bennion on Statutory Interpretation* 6th revised edn (London, Butterworths Law, 2013) ch 15.

a whole unless they know that the mistake has been corrected. The reader of the statute book will still see the incorrect words used in that statute and will not have an easy way of knowing what the judicial correction is.

If a mistake is found in legislation (by a judge or by anyone else), it is incumbent for it to be rectified *in the statute book* as soon as possible. Although the legislature may be embarrassed about a long title that includes the phrase 'An Act to rectify a mistake in [previous legislation]'[101] or 'correcting a mistake in the repeals effected by [previous legislation]'[102] it is still better to correct it than to allow the mistake to fester on the statute book.

There was an attempt in the past to pass a Bill entitled the Acts of Parliament (Correction of Mistakes) Bill. It was designed to allow for a simple procedure for Parliament to fix a mistake in an Act. The Bill was withdrawn before there was a chance to enact it, leading to the famous headline: 'Mistake Bill was a Mistake: Minister Admits'.[103]

2.4.5. Aspect 3: Law at a Point in Time

A legislative database needs to state what the law was at a particular point in time in the past. There will be many situations when past legal rights and obligations will be relevant – when a person did X, was X unlawful? For example, consider the Historical Institutional Abuse Inquiry that was obliged by statute to investigate child abuse in Northern Ireland between 1922 and 1995.[104] Part of its remit necessitated knowing what the legislative requirements were in respect of the care of children between those dates. Without knowing the legal architecture in place, the Inquiry could not effectively investigate breaches of the law.

It is unrealistic to expect legislation to stay the same forever. It needs to adapt and change as society changes. In some cases, there will be an 'arms race' as citizens take action to get around rules and then new rules emerge to stop this. However, there comes a point where frequent changes to rules make it virtually impossible to know what the rules are at any point in time.

Consider two recent poor examples of rapidly changing law. The UK Immigration Rules for 'normal' periods (UK) and the International Travel Regulations (Northern Ireland) for 'emergency periods'. In both cases the rapidity of rule changes makes it extremely hard for citizens to know what the law is. Table 1 sets out the dates when immigration rules changed (between 19 January 2012 and 16 October 2014), and when the travel rules changed (between 8 June 2020 and 27 March 2021).

[101] See the Act of 1823 4 Geo 4 c 10.

[102] Statute Law Revision (Northern Ireland) Act 1973.

[103] S Reynolds, '"You Have Committed a Great Offence and Have but a Weak Answer to Make for Yourself": When Clerks Make Mistakes' [2013] *The Table* 4.

[104] Inquiry into Historical Institutional Abuse Act (Northern Ireland) 2013.

Table 1 Rapidly changing legislation

Immigration rules amended on …	
16 October 2014	11 March 2013
10 July 2014	7 February 2013
10 June 2014	30 January 2013
1 April 2014	20 December 2012
13 March 2014	12 December 2012
10 March 2014	22 November 2012
18 December 2013	5 September 2012
10 December 2013	9 July 2012
9 December 2013	? July 2012 (actual date not specified on government website)
? November 2013 (actual date not specified on government website)	? June 2012 (actual date not specified on government website)
6 September 2013	? April 2012 (actual date not specified on government website)
10 June 2013	15 March 2012
? April 2013 (actual date not specified on government website)	19 January 2012
14 March 2013	

Coronavirus International Travel Regulations amended on …	
8 June 2020	6 November 2020
10 July 2020	14 November 2020
12 July 2020	21 November 2020
26 July 2020	24 November 2020
28 July 2020	28 November 2020
31 July 2020	11 December 2020
7 August 2020	19 December 2020
29 August 2020	23 December 2020
9 September 2020	9 January 2021
12 September 2020	12 January 2021
19 September 2020	14 January 2021
3 October 2020	16 January 2021
10 October 2020	11 February 2021
18 October 2020	20 February 2021
25 October 2020	19 March 2021
30 October 2020	27 March 2021

The immigration rules changed 27 times in three years. They changed on 9, 10 and 18 December 2013. This makes it extremely difficult for an ordinary user to know what the law is at a particular point in time. Even officials will struggle to keep up to date. The entire thrust of Yeo's analysis of immigration legislation is that it does not comply with the Rule of Law.[105] Likewise, the Public Prosecution Service in Northern Ireland felt unable to bring a prosecution for breach of coronavirus rules because they had changed so frequently. Their statement on their decision not to prosecute said 'the law as it applied to the Storey funeral was changed significantly on the evening before the funeral and further amended two days later'.[106] The rapidity of the change meant it would have been unfair to prosecute in respect of breach of the changing law.

Those charged with making legislation have a role to play here. Parliamentarians should not simply acquiesce in enacting legislation that is so volatile that it makes a mockery out of any attempt by the citizen (or immigrant) to have meaningful access to the legislation. There comes a point when incontinent legislative changes undermine the Rule of Law and legislators have to at the very least counsel that there needs to be more stability. Lord Justice Beatson expressed concern over the Immigration Rules on this very point. He stated

> The detail, the number of documents that have to be consulted, the number of changes in rules and policy guidance, and the difficulty advisers face in ascertaining which previous version of the rule or guidance applies and obtaining it are real obstacles to achieving predictable consistency and restoring public trust in the system, particularly in an area of law that lay people and people whose first language is not English need to understand.[107]

2.4.6. Aspect 4: Law in a Particular Geographical Area

The legal jurisdictions in the UK[108] are:

- England and Wales
- Scotland
- Northern Ireland

[105] C Yeo, 'How Complex Are the UK Immigration Rules and Is This a Problem?' <www.freemovement.org.uk/how-complex-are-the-uk-immigration-rules-and-is-this-a-problem/?utm_source=rss&utm_medium=rss&utm_campaign=how-complex-are-the-uk-immigration-rules-and-is-this-a-problem&utm_source=FM+master+list&utm_campaign=f5aa408822-RSS_EMAIL_CAMPAIGN_DAILY&utm_medium=email&utm_term=0_792133aa40-f5aa408822-105097653&mc_cid=f5aa408822&mc_eid=bfe873d008>.

[106] 'Public Statement Relating to Decisions Not to Prosecute 24 Individuals Reported for Breaches of the Coronavirus Regulations in Connection with Attendance at the Funeral of Bobby Storey on 30 June 2020' (Public Prosecution Service (Northern Ireland) 2021) <www.ppsni.gov.uk/sites/ppsni/files/publications/PPS%20Public%20Statement%20on%20Covid%20funeral%2030%20March%202021_0.pdf>.

[107] *Hossain v Secretary of State for the Home Department* [2015] EWCA Civ 207 at [30]. Yeo sets out a number of other cases where judges have repeated these concerns, Yeo (n 104).

[108] Excluding Crown Dependencies and British Overseas Territories.

Even though England and Wales are a single jurisdiction, it is possible to have different laws for England and Wales.[109] So a more accurate description of the different laws applying in the different parts of the UK is:

- Law of England and Wales as it applies in England and Wales
- Law of England and Wales as it applies in Wales
- Law of England and Wales as it applies in England
- Law of Scotland
- Law of Northern Ireland

The rise of devolution has increased the degree of divergence of legislation between these areas. This is not simply in terms of where they apply, but also the way in which they apply. As Watkin points out, the devolution statutes are 'inevitably silent as to how the style of the legislation made at Holyrood and Stormont or in Cardiff Bay is to relate to that enacted at Westminster and as to how the approach to the drafting of legislation for the devolved legislatures is to develop'.[110] This means that we have three jurisdictions and five geographical areas in which law can apply. This does not consider experimental/trial legislation. It also does not consider the expired jurisdictions such as legislation that applied throughout the island of Ireland before Northern Ireland was established.[111]

When the procedures for enacting legislation are considered, this becomes even more confusing. The Westminster Parliament can pass legislation for all, or any part of the UK. The Northern Ireland Assembly can only pass legislation for Northern Ireland.[112] As part of this, it can amend any UK legislation in so far as it applies in Northern Ireland. Senedd Cyrmu can pass legislation for Wales.[113] As part of this, it can amend any UK legislation in so far as it applies in Wales. It can also amend the law of England and Wales as it applies in England, if that is incidental to amending the law of England and Wales as it applies in Wales.[114] The Scottish Parliament can only pass legislation for Scotland.[115] As part of this, it can amend any UK legislation in so far as it applies in Scotland.

There is a further level of complication. The Secretary of State (for Wales) can make secondary legislation, in consequence of legislation made by Senedd Cymru, which amends the law of England, Wales and Northern Ireland (but not Scotland).[116] The monarch, by order in council (in effect the Secretary of State for Northern Ireland), can make secondary legislation, in consequence of legislation

[109] TG Watkin, *The Legal History of Wales* 2nd edn (Cardiff, University of Wales Press, 2012) 208.
[110] Watkin (n 87) 230.
[111] B Dickson, *Law in Northern Ireland* 2nd edn (Oxford, Hart 2013) 69. Dickson lists seven legislatures that have (or had) jurisdiction to pass laws for Northern Ireland, not counting secondary legislation or the European Union.
[112] s 6 Northern Ireland Act 1998.
[113] s 108 Government of Wales Act 2006.
[114] ibid.
[115] s 29 Scotland Act 1998.
[116] s 150 Government of Wales Act 2006.

made by the Northern Ireland Assembly, which amends the law of any part of the UK.[117] The monarch, by order in council or a Minister of the Crown, can make secondary legislation in consequence of legislation passed by the Scottish Parliament (presumably amending the law of any part of the UK although this isn't explicit).[118]

The net result of this is that it is hard to ascertain the geographical extent of UK laws. They may apply (or extend) to one or more parts of the UK. Sometimes they will, on their face, amend the law of the UK, but the effect is only to amend the law of the UK in so far as it applies to one particular part of the UK. The law may be repealed in one jurisdiction, but not another. For example, the Autism Act (NI) 2011 amends the Disability Discrimination Act 1995 by inserting new provisions relating to autism. But even though the 1995 Act is UK-wide, the provisions relating to autism only apply to Northern Ireland. This is further complicated by the fact that the 1995 Act has now been repealed, in relation to England, Wales and Scotland, leading to the following footnotes in the text of the online version:

> E1 In its application to Northern Ireland, this Schedule has effect subject to the modifications set out in Sch. 8; see s. 70(6)
>
> E4 Following the repeal of this Act for E.W.S. by the Equality Act 2010, this provision now extends to Northern Ireland only
>
> F5 Act repealed (E.W.S.) (1.10.2010 (except for the repeal of ss. 49A-49D) and 5.4.2011 in so far as not already in force) by Equality Act 2010 (c. 15), 216(3), Sch. 27 Pt. 1 (as substituted (1.10.2010) by S.I. 2010/2279, Sch. 2) (with ss. 6(4), 205, and with amendments and savings in the said S.I. 2010/2279, art. 16); S.I. 2010/2317, art. 2(15)(f) (with arts. 4-25, Schs. 1-16); S.I. 2011/1066, art. 2(h)
>
> F6 Sch. 1 para. 4(1)(i)(j) inserted (N.I.) (9.8.2011) by Autism Act (Northern Ireland) 2011 (c. 27 (N.I.)), ss. 1(2), 5

For someone who has spent years reading legislation, this makes sense. For the non-specialist reader, it will look like a foreign language.

What does this all mean? It means that there is no universal text of legislation. Unlike the speed of light, which is constant to all observers, legislation varies depending upon where the observer is standing. This complication is exacerbated by a particular focus on Westminster legislation that leads to consideration of devolved legislation being marginalised.[119]

A good system of legislation needs to specify to users what the law is in a particular area. As well as the temporal division in aspects 1 to 3, there is also the spatial division in aspect 4. When it comes to the form of legislation, there are two main tools used to demarcate the geographical boundaries of legislation: the extent section and the territorial limits of devolved legislatures.

[117] s 84 Northern Ireland Act 1998.
[118] s 104 Scotland Act 1998.
[119] Law Commission, 'Form and Accessibility of the Law Applicable in Wales' (Law Commission 2015) Consultation Paper No 223 15.

The extent section is the section in a (Westminster) Act setting out to what parts of the UK the Act applies.

A simple example is in the Telecommunications (Security) Act 2021.

> This Act extends to England and Wales, Scotland and Northern Ireland.[120]

A more complicated one is the Botulinum Toxin and Cosmetic Fillers (Children) Act 2021.

> (1) Subject to subsection (2), this Act extends to England and Wales only.
> (2) Sections 4(3) and 5 extend to England and Wales, Scotland and Northern Ireland.[121]

It can then get increasingly complex. The Modern Slavery Act 2015 has the following provision

> (1) Parts 1, 2 and 5 (except for section 53) and section 54A, and Schedule 4A, in Part 7 extend to England and Wales only, subject to subsection (4).
> (2) Part 3 extends as follows—
>   (a) section 35 extends to England and Wales only;
>   (b) section 36 extends to Scotland only;
>   (c) section 37 extends to Northern Ireland only;
>   (d) sections 38 and 39, and Schedule 2, extend to England and Wales, Scotland and Northern Ireland.
> (3) Part 4, section 53 in Part 5 and Parts 6 and 7 (except for section 54A and Schedule 4A) extend to England and Wales, Scotland and Northern Ireland, subject to subsections (4) and (5).
> (4) An amendment or repeal made by this Act has the same extent as the provision amended or repealed.
> (5) But the amendments and repeals made by the following provisions of Schedule 5 extend to England and Wales only—
>   (a) paragraph 2,
>   (b) paragraph 5(2),
>   (c) paragraph 6,
>   (d) paragraph 8,
>   (e) paragraph 21.[122]

Each devolved jurisdiction has the territorial limit on its legislative competence set out above. For example, the Northern Ireland Assembly can only enact legislation for Northern Ireland. It has no competence to enact legislation for any other part of the UK. This territorial limitation is contained in the legislation establishing the devolved legislatures, but it is not stated in the legislation that they enact. So, legislation of devolved legislatures will include 'Northern Ireland', 'Scotland' or 'Wales' in the title, but will not contain an express statement anywhere 'this Act only extends to Northern Ireland/Scotland/Wales'. It could therefore be assumed that if the geographical name appears in the title, the reader will know

[120] s 27.
[121] s 6.
[122] s 60.

that the legislation only extends to that area. Unfortunately, this is not so. An Act may be UK-wide even if a particular name appears in the title. For example, the Corporation Tax (Northern Ireland) Act 2015 forms part of the law of England and Wales, Scotland and Northern Ireland (it was passed by the Westminster Parliament). But the Air Passenger Duty (Setting of Rate) Act (Northern Ireland) 2012 only forms part of the law of Northern Ireland (it was passed by the Northern Ireland Assembly).

Adding complexity, there is no uniform approach between the devolved jurisdictions about where to put the name of the jurisdiction in legislation made by each devolved legislature. In Northern Ireland, the jurisdiction comes after the word Act, hence the Budget Act (Northern Ireland) 2020. But in Wales and Scotland, it comes before the word Act, hence the Wild Animals and Circuses (Wales) Act 2020 and the Tied Pubs (Scotland) Act 2021. To highlight the absurdity of this state of affairs, consider hypothetical legislation on firearms.

- Firearms Act (Northern Ireland) – made by the Northern Ireland Assembly
- Firearms (Northern Ireland) Act – made by the Westminster Parliament, but relating to Northern Ireland in some way
- Firearms Act – made by the Westminster Parliament, but title doesn't reveal if it applies in Northern Ireland (or Wales or Scotland)
- Firearms (Wales) Act – made by either the Westminster Parliament, or by Senedd Cymru, no way of knowing from the title.

This is all very confusing for the reader. In order to know if a statute applies in the area they are situated in, they need to know about extent clauses, which legislature made the statute and the territorial limitations of that legislature. These are not pieces of information that the casual reader of statutes would have access to.

There are three forms of legislation solutions available to remedy this: a presentational one and two legislative drafting ones. The presentational solution is one already adopted by the official government website on legislation. This is that the legislation is displayed with additional information setting out geographical extent. This way the reader can see at a glance to which part of the UK it applies. Subscription databases such as Westlaw also provide this service.

The first legislative drafting solution is to expressly include the geographical extent of legislation in section, chapter or part titles. For example, section 26ZB of the Children Act 1989 is entitled 'Representations: further consideration (Wales)' and the cross head before section 79N of that Act is entitled 'Inspection: England'. This immediately tells the reader what geographical area the legislation is relevant to. This is helpful if there are consecutive provisions setting out different rules for the different jurisdictions. However, this approach would quickly become cumbersome if every section title in an Act had to include the name of the jurisdiction to which it applied.

The second legislative drafting solution is more radical. Each Act of a devolved jurisdiction should include an extent clause at the end setting out the jurisdiction to which it applies. This is most definitely not the practice in any of the devolved jurisdictions, no legislation passed by them contains an extent clause. This is for the simple reason that it is unnecessary as, constitutionally, their laws can only extend to their own jurisdiction. The only exception I have seen is in a Private Members' Bill currently before the Northern Ireland Assembly that includes an extent clause stating that it extends to Northern Ireland.[123] An extent clause is constitutionally unnecessary. However, it would greatly assist the reader of legislation who is unfamiliar with all the complications around geographical application of laws set out in this section.

2.4.7. Aspect 5: Legislation in Context

A legislative system needs to be able to cite legal provisions in context. If another piece of information (legislative or otherwise) would help the reader to understand a law, it would be helpful if the reader were made aware of that information. The Interim Woolf Report expressed this aspect as follows:

> Eventually, fully integrated legal information systems will combine legislation, case law and specialist commentary, all structured in such a way that users will be able to find their way more easily through these materials.[124]

The form of legislation, in the broadest sense of how legislation is presented, can address this ambition in several ways. First, a statute could contain internal (hypertext) links to related parts of the statute. For instance, if section 2 refers to section 50, as well as a textual reference there could be a hypertext link. The National Archives and the Office of the Parliamentary Counsel carried out research in 2012 /2013 on how users interacted with The National Archives website.[125] One finding was that many users are not familiar with the structure of legislation, for example division into sections and schedules. Internal links help overcome lack of familiarity with legislative structure. An easy way to help readers unfamiliar with the relationship between sections and schedules is to have a hypertext link to the schedule in the section.

Second, the statute could contain hypertext links to related external statutory provisions. The most obvious one would be if Act X refers to Act Y, that it also includes a clickable link to Act Y. Less obvious, but potentially even more helpful, would be a link to secondary legislation made under the power of primary legislation. A factory manager reading the Climate Change (Emissions Reduction Targets) (Scotland) Act 2019 will be less interested in knowing that there is a power to make regulations changing emission targets, and more interested in clicking through to the actual text of those regulations.

[123] Climate Change Bill, currently before the Northern Ireland Assembly.
[124] Lord Woolf, 'Access to Justice: Interim Report' (1995).
[125] A Bertlin, 'Clarity in Drafting: How Can We Know What Works Best for the Reader?' (Cape Town, April 2013); Office of the Parliamentary Counsel (n 75).

External legislative links are easy to imagine when there is a direct textual reference to the provisions of another Act. They are much more difficult if there is no textual reference to the other statute, but that other statute is still connected. Take the example of section 33 of the Justice Act (Northern Ireland) 2016. That section provides for the establishment of the office of Prison Ombudsman for Northern Ireland. The reader of section 33 is unlikely to know that, under section 16 of the Interpretation Act (NI) 1954, members of a body can be appointed in advance of an enactment coming into force. The way the legislation is presented makes it nearly impossible for the casual reader to know of these interconnections. Creating this type of external link requires a certain amount of subjective judgement and is less easy to satisfy by way of algorithms.

Third, the legislation could have external links to non-legislative information that is relevant to the statute in question. Explanatory Notes are official documents, created by the government and designed to assist the reader in understanding legislation. However, technically, they do not form part of the legislation. Jenkins, former First Parliamentary Counsel in the UK, recommended that 'to make [Explanatory Notes] as widely accessible as possible, they would be made available on the internet alongside the Bill and subsequently the Act'.[126] This is current practice for UK legislation, where the official website contains both the legislation and the explanatory notes. Another type of official document is an official Impact Assessment prepared by the government to assist in the consideration of the merits of a piece of legislation. These are also now included on the official legislation website. However, the website does not as a matter of course include links to the reports of the Regulatory Policy Committee that assesses the quality of these Impact Assessments. This is an additional document would assist readers in determining the meaning, merits and purposes of legislation.

In addition to the non-legislative information suggested by Woolf above, there could also be links to Parliamentary debates, House of Commons Library Briefing Papers on Bills, etc. Irresberger states that if legislation allows for 'acceptable means of compliance', then those means must also be included or linked in some way to the legislation, otherwise accessibility is incomplete.[127] Watkin lauded the inclusion of the Convention on the Rights of the Child within a Welsh statute as 'a reader of the Measure would be able to discover what had been incorporated without having to seek out the text of the Convention and Protocols from another source'.[128] Occasionally, during a debate on a Bill, a minister won't be able to answer a point raised by a legislator and undertakes to answer the point in a letter at a later date. Greenberg points out that although the promise to write will be contained in

[126] Sir Christopher Jenkins KCB QC, Second Report of the Committee on the Modernisation of the House of Commons, HC 190 (1997–1998). Appendix, paragraph 19.

[127] K Irresberger and A Jasiak, 'Publication', in *Legislation in Europe: A Comprehensive Guide for Scholars and Practitioners* (Oxford, Hart Publishing, 2017).

[128] Watkin (n 86) 122.

the Hansard report, the actual letter won't. He argues that this letter should also be linked, in some way, to the proceedings in Parliament.[129] There is the potential for different levels of access to this information, that is, some items restricted for internal government use.

As well as external links to information that provides helpful background on legislation, or that may act as an aid to understanding it, there is also external information that is critical to the operation of the legislation. These could be things like official forms, Departmental guidance, codes of practice that must be complied with, documents or maps referred to in the legislation. If these things are not directly contained in the legislation, they must be referenced in the legislation, along with directions on how to access them. The Joint Committee on Statutory Instruments have expressly made this point, stating that

> Information on the availability of documents referred to in legislation should be included in the instrument itself (either in the footnotes or the Explanatory Note) rather than in the Explanatory Memorandum.[130]

It is perhaps when we come to consider criminal law that the need for this type of external information is most pressing. A criminal statute will tell the reader what the definition of an offence is, but it does not set out when a person will be prosecuted for that offence. That decision is a function of the Crown Prosecution Service, or the prosecuting authorities in the various devolved jurisdictions in the UK. Those prosecutors will often have key information that affects how offences will be prosecuted in practice. One of the most contentious of these types of decisions is the decision to prosecute for the offence of assisted suicide. Section 2 of the Suicide Act 1961 makes it an offence to encourage or assist in the suicide of another. It is perhaps too much to expect the Act to set out the details of when a prosecution will be launched. The factors to be considered have however been set out by the Crown Prosecution Service.[131] These include sensible factors such as the age of the victim, whether they had mental capacity etc. The difficulty is not the existence of these guidelines, but the fact that there is no reference to them in the statute law database entry for the Suicide Act 1961. This is useful contextual information and ideally should be visible and accessible alongside the legislation itself.

There are two methods for generating these links. The traditional way is the top-down approach where civil servants think through what they consider relevant to an Act and then create the links. The more innovative (and riskier) way is to use some Big Data concepts and allow links to be influenced by the choices

[129] Daniel Greenberg, *Laying Down the Law: A Discussion of the People, Processes and Problems That Shape Acts of Parliament* (London, Sweet & Maxwell, 2011) 54.

[130] Joint Committee on Statutory Instruments, *Transparency and Accountability in Secondary Legislation* (12 June 2018) para 4.8.

[131] Crown Prosecution Service *Suicide: Policy for Prosecutors in Respect of Cases of Encouraging or Assisting Suicide* (October 2014).

previously made by users. For example, if people who look at the Companies Act 2006 also usually look at the Insolvency Act 1986, then the system could automatically suggest that a reader of one also may find the other useful.

This desirability of making contextual information available is increasingly important with the rise of quasi-legislation.[132] Quasi-legislation is difficult to define, but it is essentially something that can have a legal effect without being itself legislation. Codes of practice, administrative rules, official guidance, memorandums of understanding, these are all examples of quasi legislation. Sometimes these may have statutory authority or be referred to in legislation. They can have a critical effect. For example, the codes of practice referred to in the Human Transplantation (Wales) Act 2013 set out guidance on how to handle family disputes in cases of organ donation after death. Accessibility of legislation extends to access to this type of relevant material also.

The court has recognised the importance of additional contextually relevant material. It stated in *R (Salih) v Secretary of State for the Home Department* [2003] EWHC 2273 (Admin) that

> it is in general inconsistent with the constitutional imperative that statute law be made known for the government to withhold information about its policy relating to the exercise of a power conferred by statute.

How far this extends is a question of degree. Official guidance drawn up by government in accordance with a statute does seem like precisely the kind of information that should be accessible alongside the legislation. However, what about guidance drawn up by private bodies that is referred to in the legislation? This issue arose in the Dutch Copyright Act. The Dutch Supreme Court ruled that this guidance did not constitute 'legislation' and was therefore not subject to the copyright provisions that ordinarily applied to legislation.[133] Although this decision may be correct in the narrow sense that guidance produced by a private body is not legislation, it is submitted that it is incorrect if it leads to such guidance being inaccessible. If it is directly relevant to the law, if it colours the way the law is applied, then it ought to be accessible alongside the law.

Another example is the memorandum of understanding on the role of regulators of financial services industry. Section 3E of the Financial Services and Markets Act 2000 obliges regulators to prepare a memorandum of understanding setting out their role. This must be given to the Treasury and laid before Parliament. It is clearly an important document, referred to in primary legislation, but it is not available alongside that legislation. This goes against the Rule of Law requirement of accessibility.

[132] HE Broring, 'Administrative Rules in British Law' (1994) 1 *Maastricht Journal of European and Comparative Law* 273.
[133] R van Gestel, 'Primacy of the European Legislature? Delegated Rule-Making and the Decline of the "Transmission Belt" Theory' (2014) 2 *The Theory and Practice of Legislation* 33.

2.4.8. Aspect 6: Findability

Morville defined findability as follows:

- The quality of being locatable or navigable.
- The degree to which a particular object is easy to discover or locate.
- The degree to which a system or environment supports navigation and retrieval.[134]

Lavery used the word in a legal context as long ago as 1943, considering a lawyer with a legal question, 'somewhere in that vast storehouse of the law is the answer to his problem, but he cannot find it'.[135] For Lavery the problem was the volume of law piling up, making it harder to find the desired nugget of legal information.

This requirement is the hardest of the accessibility principles to satisfy – the user ought to be able to retrieve the legislative answer to their question from a legislative database, even if the user does not know which piece of legislation contains the answer. If we start from the proposition that the user knows which section in which Act contains the answer to the question, it is relatively easy to design a legislation database that can quickly point to that section in that Act. However, it will be quite rare that the user knows the precise chapter and verse of the provision they are looking for. Much more common will be that they have an open question to which they seek an answer. The electronic system needs to facilitate easy access to help find the answer. For example, if the police arrest a child in Northern Ireland and decide not to release the child on bail, where must the child be placed in detention? The answer is contained in Article 39(8) of the Police and Criminal Evidence (NI) Order 1989. For the system to be effective, it must be able to display an accurate and up to date version of Article 39(8). But it must also be able to indicate to the user that the answer is contained within Article 39(8).

Findability flows into the form of legislation principle of navigability. Findability means the ability to find a particular piece of information whereas navigability relates to the ease of moving around the statute book. The basic concept for the legislator to bear in mind is to make it as easy as possible for the reader to find the information they are looking for.

2.4.9. Availability of Retained EU Law in the UK

Before Brexit (the United Kingdom leaving the European Union) EU legislation ran in a separate stream from domestic UK law in terms of accessibility. If an EU legislative measure wasn't transposed (directly written into domestic law), then it was only available on the EUR-lex servers hosted by the EU. In terms of availability, this was not ideal for UK citizens. There was an entire corpus of law, directly

[134] P Morville, *Ambient Findability: What We Find Changes Who We Become* (Sebastopol, O'Reilly, 2005).

[135] U Lavery, 'The "Findability" of the Law' (1943) 27 *Journal of the American Judicature Society* 25.

applicable in the UK, which nevertheless did not show up on the UK's domestic legislation website.

Paradoxically, post-Brexit there is now greater availability of EU law that is applicable in the UK.[136] The newly established category of 'retained EU law' is EU law that applied in the UK just before Brexit and that continues to apply until it is repealed.[137] The National Archives now keep a copy of retained EU law on its own website, which can be accessed alongside its records of domestic legislation. According to them

> Legislation.gov.uk is where you can find legislation originating from the EU as it now applies in the UK. This legislation will be kept up to date with any amendments made by the UK Parliaments, Governments and Assemblies.[138]

In terms of availability of legislation, this is very much to be welcomed.

However, there is now a caveat to this. Clause 56 of the Nationalities and Borders Bill reads (at present) as

> Section 4 of the European Union (Withdrawal) Act 2018 (saving for rights etc under section 2(1) of the European Communities Act 1972) ceases to apply to rights, powers, liabilities, obligations, restrictions, remedies and procedures derived from the Trafficking Directive so far as their continued existence would otherwise be incompatible with provision made by or under this Act.

This is quite a mouthful, but what it means is that if there is something in the Trafficking Directive that is incompatible with a provision in the Bill, or a provision in secondary legislation made under the Bill, then that part of the Trafficking Directive no longer has effect. This is very unsatisfactory in terms of availability of legislation. The Trafficking Directive is part of retained EU law, and therefore part of the legislation applying in the UK. If the new policy is to repeal or modify part of it, then that is a normal part of the ebb and flow of the statute book, and it should be repealed or amended in the normal way. But the provision in the Bill doesn't make a formal repeal or amendment to the Directive. There is no change to the text of the Directive, but nevertheless that text is no longer authoritative. If there is something in the Directive that is incompatible with the Bill, then that part of the Directive is no longer law. How is the citizen to make sense of this? If they look on the official government website, they will see the Directive there with no amendments. How can anyone be expected to know if a provision of it is incompatible with the Bill, if not even the government can point out any incompatibilities?[139]

[136] O Garner and T West, 'Freedoms' Risks and Opportunities? Certainty and Uncertainty in the Revision of Retained EU Law' (*UK Constitutional Law Association*, 17 February 2022) <https://ukconstitutionallaw.org/2022/02/17/oliver-garner-and-tom-west-brexit-freedoms-risks-and-opportunities-certainty-and-uncertainty-in-the-revision-of-retained-eu-law/>.

[137] Full details of this category are set out in the European Union (Withdrawal) Act 2020.

[138] See further <www.legislation.gov.uk/eu-legislation-and-uk-law>.

[139] R Cormacain and O Garner, 'Schrödinger's Trafficking Directive and the Nationalities and Borders Bill: Simultaneously Law and Not Law' (*UK Constitutional Law Association*, 17 December 2021) <https://ukconstitutionallaw.org/2021/12/17/ronan-cormacain-and-oliver-garner-schrodingers-trafficking-directive-and-the-nationalities-and-borders-bill-simultaneously-law-and-not-law-%ef%bf%bc/>.

The principles set out by Locke over 300 years ago still apply – laws must be promulgated. If the government or Parliament wants to get rid of bits of an old law, it is fully entitled to do so. But at a very minimum it must point out the bits of the old law that it is getting rid of.

2.4.10. Availability of EU Law Applicable in Northern Ireland by Virtue of the Northern Ireland Protocol

This is another Brexit related point. Although the UK (which includes Northern Ireland) has left the EU, special provision has been made for certain EU legislation to continue to apply in Northern Ireland. This has been done under the terms of the Withdrawal Agreement between the UK and the EU, and more specifically the Northern Ireland Protocol to that Agreement.[140] Annex 2 to that Protocol sets out the EU legislation that continues to apply in Northern Ireland. This is different in character from retained EU law that applies by default until it is repealed. This is EU law that has been specifically agreed between the parties to continue to apply in Northern Ireland and that cannot be unilaterally repealed by the UK. There is provision to allow additional EU legislation to be added to Annex 2 by agreement between the parties. However, there is no easy way for citizens or even legislators to know what EU law applies in Northern Ireland by virtue of the Northern Ireland Protocol. This can cause serious problems. For example, there was a proposal for a Private Member's Bill in the Northern Ireland Assembly on single use plastics, which partly sought to align Northern Ireland with EU legislation on single use plastics.[141] However, under the agreed procedure for adding EU legislation into Annex 2, the Joint Committee added the Single Use Plastics Directive EU2019/904 to the list of EU legislation applying in Northern Ireland.[142] Without any easy way to find out what is in Annex 2 a Bill was to be proposed to enact what was already obliged to be law in Northern Ireland.

The lack of availability of EU legislation applying in Northern Ireland undermines the Rule of Law. Provision ought to be made for these laws to be as easily available as other legislation applying in Northern Ireland.

2.4.11. Correction Slips

It is inevitable that legislation will sometimes contain minor mistakes. The obvious way to correct these is to make fresh legislation that rectifies those mistakes.

[140] Text of the Withdrawal Agreement available at https://ec.europa.eu/info/relations-united-kingdom/eu-uk-withdrawal-agreement_en.

[141] The proposal can be found at www.niassembly.gov.uk/assembly-business/legislation/2017-2022-mandate/non-executive-bill-proposals/.

[142] Decision No 3/2020 of the Joint Committee Established by the Agreement on the Withdrawal of the United Kingdom of Great Britain and Northern Ireland from the European Union and the European Atomic Energy Community (17 December 2020).

But sometimes if the mistake is on a technical point, such as a typographical error, or wrong cross reference, it may be possible to use the correction slip procedure. This is a UK procedure, in respect of secondary legislation only, whereby an official document is issued that 'corrects' the error. The decision on whether to use a correction slip is made by the Statutory Instrument Registrar at the National Archives, along with the Department responsible for the statutory instrument containing the error.[143]

The use of correction slips has clear implications for democratic legitimacy – officials should not be changing the law by way of an administrative procedure, only Parliament can authorise a change in the law. The Joint Committee on Statutory Instruments have identified the following circumstances where a correction slip is justified:

- Errors are small scale
- Errors are obvious
- Text and location of error are obvious
- Corrections are small scale.[144]

The key point is that the correction should not amount to a substantive change in legal rights or obligations, it ought to be limited to purely superficial or typological corrections.

In terms of availability under the Rule of Law, the following are required. First, if a correction slip is issued, then the corrected version of the statutory instrument ought to be sent to everyone who purchased it originally. This requirement is contained in the Government's manual on statutory instruments.[145] Second, the online version of the statutory instrument ought to be corrected, along with a note or chronology that shows what the original version was, what the correction was, and how the correction was effected. Third, if there is any chance at all that someone could be prejudiced by this change, or that it could amount to a substantive change of the law, then correction slips must not be used.

Mistakes in legislation are very embarrassing. But correction slips must not be used to spare the blushes of Departments or Government lawyers.

2.5. Navigability

Legislation is more accessible if it is navigable. By navigable, I mean that the user can easily move around legislation, can easily get from one part of it to another.

[143] For a fuller description of the procedure, see Joint Committee on Statutory Instruments, *Transparency and Accountability in Secondary Legislation* (12 June 2018).
[144] ibid.
[145] Statutory Instrument Practice (5th edn, 2017).

Thornton sees the benefit if users can 'find their way around the statute without difficulty'.[146] Navigability is related to findability (the ability to find a relevant provision) but also has to do with the structure, the architecture of the legislation. The closest analogy is of mapped and unmapped terrain. If there is no map, no signposts, no roads, it is very difficult for the traveller to get around. By contrast, with a map, good signposts and roads, the traveller can easily reach a destination. Well mapped legislation is more navigable and therefore more accessible, it allows 'users to find their way more easily around the statute'.[147] Navigability relates to individual statutes as well as to the statute book as a whole, so the users must be able to find the statutes they are looking for, as well as the individual provisions within those statutes. In fact, a former First Parliamentary Counsel has adopted this language of navigability:

> our legislation, complex as it is, needs a map. Lawyers have been trained in a sort of informal, passed-down map that lets you surf the wonderful web that is the statute book. But what about non-lawyers?[148]

2.5.1. Short Titles

The short title of an Act contributes to the navigability of the statute book by

- indicating the content of an Act, and
- assisting in the logical ordering of the statute book.

A title most effectively conveys meaning by being short and descriptive. It assists in the arrangement of the statute book by tessellation – fitting in harmoniously with what is already there. Duprat calls it 'a tool indicating the main issue under regulation'.[149]

The descriptive aspect of titling legislation is under threat. The trend is arguably a movement from pure description, to rhetoric as a way of persuading legislators to vote for a Bill, to bare-faced political sloganeering. The best short title (in terms of navigability) is the one that is politically neutral and best encapsulates the content of the Act in as pithy a way as possible. Orr charts how in Australia titles have become more and more tendentious, observing 'a loss of descriptiveness in titling in favour of an image-conscious and rather cynical form of political rhetoric'.[150] The classic US example is the USA PATRIOT ACT, which is an acronym for Uniting and Strengthening America by Providing Appropriate

[146] GC Thornton and H Xanthaki, *Thornton's Legislative Drafting* (London, Bloomsbury Professional, 2013). 204.

[147] Duprat and Xanthaki (n 27) 120.

[148] R Heaton, 'Innovation and Continuity in Law-Making' (Institute of Advanced Legal Studies, 2014) <www.gov.uk/government/speeches/innovation-and-continuity-in-law-making>.

[149] Duprat and Xanthaki (n 27) 116.

[150] G Orr, 'Names without Frontiers: Legislative Titles and Sloganeering' (2000) 21 *Statute Law Review* 188, 189.

Tools Required to Intercept and Obstruct Terrorism Act. It is a political argument masquerading as a title. Another argument against propagandist titles is that they clamp down on proper political debate – how can a true patriot vote against the USA PATRIOT Act? There are similar moves in the UK with the emotive use of the legally meaningless term 'veteran' in the Overseas Operations (Military Personnel and Veterans) Act 2021.[151] Strause sees this as a problem with naming conventions in American statutes, that they bring 'the law, and perhaps the lawmakers, into contempt by seeming too narrowly partisan'.[152]

This affliction of propagandist titles is global. In Australia there was the Roads to Recovery Act 2000 that is about funding expenditure on roads. The title was chosen to align with a political slogan and is criticised by Orr for being a 'corny pun'. In Canada there is the Standing up for Victims of White Collar Crime Act that amends the criminal law in respect of sentencing for fraud. The Roads (Funding) Act and the Fraud (Sentencing) Act may have been more appropriate. In Uganda, legislators did not like the title of the Marriage and Divorce Bill for religious and moral reasons. A leading daily paper called for it to be renamed the Marriage and Family Relations Bill.[153] Thankfully the drafters were successful in arguing that if it was about divorce, then divorce should be in the title.

But is this criticism too harsh? In the real world, legislation must pass (as razors must sell).[154] In order to pass, a Bill must be politically persuasive. After all, legislation also represents political vision turned into law. The Criminal Justice Act (No 2) 2003 may not inspire political interest, but the Hang Child Killers Act 2003 will. Jones has carried out some fascinating empirical research into this, and his unsurprising findings show that people are more likely to be in favour of a Bill if it has an 'evocative' title rather than a 'descriptive/technical' title.[155] But protecting the Rule of Law is more important than a transient political slogan.[156] Legislators should seek to resist government 'spin' in the wording of legislation.[157] A slogan may help an Act to pass, but this is only one instance in the life-cycle of an Act. For years to come, readers will have to struggle to navigate badly titled law.

[151] R Cormacain, 'Protecting Veterans or Protecting the Ministry of Defence? Clarity in the Overseas Operations Bill' (*UK Constitutional Law Association*, 22 January 2021) <https://ukconstitutionallaw.org/2021/01/22/ronan-cormacain-protecting-veterans-or-protecting-the-ministry-of-defence-clarity-in-the-overseas-operations-bill/>.

[152] R Strause and A Bennett, 'How Federal Statutes Are Named' (2013) 105 *Law Library Journal* 7, 30; G Orr, 'From Slogans to Puns: Australian Legislative Titling Revisited' (2001) 22 *Statute Law Review* 160.

[153] 'Marriage Bill Should Help Couples Remain Together' <www.newvision.co.ug/news/640738-marriage-bill-should-help-couples-remain-together.html>.

[154] G Engle, '"Bills Are Made to Pass as Razors Are Made to Sell": Practical Constraints in the Preparation of Legislation' (1983) 4 Statute Law Review 7.

[155] BC Jones, 'Manipulating Public Law Favorability: Is It Really This Easy?' (Social Science Research Network 2013) SSRN Scholarly Paper ID 2336895 <https://papers.ssrn.com/abstract=2336895>.

[156] Greenberg (n 129) 54.

[157] T Daintith and A Page, *The Executive in the Constitution: Structure, Autonomy and Internal Control* (Oxford, Oxford University Press, 1999) 254. Daintith gives examples of these struggles at 253, 254.

The UK is doing quite well in this regard. Although there is always a political desire towards catchy names, by and large short titles here are relatively straightforward. In fact, in Scotland, the guidance is explicit, stating that the text of a Bill 'including both the short and long titles – should be in neutral terms and should not contain material intended to promote or justify the policy behind the Bill, or to explain its effect'.[158] According to Erskine May 'the short title must describe the content of the bill in a straightforwardly factual manner. An argumentative title or a slogan is not permitted'.[159]

Being neutral doesn't necessarily mean being boring. Contrast the approaches of Hong Kong and Australia to the same problem of junk emails. In Hong Kong the legislation is the Unsolicited Electronic Messages Ordinance, whereas in Australia it is the Spam Act. Both are good and accurate titles, but the Hong Kong one is more legalistic and perhaps stuffy. The Australian one is much more quotidian and instantly tells all readers what it is about. A good example of a pithy and descriptive title is the regulations granting consumers vouchers to spend in shops as part of a covid recovery plan in Northern Ireland. The regulations are entitled the High Street (Coronavirus, Financial Assistance) Scheme Regulations (Northern Ireland) 2021.

The tessellation argument is not one that is often made in the context of legislation. Tessellation means that the individual pieces of a mosaic fit together without gap or overlap. In the context of the statute book, it means that the statute book fits together as a whole, that it is coherent. To assist in the logical ordering of the statute book, titles must follow an agreed format. They must make it easy to fit a particular statute within the general scheme of the statute book. This will help any indexing or referencing system as well as making it easy for the user to see at a glance if a particular statute falls within a group of statutes. So for example, in Northern Ireland there are the:

- Housing (NI) Order 1976
- Housing (NI) Order 1978
- Housing (NI) Order 1981
- Housing (NI) Order 1986
- Housing (NI) Order 1988
- Housing (NI) Order 1992
- Housing (NI) Order 2003
- Housing (Amendment) (NI) Order 2006.

The reader can easily identify these in an alphabetical index of statutes, as O'Brien says, 'one of the main purposes of the short title is to locate the legislation in the

[158] Directorate of Clerking and Reporting, *Guidance on Public Bills* (3rd edn, The Scottish Parliament 2007).

[159] Malcolm Jack and others (eds), *Erskine May: Parliamentary Practice* 24th revised edn (London, Butterworths Law, 2011) 527.

statute book'.[160] The reader also knows that any new legislation called the Housing Order will deal with the same subject matter as these existing orders. But if a new statute was called the Buildings for Residential Use Act, this would immediately make the statute book must less navigable. In this context, the keyword is consistency. Legislation dealing generally with the same subject matter must have generally the same name.

Personalised names in legislative titles cause problems with navigability. For example, in the US, there is the Lily Ledbetter Fair Pay Act, named after a famous litigant in an employment case. Legislation can also be named after victims, for example Megan's Law deals with making public information about sex offenders, and was named after a victim of a sex offender. It can be named after politicians closely connected with it, for example the Landlord and Tenant (Amendment) Act (Ireland) 1860 is more commonly called Deasy's Act after the Irish Attorney General of that time. Naming statutes for individuals is sometimes done posthumously, as a mark of respect, for example the Ronald W Reagan National Defence Authorization Act for Fiscal Year 2005. Jim Allister MLA in discussing a Bill before the Northern Ireland Assembly stated 'whereas the Bill must officially be called the Civil Service (Special Advisers) Bill, I trust that, in common language, it will, if passed, become known as "Ann's law"'.[161] This was in tribute to a particular victims' campaigner. Jones has written about the different approaches to what he calls 'humanised' titles in the USA and the UK:[162] he concludes that the UK establishment zealously guard the 'neutral names' approach. This non-personalised approach to short titles is one that is in accordance with the Rule of Law.

An additional barrier to navigable statutes is the overly broad and bland Act title. We know the Crime and Courts Act 2013 is about criminal law, but we don't know much more than this. We know the Northern Ireland (Miscellaneous Provisions) Act 2013 is about Northern Ireland, but we don't have an idea about the details. There isn't necessarily very much the legislator can do about this. Sometimes an Act will deal with a broad subject and make lots of different amendments to different aspects of that subject. If we were to list everything that the Act dealt with, it would be far too long a title. For example, a more descriptive short title for the Northern Ireland Act would be the Northern Ireland (Political donations, Assembly membership, Justice Minister, Excepted and Reserved Matters, Electoral Matters etc.) Act 2013 – but this is obviously far too long to be of any real use. But sometimes we can be more specific, for example most legislation amending criminal justice law is often called the Criminal Justice Act, but we also have the Criminal Justice (Evidence) (NI) Order 2004 – as that Order only deals with criminal evidence, the title can be more specific. There is no easy prescription here,

[160] P O'Brien, 'Legislative Titles – What's in a Name?' [2012] *The Loophole* 17, 20. One key recommendation of the New Zealand Law Commission was that statutes be indexed, Law Commission, *Presentation of New Zealand Statute Law* (n 33) iv.

[161] Official Report (Hansard) Session 2012/2013, Monday 3 June 2013.

[162] B Jones, 'Transatlantic Perspectives on Humanised Public Law Campaigns: Personalising and Depersonalising the Legislative Process' (2012) 6 *Legisprudence* 58.

the legislator has to balance three things: keeping the short title short, indicating its content and promoting indexing of the statute book.

2.5.2. Omnibus Bills

The section above discussed the dangers of bills dealing with a broad subject and having a bland title. Much more problematic are omnibus bills – 'a massive bulk of unrelated rules modifying numerous existing statutes'.[163] In the UK, these are sometimes termed 'Christmas tree bills' as there is something for everyone in them.[164] Popelier describes this concept as 'mosaic legislation' and they can also be referred to as programme laws.

An omnibus Bill makes navigation of the statute book very difficult. The reader has no idea of what an omnibus Bill may contain. Its title will not convey meaning and will not assist in the logical ordering of the statute book. An omnibus Bill is enacted for the benefit of legislators, not of citizens. In Belgium they are called 'Programme Laws' or 'Law holding diverse provisions' – how on earth is the user to divine content from such a broad title? Popelier directly states the disadvantages of mosaic law as the difficulty of citizens accessing the law.[165] In Israel they are called 'Arrangement Laws' and the Israeli Supreme Court heard objections about these been railroaded through the Knesset.[166] Although that case (as Bar-Siman-Tov points out)[167] was about procedural rationality in law making, it also illustrates the difficulty with navigability of the statute book. The Supreme Court in Israel has ruled 'Arrangements Law' as unconstitutional, although this is more for reasons of legislative due process than for navigability of legislation.[168]

An example of omnibus legislation in the UK is the Enterprise and Regulatory Reform Act 2013. The long title shows the diversity of subjects within it:

> An Act to make provision about the UK Green Investment Bank; to make provision about employment law; to establish and make provision about the Competition and Markets Authority and to abolish the Competition Commission and the Office of Fair Trading; to amend the Competition Act 1998 and the Enterprise Act 2002; to make provision for the reduction of legislative burdens; to make provision about copyright and rights in performances; to make provision about payments to company directors; to make provision about redress schemes relating to lettings agency work and property

[163] P Popelier, 'Mosaics of Legal Provisions' (2005) 7 *European Journal of Law Reform* 47.

[164] Office of the Parliamentary Counsel (n 75).

[165] Popelier (n 163).

[166] HCJ 4885/03 *Isr. Poultry Farmers Ass'n v Gov't of Isr.* 59(2) PD 14 [2004] (Isr.), translated in 2004 Isr L Rep 388 (2004).

[167] I Bar-Siman-Tov, 'The Dual Meaning of Evidence-Based Judicial Review of Legislation' (Social Science Research Network 2016) SSRN Scholarly Paper ID 2818007 <https://papers.ssrn.com/abstract=2818007>.

[168] HCJ 4885/03 *Isr. Poultry Farmers Ass'n v Gov't of Isr.* 59(2) PD 14 [2004] (Isr.), translated in 2004 Isr L Rep 388 (2004), see further ibid.

> management work; to make provision about the supply of customer data; to make provision for the protection of essential supplies in cases of insolvency; to make provision about certain bodies established by Royal Charter; to amend section 9(5) of the Equality Act 2010; and for connected purposes.

The sharp-eyed reader will notice a reference to the Equality Act 2010 being amended – the amendment is to make 'caste' an element of 'race' for the purposes of equality legislation. Although laudable, this has nothing to do with regulatory reform and its short title will therefore mislead the reader. This detracts from navigability and has the appearance of a provision shoved into the first available Bill.

Perhaps the only time that omnibus legislation is acceptable is the Statute Law Repeal Act. These Acts repeal vast swathes of legislation that are no longer of practical utility, and usually follow recommendations of a Law Commission. Since these laws are generally obsolete anyway, citizens are not hindered by any loss of navigability. See for example the Statute Law (Repeals) Act 2013 that got rid of a huge number of unnecessary old statutes on: benevolent institutions, criminal justice, Indian railways, the Dublin Steam Packet Company and other Irish institutions, local courts and the administration of justice, specific churches and markets, poor relief, abortive railways projects, taxation and pensions, turnpikes and more. It is a 62-page long list of laws that have had no practically utility for many years.

2.5.3. Section Headings

Short titles can assist in finding the Act sought. Headings within an Act can assist in finding the exact provision sought (I use the word heading as shorthand, these have also been called marginal notes, titles, sidebars etc). For the purposes of navigability, each part, chapter, cross heading and section heading should clearly indicate its content.

Unlike short titles, section headings can be longer and more specific. Depending upon how pithily the heading can be expressed, it can be a 'content-indicator' title or a 'rule-summary' title. A content-indicator title gives an idea of the content of the provision, whereas a rule-summary title actually summarises the rule itself. For example, when the Civil Service (Special Advisers) Bill was introduced into the Northern Ireland Assembly, clause 2 was entitled 'special advisers not to have serious criminal conviction'. This accurately reflected the content of the rule set out in clause 2, it was an abbreviated description of the rule itself. However, as the Bill passed through the Assembly the content of clause 2 was changed and there was no longer an absolute prohibition on special advisers having a serious criminal conviction. Therefore, upon enactment, the title of that clause had changed to 'special advisers: serious criminal convictions'. The new title didn't summarise the actual rule, instead it gave an indication of the subject matter of the provision. Rule-summary titles are usually more difficult to set out than content-indicator titles as it is hard to condense most rules into one line. However, rule-summary titles make it easier for the user to know the thrust of the legislation. A combination of a well-organised table of contents and descriptive titles means that reading the table of contents can be like reading a condensed narrative of the legislation.

For constitutional and historical reasons, there is a certain ambiguity about the legal status of headings in legislation in the UK. In the past they have been viewed, not as part of the legislation enacted by the legislature, but as an editorial addition inserted by the clerks and administrative staff of the legislature.[169] The actual practice of making legislation shows this to be nonsense – every part of the Bill, including all the headings, is crafted by the legislative drafter working on behalf of the legislator. However, the rule of interpretation is that section headings may be used to assist in the interpretation of the legislation, even though they are not determinative.[170] This is an eminently sensible canon of construction as three or four words in a heading can't adequately describe the entirety of the section that follows.[171] However, this rule does give the legislator an unusual opportunity for creativity and innovation, unburdened by the usual requirements of precision and legal accuracy. The purpose of a navigable heading is to convey meaning, not to be legally precise, therefore the drafter is relatively free to select headings that best convey meaning.

An example will illustrate this. The Northern Ireland Law Commission produced a Bill to amend the law on bail.[172] Clause 30 of the Bill is entitled 'repeal of street bail'. But 'street bail' has no legal meaning, the correct legal term is 'bail at any place other than a police station'. Street bail is the term used in practice, it is quicker and less cumbersome, but it is legally incorrect. However, as a title it works, the reader with a connection to the criminal justice world instantly knows what this provision is about. The detail of the provision uses the legally correct terminology, as it must, but in crafting the title, the legislator is freer to convey meaning. This practical example provides a partial answer to Heaton's concern that titles in legislation don't convey meaning to non-legal users.[173] The legal lexicon (words like tort, fee simple, actionable) are familiar and relevant to lawyers, but not to non-lawyers. So in section headings it is open to use the demotic word, not the legally precise word.

A contrasting EU legislative provision shows the benefit of this more flexible UK approach. Article 5 of Directive 2002/58/EC is entitled 'confidentially of these communications' and paragraph 3 of that Article begins

> Member States shall ensure that the use of electronic communications networks to store information or to gain access to information stored in the terminal equipment of a subscriber or user is only allowed on condition that the subscriber or user concerned

[169] Jack and others (n 159) 575.

[170] Jones (n 100) 696.

[171] Simamba discusses whether or not this is a good idea in various jurisdictions, B Simamba, 'Should Marginal Notes Be Used in the Interpretation of Legislation' (2005) 26 *Statute Law Review* 125.

[172] Northern Ireland Law Commission, 'Bail in Criminal Proceedings' (Northern Ireland Law Commission 2012) NILC 14.

[173] Heaton (n 148).

> is provided with clear and comprehensive information in accordance with Directive 95/46/EC, inter alia about the purposes of the processing, and is offered the right to refuse such processing by the data controller.

How much more navigable would this provision be if it was entitled 'no cookies without consent'? Most computer users know that websites store information about users every visit, and this information is colloquially known as a 'cookie'. The reader would instantly know the point of the provision if 'cookie' appeared in its title. In fact, the word 'cookie' even appears several times in the recital of the Directive, how much better if it had worked its way into the law itself.

2.5.4. Structure

An Act is more navigable if it is organised and structured[174] – but what does this actually mean in practice? It means that users can see at a glance the general thrust of the Act and see, again at a glance, which provisions are relevant to them. Voermans distinguished between 'structure' (division of legislation, referencing) and 'superstructure' (relation to other legislative texts, hierarchy) but I include both these here within my use of the word structure.[175] Voermans went on to say that 'the structure of an Act can act as a road map for users who want to find the relevant provisions'.[176] Onoge also saw structure as extremely important, writing that 'careful layout and design of legislation is as important as clear language'.[177]

Unless an Act is extremely short, it should have a table of contents (sometimes referred to as arrangement of sections, or contents). Like a short title, a table of contents gives the reader the gist of the Act, it also sets out the scope of the Act. So, although the Crime and Courts Act 2013 is a very broad title, looking at the table of contents reveals it is about the National Crime Agency, administration of justice, self-defence etc.

Structure is helped immeasurably by divisions and sub-divisions of the legislation – as Duprat notes these make 'the provisions easily seen by the public and to simplify the interpretation of enactments'.[178] Related material should be grouped together and listed under a separate heading. Related headings should also be grouped together and listed under larger headings. The UK taxonomy is of Parts, divided into Chapters, divided into cross headings. It is not necessary to have each of these tiers in a single Act – a short Act may only have cross headings, whereas a larger one may have multiple Parts, Chapters and cross headings. The more topically different provisions are, the higher up the tier the divisions should be.

[174] Thornton and Xanthaki (n 146).
[175] W Voermans, 'Style of Legislation and Their Effects' (2011) 32 *Statute Law Review* 38, 41.
[176] ibid 47.
[177] ES Onoge, *Structure of Legislation: A Paradigm for Accessibility and Effectiveness* (Unpublished LLM thesis 2014).
[178] Duprat and Xanthaki (n 27) 119.

For example, in the Water Act 2014, Part 1 deals with the water industry. This is conceptually very different from provisions on flood insurance, so it is quite right that flood insurance is dealt with in Part 4. Therefore, the reader interested in the new law on flood insurance doesn't have to wade (pun intended) through the other water provisions in the Act, but can dive straight to Part 4.

Different writers have suggested different ways to structure legislation. For example, Thring suggested stating the law first and then how the law was to be administered.[179] He suggested including the standard provisions first followed by the special or more complicated ones. It is also possible to take a chronological approach, such as setting out in order the steps with which a user must comply in order to satisfy a particular administrative hurdle. For example, in Part 2 of the Companies (Guernsey) Law, 2008, the first cross heading is 'conditions precedent to incorporation' and the second cross heading is 'incorporation of a company'. Bergeron suggests having permanent provisions first and temporary provisions later.[180] This practice is followed nearly all the time in the UK, where transitional provisions or transitory provisions appear at the very end of a statute. Bentham wanted to separate the 'imperative' provisions (which would be short and come first) from the 'expository provisions' that would be longer, contain more explanatory material and come later.[181]

Xanthaki proposes an innovative approach to structure, what she calls the layered approach.[182] Under this structure, legislation is drafted in different layers, corresponding to the different users of it. So, Part 1 is for lay people and sets out the basic regulatory message of the law. Part 2 is for non-legal professionals and sets out the detail that they need. Part 3 deals with issues of interpretation, application, amendments, repeals etc. It is for those lawyers who need to know the precise details of every last provision.

As with all these drafting principles, these approaches to structure are only guides and can be over-ridden. For example, in the Telecommunications Act 1984, there is a provision vesting property belonging to British Telecommunications in a successor company. Normally this sort of transitional provision is relatively unimportant and is included as a schedule at the end of the statute. However, as it was considered of crucial economic and political importance, it appeared in the body of the statute, not at the very end. The key point for the legislator is to choose a structure and an ordering of provisions that makes it as easy as possible for the reader to find their way through the statute.

The other difficulty with maintaining a sound and coherent structure is amendments, both amendments to a Bill as it passes through the legislature,[183]

[179] H Thring, *Practical Legislation: The Composition and Language of Acts of Parliament* 3rd edn (M MacKenzie ed, London, Luathe Press, 2015).

[180] R Bergeron quoted in H Xanthaki, *Drafting Legislation: Art and Technology of Rules for Regulation* 1st edn (London, Hart Publishing, 2014) 65.

[181] J Bentham, *An Introduction to the Principles and Morals of Legislation* (JH Burns and HLA Hart eds, Oxford, Clarendon Press, 1996).

[182] Xanthaki (n 180) 76.

[183] Greenberg (n 129).

and amendments to an Act after it is made. These can often wreck a carefully balanced piece of legislation by forcing new provisions into a structure that was not designed to accept them. The Aristotelian idea of the perfectly structured entity does not work when faced with the grubby realities of making law in a political legislature. One thing that those charged with preparing the law can do however, is to strongly counsel that the Bill as introduced into Parliament is the finished product, at least from the government's perspective. Introducing a Bill that even the government knows to be incomplete is a good predictor of a Bill that will be structurally unsound, with subsequent amendments stretching it out of shape. The more pre-legislative scrutiny and consultation, the less likely that the introduced Bill's structure will be deformed by amendments as it passes through the legislature. The other approach is to leave figurative 'space' for future amendments that are expected to come.

2.5.5. Parallel Structures

If an Act regulates two or more similar activities or entities in similar ways, it is made more navigable if it adopts parallel structures for that regulation. A parallel structure means that the same approach and headings (so far as possible) are used for each entity. This makes it easier for the user to follow, and they can also quickly see where the regulation differs. This is the approach taken in the Companies (Guernsey) Law, 2008. Listed in Table 2 are cross headings and section headings for Part XXVII (Protected Cell Companies) and Part XXVIII (Incorporated Cell Companies). This approach makes it easier for readers to compare and contrast these two different types of company than if the structure adopted had been wildly different.

Table 2 Protected Cell Companies v Incorporated Cell Companies

PART XXVII PROTECTED CELL COMPANIES	PART XXVII INCORPORATED CELL COMPANIES
Formation	*Formation*
437. Companies which can be protected cell companies	468. Companies which can be incorporated cell companies
438. Consent of Commission required	469. Consent of Commission required
439. Determination of applications to and other decisions of Commission	470. Determination of applications to and other decisions of Commission
440. Appeals from determinations and other decisions of Commission	471. Appeals from determinations and other decisions of Commission
	472. Incorporation of incorporated cell

(continued)

Table 2 ***(Continued)***

Status	*Status*
441. Status of protected cell companies	473. Status of incorporated cell company
442. Creation of cells	474. Status of incorporated cell
443. Demarcation of the core	
444. Cell shares and cell share capital	
Assets and liabilities	*Separate nature of incorporated cell company and its incorporated cells*
445. Cellular and core assets	475. Separation of assets and liabilities
445. Protected assets	476. Transactions

In the same vein, provisions establishing a body in legislation generally take a similar approach: setting out how people are appointed to the body, their salary, staff, reporting arrangements, budgeting, pensions, procedure, status, termination of membership etc. If a new body is set up, the reader would expect to see similar provisions in a similar order. The Office of the Parliamentary Counsel is explicit about this, setting out common provisions for the establishment of a statutory corporation.[184] This is not an argument for blindly following precedent – it is an argument for assisting readers by using a structure with which they will be familiar.

2.5.6. Sign Posting

A statute is a single document and the full meaning of that document is only apparent if the full document is read. In the same way that one line from a recipe doesn't make the meal, one section from an Act doesn't explain the Act in its entirety. In a short Act, the connection between sections is clear and obvious, and there is no need for any aids to make it more navigable. But in a longer Act, there may be a gap between two related sections – a section may make more sense if read in conjunction with another provision that may be in a different part of the Act. Take a simple example: section 10 sets out an offence and section 11 sets out the defence. It is easy for the reader to navigate from one to the other. But what if sections 10 to 15 set out the offences, and sections 30 to 32 set out the defences? Suddenly we have reduced navigability, and we have made it more difficult for readers to link together important information.

There are a number of form of legislation solutions to this. First, there is the long established adage in legislative drafting of keeping like material with like.

[184] 'Common Legislative Solutions: A Guide to Tackling Recurring Policy Issues in Legislation' (Office of the Parliamentary Counsel).

Thring, for example, recommends keeping provisions declaring the law together, and keeping them separate from provisions relating to the administration of the law.[185] The difficulty with this is that a provision may be 'like' one provision in one way, but 'like' a different provision in another way. For example, we could put all offences together because they are like each other, or we could put an offence relating to a particular subject next to the other material on that subject. This is a zero-sum game – if we put two like sections together, we automatically displace another like section and push it further away. This may be an unavoidable consequence of the interconnectedness of legislation. The rules of interpretation tell us that we can't read provisions in isolation, we need to read the entire Act.

The next solution is to try to place all relevant material together in a single section. And if material is relevant to more than one section, it can be repeated in each of those sections. There are two problems with this. First, we will dramatically extend the length of each individual provision. So, section 1 will be 10 pages long as it includes the rule, the exceptions, the defences and the definitions. A 10-page section is far too long to be easily comprehensible (see further chapter five). Second, such an approach can be repetitive and increase the chance of making copy errors. For example, if the same definitions apply to the first five rules, it would seem silly to repeat them in each of the first five rules. Even worse, we increase the risk of future errors. Say that next year we want to amend one of these definitions, we will have to amend it five times in five different places, and hope that we make exactly the same amendment in each place.

The third solution to this issue is signposting – pointing the reader to where the other relevant provisions are within an Act. So, section 1 could be set out as follows.

1. (1) This is the rule.
   (2) But this is subject to –
      (a) the exceptions in section 5, and
      (b) the defences in section 10.
   (3) The elements of the rule set out below are defined in section 50 –
      (a) element A,
      (b) element B.

This puts the user on notice that there is a context to the rule, and that the rule cannot be read in isolation. The reader is signposted to further relevant provisions. This is especially helpful for non-lawyers, particularly those not familiar with the standard structure of legislation, including its use of interpretation sections for definitions or schedules.[186] Signposting is a great aid to navigability.

[185] Thring (n 179).
[186] Bertlin (n 93).

However, there are at least two problems with signposting. The first is knowing where to stop. It is conceivable that every provision in an Act could have a bearing on every other provision in an Act – does that mean that each individual section must contain a signpost to every other section? Extending the example above, does section 1 also need to state:

> (4) The decision to prosecute a person under the rule is to be taken by the body established in section 8.
> (5) Prosecutions must be initiated within the time limits set out in section 17.
> (6) If a person is arrested under the rule, that person must be released on bail under the criteria set out in section 29.

This creates problems of undue length and complexity.

The second problem concerns the nature of legislation. If the function of legislation is to make law, everything extraneous to that is redundant and should be excised from legislation. A signpost is not law, it only clutters up the law. As Bowman put it, 'excess matter in Bills, as in people, tends to go septic'.[187]

The answer to these two problems rests in the judgement of the legislator. Balance these two problems against the need to enhance navigability. So, do not signpost everything, just those provisions that are most directly relevant (or most likely to be otherwise missed). This will sometimes mean shoehorning in a provision that is not strictly necessary from a legal perspective, just to make the reader aware of it. For a good example of legislation with signposts, see the Public Services Ombudsman Act (Northern Ireland) 2016:

> Power to investigate complaints made by a person aggrieved
>
> 5. (1) The Ombudsperson may investigate a complaint, made by or on behalf of a member of the public who claims to have sustained an injustice (in this Act referred to as 'a person aggrieved'), if the requirements of this section are met.
> (2) The complaint must relate to action taken by a listed authority (see sections 12 and 13).
> (3) The complaint must relate to a matter which can be investigated (see sections 14 to 23).
> (4) The correct procedure must have been followed (see sections 24 to 27).

In some Australian jurisdictions, navigability is taken a stage further, by making references not just to different provisions within an Act, but to provisions in different Acts. In the example below, the unauthorised version of the Children and Young People Act 2008 (as put online by the Australian Capital Territory Parliamentary Counsel's Office) is as follows:

> 356 Offence – mandatory reporting of abuse
>
> (1) A person commits an offence if –
> (a) the person is a mandated reporter; and
> (b) the person is an adult; and

[187] G Bowman, 'Why Is There a Parliamentary Counsel Office?' (2005) 26 *Statute Law Review* 69, 77.

(c) the person believes on reasonable grounds that a child or young person has experienced, or is experiencing –
  (i) sexual abuse; or
  (ii) non-accidental physical injury; and

…

Maximum penalty: 50 penalty units, imprisonment for 6 months or both.

Note 1 A person who gives information honestly and without recklessness under this section does not breach professional ethics and is protected from civil liability (see s 874).

Note 2 Giving false or misleading information to the director general is an offence (see Criminal Code, s 338).

2.5.7. Highlighting Defined Terms

Defined terms make legislation easier to read and understand. So for example, rather than using the phrase 'a person under the age of 18' throughout it, the Children Act 1989 instead uses the term 'child' and then defines it in section 105. This is both a useful shorthand term and a good way of indicating meaning to the user. But what of the reader who does not know of the existence of interpretation sections? They may be struggling to know whether a 17-year-old is a 'child' for the purposes of the Act. This is where navigability principles can assist. If a defined term is used in legislation, it can be highlighted in some way to indicate that more information is available on that term. For example, in Guernsey legislation, defined terms are in bold in the place where they are defined. This at least draws the readers' eye to the term so that they have a chance of knowing that this term has additional levels of meaning attached to it.[188] Even better would be a system whereby the casual reader would immediately be alerted (for example by 'pop-up' text) to the fact that a particular word has a precise meaning, and an easy way of getting (for example via a hypertext link) to that meaning.

2.5.8. Numbering

In physics, a quantum is the smallest size of an entity possible. So, a photon is a single quantum of light, incapable of being divided any further. However, in legislation, there is no limit to how far the gap between two sections in a statute can be divided. So, between sections 171 and 172 of the Social Security Contributions and Benefits Act 1992, there are 54 sections. The full list is as shown in Table 3.

[188] A similar practice is used in the Schedule to the High Street (Coronavirus, Financial Assistance) Scheme Regulations (Northern Ireland) 2021.

Table 3 Sections numbers between 171 and 172

s 171	s 171ZG	s 171ZC	s 171ZEE	s 171ZL	s 171ZS	s 171ZZ	s 171B
s 171ZA	s 171ZH	s 171ZD	s 171ZF	s 171ZM	s 171ZT	s 171ZZ1	s 171C
s 171ZB	s 171ZI	s 171ZE	s 171ZG	s 171ZN	s 171ZU	s 171ZZ2	s 171D
s 171ZC	s 171ZJ	s 171ZEA	s 171ZH	s 171ZO	s 171ZV	s 171ZZ3	s 171E
s 171ZD	s 171ZK	s 171ZEB	s 171ZI	s 171ZP	s 171ZW	s 171ZZ4	s 171F
s 171ZE	s 171ZA	s 171ZEC	s 171ZJ	s 171ZQ	s 171ZX	s 171ZZ5	s 171G
s 171ZF	s 171ZB	s 171ZED	s 171ZK	s 171ZR	s 171ZY	s 171A	s 172

The eagle-eyed reader may have spotted that sections 171ZA to 171ZE appear twice. This is explained by Westlaw as follows:

> Existing ss 171ZA-171ZE moved directly under Part XIIZA on the repeal of the cross-heading 'Ordinary statutory paternity pay' by Children and Families Act 2014 c. 6 Sch.7 para.11 (April 5, 2015: substitution has effect subject to transitional provisions and savings specified in SI 2014/1640 art.16)

Westlaw does a better job than the official government database of legislation, legislation.gov.uk. That database dodged the question, stating: 'This is the original version (as it was originally enacted). This item of legislation is currently only available in its original format'.

When subsections and paragraphs are factored in, this means that we have (for example) section 171ZZ5(3)(b) of this Act. How are end users meant to navigate through this? How are they meant to know that 171ZZ1 comes after 171ZA but before 171F? Although there is reason behind it, it just looks like gibberish to the ordinary citizen.

The Immigration Rules are worse.[189] We can find:

- Rules with a number, eg rule 15 is about the common travel area.
- Rules with a number with a single letter as a suffix, eg rule 20A is about non-lapsing leave.
- Rules with numbers with multiple letters as a suffix, eg rules 245ZZ to 245ZZE deal with tier 4 (child) students.
- Rules with numbers with letters as prefixes and suffixes, eg rules A57A–A57H deal with persons entering the UK for short term study.
- Rules with multiple letter prefixes eg E-ECP.3.1 deals with financial requirements.

So, in Appendix FM-SE paragraph A1 reads 'To meet the financial requirements under paragraphs E-ECP.3.1., E-LTRP.3.1., E-ECC.2.1. and E-LTRC.2.1. of Appendix FM, the applicant must meet'. The Court of Appeal in considering Immigration

[189] They can be found at www.gov.uk/guidance/immigration-rules.

Rules stated that the 'provisions have now achieved a degree of complexity which even the Byzantine emperors would have envied'.[190] The Supreme Court spoke of the difficulty for users 'to navigate their way around the requirements'.[191] These rules will most likely have been renumbered 10 times in the period between this paragraph being written and it being published.

This kind of complex numbering makes legislation extremely difficult to navigate and undermines accessibility and the Rule of Law. Although it may make things easier for government if the same numbers remain in place through many amendments, it does not help the reader. At some point the legislator has to insist that instead of the tortuous quantum fracturing of squeezing in new numbers where none ought to exist, there should instead be a fresh restatement of the legislation containing only actual numbers. And perhaps a schoolchild can advise that there is no such number as 171ZZ5.

2.5.9. 'Hidden' Provisions

Legislation is not a weapon to be used against the people, it is a tool to be used for their benefit.[192] Equally, it is not something to be 'sneaked through' the legislature, it is something to be enacted by the legislature. A statutory provision is not navigable if it is hidden somewhere within the legislation, in an unexpected place, or in a place that is out of context with its content, or with a misleading title. Thring stated that provisions shouldn't be hidden in a schedule.[193] The more important, or revolutionary a provision is, the more prominence it should have in the legislation. Take as a positive example the legislation authorising the UK Prime Minister to initiate the procedure for leaving the European Union. This fundamentally important provision is not buried in a schedule of a bill on restructuring government, it is section 1 of the European Union (Notification of Withdrawal) Act 2017.

An Italian example shows the pernicious use of hidden provisions. The Italian Prime Minister Silvio Berlusconi had lost a civil case and was obliged to pay damages totalling millions of Euro. He wanted to amend articles 284 and 373 of the Civil Code so that payment of damages would be suspended pending appeal to the Court of Cassation. In 2011 he inserted this amendment to the Civil Code into a budget bill that was being fast-tracked through the Italian parliament due to the financial crisis. It was spotted and removed.[194] Although this amendment was clearly wrong as being inserted for the personal benefit of the legislator, it was also wrong as it was in the wrong place, seriously hindering navigability.

[190] *Pokhriyal v Secretary of State for the Home Department* [2013] EWCA Civ 1568 at [4].
[191] *Mandalia v Secretary of State for the Home Department* [2015] UKSC 59 at [2].
[192] Locke (n 4).
[193] Thring (n 179).
[194] G Negri, 'Nella Bozza Della Manovra Sospensione per Le Condanne Superiori a 20 Milioni. Vi Può Rientrare Il Lodo Mondadori' *Il Sole 24 Ore* (4 July 2011).

2.6. Inclusivity

For legislation to be accessible, the legislation must contain within it all relevant legal information. If a piece of legislation only includes 90 per cent of the information on how that law is going to be applied, then this undermines the values that accessibility promotes. To put it bluntly, if the statute doesn't give the citizen the full picture, then the citizen can't properly follow the law. If the citizen is held liable for something that isn't effectively disclosed within the law, this would be unfair. Citizens can't make decisions based on rules outside their knowledge. There is no certainty if the individual doesn't know the rules, and it is impossible to hold parliament to account for a rule if parliament hasn't fully set out the rule in the legislation. From this is derived the form of legislation principle of inclusivity. By this I mean that the legislation must itself include a reasonably complete statement of all the rules and other matters that affect its application. Nothing extraneous to the legislation should fundamentally change the meaning of that legislation.

Inclusion can be direct by means of the legislation physically containing the material, or indirect, by means of the legislation including a reference or pointing to the material. The reader ought not to be surprised by the legislation applying in a way that is not disclosed or easily inferable from the face of the legislation. In fact, this is already a ground for parliament to question subordinate legislation – if 'it appears to make some unusual or unexpected use of the powers conferred by the statute under which it is made'.[195]

If this is the case, then the statute as it appears on screen is misleading and the legislation is not truly accessible. This chimes with Thring's comment over a century ago that readers ought not to 'have to look beyond the four corners of the Bill in order to comprehend its meaning'.[196] This form of legislation principle can be summed up as follows – if it is important, or if it will colour how the Act will be applied, then it should go into the Act.

This is related to aspect 5 of availability – legislation in context. The legislator may not be able to make sure that contextually relevant material is linked to the statute as it appears on screen. However, the legislator does have a role in ensuring that such material is included (either directly or indirectly) in the legislation. This is a key form of legislation principle – that the legislation ought to include all important relevant information. Readers ought to have a reasonable idea of how the law will be applied in practice and know what other sources of information will shed light upon this application. Set out below are three examples of the kinds of situations where this principle is not respected.

[195] Standing Order 151(1)(B)(vi).

[196] H Thring, *Practical Legislation: The Composition and Language of Acts of Parliament* 3rd edn (M MacKenzie ed, London, Luathe Press, 2015) 25.

2.6.1. Tax Legislation and Extra-Statutory Concessions

It is a fundamental principle of UK tax law that we can only be taxed in accordance with legislation laid down by Parliament.[197] However, for at least 100 years, we can now be 'untaxed' (or excused of an obligation to pay tax) by an Extra-Statutory Concession (ESC) granted by the government.[198] As its name indicates, this is a situation, not provided for in legislation, where the government does not insist on applying the full rigour of the law, and thus reduces the tax liability of an individual. ESCs have been given (sometimes begrudgingly) a seal of approval by the judges.[199]

Extra-statutory rules are anathema to the general principle of the Rule of Law that we are all subject to the law. They are also anathema to element 1 of Bingham's definition of the Rule of Law as they are not accessible alongside the legislation. Having said this, the government do publish the list, together with details, of all ESC annually. The government do have a rolling programme to turn some ESCs into actual legislation. There is legislative power to give effect to ESCs, including turning them into statutory concessions.[200]

In discussing ESCs, Freedman's main objections are in terms of lack of certainty and clarity over the law.[201] Tax-payers could not be sure how much they could rely upon these ESCs. Freedman suggests that 'one way forward would be for all concessions and guidance to have a statutory basis'.[202] However she sees this as a counsel of perfection and not feasible for the small, transitory and complex areas in which ESCs normally operate.

Three recommendations can be made. First, so far as possible, there should be nothing outside the statute book that denudes the contents of the statute book – the principle of inclusivity requires that concessions ought to be contained within the statute book. Second, where this is not possible, the reader ought to be alerted at the very least to the existence of such things as extra-statutory concessions when they are reading the tax statutes. Third, those ESC must be easily accessible in full.

2.6.2. Broadly Drafted Legislation Constrained by Non-legislative Indications of Narrow Application

On occasion, legislation on its face has a broad remit, but the persons introducing the Bill into Parliament state that it will only be applied in narrow circumstances.

[197] Article 4, Bill of Rights 1689.
[198] D Williams, 'Extra-Statutory Concessions' [1979] *British Tax Review* 137.
[199] See for example *R v IRC ex parte Wilkinson* [2005] UKHL 30.
[200] s 160 Finance Act 2008.
[201] J Freedman and J Vella, *HMRC's Management of the UK Tax System: The Boundaries of Legitimate Discretion* (Oxford University Centre for Business Taxation 2010).
[202] ibid 38.

If the intention is that it will only be applied in narrow circumstances, then this should be stated on the face of the Bill and should not be reliant upon political whim. There are two problems with this kind of extra-statutory statement. First, as they are not included with the legislation, they are inaccessible to the reader. Second, they are not legally binding and can be treated as effectively flim-flam.

As an example, consider the Anti-Terrorism Crime and Security Act 2001. This was enacted in response to the terrorist bombings on 11 September 2001.[203] When introduced, the Home Secretary David Blunkett used the following phrases in Parliament to describe it:

- 'legislative steps necessary to counter the threat from international terrorism';
- 'we will reinforce action against the perpetrators of organised crime, drugs and people trafficking';
- 'the emergency legislation will build on the provisions of the Proceeds of Crime Bill to deal specifically with terrorist finance through monitoring and freezing the accounts of suspected terrorists'.[204]

From the general tenor of the debate, it was quite clear that the powers contained within this bill, in particular the power to freeze assets, were to be used for the purposes of defeating terrorism. The actual legislation contained the following as one condition for making an order freezing assets of someone outside the UK:

> The first condition is that the Treasury reasonably believe that—
>
> (a) action to the detriment of the United Kingdom's economy (or part of it) has been or is likely to be taken by a person or persons ...[205]

However, during the financial crisis, there was a risk to UK money held by the Icelandic bank Landsbanki. The government made an order under this provision freezing money belonging to the bank. There was no suggestion of terrorist activity on the part of the Icelandic banks, instead this was a measure used as part of the response to the economic crisis of the time. Although the actual action done may have been necessary and even laudable in economic terms, the fact remains that legislation with an ostensibly narrow remit (terrorism) was used for a much broader purpose. There was no requirement for there to be terrorist activity under the terms of the Act in order for the freezing powers to be used, but the idea that it be used for purely economic reasons seems out of keeping with how a reasonable person would expect the legislation be used. As Smyth stated 'it was controversial because it was made under the Anti-terrorism, Crime and Security Act 2001'.[206]

Terrorism powers being used for non-terrorism purposes is the most egregious example of this kind of abuse. But it can happen in other circumstances where

[203] H Fenwick, 'Anti-Terrorism, Crime and Security Act 2001: A Proportionate Response to 11 September, The' (2002) 65 *Modern Law Review* 724.

[204] HC Debs 15 Oct 2001 col 923.

[205] Section 4(2) Anti-terrorism, Crime and Security Act 2001.

[206] M Smyth, 'The Public Law of Commercial Regulation' (2009) 14 *Judicial Review* 197, 208.

a Minister seeks a broad power in legislation, but then gives an undertaking in Parliament that it will only be used for a particular purpose. To make an analogy, once you give the solider a weapon, he is going to use it against all enemies, not simply those you tell him to use it against at the start.

Baroness Chakrabarti was alive to this problem when debating legislation in the House of Lords. She stated

> When a Minister has to stand up and say, 'Yes, this offence is really broad but don't worry because we intend for it to be prosecuted only in a subset of places', that is the very definition of an overbroad criminal offence, and it should be tightened up to cover the egregious cases that are on the Minister's mind.[207]

This form of legislation principle is a matter of degree and balance. If the legislator is aware of some important limitation to the way the legislation is to be applied, then that limitation ought to be contained in the legislation itself. To do otherwise is to mislead users and subvert the legitimacy of the law-making process.

2.6.3. Broadly Drafted Legislation Due to the Difficulty of Defining Exactly What is to be Covered

Sometimes it can be very difficult to enact a law in such a way that it will cover all the cases that are intended to be covered, while excluding all the cases that are not intended to be covered. This was precisely what happened with the Sexual Offences Bill in the UK Parliament. The main thrust of the law was to protect children from sexual assault. The thing that was meant to be excluded was children involved in natural, low-level, sexual experimentation with other children. One specific difficulty that exercised Parliament greatly was whether the law really ought to be criminalising consensual kissing or petting among 14- and 15-year-olds. The entire debate in Parliament is extremely interesting. The Minister responsible for piloting the legislation through Parliament was David Blunkett, the Home Secretary, and he said that 'it is extremely difficult to come up with a formulation'[208] that includes and excludes the right activities. He said that the government simply could not craft a provision that protected those who ought to be protected, but would not allow for prosecutions of those who ought not to be prosecuted. In fact he went on to say that he would offer 'a flagon of champagne for anyone who comes up with a satisfactory answer'.[209] Dominic Grieve MP (who later went on to become the Attorney General) stated that:

> I have an inherent anxiety about administrative discretion. I accept that administrative discretion may be the only remedy in cases where the CPS will not charge. Nevertheless, when such matters are put on to the statute book in such stark terms, I always fear that,

[207] Hansard 8 February 2022 Column 1514.
[208] Hansard 15 July 2003 Column 178.
[209] Hansard 15 July 2003 Column 195.

> at some point, something will not work properly and that we will end up with prosecutions that cause serious problems. I admit to the Secretary of State that I am not sure that I know the answers, and I suspect that, if he had known the answers, he would have already put them on the statute book.[210]

One solution proposed to this problem was that the Director of Public Prosecutions would offer guidelines on what activities should be prosecuted and what not. To my mind, this breaks the principle of inclusivity – an important limitation on the legislation is placed, not within the legislation, but outside it. The person reading the legislation would come away with the misleading impression that if they did X they would be prosecuted, even though the defence of Y existed somewhere outside the statute book. I can only agree with Sandra Gidley who said in the debate that 'I feel that we need to deal with that matter in the Bill'.[211]

Conclusion

Knowing what the law states is a prerequisite to following that law. Without an easy way for users to access legislation, that legislation becomes irrelevant. Accessibility is therefore an important element of the Rule of Law. This is basic fairness – one shouldn't be prosecuted under a law that one was unaware of. But it is also pragmatic – if legislators enact law for the purpose of it being obeyed, then they want the people who are meant to obey it to be aware of it.

Accessibility means that the text of the law is available, in the sense that people can easily find and read that text. Not only do they need to be able to read what the law is today, but also what the law was at any point in time in the past, and what the law is in the particular part of the country where they live. Availability also means that important related legislative material is also available to the reader, they need to know not just a single provision, but the legislation in its context, in order to more properly understand their rights and duties.

Accessibility also means that readers be able to navigate around an individual statute, and around the statute book as a whole. Simply being presented with a 100,000 page statute book does not give true accessibility. Accessibility is only meaningful when there are ways that readers can navigate around that mass of information and reach the provision that is relevant to them. There are many form of legislation techniques that can enhance that degree of navigability.

Finally, legislation is only accessible if it is inclusive of all the relevant information. There should not be something outside the legislation that has a substantial impact on its meaning or how it will be applied.

[210] Hansard 15 July 2003 Column 194.
[211] Hansard 15 July 2003 Column 224.

3

Prospectivity of Legislation

Introduction

The Rule of Law requires that legislation ought to generally be prospective, that is, it only applies forwards in time from the point when it is made.

In Part 1 of this Chapter I examine the theory of prospectivity within the context of the Rule of Law and set out a new taxonomy for considering what I call 'Janus-faced' legislation. There are three types of Janus-faced legislation: retroactive legislation (which looks to the past and applies in the past), retrospective legislation (which looks to the past and applies in the future) and legislation that interferes with existing rights (which only looks forward, but which is affected by what has been done in the past).

Part 2 examines the drafting principles we can derive from the requirement of prospectivity. The first is that there is a need to be explicit about the time period in which, and in respect of which, legislation applies. The second is the use of transitional and savings provisions to deal with backwards-facing components of legislation. The third is the use of substantive criteria for determining when it is appropriate for legislation to have a backwards-facing component.

Part 1: The Theory of Prospectivity

3.1. The Importance of Prospectivity

In his overall definition of the Rule of Law, Tom Bingham stated that laws should take effect '(generally) in the future'.[1] In element one of his definition he stated that law should be predictable,[2] and in a judicial capacity he added that law should be 'foreseeable'.[3]

Lon Fuller's first desideratum of a good law is prospectivity.[4] Fuller states that retroactive laws (the opposite of prospective laws) are a monstrosity.[5] He states

[1] T Bingham, *The Rule of Law* (London, Penguin UK, 2011).

[2] ibid 37.

[3] *Gillan v Commissioner of Police* [2006] UKHL 12, para [34].

[4] LL Fuller, *The Morality of Law: Revised Edition* (Revised, New Haven, Yale University Press, 1969) Desideratum 3, no retroactive laws.

[5] ibid 53.

that laws are there to govern human conduct, and we can't govern today's conduct by tomorrow's rules. However, as with Bingham he also acknowledges that there can't be a blanket ban on retroactive laws. Criminal law ought never to be retroactive, but in other spheres, there can sometimes be a need for curative retroactive laws 'because their draftsmen commonly overlook the occasional need for "curative" laws, flat constitutional prohibitions of retroactive laws have sometimes had to be substantially rewritten by the courts'.[6] As an example of a curative law, he cites a marriage law that was poorly executed, resulting in many proper marriages being declared void. A curative retroactive law would go back in time and deem all those void marriages valid.

Joseph Raz says in his principle 1 that laws should be prospective, as a retroactive law cannot guide behaviour.[7] Retrospective legislation can change the legal nature of a past event. This is frowned upon because it is seen as both unfair and artificial. It is unfair because the legislature changes the rules after the game has been played. It is artificial because it deems something to be that wasn't. There is a wealth of judicial opinion supporting the proposition that retrospective legislation is to be avoided.[8] It is

> contrary to the general principle that legislation, by which the conduct of mankind is to be regulated ought, when introduced for the first time, to deal with future acts and ought not to change the character of past transactions carried out upon the faith of the then existing law.[9]

The Israeli Supreme Court listed the problems caused by retrospective legislation 'the application of a statute retroactively may cause an injustice, violate rights that have been acquired, undermine stability and certainty in interpersonal relationships and harm just expectations'.[10]

The persuasiveness of these arguments against retrospective legislation is reflected in the various restrictions and prohibitions of this type of legislation. The power of these restrictions is evidenced by the relative rarity of retrospective legislation. Many constitutions expressly prohibit it, particularly in the field of criminal law, although less so in civil law.[11]

[6] ibid 54.

[7] J Raz, 'The Rule of Law and Its Virtue', in *The Authority of Law: Essays on Law and Morality* (Oxford, Oxford University Press, 1979) 214.

[8] See for example, *EWP v Moore* [1992] QB 460, 474; *L'Office Cherifien des Phosphates v Yamashita-Shinnihon Steamship Co Ltd* [1994] 1 AC 486, 525; *Secretary of State for Social Security v Tunnicliffe* [1991] 2 All ER 712.

[9] *Philips v Eyre* (1870) LR 6 QB 1, 23.

[10] *Ganis v Ministry of Building and Housing* [2004] Israel Law Reports 505, 522.

[11] See for example Article 50 of the Kenyan Constitution, Article 1, Section 9 of the American Constitution and Article 28I of the Indonesian Constitution. Kyrvoi and Matos argue that there is no general principle in international law that prohibits retroactive civil law though, Yarik Kryvoi and S Matos, 'Non-Retroactivity as a General Principle of Law' (2021) 17 *Utrecht Law Review* 46.

3.2. The Nature of Prospectivity

Prospectivity is a long-established legal principle.[12] The Latin expression is *lex prospicit non respicit* (law looks forwards not backwards). Prospectivity means that legislation applies from the date it is made forwards.[13] Under the aegis of the Rule of Law, the House of Lords has stated that 'enacting legislation with retrospective effect should be avoided'.[14] Likewise in the US Congress, the general approach is to avoid it.[15] Prospective law does not apply to a time before the law was made. This is different from the principle of stability (see further chapter four). Stability means that the law today will be roughly the same as the law tomorrow. Prospectivity means that if the law changes tomorrow, those changes will only take effect from tomorrow.

Article I, section 10 of the United States Constitution bluntly provides that 'no state shall pass an ex post facto law' (ex post facto being another way of referring to retrospective laws).

3.2.1. Conceptual Blind Spot at the Heart of Prohibition on Prospectivity

For all the strength of words in favour of legislation being prospective, there is a rather large blind spot – the absence of a coherent and consistent test for when it is acceptable for legislation not to be prospective. Bingham says that legislation should 'generally' be prospective.[16] Bennion says that it is presumed as a matter of statutory interpretation that legislation is prospective, but that this is only a presumption capable of being overturned.[17] Nehushtan and Davidson attempt a test, which assesses fairness, morality and constitutionality of retrospective laws, but their criteria are of degree: (1) how severe are the implications of a retrospective rule, (2) how difficult is it to change behaviour in response to a retrospective rule and (3) would a person have changed their behaviour in the past had they known a retrospective rule is coming.[18] Prospectivity is not an absolute Rule of Law value, but there is no easy test setting out when legislation can look backwards in time.

[12] Hayek states that rules should be fixed and announced beforehand, F Hayek, *The Road to Serfdom* (London, Routledge, 1944) 22. The Venice Commission stated that retroactivity offends against legal certainty, Venice Commission, 'Report on the Rule of Law' (2011) [46]. For Northern Ireland, Dickson describes this as a legal convention, B Dickson, *Law in Northern Ireland* 2nd edn (Oxford, Hart Publishing, 2013) 48.

[13] This chapter develops ideas I previously published in R Cormacain, 'Retroactivity, Retrospectivity, and Legislative Competence in Northern Ireland: Determining the Validity of Janus-Faced Legislation' (2015) 36 *Statute Law Review* 134.

[14] J Simson Caird, R Hazell and D Oliver, *The Constitutional Standards of the House of Lords Select Committee on the Constitution* (London, University College London, 2014).

[15] J Lampe, 'Retroactive Legislation: A Primer for Congress' [2019] *Congressional Research Service.*

[16] Bingham (n 1).

[17] O Jones, *Bennion on Statutory Interpretation* 6th revised edn (London, Butterworths Law, 2013) 184.

[18] Y Nehushtan and M Davidson, 'Retrospective Rule Making and the Rule of Law: Between Fairness, Morality and Constitutionality' (2017) 2 *Indian Journal of Constitutional and Administrative Law* 27.

It is my contention that one reason for this disconnect between the abstract theory that law should be prospective only, and the practical reality of legislation not being prospective is the terminological inexactitude of the term 'retrospectivity'. This term lumps together too many different concepts and makes it impossible to have a single clear rule 'against retrospectivity'. Instead, courts tie themselves in knots in trying to rule that a law that clearly looks back in time is actually prospective and therefore valid.

3.3. The Nature of Retrospectivity: Janus-faced Legislation

In seeking to define an ex post facto law, Crosskey said it 'is simply a law that is retrospective; that is, a law made after the doing of the thing to which it relates, and retroacting upon it'.[19] This illustrates the definitional problem – these three things are said to be equivalent: ex post facto, retrospective and retroacting. The different shades of meaning over what exactly is 'retrospective' legislation make it very difficult to set out clear guidelines on how and when this type of legislation is acceptable. I therefore set out below a new taxonomy.

I use the term 'Janus-faced legislation' to mean legislation that has both a forward and backwards-facing component. Janus-faced legislation stretches into the future and into the past. Janus is the Roman god of beginnings and time, and the entity after whom the month of January is named. He has two faces, one that looks forwards to the future and one that looks back to the past. Janus-faced legislation can be (1) retroactive, (2) retrospective or (3) can interfere with existing rights, and I analyse below the nature of these three sub-sets. This taxonomy allows for a more nuanced consideration of when it is permissible under the Rule of Law to have backwards-facing legislation.

3.3.1. Retroactive Legislation

Retroactive legislation has effect before it was actually made. This is chronologically impossible, but legislation does not always respect the laws of physics and it solves this impossibility by deeming legislation to have had effect before it was made. It goes back in time and states that the law at that time is what we now say that it was. To put this another way, the date that it comes into effect is earlier than the date it is made. Retroactive legislation is the Dr Who of the legal world. It applies to the past and in the past. It is blatantly artificial as it states something to exist when it did not exist. It is the easiest type of Janus-faced legislation to

[19] WW Crosskey, 'The True Meaning of the Constitutional Prohibition on Ex-Post-Facto Laws' (1947) 14 *University of Chicago Law Review* 539.

recognise and often the hardest to justify. Perhaps for this reason, it is also the least common type of Janus-faced legislation.

Some brief examples of retroactive legislation in the UK are as follows. The Local Government (Miscellaneous Provisions) Act (Northern Ireland) 2010 contained a provision that certain council contracts are deemed always to have had effect as if the council had power to make them.[20] In the Child Support, Pensions and Social Security Act (Northern Ireland) 2000, certain provisions were deemed always to have had effect.[21] These are what Fuller called curative provisions – fixing a problem after the problem occurred. As individuals we don't have the ability to go back in time and unsay that thing that we now regret saying, but with retroactive legislation, that is exactly what it does do – goes back and unsays the thing.

The War Crimes Act was made in 1991 but criminalises actions carried out in World War II. Persons can be punished under a law that did not exist at the time they carried out the impugned acts, and enacted by those who were probably not alive when those acts took place. When this Act passed through Westminster, the House of Lords did raise objections based on its retroactive nature. However, as Ganz pointed out, it did not cause a constitutional crisis.[22]

The International Criminal Court Act 2001 is also expressly retroactive as it applies to acts committed from 1 January 1991 onwards. Interestingly, the retroactive provisions were only added by way of amendments to the 2001 Act by the Coroners and Justice Act 2009.[23] So a 2009 Act amended a 2001 Act to deem criminal certain actions as far back as 1991. This is not curative in the sense of fixing an earlier administrative mistake, or done for administrative convenience. But it is done to correct an historic injustice, or to prevent people getting away with monstrous actions.

The Court of Appeal has adjudicated upon a particular instance of retroactive legislation – this is retroactive tax legislation that has effect from the date that the announcement about the new tax law is made in Parliament, rather than the (later) date of when the tax law is enacted.[24] The court ruled that this particular type of retroactive legislation was in accordance with human rights law.

3.3.2. Retrospective Legislation

Retrospective legislation bases future legal consequences upon events that occurred before the legislation was made. It looks back to the past and although it

[20] s 2.
[21] s 35.
[22] G Ganz, 'The War Crimes Act 1991 – Why No Constitutional Crisis?' (1992) 55 *Modern Law Review* 87.
[23] R Cryer and P Mora, 'The Coroners and Justice Act 2009 and International Criminal Law: Backing into the Future?' (2010) 59 *International and Comparative Law Quarterly* 803. R Cormacain and N Donovan, *Suspected War Criminals and Génocidaires in the UK: Proposals to Strengthen Our Laws* (Newtown, Aegis, 2009).
[24] *R v HMRC ex p Huitson* [2011] EWCA Civ 893.

doesn't apply in the past, it does apply future consequences to what happened in the past. To put this another way, a provision will be retrospective if it is impossible to avoid the legal consequences of a past action. The action carried out before the legislation is made has a binding and irreversible legal impact. This means that at the time you do an action, you cannot predict its legal effect.

One common application of retrospective law is legislation that states that a past event disqualifies a person for some future job. In the Safeguarding Vulnerable Groups (Northern Ireland) Order 2007, paragraph 3 of Schedule 1 contains a retrospective provision. A person may be placed on the Children's Barred List due to conduct the person has engaged in at any time. No matter what actions the person undertakes in the present, they will still be bound by the consequences of a pre-commencement action.

Laws often set out qualifying or disqualifying conditions for the application of a particular rule. The fact that these conditions may have been satisfied in the past, before the law commences, makes the law retrospective rather than retroactive. Bennion put it thus:

> Changes relating to the past are objectionable only if they alter the legal nature of a past act or omission in itself. A change in the law is not objectionable merely because it takes note that a past event has happened, and bases new legal consequences upon it.[25]

Retroactive legislation is easy to identify, as it will normally expressly state that it has effect on a date before it was made. Retrospective legislation won't necessarily make its backwards-facing component obvious on its face. It commonly arises when past conduct determines eligibility for a post. For instance, the Police Reform and Social Responsibility Act 2011 provided for the election of police and crime commissioners. Under section 66(3)(c), a person is disqualified from being a commissioner if the person has been convicted of an imprisonable offence. Although this provision has been criticised as being disproportionately harsh, it has not been criticised as being retroactive.[26] The provision takes note of a past event and bases a current disqualification upon it. It doesn't retroactively change the legal character of that past event, but it does base future legal consequences upon it.

The courts considered this point in *R v Field*.[27] The legislation in that case disqualified people from working with children if they had certain criminal convictions. The convictions could have been incurred before the legislation commenced. The court accepted the submission that 'the effect of disqualification orders is entirely prospective, because it only affects future conduct'.[28] I would rephrase this slightly in order to fit in with the taxonomy being suggested in this section. That legislation falls into the retrospective subset of Janus-faced legislation, it isn't solely prospective as it does look back to the past before determining future eligibility.

[25] F Bennion, *Bennion on Statutory Interpretation* 5th edn (London, LexisNexis, 2008) 317.
[26] T Thomas, 'Old Criminal Records Playing a Familiar Tune' (2012) 176 *Criminal Law and Justice Weekly* 539.
[27] [2003] 3 All ER 769.
[28] ibid para 60.

In practical terms, it makes social regulation very difficult if only conduct after and not before commencement of a new law can be considered. The court in *Antonelli* considered whether convictions incurred before commencement of the Estate Agents Act 1979 would render a person ineligible to be an estate agent.[29] The court ruled that

> it would be quixotic to suppose that Parliament intended that the public should be protected from the activities of a practitioner convicted a week after the Act came into force, but not from those of the practitioner convicted a week before.[30]

It is also possible that this type of retrospectivity works in reverse; to deem that what was unlawful conduct at the time it was committed is now to be regarded as lawful. It doesn't deny that an offence was committed in the past, but states that the future consequences of that offence are to be cancelled out or disregarded. This was the approach taken to consenting homosexual acts that were historically unlawful, but convictions for which are now to be disregarded.[31] The Secretary of State is to direct that such convictions are to be deleted from the record. Furthermore, 'A person who has a disregarded conviction or caution is to be treated for all purposes in law as if the person has not committed the offence'.[32] This is a retrospective provision because it alters the legal consequences of a past action.

3.3.3. Legislation that Interferes with Existing Rights

Even though legislation only takes effect in the future, it can affect historic rights, or in other words, interfere with rights being exercised before the legislation commences. This type of legislation takes effect in the future, but may prejudice rights accrued or enjoyed in the past. Citizens might have done something in reliance upon a particular law, and when a new law is made, it might affect their existing activities. This can be distinguished from retrospective legislation. If it is possible to avoid the legal consequences of a past action, but even so, the person suffers some disadvantage, this is an interference with existing rights. Nehushtan and Davidson give this concept a different name, calling it 'weak retrospective rule making' and defining it as

> a rule that changes the legal status or legal consequences of an act that has started before the rule was created, yet this is an ongoing act that is still being committed in the present and continues into the future; or a rule that changes the legal status or legal consequences of a state of affairs that existed before the rule was created – and continues to exist after the rule was created.[33]

The Firearms (Northern Ireland) Order 2004 required persons possessing a firearm to hold a firearms certificate. If X possessed a firearm before commencement,

[29] *Antonelli v Secretary of State for Transport* [1998] 1 EGLR 9.
[30] ibid 13.
[31] Part 5, Chapter 4 of the Protection of Freedoms Act 2012.
[32] s 96 Protection of Freedoms Act 2012.
[33] Nehushtan and Davidson (n 18) 29.

then upon commencement, X has three choices: (1) get rid of the firearm, (2) keep the firearm and break the law or (3) keep the firearm and get a licence. X has a choice, an opportunity to avoid the legal consequences of having a firearm without a certificate. The Order interferes with existing rights, but the legal consequences are avoidable. Contrast this with the Safeguarding Vulnerable Groups (Northern Ireland) Order 2007 – if X had engaged in certain conduct with a child in the past, X could not avoid the legal consequences of that conduct.

The courts have drawn a clear distinction between retroactivity and interference with existing rights.[34] The distinction was confirmed in the *Axa* case by Lord Reed. He held that 'A distinction might, however, be drawn between laws which alter prospectively the rights and obligations arising from pre-existing legal relationships, and laws which alter such rights and obligations [retroactively].'[35] It is when there is an interference with an existing right combined with the interference being conditional upon past conduct that the blurring between the different subtypes of Janus-faced legislation is most pronounced. The Solicitors (Amendment) Act 1956 contained a provision requiring disqualification as a solicitor's clerk for certain offences. A clerk had a conviction from 1953, before the Act was made, but was nevertheless disqualified from acting under the auspices of the Act. The Court of Appeal in *Re A Solicitor's Clerk* ruled that the Act

> is not in truth retrospective. It enables an order to be made disqualifying a person from acting as a solicitor's clerk in the future and what happened in the past is the cause or reason for the making of the order, but the order has no retrospective effect. … This Act simply enables disqualification to be imposed for the future which in no way affects anything done by the appellant in the past.[36]

In this case, the legislation was both retrospective (applying to pre-commencement acts) and interfered with existing rights (affecting persons currently practising as solicitor's clerks).

The Estate Agents Act 1979 was construed in a similar way. It contained provisions prohibiting persons from being estate agents if they had certain criminal convictions. The person in *Antonelli* was already an estate agent and already had a conviction before the Act was commenced. Nevertheless, the Court of Appeal held that the Act applied to persons already acting as estate agents and to convictions incurred before the Act commenced.

3.3.4. UK Terminology to Describe Janus-faced Legislation

There is no consensus on the terminology used in the UK to describe Janus-faced legislation. The most common term is 'retrospective'. Bobbett analysed terminology

[34] *West v Gwynne* [1911] 2 Ch 1, 11.
[35] *Axa Insurance* [2011] UKSC 46 [121].
[36] [1957] 3 All ER 617.

used in House of Lords judgments since 1900 and reported that 'retrospective' appears 826 times with 'retroactive' appearing 167 times.[37] In a search of the database UK legislation, 'retrospective' appears in over 200 statutes whereas 'retroactive' appears in only one piece of primary legislation.[38] Greenberg accurately describes the UK approach when he states that 'the terms "retrospective" and "retroactive" are generally used either interchangeably or, at least, without clear difference'.[39]

For reasons I have discussed more fully elsewhere,[40] I favour the taxonomy adopted in this section, which follows on from the taxonomy of Driedger,[41] Sullivan,[42] Salembier[43] and Twining and Miers.[44] A proper and accurate classification allows a more nuanced approach to how to deal with the different types of Janus-faced legislation.

Part 2: Form of Legislation Principles for Promoting Prospectivity

3.4. Explicitness About the Time Period to Which the Legislation Applies

Legislation ought to be explicit about the time period to which it applies. In chapter four I will examine the relatively straightforward issues around a clear commencement date and a clear repeal date. But in this chapter, I am addressing the more complex recommendation that legislation ought also to be explicit about whether it is looking back to past events as well as forward to future ones. The reader ought to be confident that legislation is prospective, unless it contains an express and obvious provision that states that it also has a backwards-facing component. Since Janus-faced legislation can be problematic from a Rule of Law perspective, it should not be hidden away from view in legislation, but be openly expressed. This is for two reasons. First, if it is not explicit, courts may be unwilling to accept that an Act is intended to have retrospective effect. As prospectivity is the default setting, there needs to be express words in law to make it clear that the legislation also looks backwards. Second, if it is to be voted on by parliamentarians,

[37] C Bobbett, 'Retroactive or Retrospective? A Note on Terminology' (2006) 1 *British Tax Review* 15.
[38] Geneva Conventions Act 1957.
[39] D Greenberg, *Craies on Legislation* 10th edn (London, Sweet & Maxwell, 2012) 492.
[40] Cormacain (n 13).
[41] E Driedger, 'Statutes: Retroactive Retrospective Reflections' (1978) 56 *Canadian Bar Review* 264.
[42] R Sullivan, *Sullivan and Driedger on the Construction of Statutes* 4th edn (London, Butterworths Law, 2002).
[43] JP Salembier, 'Understanding Retroactivity: When the Past Just Ain't What It Used to Be' (2003) 33 *Hong Kong Law Journal* 106.
[44] W Twining and D Miers, *How to Do Things with Rules* 5th edn (Cambridge, Cambridge University Press, 2010) 233.

they should know that they are voting for provisions that have the potential to undermine the Rule of Law. This is a clear case where the form of legislation can promote the Rule of Law.

A good example of this is contained in the Criminal Justice Act 2003 where it states that 'An offence is within this subsection (whether it was committed before or after this section comes into force)'.[45] This makes it clear that this is retrospective in the sense that it looks back to past events and sets out future consequences for them. If the intention is that a provision should cover pre-enactment offences, then this should be explicit on the face of the legislation.

An even better example is if the section title advertises its retrospective nature. See for example a section title like 'Retrospective application of certain offences'.[46] Such a title ought to act like a red flag to parliamentarians – caution: this provision is doing something unusual. They may still decide to pass it, but they know that in passing it, they are doing something that goes against the normal rules on prospectivity.

Attention to detail in the actual words of legislation is crucial here. The precise words used can often have important repercussions. Consider section 132 of the Serious and Organised Crime and Police Act 2005. Subsection (1) provides that

> (1) Any person who—
>
> (a) organises a demonstration in a public place in the designated area, or
> (b) takes part in a demonstration in a public place in the designated area, or
> (c) carries on a demonstration by himself in a public place in the designated area,
>
> is guilty of an offence if, when the demonstration starts, authorisation for the demonstration has not been given under section 134(2).[47]

The context for this provision, and perhaps even the reason for its enactment, was Mr Haw. Mr Haw was a protestor who occupied Parliament Square to complain about UK foreign policy, in particular wars in the Middle East. In response, the government introduced, and Parliament enacted, section 132 to ban all unlicensed protests in Parliament Square. However, despite their clear intention to get rid of Mr Haw, the actual words used in the legislation applied only if 'when the demonstration starts' it didn't have authorisation. Mr Haw's protest started long before the Act commenced, so he would only be guilty of an offence if the Act had retroactive effect. If Parliament wanted it to apply to Mr Haw, they should have made it apply in respect of a protest that doesn't have authorisation when it 'starts, or continues'.

Unfortunately for Mr Haw, the Court of Appeal looked at what Parliament intended, rather than what it actually said.[48] Although the Divisional Court ruled that 'starts' meant 'starts',[49] the Court of Appeal ruled that 'starts' meant 'starts or continues'. Despite the explicit wording in the legislation about the time period to which the law applied, the court ultimately took a different approach in ruling in

[45] s 247A(1) Criminal Justice Act 2003.
[46] s 9A International Criminal Court (Scotland) Act 2001.
[47] s 132(1), Serious and Organised Crime and Police Act 2005.
[48] *Haw v Secretary of State for the Home Department* [2006] EWCA Civ 532.
[49] [2005] EWHC 2061 (Admin).

favour of the government. As a side point, the use of 'serious and organised crime' in the short title of the Act does not accurately describe the behaviour of a single non-violent protestor, no matter how annoying the authorities may have found him.

3.5. Transitional and Savings Provisions

The perceived unfairness of a new law interfering with existing rights is well recognised in the development of legislative policies. So much so, that there is an established mechanism for dealing with it – by way of transitional and saving provisions. Transitional and savings provisions normally come at the end of a piece of legislation and set out safeguards or protections, or simply instructions on how to deal with the old law that the new law is repealing.

Transitional provisions govern the transition from an old regime to a new one. They are normally temporary in nature, applying only for a short period until the new law fully takes effect. For Xanthaki they 'deal with the passage from the previous regulatory regime to the new one'.[50] Savings are similar, and protect existing rights that may be affected by the new regime. For Xanthaki 'saving provisions keep in being laws, rights or obligations that would otherwise disappear when an existing law is repealed'.[51] Unlike transitional provisions, savings provisions have the potential to last much longer, they may preserve existing rights indefinitely, not merely for a short period while the new regime beds down.

Where an existing right would be interfered with by new legislation, transitional and saving provisions often soften the blow. Even more specifically, there are 'grandfather' clauses – if your grandfather was allowed to do a thing under the old law, then you as his descendant can continue to do that thing.[52]

Within transitional and savings provisions there are five specific legislative techniques to ameliorate the harshness of Janus-faced legislation. First, an authorisation for an action granted under the previous law can be treated as if it was an authorisation under the new law. The Firearms (Northern Ireland) Order 2004 has already been mentioned in the context of interference with existing rights. There is an additional piece of legislation that ameliorates the position for persons already possessing firearms who held a certificate under the previous legislation. The Firearms (Northern Ireland) Order 2004 (Commencement and Transitional Provisions) Order 2005 provided that firearms certificates granted under the old regime were to be treated as if they had been granted under the new regime. This is a classic example of a grandfather clause. This 2005 Order was a separate and distinct piece of legislation from the 2004 Order. The 2005 Order was only

[50] H Xanthaki, *Drafting Legislation: Art and Technology of Rules for Regulation* 1st edn (Oxford, Hart Publishing, 2014) 179.

[51] ibid 176.

[52] JW Summers, 'The "Grandfather Clause"' (1914) 7 *Lawyer and Banker and Southern Bench Bar Review* 39 sets out the historical background to this type of clause.

enacted to set a commencement date for the 2005 Order, and to deal with some transitional provisions.

Second, if you have previously done the thing lawfully, and no authorisation was required, then you can continue to do the thing lawfully under the new law, even though you don't have an authorisation under the new law. Consider a hypothetical example of a person who became a barrister before there was a requirement to hold a law degree. If the law was changed and required all barristers to hold a law degree, a savings provisions could exempt all existing barristers.

Third, a person already doing the thing lawfully could be given additional time to comply with a new requirement under the new legislation. For example, if a new law prohibits a particular type of weapon, existing owners of that weapon could be given a six-month grace period in which to dispose of the weapon before they face the full rigour of the law.

Fourth, a person could be compensated for the law interfering with existing rights, or for depriving them of their property. Unbelievable as it may seem today, when slavery was abolished, slave owners were 'compensated' for losing their slaves. So, the Slavery Abolition Act 1833 abolished slavery, but then in section XXIV went on to state:

> And whereas, towards compensating the persons at present entitled to the Services of the Slaves to be manumitted and set free by virtue of this Act for the Loss of such Services, His Majesty's most dutiful and loyal Subjects the Commons of Great Britain and Ireland in Parliament assembled have resolved to give and grant to His Majesty the Sum of Twenty Million Pounds Sterling.

The subject matter is repugnant to us today, but the principle remains the same, if legislation takes away your property, you are entitled to compensation for it.

A more modern example is the Civil Service (Special Advisers) Act (Northern Ireland) 2013. Under that Act, a person with certain serious criminal convictions could not act as a special adviser to a government minister. This was prospective in that it applied to people not yet appointed, but also interfered with existing rights as it applied to advisers already in post. Anyone already in post with a serious criminal conviction was essentially 'fired' by an Act. Recognising the potential unfairness of this Janus-faced legislation, there was a saving provision that gave compensation to individuals in this position.

Fifth, the legislation can create a separate and special regime to deal with existing cases. Rather than the standard regime applying to existing cases, a separate regime could apply to them.

3.6. Substantive Criteria for Determining Whether Janus-faced Legislation is Acceptable

This book deals only with the Rule of Law and the form of legislation, not the substance of legislation. In any event, as set out above, there is a blind spot and there is no clear single answer to the question when can Janus-faced legislation be in compliance with the Rule of Law. However, it is possible to sketch out very briefly the main point substantive criteria for determining whether Janus-faced legislation breaches the Rule of Law.

3.6.1. Common Law Substantive Criteria

Salembier directly links common law temporal presumptions to the Rule of Law.[53] Chaturvedi sets out the parameters of his discussion on retrospectivity in India by reference to the Rule of Law.[54] Sampford sets out a classification of Janus-faced legislation that may make it more amenable to Rule of Law evaluation.[55]

The common law approach of the Rule of Law with respect to Janus-faced legislation in the UK can be simplified out as follows.[56] If a provision can be classified as retroactive, it could undermine the Rule of Law. If it is retrospective or interferes with existing rights, it does not offend against the Rule of Law. If it is retroactive but deals with procedural matters, it is not problematic – retroactive changes to procedure are assumed to be of benefit to the individual. If it is retroactive and makes a substantive change to the law, it is problematic. If the substantive retroactive change is to civil law, it is less problematic for the Rule of Law. If the substantive retroactive change is to criminal law and is to the detriment of the individual, it is very problematic. This is a general approach, so all the preceding propositions should be read as subject to the word 'usually'. Given the sovereignty of Parliament in the UK, these are all merely presumptions, Parliament is free to legislate retrospectively if it makes its intentions clear.

This final prohibition on retroactive criminal legislation is probably the most important and deserves to be analysed in slightly more detail. Mokhtar traced its roots back to antiquity.[57] The prohibition can be divided into two related principles. The first is *nullem crimen sine lege*, no crime without law. The impugned act must have been a crime at the time when it was committed. The second is *nulla poena sine lege*, no punishment without law. A heavier penalty for a crime cannot be imposed than the penalty that existed at the time the crime was committed. Since at least the time of the Nuremburg War Trials, this has been subject to a caveat that some things have always been crimes, regardless of what the domestic law says. For a legislative example of *nullem crimen*, see paragraph 1(4) of Schedule 2 to the Human Rights Act 1998, which provides that where a minister makes a remedial order (remedying some human rights defect), the order cannot retroactively make a person guilty of an offence.

[53] Salembier (n 43).
[54] K Chaturvedi, 'Legislative Retrospectivity and Rule of Law' (2013) 34 *Statute Law Review* 207.
[55] C Sampford, *Retrospectivity and the Rule of Law* (Oxford, Oxford University Press, 2006).
[56] This distillation relies upon the analysis set out in Jones (n 17).
[57] A Mokhtar, 'Nullem Crimen, Nulla Poena Sine Lege' (2005) 26 *Statute Law Review* 41. See also R Ticehurst, 'Retroactive Criminal Law' (1998) 9 *KCLJ* 88.

The main difficulty with using the Rule of Law as a criterion on prospectivity, is that there is a binary decision about whether to classify something as 'retrospective' in which case it may be problematic, or 'prospective' in which case it is fine. This does not recognise the subtleties between the different sub-sets of Janus-faced legislation. Nor does it recognise that retrospective legislation and legislation that interferes with existing rights might sometimes be more unfair than retroactive legislation. Salembier considers this as a valid criticism of the Canadian presumption against retroactive legislation.[58] Turatsinze argued that the theoretical differences between retroactive and retrospective legislation did not lead to practical differences in terms of their impact on individual rights.[59]

3.6.2. Human Rights Substantive Criteria

There is a specific prohibition on substantive retroactive criminal law in Article 7 of the ECHR. However, there is no general prohibition on Janus-faced legislation. Rather, there are specific rights that could in theory be infringed by such legislation. Therefore, unlike the common law criteria, there is no binary logic stating that if a provision is retroactive it is problematic, but if not, then it isn't. The key criterion for human rights jurisprudence is not the sub-type of Janus-faced legislation that a legislative provision falls into, rather the matter is determined by the substance of the provision itself and the nature of the right infringed. The following paragraphs set out some human rights jurisprudence that touch upon Janus-faced legislation as it applies to specific rights.

Article 6: Right to a Fair Trial

If the legislature changes the law upon which a party to a case relies, then that party may not get a fair trial. According to Knight, 'where the state legislates retrospectively on a matter which effectively determines the substance of an existing dispute, making it pointless for proceedings to continue, that can be a breach of Article 6'.[60]

Therefore, if the legislature retroactively changed the law to pre-determine the outcome of a particular case, that would infringe Article 6 unless there was a compelling public interest.[61] However, if a retroactive Bill incidentally affected existing cases along with future cases, the Bill would only infringe Article 6 if it was 'manifestly without reasonable justification'.[62] The key question is not where

[58] Salembier (n 43) 115.

[59] E Turatsinze, 'The Pursuit of Clarity, Precision and Unambiguity in Drafting Retrospective Legislation' (Thesis, 2012) <http://sas-space.sas.ac.uk/4711/>.

[60] CJ Knight, 'Taking an AXA to Acts of the Scottish Parliament' [2010] *JR* 163, 166.

[61] *Zielinski & others v France* (2001) 31 EHRR 19.

[62] *James v United Kingdom* (1986) 8 EHRR 123, para 46.

on the spectrum of Janus-faced legislation a provision lies, but the justification and fairness of it.

Article 7: No Punishment without Law

The European Court of Human Rights held that Article 7 embodied the Rule of Law principle of *nullem crimen*.[63] The Convention only allows one exception to the prohibition on retroactive criminal legislation – if the act was, at the time it was committed, 'criminal according to the general principles of law recognised by civilised nations'. This is the exception relied upon in the two Acts previously discussed, the War Crimes Act 1991 and the International Criminal Court Act 2001 and follows the precedent set out in the Nuremberg War Trials.

The ECHR approach asks whether a criminal penalty is now being imposed for a past action. The test is as follows:

> The court must therefore verify that at the time when an accused person performed the act which led to his being prosecuted and convicted, there was in force a legal provision which made that act punishable, and that the punishment imposed did not exceed the limits fixed by that provision.[64]

Imprisonment for non-payment of a customs fine was not simply a matter of enforcement of payment, but a punitive sanction.[65] Changing the prison rules on the meaning of 'life imprisonment' post-conviction did not amount to retroactively changing the law.[66] Changes to the sentencing or release regime for prisoners are within Article 7 if the changes are within what could have been imposed originally (changes to the manner and execution of the penalty),[67] but not if they change the scope of the penalty.[68] The Terrorist Offenders (Restriction of Early Release) Act 2020 trod this fine line here in changing the way that early release schemes worked for persons convicted of terrorist offences.[69] Disqualification from a post is not a criminal penalty.[70]

Article 8: Right to Private and Family Life

Janus-faced legislation can infringe upon this right if something done in the past constitutes a legal impediment to enjoying your private and family life. Banning all former KGB members from jobs in the public sector in Lithuania has been

[63] *SW v UK* (1995) 21 EHRR 36 at para [35].

[64] *Achour v France* (2007) 45 EHRR 2 at [43]. See also *Welch v UK* (1995) 20 EHRR 247 on the meaning of a 'penalty'.

[65] *Jamil v France* (1995) 21 EHRR 65.

[66] *Kafkaris v Cyprus* (2009) 49 EHRR 35.

[67] *R v Uttley* [2004] UKHL 38, and upheld by the European Court of Human Rights in *Uttley v UK*, App no 36946/03 (29 November 2005).

[68] *Del Rio Prada v Spain* (Application No 42750/09 – 2013).

[69] R Cormacain and M Hunt, 'Terrorist Offenders (Restriction of Early Release) Bill A Rule of Law Analysis' (Bingham Centre for the Rule of Law 2020).

[70] *R v Field* [2003] 3 All ER 769.

ruled unlawful.[71] The Court found that Lithuania did have a legitimate right to regulate both private and public sector employment. However, the breadth of the prohibition was disproportionate. The particular provision could be characterised as retrospective (future consequences of past actions) and interfering with the existing rights of those already in post. However, this was not the key criterion upon which the judgment was based. Judgment was based upon the breadth of the prohibition, not its location in the Janus-faced legislation spectrum.

Article 9: Freedom of Thought, Conscience and Religion

Janus-faced legislation can interfere with this if past conduct exercising this right colours the enjoyment of some current right. A blanket ban on being a chartered accountant if the applicant had a criminal conviction was not unlawful if the conviction in question was for refusing to wear a military uniform for religious reasons.[72]

The European Court of Human Rights held that the general rule of prohibiting persons with convictions for serious crimes was legitimate. However, the Court ruled that the legislation should have differentiated between different cases. In a case where the conviction arose from the right to freedom of religion, it was not justified to disqualify the person. There was no objective justification for treating conscientious objectors the same as other criminals. Article 9, in conjunction with Article 14, had been infringed. The question of whether the legislation was retroactive, retrospective or interfered with existing rights did not arise. At issue was whether or not Article 9 was breached, and if the legislation was objectively justified in treating different people the same.

Article 10: Freedom of Expression

Similarly to the Article 8 rights, this right can be infringed where the past exercise of the right can mean disqualification from a particular job. Two cases from Germany where past political activities (related to Communism) meant legislative disqualification from teaching jobs gave differing answers.[73] The arguments in both cases were not focused on when the communist activity took place. The arguments were focused on whether the right to freedom of expression had been interfered with and whether such interference was justified. However it also fits within the Janus-faced legislation taxonomy of retrospective legislation (past behaviour has future consequences) and interference with existing rights (they were already teachers).

[71] *Sidabras and Dziautas v Lithuania* 27 July 2004, Application nos 55380/00, 59330/00.
[72] *Thlimmenos v Greece* 6 April 2000, Application no 34369/97.
[73] *Glasenapp v Germany* 28 August 1986, Application no 228/80, *Vogt v Germany* 26 September 1995, Application no 17851/91.

Article 1 of Protocol 1: Right to Property

When the state seeks to interfere with property rights, human rights jurisprudence has distilled the matter to: (1) is the interference for a legitimate aim? And (2) is the interference proportionate to achieving that aim?

The case of *Mellacher v Austria* concerned rent control legislation that applied to existing leases.[74] Although Lord Reed characterised this as a civil law with retroactive effects,[75] I would respectfully disagree. It is a law that interferes with existing rights. The European Court of Human Rights itself observed that 'in remedial social legislation … it must be open to the legislature to take measures affecting the further execution of previously concluded contracts in order to attain the aim of the policy adopted'.[76] The backwards-facing nature of the rent control legislation was one factor to consider in deciding upon its validity, but the main criteria were as set out in the previous paragraph: was the interference legitimate and proportionate?

The legislation in *Bäck v Finland* allowed courts to modify pre-existing creditor/debtor arrangements.[77] The European Court again noted that the legislation authorised interference with existing rights. This could be acceptable under the ECHR, but there would need to be 'special grounds of sufficient importance to warrant it'.[78] Although the Janus-faced nature of the legislation was relevant, the main criteria remained the same as for any decision under Article 1 of the First Protocol: was the interference legitimate and was it proportionate?

In *Axa Insurance* the UK courts adopted the ECHR reasoning to rule that retrospective civil legislation was in accordance with the Rule of Law and the ECHR.[79] This reasoning was followed in *Re Forgave (RHI Scheme)* that concerned the payment of subsidies for renewable heat sources.[80] A legislative scheme known as the Renewable Heat Initiative (RHI) had been introduced in Northern Ireland to encourage the use of biomass boilers. The scheme was fatally flawed and would have led to a massive overspend by government. The Northern Ireland Assembly eventually enacted legislation to reduce the subsidies to more manageable levels. It was argued in doing so that it prejudiced the property rights of those who had signed up to the scheme. This was a law that clearly interfered with existing rights, but the court found that the amended scheme constituted a legitimate aim, was proportionate and struck a fair balance between the interests of the individual and the community.

[74] *Mellacher v Austria* (1989) 12 EHRR 391.
[75] *Axa Insurance* (n 35) [122].
[76] *Mellacher* (n 74) [51].
[77] 20 July 2004, Application no 37598/97.
[78] ibid [68].
[79] *Axa Insurance v Lord Advocate* [2011] UKSC 46.
[80] *Re Forgave*, Northern Ireland High Court, 14 October 2021.

Conclusion

Legislation ought, as a general rule, take effect only in the future. That is to say, when we make legislation today, it ought only to affect our actions from today on, and shouldn't colour or impact upon our past actions. Although this is a superficially attractive element of the Rule of Law, upon closer inspection there are instances when it is appropriate for legislation (other than criminal legislation) to have a backwards-facing component, or what I term Janus-faced legislation.

An important form of legislation principle is therefore to be explicit about the time period to which a statute will apply. If it will have a backwards-facing component, then it should be clear on the face of the statute what that is: does the law take effect in the past, does it look to past events but take effect only in the future, or does it interfere in some way with pre-existing rights?

Transitional and savings provisions are normally seen as boring technical provisions placed in legislation as an afterthought. But they are important ways to ameliorate any potential unfairness in Janus-faced law, or any difficulties caused in moving from an old legislative regime to a new legislative regime.

Finally, both the common law and human rights jurisprudence have developed specific guidance and tools on how to justify and ensure fairness for legislation with a backwards-facing component.

4

Predictability of Legislation

Introduction

The Rule of Law requires that legislation be predictable. The term predictability is used here in a very broad sense so as to include the concept of certain, fixed and stable law. Legislation is predictable if you know its effect. More specifically, it is predictable if you can read the legislation and then know in advance what the legal effect of your actions will be. For example, if rules on broadcasting are so vague that a broadcaster cannot predict if a particular program will be sanctioned for being 'indecent', then those rules ought not to stand.[1] Predictable law means law that can be used as a guide for future conduct.

In Part 1 of this chapter, I examine the meaning of the concept of predictability, within context of the Rule of Law. Part 2 is the main part of this chapter. It examines the drafting principles we can derive from the requirement of predictability. These are as follows. Determinacy means that the law is certain, precise and exact. Stability means that the law doesn't change too much, and when it does change, the effect of the change is ameliorated. Clear commencement means that the date the law has effect from is clear. Consistency means both that there are no contradictions within a statute, and also that the statute book as a whole is generally harmonious. Application in the real world means that the law on the statute book is the same as the law as it applies in practice. Implementation means that there are effective means for implementing the law within the legislation.

Part 1: The Theory of Predictability

4.1. The Nature and Importance of Predictability

Tom Bingham said that laws must be, so far as possible, predictable.[2] As with accessibility, he didn't deconstruct this. His reasons for predictability were subsumed into the reasons for accessibility as set out in chapter two. However, unlike accessibility, predictability is not an absolute value. Instead, it need only

[1] 'Constitutional Law – Vagueness – Second Circuit Strikes Down the FCC's Indecency Policy as Void for Vagueness' (2011) 124 *Harvard Law Review* 835.

[2] T Bingham, *The Rule of Law* (London, Penguin UK, 2011) 37.

be done 'so far as possible'. Bingham does not set out any criteria for determining whether or not something is 'possible'. Developing Bingham's argument, Laws stated that 'an element of predictability and permanence is an essential contributor to the role of law in preserving social cohesion and doing justice.[3] Xanthaki cites unambiguity and precision (two aspects of predictability as derived in this chapter) – 'this promotes the Rule of Law'.[4]

John Locke didn't use the word predictability when discussing legislation. However, his manifesto in favour of the Commonwealth argued for much the same thing. He argued that people should be safe and secure in the knowledge of their duties under the law[5] and that the rules ought not to be varied in individual cases.[6]

For Lon Fuller, desideratum 7 of his ideal legal system is the need for constancy of law through time.[7] If laws are constantly changing, then it is hard for people to predict the legal effect of their actions. Again, this is not an absolute for Fuller as it 'seems least suited to formalization in a constitutional restriction'.[8] It is difficult to know how much legislative change is 'too much'.

The second desideratum on this point for Fuller is desideratum 8, congruence between official action and declared rule. Legislation gives predictable results if the state follows the actual rules in the statute book. There are two aspects to this. First, the broader respect for the Rule of Law in terms of the state obeying the law. Second, regarding statutory interpretation, that society and the state (including judges) follow the obvious and natural meaning of the words used in a statute. As Fuller says, 'if the legislative draftsman is to discharge his responsibilities he, in turn, must be able to anticipate rational and relatively stable modes of interpretation'.[9]

Joseph Raz doesn't say that laws should be predictable. However, in principle 2 of his explanation of the Rule of Law, he states that laws should be relatively stable: 'stability is essential if people are to be guided by law in their long-term decisions'.[10] He doesn't see stability as an absolute value. Bingham's recommendation for predictability is therefore reflected in Raz's own recommendations.

Lady Hale tied these points together, ruling that

> The foundation of the principle of legality is the rule of law itself … that [law] must be sufficiently precise to enable a person – with legal advice if necessary – to regulate his conduct accordingly. The law will not be sufficiently predictable if it is too broad, too imprecise or confers an unfettered discretion on those in power.[11]

[3] S Laws, 'Plus ca Change – Continuity and Change in UK Legislative Drafting Practice' (2009) 11 *European Journal of Law Reform* 139, 140.

[4] H Xanthaki, *Drafting Legislation: Art and Technology of Rules for Regulation* 1st edn (Oxford, Hart Publishing, 2014) 86.

[5] J Locke, *Locke: Two Treatises of Government* (London, Awnsham Churchill, 1689) Section 137.

[6] ibid section 142.

[7] LL Fuller, *The Morality of Law: Revised Edition* (Revised, New Haven, Yale University Press, 1969).

[8] ibid 79.

[9] Fuller (n 7) 91.

[10] J Raz, 'The Rule of Law and Its Virtue', in *The Authority of Law: Essays on Law and Morality* (Oxford, Oxford University Press, 1979) 215.

[11] *In the matter of an application by Gallagher* [2019] UKSC 3, para [73].

4.1.1. Why is Legislation Sometimes Not Predictable?

All the writers cited above have stated that legislation ought to be generally predictable. This means that if you read the legislation, you will know how it will be applied (the two assumptions underlying this are that the legislation is accessible, as discussed in chapter two, and that the legislation is intelligible, which will be discussed in chapter five).

This is the theory (or what Fuller would call the morality of aspiration). However, why does the practice sometimes differ – that is, why is the effect of legislation sometimes not predictable? To put this another way, why is legislation sometimes vague or ambiguous? There is one very pragmatic reason for this. Legislation represents difficult political choices. Sometimes the choice between two alternatives is too difficult a political compromise, so rather than make that choice, it is fudged by politicians, and this fudge ends up in the legislation. Or sometimes legislators don't want to be seen to be doing something unpopular, so they try to introduce obfuscatory language into the legislation to hide its true effect. Hedlund and Zamboni describe this as 'initial political ambiguity'.[12] VanSickle-Ward's argument is that 'ambiguity serves as a vehicle for compromise when key participants disagree over details'.[13] In the context of Brazilian law-making, this was the conclusion of de Paula: 'ambiguity is a usual escape for political conflicts'.[14]

Take an example from international law, the UN Security Council Resolution following the 1967 Arab-Israeli war. The text in English calls for 'withdrawal of Israeli armed forces from territories occupied in the recent conflict'.[15] The word 'territories' can be seen as ambiguous, does it mean 'some of the territories' or 'all of the territories'? I would suggest that the answer is politically controversial, so the resolution was drafted in an ambiguous way to cover both possibilities. In an example closer to home, the Downing Street Declaration (part of the Northern Ireland Peace Process) states that the UK has no 'selfish strategic or economic interest' in Northern Ireland.[16] Does 'selfish' qualify 'strategic', or are they stand-alone adjectives – that is no selfish interest and no strategic interest, or no selfish strategic interest? The phrase is ambiguous, perhaps because it needed to be equivocal in order to keep the peace process going and say something that both sides could agree with.

It needs to be remembered that legislation is a political output as well as a legal one. Primary legislation must be enacted by a legislature. For Stephen Laws, this

[12] D Hedlund, AC Cederborg and M Zamboni, 'The Art of the (Im)Possible: Legislators' Experiences of the Lawmaking Process When Reforming Migration Law' (2016) 4 *The Theory and Practice of Legislation* 45, 53.

[13] R VanSickle-Ward, *The Devil Is in the Details: Understanding the Causes of Policy Specificity and Ambiguity* (Albany, SUNY Press, 2014) 22.

[14] F de Paula, 'Does Brazil Have a Legislative Policy?' (2016) 5 *Theory and Practice of Legislation* 329.

[15] UN Security Council Resolution 242 (S/RES/242).

[16] Downing Street Declaration, Wednesday 15 December 1993.

means that political necessities must also be borne in mind alongside legal ones.[17] The consequences of this are as Greenberg points out, 'expressions that are deliberately ambiguous or vague because clarity would require coming down on one side or another of a politically intractable argument'.[18] Xanthaki takes a practical view on this, arguing that sometimes it is better to have vague legislation than no legislation at all.[19] Schiemann goes so far as to make a virtue of this when he argued that ambiguity allowed things to be done, whether that be the writing of a judgment of a court containing several judges, or the passing of legislation accommodating mutually exclusive viewpoints.[20]

These political difficulties are evidenced by the convoluted, ambiguous and conflicting messages emerging from the Northern Ireland Protocol, part of the deal agreed between the UK and the EU on the UK's withdrawal from the EU.[21] At heart the Protocol claims to reconcile two competing needs: that there be no border between Northern Ireland and Ireland, and no border between Northern Ireland and the UK. Or to put it in the language of the Protocol,

> Nothing in this Protocol shall prevent the United Kingdom from ensuring unfettered market access for goods moving from Northern Ireland to other parts of the United Kingdom's internal market …[22]

And

> the commitment of the United Kingdom to protect North-South cooperation and its guarantee of avoiding a hard border, including any physical infrastructure or related checks and controls …[23]

The Protocol is not predictable because on the face it claims to do two things that are not quite compatible with each other. As Murray says 'The Protocol too often seems to say one thing in terms of trade, but operate in a different way in practice.'[24]

In my view, deliberate ambiguity in legislation is wrong. The legal effect of legislation ought to be predictable, in this way it can guide behaviour. But if legislation is ambiguous, it cannot guide behaviour. There may certainly be political difficulties in agreeing a particularly thorny point, but it is the job of politicians to make these agreements, and it is an abdication of responsibility if they pass this job to judges and ultimately to citizens to resolve. In discussing a vague American law on climate change, VanSickle-Ward stated that 'it merely moved [key disagreements]

[17] S Laws, 'Legislation and Politics', in *Law in Politics, Politics in Law* (Oxford, Hart Publishing, 2015).

[18] D Greenberg, *Laying down the Law: A Discussion of the People, Processes and Problems That Shape Acts of Parliament* (London, Sweet & Maxwell, 2011) 151.

[19] Xanthaki (n 4) 87.

[20] Sir K Schiemann, 'The Advantages of Obscurity: The Drafting of EU Legislation and Judgements' (Institute of Advanced Legal Studies, 13 June 2013).

[21] Agreement on the withdrawal of the United Kingdom of Great Britain and Northern Ireland from the European Union and the European Atomic Energy Community2019/C 384 I/01.

[22] Northern Ireland Protocol, Article 6.

[23] Northern Ireland Protocol, preamble.

[24] Colin Murray, 'Vichy France and Vassalage: Hyperbole versus the Northern Ireland Protocol' (*UK Constitutional Law Blog*, 1 July 2021) <https://ukconstitutionallaw.org/>.

to new venues, agencies and the courts'.[25] In the field of peace processes, it may be just about acceptable to temporarily fudge matters in order to gloss over political differences. In the field of domestic legislation, this is not acceptable, as domestic legislation will have a direct impact upon people's lives.

4.1.2. Predictability in Primary Legislation, or in the Legal System as a Whole?

Does it make a difference where the lack of predictability is? Can a lack of predictability in primary legislation be cured by introducing predictability at some other point in the legal system?

Strauss refers to this as a lack of specificity in the legislation – that the primary legislation does not specify precisely what course of action ought to be followed.[26] He cites the case of *Chevron USA v National Resources Defence Council* where the US court stated 'perhaps Congress was unable to forge a coalition on either side of the question, and those on each side decided to take their chances with the scheme devised by the agency'.[27] The agency in this case was the governmental body responsible for implementing the primary legislation. Strauss does accept ambiguity in primary legislation, but only if the legal system as a whole (including secondary legislation and administrative actions) is precise – 'vagueness or a lack of clarity in modern legislation is tolerable because it exists within a system that does give legal obligations or restrictions more precise shape before the citizen is asked to act'.[28]

I think that Strauss is half-right here. If the primary legislation is vague (and thus its effects unpredictable) but the secondary legislation made under it is specific, then the individual can read the law and predict its results. However, if the specificity rests on the layer underneath, the layer of administrative action, then the legal effect is not predictable. The Advocate General of the European Union has come to the same conclusion, albeit on slightly different reasoning. If the primary legislation gives too wide a power to make delegated legislation, then this will be unconstitutional as it gives an unwarranted power to the executive to make law:

> a legislative provision empowering an EU level implementing authority to prohibit short selling 'where necessary', would represent an unconstitutional conferral of excessive implementing powers, irrespective of whether they were conferred on the Commission or an agency. This reflects the general principle of the primary role of the democratic legislature, recognised in the constitutions of several Member States, and in Article 290 TFEU, to the effect that *legislation may not be so vague or open-ended that essential policy choices or value judgements remain to be decided at the implementation phase.*[29]

[25] VanSickle-Ward (n 13) 58.
[26] P Strauss, 'Legislative Theory and the Rule of Law: Some Comments on Rubin' (1989) 89 *Columbia Law Review* 427.
[27] 467 US 837, 865.
[28] Strauss (n 26) 445.
[29] Opinion of Advocate General Jääskinen C-270/12 (2013) (my emphasis).

Although the reasoning here is based on the constitutional law of the EU (van Gestel argues in favour of greater transparency for rule-making authorities within the EU),[30] I think it can equally rest on the quality of predictability. A person cannot predict the legal effect of law if the implementing authority is given too wide a discretion on how the law will be used.

4.1.3. The Qualifier: 'So Far as Possible'

What then is to be said about Bingham's qualifier that law must be predictable 'so far as possible'? There are two aspects to this.

First, there is no binary choice between legislation being predictable or unpredictable. It is a matter of degree. Unlike something like availability (either the legislation is available, or it is not available), predictability is measured on a scale of how predictable is the legal effect of legislation. So, we are aiming for maximum predictability, balancing the other Rule of Law requirements such as accessibility, brevity, intelligibility etc. For example, a long and exhaustive list of how legislation will be applied in different circumstances may enhance predictability, but at the expense of intelligibility.

The second aspect is real world political pragmatism. If a requirement for specificity would cause a Bill to fail to be enacted, then it might be necessary for a legislative drafter to swallow some pride in craftsmanship, and include an ambiguous provision. There are no easy answers to this question, and this aspect of the form of legislation is more a question for politicians than lawyers.

Part 2: Promoting Predictability in the Form of Legislation

4.2. Determinacy

Legislation is predictable if it is determinate. Determinacy means that a law has fixed or exact limits, it is certain and precise. According to Simson Caird 'the Rule of Law requires laws to be reasonably certain'.[31] Determinacy is concerned with the words used in the legislation, and the construction of those words into sentences. Provided the legislation is intelligible, determinacy means that there is no doubt about what it means, there are no grey areas. Readers can examine the legislation and can then be certain of the legal effect of their own actions.

[30] R van Gestel, 'Primacy of the European Legislature? Delegated Rule-Making and the Decline of the "Transmission Belt" Theory' (2014) 2 *The Theory and Practice of Legislation* 33.

[31] J Simson Caird, R Hazell and D Oliver, *The Constitutional Standards of the House of Lords Select Committee on the Constitution* (London, University College London, 2014) 11.

There are two aspects to determinacy: legislation must be unambiguous and legislation must be precise. Xanthaki argues for unambiguity and precision because 'they render the law predictable',[32] and Dickerson includes vagueness and ambiguity in his list of 'drafting diseases'.[33] In fact, virtually all of the major works on legislative drafting include strong requirements in favour of unambiguity and precision.[34] Indeterminacy can also arise from a wide degree of discretion of legislation, but this is considered separately in chapter six.

There are limits to what can be done to combat indeterminacy where the policy itself is indeterminate. VanSickle-Ward has investigated the causes of a lack of specificity in statutes. Her conclusion is that the greater the degree of fragmentation in a state (partisan legislators, division between different arms of government, powerful and heterogeneous interest groups etc) then the more likely the legislation is to be vague.[35] Her analysis is from the political science perspective, but her findings indicate the limits of the form of legislation – if the policy is vague, then there is little that can be done to make the legislation specific. Depending upon the perspective of the legislator, this can set up a tension between legislator and drafter, with the legislator seeking vagueness in order to keep political supporters on board, with the drafter seeking determinacy in order to satisfy the Rule of Law.

4.2.1. Unambiguity

What is Unambiguity?

A legislative provision is ambiguous if it can have more than one meaning.[36] This isn't a question of nuance or shades of meaning, it is a clear distinction between two completely separate and distinct meanings, both of which could legitimately be argued as the 'correct' meaning. This is an important qualifier, that the interpretation is 'legitimate'. Language, by its very nature, is not 100 per cent precise as there is no such thing as perfect communication whereby 100 per cent of the meaning intended by one person by the use of a word will be 100 per cent understood by the observer of that word in that way. I am discounting what could be

[32] Xanthaki (n 4) 85.

[33] R Dickerson, 'The Diseases of Legislative Language' (1964) 1 *Harvard Journal on Legislation* 5.

[34] See chapter 1 under the heading of words in GC Thornton and H Xanthaki, *Thornton's Legislative Drafting*. (London, Bloomsbury Professional, 2013). See chapter 6 under the heading of writing effectively in T Dorsey, *Legislative Drafter's Deskbook: A Practical Guide* (Alexandria, The CapitolNet, 2006). See chapter 9 under the heading of ambiguity, vagueness and generality in R Martineau and M Salernon, *Legal, Legislative and Rule Drafting in Plain English* (Toronto, Thomson West, 2005). See Xanthaki at page 115 under the heading of quality in legislation in H Xanthaki, 'Drafting Manuals and Quality in Legislation: Positive Contribution towards Certainty in the Law or Impediment to the Necessity for Dynamism of Rules?' (2010) 4 *Legisprudence* 111.

[35] VanSickle-Ward (n 13).

[36] J Evans, *Statutory Interpretation: Problems of Communication* (Oxford, Oxford University Press, 1988) 73. Xanthaki (n 4) 90.

termed fanciful or absurd constructions of a word leading to it being considered as ambiguous.

If a legislative provision is ambiguous, then the reader cannot predict its legal effect, and cannot use it as a guide to conduct. Xanthaki uses the analogy of overlapping circles of meaning, the ambiguous word could fall equally within either circle. Take the example of a 'light' truck – the word light could mean light in terms of weight, or light in terms of colour. If we draw a circle entitled 'colour' and a circle entitled 'weight' then the word 'light' could be placed in the intersection of these two circles.

Xanthaki includes the quality of unambiguity as one of the criteria for quality of legislation in her hierarchy.[37] She proceeds on the basis that law is there in order to have effect, and if it is ambiguous, it cannot have effect. My underlying rationale is different, that legislation ought to be in accordance with the Rule of Law, but the end result of these positions is the same, that legislation ought not to be ambiguous.

There are two different types of ambiguity – semantic and syntactical. Semantic ambiguity is at the level of individual words – the words can have different meanings. Many words are polysemous in the English language – they have multiple meanings. Using Dorsey's example, a seal is both a marine mammal and also a form of official approval on a document, so a legislative requirement for a 'seal' is, by reference solely to that word, ambiguous.[38] 'Tata Jesus is bangala' says the missionary in the Congo in *The Poisonwood Bible*, an unfortunately ambiguous word as it can either mean that Jesus is precious, or Jesus is poisonwood.[39]

Syntactical or grammatical ambiguity arises from the construction of words into phrases. The phrase itself can mean more than one thing, either by regards to the placement of the words alongside each other, or the use of punctuation. For example, if a sentence contains two nouns and one pronoun, which of the nouns does the pronoun refer to? Or if there is an adjective followed by two nouns, does the adjective refer to the first noun, or both nouns?

There is a particular form of semantic ambiguity when a word is used that has a general meaning, but also one that is particular to a specific semiotic community. There will be such a community if 'they share a common understanding of words and phrases which the larger community do not share'.[40] Thornton gives the example of 'issue', which will mean a point of argument for most people, but for chancery lawyers it will mean offspring, and for philatelists an issue of stamps.[41] But what meaning should be followed when such a word appears in legislation, the 'ordinary' meaning or the 'technical' one? For Sullivan, as a matter of statutory interpretation the 'ordinary meaning of a legislative text is the meaning intended by the legislature. In the absence of a reason to reject it, the ordinary meaning prevails'.[42] Emon argues

[37] See for example Xanthaki (n 34).
[38] Dorsey (n 34) 174.
[39] B Kingsolver, *Poisonwood Bible* (New York, Harper Collins Publishing USA, 2012).
[40] R Cormacain, 'A Plain Language Case Study: Business Tenancies (Northern Ireland) Order 1996' [2012] *The Loophole* 33, 42.
[41] Thornton and Xanthaki (n 34) 133.
[42] R Sullivan, *Sullivan on the Construction of Statutes* 5th edn (Toronto, LexisNexis Canada, 2008) 24.

that this difficulty is to be resolved by looking at the audience of the statute, so if the statute is directed at a technical audience, then the technical meaning must prevail, but if directed at the populace at large, then the ordinary meaning must prevail.[43] The courts can sometimes take a different approach, as in *Will-Kare* where the courts took a technical meaning of the word 'sale or lease' even though it appeared in the Income Tax Act, a statute applying to everyone.[44]

Is Unambiguity Always Necessary?

Although there may be times when vagueness/lack of precision may be regarded as acceptable, it is hard to see any circumstances in which ambiguity is acceptable in legislation. The alternative meanings of ambiguous legislative provisions can be equally reasonable and this makes it impossible for people to know what the actual law is. The only justification is political, as set out in Section 4.1.1 – ambiguous legislation to ensure that a contested statute is enacted.

Form of Legislation Measures to Enhance Unambiguity

Having established that legislation ought to be unambiguous, how can the form of legislation address this? There are several techniques.

First, where possible, avoid ambiguous words. So if the reasonable reader would be confused by the meaning of a word in a statute, use a word that is not ambiguous. For example 'partner' could mean business partner or romantic partner, so if the second meaning is intended, use 'spouse'.[45] However, this is not a very strong abjuration, as many words in English are polysemous, and avoiding them all would make drafting very difficult.

Second, consider the context. This is probably the key concept, which saves many provisions from being ambiguous. Going back to Dorsey's example, if a document is required to have an official seal, it is abundantly clear from the context that this means a stamp, not a marine mascot. The words in context (both the sentence and the statute as a whole) will remove many ambiguities. This chimes with Watkin's advice that 'clarity of expression therefore requires that it should be clear which of the several meanings which a word may bear is intended in a particular context'.[46] So the context within which a polysemous word is set resolves any potential ambiguities. This requires a holistic appreciation of the text as a whole. So a bald requirement that 'Each customer must be supplied with a fork' is ambiguous, but that ambiguity is resolved if the title of that provision is 'Requirements

[43] A Emon, 'On Statutory Interpretation and the (Canadian) Rule of Law: Interpretive Presumptions as Boundary Setting' (2015) 3 *Theory and Practice of Legislation* 45, 68.

[44] *Will-Kare Paving and Contracting v Canada* [2001] 1 SCR 915.

[45] Or depending on the policy, spouse, civil partner, or persons living together as spouses or civil partners.

[46] TG Watkin, 'Bilingual Legislation: Awareness, Ambiguity, and Attitudes' (2016) 37 *Statute Law Review* 116, 120.

for a restaurant' or 'Requirements for a gardening centre'. The context tells the reader if it is a fork for eating, or a fork for gardening.

Third, use definitions. If there could be a doubt over the light truck, then include a definition that 'light truck means a truck under 1,000 kg'. Readers will normally expect words to have the ordinary, dictionary meaning. If a word is intended to have a different meaning, or a particular technical meaning, then that meaning should be given in a definition section.

Fourth, use grammar and punctuation appropriately. The running joke in Truss's popular book on punctuation is on the meaning of the sentence 'the giant panda eats shoots and leaves'.[47] Including a comma after 'eats' gives the sentence a completely different complexion. Grammar does supply rules that allow for unambiguity. Take for example the rule of the last antecedent. This rule states that where there is a list followed by a qualifier, the qualifier applies only to the last item on the list. This can be illustrated by the contract law dispute described by Adams.[48] The contract provision stated:

> Subject to the termination provisions of this Agreement, this Agreement shall be effective from the date it is made and shall continue in force for a period of five (5) years from the date it is made, and thereafter for successive five (5) year terms, unless and until terminated by one year prior notice in writing by either party.

At issue was whether the qualifying phrase (terminated by one-year notice) applied only to subsequent contract periods, or also to the first contract period. The rule of last antecedent indicates that it applies only to the last item in the list. This contract provision contains a syntactical ambiguity that can be resolved by application of the rule of last antecedent.[49]

However, this is a perfect example of a failure of form of legislation. The provision was so ambiguous it required court proceedings to determine the full meaning, and only then by reliance on an obscure grammatical rule. People should not be subjected to this level of unpredictability. Instead of relying on arcane grammar points to resolve ambiguity, the ambiguity should be written out in the first place. This leads onto the fourth way to remove ambiguities – by proper formatting. Formatting is an easy way to remove ambiguity of this sort. Thus, the provision should have read:

> Subject to the termination provisions of this Agreement, this Agreement shall be effective from the date it is made and shall continue in force
>
> (a) for a period of five (5) years from the date it is made, and
> (b) thereafter for successive five (5) year terms,
>
> unless and until terminated by one year prior notice in writing by either party.

[47] L Truss, *Eats, Shoots and Leaves* (New York, Fourth Estate, 2009).

[48] K Adams, 'Behind the Scenes of the Comma Dispute' *Globe and Mail* (28 August 2007) <http://adamsdrafting.com/downloads/g-and-m-082807.pdf>.

[49] For a statutory example of the importance of commas, see *R v Casement* [1917] 1 KB 98 and the interpretation of the Treason Act 1353.

If the termination clause is intended to apply to only (b), then it can be reformatted so that it only appears in relation to (b).

Polysemous words and ambiguous language are precisely the sort of area where the unreasonable reader can make mischief by misconstruing the statute. So, if there is a reasonable argument that a provision is ambiguous, this ought to resolved by context, by definitions, by grammatical rules or by proper formatting.

4.2.2. Precision

What is Precision?

Legislation is precise (and thus predictable) if it is fixed and certain – the reader knows both the limits of the law and its details. The reverse is imprecise or vague legislation – legislation that doesn't contain sufficient specific information to allow a person to know what its effect will be. Writing in the context of legal determinacy, Dorf stated that 'if the application of a rule requires deliberation about its meaning, then the rule cannot be a guide to action in the way that a commitment to the rule of law appears to require'.[50] There are two broad ways in which legislation can fail to be precise, first by using vague words or phrases, and second by a lack of specificity or detail.

Beginning with vagueness, vagueness means that the boundaries of a word or phrase are in doubt.[51] The core meaning may be clear, but the outer limits, or the length that the word extends to are not certain. Xanthaki's example is the word 'vehicle'. Most people would agree that it includes a car, but does it include a motorbike, or a snow-mobile, or a horse drawn carriage? Like a stone thrown into a pond, the ripples of meaning spread far and wide – how do we know where the ripples stop? The core of the word is clear, so most people would agree that vehicle includes cars, lorries and motorbikes. But it is at the edges that the meaning of the word becomes blurred and indistinct.

Nouns like 'vehicle' have a reasonably distinct core meaning that most people would be able to agree upon. But there are other more general words where the boundaries of the word are much less distinct. These words can cover different types of activities and are, of their nature, more indeterminate. Words like 'reasonable', 'necessary', 'appropriate' or 'due care' give rise to a much wider spectrum of possible interpretation. People will know that they need a licence to drive a car, because:

> It is an offence for a person to drive on a road a *motor vehicle* of any class otherwise than in accordance with a licence authorising him to drive a motor vehicle of that class.[52]

[50] M Dorf, 'Legal Indeterminacy and Institutional Design' (2003) 78 *NYUL Review* 875, 877.
[51] Xanthaki (n 4) 90.
[52] s 87 Road Traffic Act 1988.

But people may not know precisely what kind of activity is prohibited by the following:

> If a person drives a mechanically propelled vehicle on a road or other public place *without due care and attention*, or *without reasonable consideration* for other persons using the road or place, he is guilty of an offence.[53]

Then there are words that are so broad that they lack sufficient determinacy to allow people to set their affairs in order. Lord Rodger criticises words like 'almost' or 'perhaps' in legislation 'since legislation is meant to delimit rights and duties exactly'.[54] In my own research of the statute book, I haven't found the word 'almost' and only a few uses of 'perhaps' in EU legislation, but there are other provisions that are equally vague. For example, Standing Order 42A(8) of the Northern Ireland Assembly states that 'A legislative consent motion shall not *normally* be moved …'. This is not a rule – it lacks detail and obligation. It is instead simply a description of what sometimes happens.

Turning next to lack of specificity. Legislation ought to set out the details of the law, rather than leave people to guess at those details. Legislation is not a sketch, nor a rough guide to legal obligations, it is a detailed, exact and precise list of those obligations. It is not the job of individuals to fill in the blanks left by a statute – how are they meant to follow the law if the law doesn't specify what they are meant to do? The Supreme Court has considered this particular point in *Reilly*.[55] That case revolved around the lack of specificity in Regulations. Section 17A of the Jobseeker's Act 1995 stated that

> Regulations may make provision for or in connection with imposing on claimants in prescribed circumstances a requirement to participate in schemes of any prescribed description that are designed to assist them to obtain employment.

Regulation 2 of the Jobseeker's Allowance (Employment, Skills and Enterprise Scheme) Regulations 2011, made under section 17A, stated that

> 'The Employment, Skills and Enterprise Scheme' means a scheme within section 17A … known by that name and provided pursuant to arrangements made by the Secretary of State that is designed to assist claimants to obtain employment or self-employment, and which may include for any individual work-related activity (including work experience or job search).

The Supreme Court held that regulation 2 was ultra vires because it wasn't precise enough, it didn't actually specify any scheme, all it did was mention a scheme. The Court of Appeal stated

> The question as to precisely how much detail must be included in the Regulations in order to comply with the requirements of the Act does not arise for consideration in this appeal, since the Regulations contain none.[56]

[53] s 3 Road Traffic Act 1988.

[54] Lord Rodgers, 'The Form and Language of Legislation' in D Feldman (ed), *Law in Politics, Politics in Law* (Oxford, Hart Publishing, 2015) 74.

[55] *R (Reilly) v Secretary of State for Work and Pensions* [2013] UKSC 68.

[56] [2013] EWCA Civ 66.

In agreeing with this decision, the Supreme Court spoke of 'the importance of legal certainty' particularly where a statute has a significant impact upon a person's livelihood.[57] Another example of lack of specificity from Northern Ireland is abortion law, where there has been a long-standing argument that the legislation is too imprecise for people to know what the actual law on abortion is.[58]

Is Precision Always Necessary?

The starting point of the Rule of Law is that law should be precise. The courts have been quite clear about this, ruling that

> 'John Citizen' should not be in complete ignorance of what rights over him and his property have been secretly conferred by the Minister … for practical purposes, the rule of law … breaks down because the aggrieved subject's legal remedy is gravely impaired.[59]

The US courts have gone a step further, developing the 'void for vagueness' doctrine.[60] This doctrine means that a court can strike down any statute that is too vague. Legislation is void for vagueness if it 'fails to provide a person of ordinary intelligence fair notice of what is prohibited, or is so standardless that it authorizes or encourages seriously discriminatory enforcement'.[61] Cunnion specifically points the finger at bad rule making if a statute is void for vagueness.[62] This doctrine is not available to UK courts, although they did strike down the Regulations in *Reilly* for being ultra vires.[63]

However, precision is not an absolute value. In general terms, it is better for law to be precise than for it to be imprecise. There are four reasons why absolute precision is not always a good thing.

First, precision can sometimes lead to over-precision or prolixity. According to the Chief Parliamentary Counsel of Ireland, 'It is frequently unnecessary to name every single thing you are forbidding or requiring. An overzealous attempt at precision may result in redundancy and verbosity. Drafting too precisely may create unintended loopholes'.[64] Xanthaki speaks of the 'trap of over-exhaustiveness'.[65]

[57] n 55 [47].

[58] See for example *Family Planning Association v Minister for Health, Social Services and Public Safety* [2004] NICA 39, *Northern Ireland Human Rights Commission's Application* [2015] NIQB 96.

[59] *Blackpool Corporation v Locker* [1948] 1 KB 349, 362.

[60] C Lockwood, 'Defining Indefiniteness: Suggested Revisions to the Void for Vagueness Doctrine' (2009) 8 *Cardozo Public Law, Policy, and Ethics Journal* 255.

[61] *United States v Williams* 128 S Cr 1830, 1845 (2008).

[62] KR Cunnion, 'Earning a C for Rulemaking: The Ambiguity and Potential Impact of a Recent SEC Rule Governing Nationally Registered Statistical Rating Organizations' (2014) 93 *North Carolina Law Review Addendum* 150.

[63] *R* (n 55).

[64] Unpublished Legislative Drafting Manual, Dublin 2001, para 4.4.

[65] Xanthaki (n 4) 91.

As a hypothetical example, consider if a government wants to ban people from destroying polling cards. The simple way to present this is:

> It is an offence to destroy a polling card.

An overly-precise way is

> It is an offence to burn, tear, immolate, rip, or chew a polling card.

In trying to cover all eventualities, in trying to be too specific, two problems have arisen here, (a) that the sentence is longer to read and harder to understand, and (b) it has inadvertently left out some means of destruction, for example by dipping the polling card in acid. Bingham himself, in a judicial capacity, criticised a style of interpretation that leads to over-precision:

> that is not to say that attention should be confined and a literal interpretation given to the particular provisions which give rise to difficulty. Such an approach not only encourages immense prolixity in drafting, since the draftsman will feel obliged to provide expressly for every contingency which may possibly arise. It may also (under the banner of loyalty to the will of Parliament) lead to the frustration of that will, because undue concentration on the minutiae of the enactment may lead the court to neglect the purpose which Parliament intended to achieve when it enacted the statute.[66]

Schulz criticises ancient Roman drafting as well as modern UK drafting for the tendency towards exhaustiveness 'legal science was convinced that unambiguous expression of thought could only be attained through the medium of pedantic, circumstantial phrasing', adding in a footnote 'the nearest parallel is the form of the English statute'.[67]

Second, it can be hard to set out in minute detail all the individual ways in which a statute can be breached. Sometimes it is better to use a broad and general term. Going back to the offence of driving without due care and attention,[68] most people will have a general idea of what that means – driving without the appropriate level of care, or driving carelessly. The other way to approach it would be to say

> It is an offence –
>
> (a) to drive while talking on a mobile phone,
> (b) to overtake going around a bend,
> (c) to overtake on the brow of a hill,
> (d) to root around in the glove compartment for a CD while driving,
> (e) to hold a cigarette in one hand and a drink in the other instead of having both hands on the wheel,
> (f) etc.

[66] *Quintaville v Secretary of State of Health* [2003] UKHL 13 [8].
[67] F Schulz, *Principles of Roman Law* (Oxford, The Clarendon Press, 1936) 79–80.
[68] s 3 Road Traffic Act 1988.

It will swiftly become apparent that there are a myriad of types of behaviours or actions that we want to prohibit, and that the catch-all of 'driving without due care and attention' is the most effective way to describe them.

Third, with laws that regulate the activities of government, it can sometimes be necessary to have a level of flexibility, so that they can take whatever action is appropriate in the circumstances. This can be contrasted with the precision necessary when a person is told to do something on peril of breaking the criminal law. See for example section 6(2)(b) of the Financial Services and Markets Act 2000 that states:

> (2) In considering that objective the Authority must, in particular, have regard to the desirability of—
>
> (b) regulated persons taking appropriate measures (in relation to their administration and employment practices, the conduct of transactions by them and otherwise) to prevent financial crime, facilitate its detection and monitor its incidence …

'Appropriate measures' is an extremely broad term here. VanSickle-Ward's measurement of lack of specificity includes the use of terms like: where appropriate, deemed necessary, reasonable charges and generally accepted.[69] However, it is used in connection with the duties of the Financial Services Authority and does not impose duties on individuals. Likewise, the Secretary of State may do certain things for 'the purpose of ensuring that all appropriate measures are taken to avoid damage to the environment'.[70] As this gives a power to government rather than placing a duty on a person, the benefits of flexibility outweigh the disadvantages of a lack of precision. This was accepted as a valid point in the *Reilly* case:

> the self-evident need for flexibility in the precise characteristics of any scheme introduced under section 17A render it unlikely that Parliament can have intended much, if anything, in the way of specific information about any scheme to be included in any regulation made thereunder.[71]

Fourth, it is not always possible for the legislators to know in advance about the way in which individuals, entities or society will respond to a particular law, or know the different kind of factual situations that may arise. Although legislators ought to turn their mind to the impact of a law, it isn't always possible to effectively predict every response. This means it isn't always possible to specify what is to apply in every single case. The US courts have recognised this, stating that

> most statutes must deal with untold and unforeseen variations in factual situations, and the practical necessities of discharging the business of government inevitably limit the specificity with which legislators can spell out prohibitions. Consequently no more than a reasonable degree of certainty can be demanded.[72]

[69] VanSickle-Ward (n 13).
[70] s 112(1) Environmental Protection Act 1990.
[71] *Reilly* (n 55) [46].
[72] *Boyce Motor Lines Inc v United States* 342 US 337 (1952) at 340.

Commenting upon this topic, Lockwood stated that it is impossible for legislation to achieve what she called 'mathematical certainty'.[73] Developing this argument, Soames[74] (as summarised by Asgeirsson) states that 'under certain circumstances, it is a good idea for lawmakers to formulate laws in vague terms and thereby facilitate their incremental, case-by-case precisification, resulting from adjudication of borderline cases aimed at furthering their rationale'.[75] However, I think this argument fails (in democratic terms) in its reliance on judges making law. It also fails as it considers that the application of law is unknowable at the time the law is made – this is the very opposite of predictability.

This can come down to a judgement call, balancing the need for precision against the arguments set out above. The guiding principle should be the Rule of Law, specifically predictability in this case – the law should be sufficiently precise so that reasonable people can predict the legal effect of their actions by reference to the words in the statute book.

Form of Legislation Measures to Enhance Precision

Many of the techniques discussed in relation to unambiguity apply equally here. In addition, the following techniques can assist with precision.

First, the use of a general term followed by a non-exhaustive list. A non-exhaustive list sets out a certain level of detail, but states that there may be other points of detail that are not included in the list, and the fact that something isn't included specifically, doesn't mean that it is excluded. Taking the polling card example, it could be phrased as

> It is offence to destroy a polling card, including destroying it by burning, ripping, tearing or immolating.

The fact that we haven't specifically mentioned 'or by dipping it in acid' is no longer problematic now, as 'dipping in acid' falls within the general heading of 'destroying'. There are many ways to set up non-exhaustive lists:

- Without prejudice the generality of the foregoing, X means …
- Including, without limitation …
- For example, …

This point can be evidenced by comparing the Commissioner for Complaints (NI) Order 1996 with its successor, the Public Services Ombudsman Act (NI) 2016. In the 1996 Order, the Commissioner is given powers to effect a fair settlement.

[73] Lockwood (n 60) 271.

[74] S Soames, 'Vagueness and the Law' in A Marmor (ed), *The Routledge Companion to Philosophy of Law* (Abingdon, Routledge, 2012).

[75] H Asgeirsson, 'Can Legal Practice Adjudicate between Theories of Vagueness?' (Social Science Research Network 2015) SSRN Scholarly Paper ID 2687091 <http://papers.ssrn.com/abstract=2687091>.

In the 2016 Act, the Ombudsman is given the same power, but with an addition 'including by recommending that the listed authority make a payment to the person aggrieved'.[76] In adjudicating upon the 1996 Order, the courts wrestled with the question if the Commissioner had a power to recommend a financial payment.[77] However, the 2016 Act completely avoids the need for litigation as it expressly includes powers to recommend payment. Kirkham, in writing about the case, rather misses the point.[78] His focus is on statutory interpretation when the legislation is unclear, rather than on good form of legislation to make the legislation clear in the first place.

Second, avoid indeterminate or subjective language where it would place a undue burden on the person to understand, and where the consequences of failure to understand would be severe. So, whilst it may be appropriate to require government to take 'appropriate measures' it would not be sufficiently precise to require people to take 'appropriate measures' on peril of breach of the criminal law.

Third, encourage the appropriate use of extra-statutory guidance. An indeterminate word or phrase may be fleshed out by official guidance. This goes slightly beyond being a form of legislation principle as it is external to the legislation, but those enacting it can provide for its use. For example, there is a test for obscenity in the Obscene Publications Act 1959

> For the purposes of this Act an article shall be deemed to be obscene if its effect or (where the article comprises two or more distinct items) the effect of any one of its items is, if taken as a whole, such as to tend to deprave and corrupt persons who are likely, having regard to all relevant circumstances, to read, see or hear the matter contained or embodied in it.[79]

Without anything more, the test of what is obscene could be as unhelpful to the people as the test in the American case of *Jacobellis v Ohio* – 'I know what it is when I see it'.[80] However, the Crown Prosecution Service in the UK have written guidance on when they will normally prosecute:

> It is impossible to define all types of activity which may be suitable for prosecution. The following is not an exhaustive list but indicates the categories of material most commonly prosecuted:
>
> - sexual act with an animal
> - realistic portrayals of rape
> - sadomasochistic material which goes beyond trifling and transient infliction of injury
> - torture with instruments
> - …[81]

[76] s 11(b).
[77] *In the matter of an application by JR55 for judicial review (Northern Ireland)* [2016] UKSC 22.
[78] R Kirkham, 'JR55, Judicial Review and the Limits of Textual Reasoning' [2017] *Public Law* 46.
[79] s 1(2) Obscene Publications Act 1959.
[80] 378 US 184 (1964).
[81] 'Obscene Publications: Legal Guidance: The Crown Prosecution Service' <www.cps.gov.uk/legal/l_to_o/obscene_publications/>.

4.3. Stability

Law is predictable if it is stable. This means that the law today is reasonably similar to the law tomorrow. The Law Society has pointed out (in relation to Rule of Law problems in Fiji) that 'practical difficulties are created by the frequent amendment of decrees'.[82] However, laws cannot be expected to remain static forever. Fuller dismisses the argument that laws must never change so as to avoid prejudice to people who entered into contracts on the faith of an existing law.[83] That way lies ossification and a refusal to let the law evolve in response to changing social circumstances, or as the House of Commons Energy and Climate Change Committee put it 'policy changes are a fact of life in a democracy'.[84] People cannot expect the law to remain static and that a social activity will always be regulated in the same manner. In a Canadian case, Dickson J observed that 'No one has a vested right to continuance of the law as it stood in the past'.[85]

In fact, the question of how often a law ought to change isn't really a form of legislation question, it is a political question to be determined by reference to social pressures. Tax law changes every year in response to changing financial pressures – the need for stability does not over-ride the need for a balanced budget. Criminal law changes regularly in response to different political priorities, and again, this is entirely appropriate. For example, if society/legislators see a heightened problem with knife crime, then it is perfectly acceptable for the law on knife crime to change in response.

Therefore, we can say that stability is a weak form of legislation principle as it can be displaced if there is a good enough reason for doing so.

4.3.1. The Nature of Legal Change

A stable law remains relatively constant over time. Laws can be unstable in two ways: (a) if the magnitude of the change is large, or (b) if the law changes frequently.

A stable law is a law with small changes in magnitude happening relatively infrequently. A quantitative example could be the tax rate for a particular economic activity – it changes by a few percent points every couple of years. A flip-flop law is a law with large changes in magnitude. This could mean a complete reversal of a previous policy. An example could be same-sex marriage: it is unlawful, and then it is lawful, a complete change from the previous position, so the magnitude of change is large. A frequently changing law is a law that changes with great frequency. Every year the law changes (the magnitude of the changes could be

[82] The Law Society Charity, 'Fiji: The Rule of Law Lost' (The Law Society Charity 2012) 5.

[83] Fuller (n 7) 60.

[84] Energy and Climate Change Committee, 'Investor Confidence in the UK Energy Sector' (House of Commons 2016) Third Report of Session 2015–16, 9.

[85] *Gustavson Drilling v Department of National Revenue* [1977] 1 SCR 271, 282.

large or small). An example could be laws on criteria for welfare payments. Each year the amount of welfare payments, their type and the criteria for eligibility may change.

4.3.2. Ameliorating the Effects of Unstable Law

If there is a good reason why the law should not be stable, then it follows that legislation must be enacted to change the law. However, there are form of legislation tools to ameliorate the difficulties caused by unstable law. These are set out below.

4.3.3. Highlighting the Change

The greater the magnitude of the change in the law, the more prominent the change should be in the legislation. If a new provision represents a radical departure from the old law, then it should be flagged or highlighted within the legislation. A large change makes law unpredictable, but we can ameliorate this unpredictability by telling people in the legislation itself that this is a large change. Legislation should strive to communicate its central messages, this goal is even more important when the central message is a large change to the legal system. A legal provision can be given greater prominence in several ways: being included in the title of the Act, being included as part of a section heading, or its relative place in the legislation (towards the start, not at the end).

Take as an example the abolition of the death penalty in the UK. This could have been done via a standard Criminal Justice Act. Instead, it was done in the Murder (Abolition of the Death Penalty) Act 1965. Abolishing the death penalty was a major change and this was made clear at the very outset of the legislation. As another example, consider Scottish devolution, contained in the Scotland Act 1998. The very first section states 'There shall be a Scottish Parliament'.[86] As Lord Rodger points out, this is a brilliant opening line.[87] It is short, clear and resonant. However, for the purposes of predictability it is also excellent because it makes clear at the very outset the revolutionary changes that the Act is making.

4.3.4. Advertising the Change

Legislation making major change can include an obligation to inform the public at large about that change. The previous technique concerns making clear the nature of the legal change within the legislation. But this technique inserts an

[86] s 1(1) Scotland Act 1998.
[87] Rodger in Feldman (n 54) 69.

obligation within the legislation to advertise the change. This is perhaps best illustrated by way of an example. When the Human Transplantation Bill was before the Northern Ireland Assembly it stood to make a substantial change to the law on organ donation. Previously a person would have to opt in (or actively consent) to their organs being donated after they die. Under the Bill, a person would have to opt out (or they would be deemed to consent) to donating their organ after they die. This is a complete change in the law and would have a major impact upon people. Therefore, in clause 1 of the Bill, there was included a duty upon government to 'inform the public about the circumstances where consent to transplantation is deemed to be given, and the role of relatives and friends in affirming that deemed consent'.[88]

Thus, the unpredictability caused by a large change in the law is ameliorated by including an express duty upon the state to tell the public about that change. Jowell, in expanding upon Bingham's definition calls for precisely such clauses, arguing that the rule of law requires that 'fair warning should be given about any change in the law'.[89]

4.3.5. Long Lead-in Time to Change

Thring stated that laws shouldn't be commenced immediately after being made, that people should be given a chance to understand the law first.[90] If the magnitude of change is large, then it is advisable for there to be a long period between the law being made and the law coming into force. This gives more time for people and the government to acclimate and to make full preparations for the change. The unpredictability is smoothed out by allowing time for people to be made fully aware of the change. Taking again the organ donation legislation example, when this law was introduced into Wales, there was a provision within the legislation that stated that the law couldn't be commenced until at least two years after it was made.[91] This was inserted to give enough time for the population to be effectively informed about the radical nature of the change.

Investors and those in the business community argue for this kind of stability also:

> if policy changes are announced with sufficient lead time, are in line with the overall direction of energy policy, are not retroactive and result from an extensive and objective consultation they are acceptable to investors.[92]

[88] Human Transplantation Bill clause 1(1)(c).

[89] J Jowell, 'The Global Economy and the Rule of Law' (Global Law Summit, London, 25 February 2015) 1 <www.biicl.org/documents/504_sir_jeffrey_jowell_qc_-_global_law_summit_paper_25_feb_2015.pdf>.

[90] H Thring, *Practical Legislation: The Composition and Language of Acts of Parliament* 3rd edn (M MacKenzie ed, London, Luathe Press, 2015).

[91] Human Transplantation (Wales) Act 2013, s 21(2).

[92] Energy and Climate Change Committee (n 84) 9.

Stepping outside the form of legislation, substantial changes to the rules on petrol and diesel cars have been announced long in advance, before the legislation has even been drawn up.[93] Ten years before the ban is expected to come into effect, it has been officially confirmed by the Government.

4.3.6. Dealing with Rapid Technological Changes

One reason for frequent change in law is in order to respond to technological change. So, if a new technology is created, or allows for doing something in a different way, it requires new legislation to regulate it. Take as an example medicines law – the law that regulates pharmacies and the sale and use of medicines for human use. The law on prescription only medicines for human use is contained in the Human Medicines Regulations 2012. The following Table 4 sets out how many times it was amended in the three years since it was enacted.[94] These amendments are necessary as new types of medicines are constantly being created.

Table 4 Amending the Human Medicines Regulations 2012

Year	Times Amended
2015	6
2014	4
2013	3

There has always been a race between societal innovation and legislative response. By this I mean that society finds a new way to do something (or a new loophole) and then legislation is enacted to regulate it (or plug the loophole). This then leads to fresh innovation and the cycle continues.

This is not a new phenomenon, Rodger gives examples going back to Roman times of laws regulating the sale of slaves being abused and then recast to combat the abuses.[95] However, there is an argument that technological advances speed up this race. Thus, according to Wadhwa, 'these regulatory gaps exist because laws have not kept up with advances in technology. The gaps are getting wider as technology advances ever more rapidly'.[96] So previously, law might need to change once every 10 years in response to societal change, now it needs to change every one year in response to technological change. This can be condensed down to the common

[93] 'Ban on New Petrol and Diesel Cars in UK from 2030 under PM's Green Plan' *BBC News* (18 November 2020) <www.bbc.com/news/science-environment-54981425>.

[94] Including amendments to the Northern Ireland equivalent regulations.

[95] Rodger in Feldman (n 54) 77.

[96] V Wadhwa, 'Lawmakers Can't Keep Up with Technology' (*MIT Technology Review*) <www.technologyreview.com/view/526401/laws-and-ethics-cant-keep-pace-with-technology/>.

trope that law is not 'keeping up', or 'keeping pace' with technological change.[97] Voermans presents a novel solution that partly addresses this problem. He advocates greater use of information technology in order to speed up the process for making legislation,[98] allowing a more rapid response to technological change. However, this does not address the issue of stability in terms of the law changing too frequently.

The interaction of technological change and legislation is clearly a broad field of enquiry. In this section, I consider only one aspect, that is how to maintain stability (and thus predictability) in the law in the face of technological change. On the face of it, there are two options, both of which lead to bad results. The first option is to repeatedly change the law to react to new technologies. This makes legislation unstable and unpredictable as it is constantly changing. The medicines law quoted above is an example of unstable legislation that is constantly changing. The second is to leave the law as it is. This results in uncertainty as people don't know if the old law applies to new technologies. For example, does the Theft Act 1968 apply to 'stealing' someone's wifi connection?

The most common solution that is proposed to this problem is to enact legislation in a way that future-proofs it. This means that current legislation will apply in the future, even if there are technological changes. This can be done by preparing legislation in such a way that requires the least amount of subsequent change in response to future technologies – what is generally called 'technology neutral' legislation. Legislation is technology neutral if it 'neither imposes nor discriminates in favour of the use of a particular type of technology'.[99] The theory is, that if the legislation simply specifies the end result, without specifying the means to that end result, it will not need to change as the different means to that end change.

Take a simple example, communicating a notice to a department. Table 5 below sets out the different ways this requirement can be satisfied. As can be seen, there is a spectrum of ways to refer to technology. This links into the argument made by Whitley, that there isn't a simple binary choice between technology specific or technology neutral legislation, it is more a question of degree.[100]

[97] L Moses, 'Adapting the Law to Technological Change: A Comparison of Common Law and Legislation' (2003) 26 *University of New South Wales Law Journal* 417. M Shapiro, 'Is Bioethics Broke?: On the Idea of Ethics and Law "Catching Up" with Technology' (1999) 33 *Indiana Law Review* 17. L Moses, 'Recurring Dilemmas: The Law's Race to Keep up with Technological Change' [2007] *University of Illinois Journal of Law, Technology and Policy* 239.

[98] W Voermans, HM ten Napel and Reijer Passchier, 'Combining Efficiency and Transparency in Legislative Processes' (2015) 3 *Theory and Practice of Legislation* 279. I don't fully agree with him that 'faster' legislation makes for better legislation as it may reduce the scope for mature deliberation and debate over whether a particular law is a good idea. However, he finds ways in which ICT can enhance consultation and deliberation while at the same time speeding up the process.

[99] EU Directive 2002/21. Paragraph 18 of the preamble.

[100] E Whitley, 'On Technology Neutral Policies for E-Identity: A Critical Policy Based on UK Identity Policy' (2013) 8 *Journal of International Commercial Law and Technology* 134, 143.

Table 5 Ways to Give Notice

Technology status	Requirement in Legislation	Methods that can be employed
Technology specific	Notice must be posted	Written hard copy, sent through the post
Partially specific	Notice must be in writing	Hard copy letter Email Fax Text message
Technology neutral	Notice must be communicated	Hard copy letter Email Fax Text message Phone call Online form filled in (boxes ticked etc) Facebook poke New forms of communication

In order to make legislation technology neutral, it is often necessary to focus more on principles rather than details. In this way, if the technology changes, the principles will remain constant and will be able to guide the interpreter. This is certainly the conclusion that John reaches: 'rapid change is also a situation in which a non-detailed law is ideal'.[101] This requires consideration of the justification behind a suggested policy and consideration of how to enact the rule in a way that reflects the justification, rather than simply looking at how the policy will be implemented with today's technology. Taking a facile example, the justification behind a rule making it a crime to shoot people is that we don't want people to be injured. So, the principle is 'don't injure people with a weapon', and the detail is 'don't shoot people with a gun'. In order to future-proof this rule, we can use the principle as our rule, rather than the detail, so the rule will be 'it is an offence to injure a person with a weapon'. If a new technology comes along (say the Taser), our broad principle rule will cover it. However, if we had drafted in a detailed way ('it is an offence to injure a person with a gun') then Tasers will cause problems as we don't know if they fall within the detailed definition of 'gun'.

Technology neutral legislation is a useful technique to bear in mind and it can work in some circumstances. However, to my view it is a weak principle as there are four problems arising from it. First, we can't know with certainty what

[101] J Ubena, *How to Regulate Information and Communications Technology: A Jurisprudential Inquiry into Legislative and Regulatory Techniques* (Stockholm, Jure, 2015) 101.

future technology will do. Our mode of thinking is constrained by current paradigms that may be rendered obsolete by future technologies. Or, as Moses puts it, 'the rule may also apply to conduct outside what could have been foreseen at the time of its creation'.[102] Bingham himself specifically addressed this issue in relation to legislative drafting, stating that 'the situation which has arisen is one which the draftsman could not have foreseen and for which accordingly he has made no express provision'.[103] For example, laws preventing threatening communications would work 100 years ago with regards to threatening letters and will work today with regards to threatening emails. But we had no concept of 'spam' communications 100 years ago so the laws of then couldn't possibly cope with spam emails today. So, even if we think we are writing technology neutral law today, the environment in which it operates tomorrow may have so fundamentally changed that the law will be out of date, no matter how technology neutral we may think it is.

Second, the more general the legislation becomes, the more it risks becoming vague and unfocused. If we wanted to really future-proof criminal law, we would have a single law that states 'it is an offence to harm another person'. Yes, this would always work, but it allows for no nuance, no way of reflecting different sorts of crime and harm.

Third, in order to make something technology neutral, we may have to enact abstract laws. For example, if we specifically refer in legislation to 'a smartphone' then everyone can understand, but if we try to cover future technologies and refer to 'a hand-held portable electronic communication device' we introduce confusion. This is exactly the problem with the Regulation of Investigatory Powers Bill.

> The instructions to parliamentary draftsmen were to make it technology-neutral, because everyone could see that the technology was moving very fast. Parliamentary draftsmen did an excellent job in doing that, but as a result I do not think the ordinary person or Member of Parliament would be able to follow the Act without a lawyer to explain how these different sections interact.[104]

Intelligibility is dealt with in depth in chapter five, but it touches directly here on future-proofing law. On this point, Smith stated that 'unintelligibility is a direct consequence of the attempt to future-proof by technologically neutral, abstract drafting'.[105] Smith went on to directly link this to the Rule of Law requirement that people be able to understand law.

[102] Moses, 'Adapting the Law to Technological Change: A Comparison of Common Law and Legislation' (n 97) 400.

[103] *Quintaville* (n 66) [7].

[104] Sir David Omand, giving evidence in Home Affairs Select Committee, 'Uncorrected Transcript of Oral Evidence' (House of Commons 2014) HC 231-vii <www.publications.parliament.uk/pa/cm201314/cmselect/cmhaff/uc231-vii/uc23101.htm>.

[105] G Smith, 'Future-Proofing the Investigatory Powers Bill' (BILETA, 11 April 2016) <www.slideshare.net/GrahamSmith9/futureproofing-the-ipbill-60769756>.

The fourth problem has more to do with democracy than the Rule of Law. If we have technology neutral, general principles law, then we are passing on the responsibility to react to new technologies to judges rather than legislators. We are leaving the job of regulating future technologies to judges on a case by case basis. This is what happened in *Quintaville*.[106] In that case, the question for the court was whether the Human Fertilisation and Embryology Act 1990 (which covered certain types of reproductive technologies) applied to a new type of reproductive technology. The court, taking a liberal and purposive interpretation, and looking at the intention of Parliament, held that it did. In my view, *Quintaville* falls on the correct side of the line as the new technology was close enough in type to the old technology, requiring no fresh moral or ethical decision making – it was clear that as Parliament was intent on regulating similar reproductive technologies, and would have wished to regulate this reproductive technology if it had existed at the time the legislation was enacted.

However, it is a rather different proposition when a 'new' problem arises out of new technology. In that case, there is much less scope for extending the words of an Act to a novel problem. So, taking the example of piggy-backing on someone's wifi, this is quite different from the law of theft in the Theft Act 1968, and it would be wrong for judges to decide on this rather than Parliament. Lord Wilberforce said:

> there is one course which the courts cannot take, under the law of this country; they cannot fill gaps; they cannot by asking the question 'What would Parliament have done in this current case – not being one in contemplation – if the facts had been before it?' attempt themselves to supply the answer, if the answer is not to be found in the terms of the Act itself.[107]

One of Moses' arguments is that courts are better than legislators at dealing with technological change, because they are quicker and can deal with new cases incrementally and by analogy.[108] This is true, but it is a question of degree. If a judge can deal with a small jump in technology by a purposive and broad reading of existing legislation (what is termed ambulatory interpretation),[109] then this may be a cost effective way to deal with the problem. But anything more than a small jump, and anything that would require twisting the current legislation to fit the new facts, would be undemocratic.

Drawing the line between acceptable and incremental extension of statute law by judges, and unacceptable new law-making by judges is very difficult. The Rule of Law principle for the form of legislation is therefore to use technology neutral

[106] *Quintaville* (n 66).

[107] *Royal College of Nursing of the United Kingdom v Department of Health and Social Security* [1981] AC 800, 822.

[108] Moses, 'Adapting the Law to Technological Change: A Comparison of Common Law and Legislation' (n 97).

[109] M Bradley, 'Ambulatory Approach at the Bottom of the Cliff: Can the Courts Correct Parliament's Failure to Update Legislation?' (2003) 9 *Canterbury Law Review* 1.

legislation where this is feasible without (a) making uncertain law, and (b) delegating power to make new law to judges.

4.3.7. Procedural Rules for Law-making and Time Taken to Make Legislation

In this context, it is worth noting the Rule of Law requirement of 'clear constitutional rules on the legislative process'.[110] These are the rules about rules. Bar-Siman-Tov argues that 'the rules that confer the necessary powers for making valid law and the rules that instruct lawmakers how to exercise their lawmaking power are both essential components of the Rule of Law'.[111]

This Rule of Law requirement on legislative due process dovetails very well with the Rule of Law requirement of stability of laws. Detailed procedural rules make the process of law-making long and painstaking. This is the very thing to promote stability in the law and to reduce kneejerk legislative responses. Bar-Siman-Tov states that 'these rules ensure, *inter alia*, that laws will not change too frequently or too hastily, thereby promoting the Rule-of-Law principle of stability'.[112] Arguing for fast and nimble law-making can be counter-productive since quick rule changes are the opposite of stability in law.

4.4. Clear Commencement

Legislation rarely comes into force immediately when it is made (although see further chapter three). Instead, there will be a period between its making and its commencement (also referred to as coming into force, coming into operation or coming into effect). As well as making the legislation less navigable, commencement provisions can make the legislation less predictable – how is a person to know when a new law will come into force? Consider an investor making a decision about whether to buy widgets. The law regulating the sale of widgets has changed, but that change has not yet been commenced. The legal position is therefore unpredictable and the investor does not have sufficient information on which to make a rational business decision. If she knows the commencement date of the new regulation, then she can plan accordingly (for example by increasing or decreasing the size of her offer). This unpredictability is entirely state imposed and should be eliminated so far as is possible.

[110] Benchmark A5, Venice Commission, 'Report on the Rule of Law' (2011).
[111] I Bar-Siman-Tov, 'The Puzzling Resistance to Judicial Review of the Legislative Process' (2011) 91 *Boston University Law Review* 1915, 1932.
[112] ibid 1933.

Predictability will be enhanced if a person knows at the outset when the new law will come into force, or is given clear information about the commencement date. This can be achieved in several ways.

4.4.1. Commencement Date on Act When Act is Made

When legislation is enacted, it ought to state on its face the actual date it comes into force. This is the gold standard for predictability. If different provisions are to be commenced on different dates, this should be done as simply as possible, and should be represented as clearly as possible, for example in a table.

On some occasions, there may be a desire from within government to allow for some flexibility on commencement dates, thus there may be a request that a Minister is given a power to determine the commencement date at some point in the future. According to Leigh, 'this allows for flexibility, giving time for necessary administrative changes and for the law to be introduced according to political expediency'.[113] As an example, see the Civil Evidence (Witnesses) Bill.[114] This Bill allowed for (amongst other things) witnesses to give evidence via a video link. Because it was not clear how long it would take to set up video links in all the courts in Northern Ireland, there was a power to commence on a day determined by the Department of Finance and Personnel. So, when the technology was ready, the Bill would be commenced.

This practice provides an excuse for government inaction – without a fixed date, government may drag its heels in establishing the necessary machinery for the Act to be effective. Worse still, this makes legislation subject to executive caprice – if a Minister decides she doesn't like a particular statute, then she may simply decide not to commence it. The courts have directly addressed this point. In the *Fire Brigades Union* case they held that it was unlawful for the Minister to decide never to commence a statute, he was under an on-going obligation to at the very least consider commencing a statute.[115] More recently, the Outer House of the Court of Session in Scotland ruled that it was unlawful to make a commencement order in respect of England, Wales and Northern Ireland without also commencing the provision for Scotland.[116] However, that was only because the enabling power only authorised UK-wide commencement, without allowing different commencement for different parts of the UK.[117]

[113] I Leigh, 'The Prerogative, Legislative Power, and the Democratic Deficit: The Fire Brigades Union Case' (1995) 3 *Web Journal of Current Legal Issues*.
[114] Northern Ireland Law Commission, NILC 10 (2011).
[115] [1995] 2 AC 513.
[116] *Craig v Advocate General for Scotland* [2018] CSOH 117.
[117] s 61, Crime and Courts Act 2013.

4.4.2. Presentation of Commencement Dates

If the actual commencement date does not appear on an Act, it is difficult for people to know if it has commenced. This lack of predictability has now been ameliorated by section 104 of the Deregulation Act 2015. This section provides that a commencement provision can be amended after the event to include the actual date of commencement.

4.4.3. Clear Repeal Date

It is equally important that the end date of a law is clear and certain. There are several ways that legislation can cease to have effect. The most common way is express repeal by another statute. So, a new law will make new provision about a subject, and it will then expressly repeal the old law regulating that subject. This gives the reader certainty. The bad way is implied repeal, where the new law is incompatible with the old law, and it therefore impliedly repeals the old law to the extent of that incompatibility. This is lazy law-making that leaves the reader uncertain about what the actual law is and what the law prescribes. I agree with de Paula's conclusion that 'explicit clauses are always preferable to general revoking'.[118]

There has been a recent attempt at a novel mechanism for bringing old law to an end, what may be called a disapplication model, as set out in the Nationalities and Borders Bill. Under that Bill, any provision of the Trafficking Directive that is incompatible with the Bill will cease to have effect. There is no express repeal or modification, instead a blanket statement that any (unspecified) provision in the Directive no longer has effect if that provision is incompatible with the new law. I have previously described this as Schrödinger's legislation – because it means that the Trafficking Directive is simultaneously law and not law.[119] There is no clear repeal, instead the reader is left scratching their head wondering if the Directive is in force or not.

A relatively uncommon way to end law is the sunset clause. This is a clause in a statute that states when that statute will expire. In many ways, this is an excellent tool for assisting predictability, as the user will know in advance when the statute will cease to have effect.[120] However, as Bar-Siman-Tov points out, in many cases the point of temporary legislation isn't to give a definite end date to the legislation,

[118] de Paula (n 14).

[119] R Cormacain and O Garner, 'Schrödinger's Trafficking Directive and the Nationalities and Borders Bill: Simultaneously Law and Not Law' (*UK Constitutional Law Association*, 17 December 2021) <https://ukconstitutionallaw.org/2021/12/17/ronan-cormacain-and-oliver-garner-schrodingers-trafficking-directive-and-the-nationalities-and-borders-bill-simultaneously-law-and-not-law-%ef%bf%bc/>.

[120] See further for example, S Ranchordas, *Constitutional Sunsets and Experimental Legislation: A Comparative Perspective* (Cheltenham, Edward Elgar Publishing, 2015).

but to experiment to see if the temporary legislation actually works.[121] In fact a sunset clause can be misleading if the sunset date is continually extended, or the legislation continually renewed.[122]

The final way is the very undesirable situation where a law simply becomes obsolete or falls into disuse. This makes predictability difficult because the reader has little way to know if the statute on the page will actually still be applied in practice. This is where Law Commissions provide a valuable function; promoting statute law repeal Acts, or other legislation that tidies up the statute book.

4.5. Consistency

Consistency in legislation promotes predictability. The most basic principle here is that a statute should not contradict itself – it shouldn't have 'simultaneous, mutually inconsistent meanings'.[123] Kecskés points out that the Sarbanes-Oxley Act has internal inconsistencies due to its hasty transit through the legislature: 'proper attention was not given to the text of the bill, thus the approved Act contained duplicate provisions on sentencing which were likely to cause confusion'.[124] Watkins points out the efforts made by medieval lawyers to resolve inconsistencies in the text of the Justinian Digest:

> Faced with contradictions and inconsistencies in the Digest, the jurists who studied it responded with a humility to match that of the theologians, believing that through the application of reason, the essential consistency and unity of the compilation could be demonstrated.[125]

But in my view, this is a wasted effort. It would be much better to delete or avoid inconsistencies than to try to use sophistry to reconcile them.

Consistency means much more than simply avoiding direct contradictions within a single statute. If a novel statutory provision is introduced then people may not know how it will be applied. But if a statutory provision is introduced that is in resonance with previously interpreted and applied provisions, then people will have a reasonable assumption that this provision will be interpreted and applied in a similar way. For example, the UK statute book is littered with 'it is an offence to …' and 'a person commits an offence if …'. This consistency of language helps readers to quickly understand that an offence is being created. But if the provision states 'a crime has the following elements …', then this lack of consistency with

[121] I Bar-Siman-Tov, 'Temporary Legislation, Better Regulation and Experimentalist Governance: An Empirical Study' (2017) 11 *Regulation and Governance* 192.

[122] ibid.

[123] Dorsey (n 34) 175.

[124] A Kecskés, 'The Sarbanes-Oxley Act from a Legislative Viewpoint' (2015) 4 *Theory and Practice of Legislation* 27.

[125] TG Watkin, 'Publication Review: Law and Theology in the Middle Ages' [2004] *Ecclesiastical Journal* 353, 354.

other statutes creates unpredictability – why this difference, is an offence being created?

However, consistency is not a strong form of legislation principle. As with predictability it is subject to the 'so far as is possible' caveat. Absolute consistency across the statute book, and blindly following precedent stifles innovation and the development of new legislative techniques. Greenberg entitles one of his chapters 'the pestilential power of precedent'[126] and argues strongly in favour of individuality in enacting new provisions. Undue consistency also corrals legislation into existing paradigms that may not effectively deal with the exigencies of emerging social problems. Watkin questions whether 'received tradition can become invalid by the passage of time',[127] his point is more about whether old accepted practices can continue in the modern age, but it applies equally to old accepted precedents.

What then does it mean to have consistent legislation? I submit that it means (a) similar policies in different statutes are given effect by similar legal provisions, (b) similar words used in statutes are intended to have similar meanings and (c) the statute book as a whole is generally harmonious. As will be explained further below, I have deliberately said 'similar' rather than 'the same'. Consistency is not the same as continuity or stasis. It doesn't mean that there is no change at all. Every statute is enacted to effect legal change (otherwise there would be no point in enacting new legislation). Legislators are not in the business of keeping the law static. Consistency means that we enact legislation in a similar manner over time. Laws uses a colourful metaphor to describe this, legislative drafters must not 'debase the coinage of communication'.[128] Words are what we use to communicate, we must use them consistently and with respect in order that we are able to continue to use them (and for them to have the same meaning) in the future.

This is the theory on consistency, but how do we give effect to it?

4.5.1. Words Mean the Same Thing

Within a single statute, it is imperative that words have exactly the same meaning throughout the statute. So, if a child is defined as someone aged under 18 in one part of a statute, then that meaning should be used throughout the rest of the statute. If you mean the same thing, use the same word, but if you mean a different thing, use a different word. 'Consistency in this context means being repetitive, that is using the same word rather than a synonym'.[129] Unlike in literature where a synonym may stop the text from being boringly repetitive, in legislation repeating the word shows you intend the same meaning to apply. Elizabeth Barrett Browning

[126] Greenberg (n 18) chapter 27.
[127] TG Watkin, 'Consensus and the Constitution' [1994] *Ecclesiastical Journal* 232, 235.
[128] Laws (n 3) 142.
[129] Martineau and Salernon (n 34) 59.

could write 'How do I love thee? Let me count the ways' and then go on to enumerate them.[130] Good for poetry, bad for legislation.

An example of how confusing it can be to use the same phrase to describe two different things can be found in the Consumer Credit Directive.[131] Article 14 is entitled 'right of withdrawal' and deals with the right of a consumer to withdraw from a credit agreement within 14 days. However, article 15 then goes on to talk about a 'right of withdrawal, based on Community law'. However, this right of withdrawal does not mean the same thing as the article 14 right of withdrawal, instead it refers to a separate and distinct right of withdrawal from a contract for the supply of goods and services. The reader is left scratching her head trying to figure out the meaning, before (hopefully) eventually realising that notwithstanding that the same words are used, the meanings are completely different.

It is superficially attractive to argue that words must also mean the same across the entirety of the statute book. So, if we say 'child' anywhere in legislation, it will always mean someone under the age of 18. However, this would not allow for necessary distinctions to be made in those different statutes. Take tax, electoral and immigration law and their definitions of 'resident' as an example. The word 'resident' may mean quite different things in each of these statutes. This is quite right and proper as it reflects the different purposes behind each of these subjects. The criteria for taxing someone as a resident may be quite different from the policies behind letting them vote as a resident, or allowing their spouse to qualify as the spouse of a resident. The English word 'resident' is the best word to use in each of those separate statutes as it indicates to the reader what type of concept we are discussing. We would quickly run out of synonyms if we couldn't reuse a word already used in another statute.

What applies to words specifically defined in different statutes applies less so to ordinary 'working' words that aren't defined. Ordinary words should generally have the same meaning across the statute book. So, 'contravene' in one law should generally mean the same as 'contravene' in another law. This allows us to use words as the common currency of communication – they mean the same and can be exchanged easily across the statute book. So, when we use 'shall' or 'must' in different contexts in different laws it always indicates obligation, whereas when we use 'may' in different laws, we know that it always means discretion. But if we start being inconsistent, or giving words an unnatural meaning, we lose the predictability of repeated use and understanding. Sarat went further and argued that

> when words lose their meaning and their capacity to bind those who use them, neither democracy nor the rule of law can long survive. In contrast, when citizens and officials insist on the integrity of language they nourish the hope that both will outlive current assaults on them.[132]

[130] E Barrett Browning, 'How Do I Love Thee (Sonnet 43)'.

[131] Directive 2008/48/EC.

[132] A Sarat, 'Loose Talk Came Back to Haunt Trump in Judge's Travel Ban Ruling' *The Guardian* (16 March 2017) <www.theguardian.com/us-news/2017/mar/15/trump-travel-ban-muslims-hawaii-judge-power-words>.

There is a further complication with requiring a consistent meaning of words across the statute book. The meaning of words changes over time. So, if we used a word simply because it has appeared in an older statute, we may not get the same meaning. An extreme example can be used here by comparing the words we use to describe roads and bridges. In the Preamble to the Statute of Pious Uses 1634 the following purpose appears 'for the erection, building, maintenance, or repair of any bridges, causeyes, cashes, paces and highways within this realm'. O'Halloran and I give a brief indication of the etymology here: 'causeye' is the root of the word causeway, 'cash' probably comes from cashel – a wall around a group of churches and 'pace' is a passageway.[133] However, by the time we reach 1993, the following definition appears:

> 'road' means a public road, that is to say a road which is maintainable by the Department, and includes—
>
> (a) a road over which the public have a right of way on foot only, not being a footway;
> (b) any part of a road; and
> (c) any bridge or tunnel over or through which a road passes ...[134]

To use the words cash, causeyes and paces today would be meaningless. As Xanthaki says, 'semantic change is one important aspect of the fluidity and instability of the vocabulary we use'.[135] Consistency of language does not mean blind and unthinking repetition of older words, that way lies not just stasis but obsolescence.

4.5.2. Consistent Grammar

The rules of grammar allow us to reduce word length by using accepted shortcuts. For example, we can say 'the defendant's possessions' rather than 'the possessions of the defendant' because we know how apostrophes work. In the same way as with words, consistently using grammatical rules correctly means that people have a better chance of understanding what we mean – they can predict the effect of our words and grammar. The same applies with punctuation.[136] But if we start abusing the rules of grammar, people cannot trust them as a reliable means of predicting the meaning of a statute. This doesn't quite go as far as 'bad grammar leads to bad men',[137] but it does bear witness to Orwell's comment that slovenliness of language leads to foolishness of thought.[138]

Overall, consistent grammar is a weak form of legislation principle. It should be followed as a general rule, provided that there is no good reason to

[133] K O'Halloran and R Cormacain, *Charity Law in Northern Ireland* (Dublin, Round Hall Ltd, 2001) 253.
[134] Roads (Northern Ireland) Order 1993, Art 2(2).
[135] Thornton and Xanthaki (n 34) 15.
[136] Martineau and Salernon (n 34) 68.
[137] H Jacobson, *Pussy* (London, Jonathan Cape, 2017).
[138] G Orwell, *Politics and the English Language* (London, Penguin, 2013).

break it. Grammar is a good servant but a bad master. The other example is the grammatical rule against starting a sentence with a conjunction (although it isn't quite the rule that it is sometimes thought to be). Sometimes effective communication of an idea is aided by starting the sentence with a conjunction. For example:

> (1) It is an offence to have a weapon in a public place.
> (2) But this does not apply to police officers.

4.5.3. Do Similar Things in Similar Ways

There are many common tropes in legislation: establishing a body corporate, granting a right of appeal, creating a criminal offence etc. If these are done in broadly similar ways, then it makes the legislation consistent and thus predictable. If a person is familiar with procedure X1 in a statute and then sees procedure X2 in a new statute, then they can be reasonably confident, based on their knowledge of X1 of how X2 will be applied.

An example is how the prohibition on extra-territorial legislation is expressed in relation to the Scottish Parliament and the Northern Ireland Assembly. Section 6(2)(a) of the Northern Ireland Act 1998 states:

> (2) A provision is outside that competence if any of the following paragraphs apply—
> (a) it would form part of the law of a country or territory other than Northern Ireland, or confer or remove functions exercisable otherwise than in or as regards Northern Ireland …

Section 29(2)(a) of the Scotland Act 1998 states:

> (2) A provision is outside that competence so far as any of the following paragraphs apply—
> (a) it would form part of the law of a country or territory other than Scotland, or confer or remove functions exercisable otherwise than in or as regards Scotland …

The words used are nearly exactly the same. This consistency means that anyone familiar with how extra-territoriality works in Scotland will be able to predict how extra-territoriality works in Northern Ireland. As with parallel structures discussed in chapter two, using the same phrases makes interpretation easier for the reader. The provisions on extra-territoriality in Wales are quite different, reflecting the special nature of the Welsh legal jurisdiction (Wales isn't a separate jurisdiction, it is part of the legal jurisdiction of England and Wales, so the rules on extra-territoriality need to reflect this).

A bad example, drawn from these above three Acts, is the power of the Secretary of State to make changes to the legislation of other parts of the United Kingdom that are consequent upon the changes made by the devolved legislatures, but that those devolved legislatures have themselves no power to make. So, in Northern Ireland, section 84(2) of the Northern Ireland Act 1998 states:

> (2) Her Majesty may by Order in Council make such amendments of the law of any part of the United Kingdom as appear to Her Majesty to be necessary or expedient in consequence of any provision made by or under—
>
> (a) Northern Ireland legislation; or …

In Wales, section 150 of the Government of Wales Act 2005 states:

> (1) The Secretary of State may by order make such provision as the Secretary of State considers appropriate in consequence of—
>
> (a) any provision made by an Assembly Measure or Act of the Assembly …

In Scotland, section 104(1) of the Scotland Act 1998 states:

> (1) Subordinate legislation may make such provision as the person making the legislation considers necessary or expedient in consequence of any provision made by or under any Act of the Scottish Parliament or made by legislation mentioned in subsection (2).

These three different provisions are all directed at the same end goal – a power to fix legislation in other parts of the UK in consequence of something done by one of the devolved legislatures. But the ways in which they are structured are all quite different. Doing a different thing will of course require different words, but doing the same thing should require fairly similar words. The divergence between these three provisions doesn't seem to reflect any policy deviation, and the lack of consistency makes it hard for the reader to discern if different procedures are to apply in each of the different jurisdictions.

Sheridan approaches this from a technological and informatics perspective – identifying patterns in legislation to discern what works and what doesn't work.[139] He sees pattern language as a method of describing good design practices, or a common vocabulary between users and professionals.[140] This reflects the fact that legislation normally follows consistent patterns, so repeating familiar patterns makes for greater consistency. Moving back to law, Spencer argues that we should have standardised templates in criminal law – a standard way of setting out the elements of an offence, the actus reus, mens rea, defences, exceptions, penalties etc – these make it much easier for the reader to understand and follow.[141]

[139] J Sheridan, 'People, Patterns and Data – the Story of Legislation.Gov.Uk People, Patterns and Data – the Story of Legislation.Gov.Uk' (*Social Tech Guide*, 2014) <www.socialtech.org.uk/blog/people-patterns-and-data-the-story-of-legislation-gov-uk/> accessed 20 January 2016.

[140] J Sheridan, 'Using Data to Understand How the Statute Book Works' (2014) 14 *Legal Information Management* 244. See further Big Data on the government legislation website dealing with pattern language for legislation, <www.legislation.gov.uk/projects/big-data-for-law>.

[141] JR Spencer, 'Criminal Justice Legislation That Everyone Can Understand: A Flying Pig or a Realistic Aspiration' (Institute of Advanced Legal Studies, 25 January 2016).

Sheridan's work for the National Archives led directly to guidance issued by the Parliamentary Counsel Office on 'Common Legislative Solutions: A Guide to Tackling Recurring Policy Issues in Legislation'.[142] As set out in the foreword to this work, its purpose is 'to deliver legislative drafting more efficiently and effectively and to help the users of legislation by making it more consistent'. If the form of legislation seeks to do similar things in similar ways, it makes it easier for those drafting it and easier for those reading it.

4.5.4. Consistent Presentation

Similar to the above point but broader, legislation should generally be presented in a consistent fashion. So if it normally begins with a preamble, enacting words then introductory provisions, then it should continue to do so. If the layout is left-aligned with section titles in bold and chapter heads centred, it should continue to be so. This kind of consistency also helps with navigability.

4.5.5. Address the Same Issues

The above advice applies when legislation is attempting to do similar things in different areas. On many occasions the legislation will be doing different things in similar areas because there is a different policy imperative. However, if similar issues will arise in each of these areas, then it is advisable to at least address each of these issues. So, if statute A establishes a body corporate X and sets out pay, pensions, legal status etc, then if statute B establishes a body corporate Y, it should also set out pay, pensions, legal status etc. These provisions may be quite different from each other, but at least the same headings, the same categories are being addressed.

4.5.6. Consistency and the Development of New Ideas

The greatest challenge faced by consistency is new ideas, new solutions and new ways of doing things. It has to be accepted that if the policy changes, then the legislation must change. But what if the policy doesn't change, but there is a better way of preparing the legislation? Or, half way between these two ends, the policy hasn't really changed, but in a new iteration, it can better cover some potential loopholes in the old law? Take the example of pre-emption rights in legislation privatising various public utilities. In the British Telecommunications Act 1981, Schedule 2 doesn't really deal with pre-emption rights at all. But by the time we reach privatisation of water in the Water Act 1989, schedule 2, paragraph 2(6), does deal with

[142] Parliamentary Counsel Office, 'Common Legislative Solutions: A Guide to Tackling Recurring Policy Issues in Legislation' (The Cabinet Office 2021).

pre-emption rights. Then in the Coal Act 1994, schedule 2, paragraph 3(3), deals with pre-emption rights slightly differently. This is what Laws is describing when he states 'just as an innovation in drafting may commit future drafters to a particular approach for the future, it can also condemn them for not having adopted a particular approach in the past'.[143]

Does a change (or an 'improvement') in a new statute mean that the old statute was wrong? If a new statute plugs a loophole, does this mean that in the act of doing so, the legislature is acknowledging that there was a loophole in the old statute? In my view, the decision must generally be taken in favour of the new, otherwise consistency would oblige us to continually wallow in the mud of unsatisfactory older law. But this also requires the assistance of judges who must accept that just because a thing is being done in a new way, it doesn't mean that the old way is wrong.

4.5.7. Consistency and Changes in Legal Culture

The other challenge to be addressed in making legislation consistent is in dealing with changes in the legal culture that form the background and context in which the legislation must be interpreted and applied. The most obvious recent change in the UK is the influx of human rights jurisprudence following the enactment of the Human Rights Act 1998. An older piece of law may have been perfectly acceptable when it was made, but if we try to be consistent and replicate it now, it may fall foul of the new imperative to make legislation that is in accordance with human rights. So, if an old precedent is being dusted off and inserted into a new statute, the classic modification to be made is to insert a right of appeal into it.

It is this argument that led the Attorney General for Northern Ireland to discount old cases and legislation when considering the validity of a new piece of legislation. He stated in evidence to a committee of the Northern Ireland Assembly

> [the old Acts] antedate the Human Rights Act 1998 and particular provisions in that that deal with retrospectivity. So, I do not think that those old statutes offer us any assistance about what might happen now.[144]

Chapter seven deals further with this point, and in particular changes to legal culture and an acceptance of gender equality, meaning that old ways of doing things are no longer satisfactory.

4.5.8. Need for Consistent Interpretation by Judges

Consistent form of legislation is only one side of the equation. For legislation to be predictable, there must also be consistent interpretation by judges. So, words must be given their normal meaning by the courts, the meaning that has been given to

[143] Laws (n 3) 143.
[144] Report on the Civil Service (Special Advisers) Bill, 13 February 2013, NIA 97/11-15, page 75.

them in the past. In addition, judges should be aware of the efforts to make legislation predictable. This is generally the case in the UK, for example Gillen J stated that 'precision drafting rather than disorganised composition is presupposed' when it comes to the words of a statute.[145] However, consistency in language is thwarted when judges take a perverse approach to interpreting the clear words in a statute. Perhaps the nadir of perverse judicial interpretation was reached in *Liversidge v Anderson*.[146] It was in this case that Lord Atkin made one of the most famous dissenting speeches of all time. In criticising the interpretation placed on a phrase by his fellow judges, Lord Atkin said

> I know of only one authority which might justify the suggested method of construction: 'When I use a word' Humpty Dumpty said in a rather scornful tone, 'it means just what I chose it to mean, neither more nor less'.[147]

However, the need for consistent interpretation by judges is not form of legislation principle. Although there is an on-going dialogue between the legislature and the judiciary, it is beyond the scope of this book to investigate how judges reach their decisions.

4.6. Application in the Real World

The law as stated on the statute book ought to be the same as the law applied in the real world. If this is not so, then legislation cannot be used to predict the legal effect of actions and the Rule of Law is breached. Although this may appear self-evident, there are many instances where the law on the statute book is not the same as the law applied. Set out below are some of the more prominent examples of this.

4.6.1. Law is Ignored

In a state where the Rule of Law is not respected, the government will flout legislation. In a state without effective Rule of Law, people will ignore the law. There is little any form of legislation principle can do to combat such outcomes.

4.6.2. 'The Law is an Ass'

The state ignoring the law is normally seen as a bad thing. However, there are occasions where 'the law is an ass' and to ignore it seems sensible.[148] Even if this

[145] *In the matter of an application by Christine Forde for judicial review* [2008] NIQB 40 at para [47].
[146] (1942) AC 206.
[147] ibid, 245.
[148] The expression 'the law is an ass' means that the law is idiotic or asinine, rather than the modern, cruder meaning. The expression was first disseminated to a wider audience in the 1800s by C Dickens, *Oliver Twist* New Ed edn (London, Penguin Classics, 2007).

is done for the benefit of citizens, it seriously undermines respect for the Rule of Law. Greenberg cites an example where a new piece of legislation would prohibit Community First Responders (ie volunteer ambulances) from using the traditional Battenburg-style panels on their ambulances.[149] This would have a serious impact on their ability to help people in an emergency. The police stepped in, and recognising the sterling work done by these organisations, stated that they would not prosecute anyone during an informal transitional period. This gave time to the organisations to re-organise how to provide their vehicles. Yet, the legal basis for an 'informal transitional period' as granted by the police is flimsy at best, as there were no transitional provisions in the legislation. In fact, it is a complete breach of the Rule of Law for the police to decide not to enforce the law. Greenberg, somewhat tongue in cheek, suggests that the best way to deal with bad law like this is simply to ignore it.[150] This is a pragmatic solution – if everyone knows the law is an ass, then everyone can simply ignore it. The major drawback to this is that it seriously weakens respect for the Rule of Law.

Enright gives an historical example of this when Creon, the ruler of Thebes, decrees that it is unlawful for Antigone to bury her brother's body.[151] Antigone refuses to comply – 'she does not seek to justify her actions with the terms of Creon's law: she negates the law by handing it back to him, intact'.[152]

There is one rather blunt form of legislation technique to deal with this problem – enact the law properly in the first place. If the legislation in Greenberg's example had included an exemption for Community First Responders, or allowed for a formal transitional period, then the law would not have been stupid, and it would have been obeyed. Respect for the Rule of Law is enhanced if the law is not an ass.

4.6.3. Impossible Law

In the world of the White Queen 'the rule is, jam tomorrow and jam yesterday – but never jam today'.[153] As well as diminishing respect for legislation, impossible law is unpredictable as it is incapable of being applied in the real world.

4.6.4. Panglossian Law

Panglossian legislation is legislation that assumes that all is for the best, in this the best of all possible worlds. So, it sets legal obligations that are wildly

[149] D Greenberg, 'Coping with Bad Legislation: Strategy No. 1 – Ignoring It' (2015) 36 *Statute Law Review* v.
[150] ibid.
[151] A Enright, 'Antigone in Galway: Anne Enright on the Dishonoured Dead' *London Review of Books* (17 December 2015) 11.
[152] ibid.
[153] L Carroll, *Through the Looking Glass* (London, Collector's Colour Library, 2011) 206.

over-optimistic, if not impossible. So, reducing carbon dioxide emissions to 80 per cent of what the emissions where in 1990 may be a tough target, but it is doable.[154] However, a requirement that all homes are immediately carbon neutral right now would be impossible. The undesirability of Panglossian law is reflected in the Environment Act 2021. There is a power to set certain environmental targets, but: 'Before making regulations under sections 1 to 3 which set or amend a target the Secretary of State must be satisfied that the target, or amended target, can be met'.[155]

Calabresi decried what he saw as a Panglossian view of what administrative agencies could actually accomplish within the legal framework.[156] In the UK this kind of legislation doesn't really exist, and targets in legislation, although sometimes challenging are normally at least realistic.

The form of legislation principle here is simple; ensure that requirements and assumptions contained within the legislation are realistic and achievable.

4.6.5. Law is Inaccessible

If people can't access the law, they can't follow it. Chapter two sets out principles to combat this.

4.6.6. Law is Unintelligible

If people can't understand the law, they can't follow it. Chapter five sets out principles to combat this.

4.6.7. Disconnect between Language of the Law and Practice on the Ground

Legislators must ensure that legislation is directly connected to the behaviour that it seeks to modify. The law was made for man, not man made for the law. Therefore, it is incumbent upon the legislator to determine what the actual intention of the law is and accurately reflect that intention rather than force people to do something that wasn't intended. So, if people are doing action X and we wish that to be lawful, then legislation must authorise action X. There is no point in the law authorising Y when everyone (individuals and the state) wants X to be done. In this case everyone will follow Y even though the law actually says X. In discussing the Sexual Offences Bill, one parliamentarian stated: 'we need to reflect on what is happening out there in the real world and ensure that our laws do not

[154] Climate Change Act 2008.
[155] s 4(2), Environment Act 2021.
[156] G Calabresi, *A Common Law for the Age of Statutes* (Clark, The Lawbook Exchange, Ltd, 1982) 45.

attract ridicule'.[157] More recently an editorial in the *New Scientist* objected to the Investigatory Powers Bill because it 'asks for some powers that are nonsensical, because they bear little relation to how digital communications actually work'.[158] Law is not predictable if there is a disconnect between the language of legislation and lived reality.

The object and the legal description of the object should be the same. They should map as closely as is possible onto each other, otherwise the law moves into a parallel dimension divorced from reality. This means that legislators should strive to avoid a two- stage process of taking the thing, converting it into legal description, then when we come to apply it, comparing the thing to the legal description to see if it fits. The legal description of the thing should relate as directly as possible (linguistically and practically) to the thing itself. So, if we mean horse say horse, not a four-legged grazing animal. If we mean cookie say cookie, not 'the use of electronic communications networks to store information or to gain access to information stored in the terminal equipment of a subscriber or user'.[159]

Greenberg puts it this way: 'everyone knows this is what is meant to happen even though the law says something different'.[160] The example Greenberg gives is *Vehicle and Operator Services Agency v Kayes*.[161] In that case, a particular industry (the Showman's Guild) had a long-standing agreement with the Agency that a particular type of vehicle (adapted for carrying showman equipment) was not to be regarded as a goods vehicle by virtue of falling under a particular statutory exception. When the court examined that particular statutory exception, it was quite clear that the vehicle did not fall within that exception. The court was able to find a reason to find this particular showman not guilty of not holding a licence for a goods vehicle. However, it had clear difficulties with this agreement, stating:

> I would very much doubt whether that would stand up to a legal challenge if such were brought because clearly it is very difficult to conceive that any showman's goods vehicle which would carry any sort of equipment for a show could be properly regarded as [falling within the exemption].[162]

What is the form of legislation solution to this? I suggest it is the same blunt answer as was given in relation to the law being an ass – enact the law correctly in the first place (or amend any mistakes). The judge in *Kayes* put this rather more diplomatically, saying:

> I need do no more than to suggest that it would be sensible for that matter to be put on a proper legislative basis, maybe by some amendment to the relevant regulations, because

[157] Sandra Gidley, Hansard 15 July 2003 Column 224.

[158] Editorial, 'No Art to the Impossible' *New Scientist* (30 January 2016) 5.

[159] Art 5(3) Directive 2002/58/EC of the European Parliament and of the Council of 12 July 2002 concerning the processing of personal data and the protection of privacy in the electronic communications sector.

[160] D Greenberg, 'A Refreshing Decision; Or the Rule of Law in Action' (2012) 33 *Statute Law Review* 409.

[161] [2012] EWHC 1498 (Admin).

[162] ibid [16].

> I suspect the time may well come when someone challenges the agreement and I very much doubt whether it would survive any such challenge.[163]

Bad law is one of the best ways to diminish respect for the Rule of Law. If everyone 'knows' what the law is (whether by reference to convention, or official guidance), regardless of what the law actually states, then we undermine the basis of even having law.

4.6.8. Things that are Not in the Law, but that are Intended to be Applied in Practice

If we want the law to be applied in a particular manner, then we should make that clear in the law. This is another way of saying that the law must be inclusive of all relevant material. The form of legislation principle of inclusivity is dealt with in chapter two.

4.6.9. Legislative Provisions that are Not Intended to be Applied in Practice

If we want the law to reflect reality, then legislation must only contain provisions that it is intended will apply in practice. So, if an individual sees provision X in the law, she will expect X to apply in practice. And if X doesn't apply in practice, then the legislation cannot be used to predict the legal effect of the individual's actions. Stepping back in time in the legislative process, if the legislators want a particular thing, then include that thing in the law. But if they don't actively desire that thing, then don't include it in the law. Legislative drafters have long said that excess matter in Bills, as in humans, goes septic.[164] This applies doubly if the excess material is unused material.

There are three circumstances where provisions in the statute book may not be applied in practice. First, powers that are only to be exercised in certain circumstances, or upon certain criteria being satisfied. The most obvious instance of this are powers to be exercised in the case of an emergency. The Civil Contingencies Act 2004 is a good example of this. It makes express provision for a power to make regulations, but only in the case of an emergency. The reader will not be confused

[163] ibid.

[164] The source of this quote is hard to find. Bowman used it in 2005, G Bowman, 'Why Is There a Parliamentary Counsel Office?' (2005) 26 *Statute Law Review* 69, but ascribed it to an unnamed drafter. Carter referred to it in 2007, R Carter and M Green, 'The Act Is Self-Explanatory … or Is It? Explanatory Notes in New Zealand Legislation' (2007) 28 *Statute Law Review* 1. Laws used it in 2011, S Laws, 'Giving Effect to Policy in Legislation: How to Avoid Missing the Point' (2011) 32 *Statute Law Review* 1.

into thinking that these powers always apply. It is clear that they can only be exercised in an emergency. As long as the criteria for exercise of these powers is clear, then the legislation is predictable. Unpredictability only arises when the criteria for exercise of a power are vague.

Second, we can have 'just in case' provisions in a statute. Thornton argues that there must be a necessity for a power in legislation, his point being that if the power is already contained (expressly or impliedly) elsewhere, that there is no need for it.[165] But my point goes further; it isn't about unnecessary duplication, but about actual use. A just in case power is inserted when a legislator doesn't think there is a current need for a particular power, but wants it inserted just in case it is necessary at some point in the future. As well as cluttering up the statute book, this makes legislation unpredictable as readers will assume that powers contained in the statute book are there for a reason, they are there to be used. But if they have only been inserted 'just in case' then the reader has a false impression of how the law will be applied in practice.

It is difficult to determine whether a general power in a statute has been used as it will depend on the history of how that power has been applied in practice, and these things are not recorded in an easily searchable format. However, it is much easier to determine whether a power to make subordinate legislation has been used: the exercise of powers to make regulations are recorded.[166] Take therefore as an example powers to make regulations under the Licensing (Northern Ireland) Order 1996. There are powers to make an order to vary opening hours,[167] to make regulations relating to places of public entertainment where alcohol can be served,[168] to make regulations relating to sale of alcohol at international airports,[169] etc. However, none of these powers have been exercised. Why is a power inserted if it is never exercised? If people read the legislation they will not be able to predict its effect as it is subject to a possible change. Why introduce that element of unpredictability if that change will never arise? Of course, it is very difficult to say at the outset, when a Bill is being prepared – 'do we really need this power?' However, the momentum seems to be in favour of automatically including powers that are never exercised. In the Licensing Order example, these powers to make regulations were originally contained in the Licensing (Northern Ireland) Order 1990. They were not exercised under the 1990 Order, but in spite of this, they were then included in the 1996 Order (where they remained unexercised).

The next example also has to do with alcohol, but the unpredictability is more obvious and more serious. The Scotch Whisky (Northern Ireland) Order 1988 regulates the sale of Scotch whisky in Northern Ireland. Whisky is defined in Article 2(2), but Article 2(3) then goes on to say: '(3) The Department may by

[165] Thornton and Xanthaki (n 34) 268.
[166] Statutory Publications Office, *Index to the Statutory Rules and Orders: Northern Ireland* (28th edn, The Stationery Office 2007).
[167] Art 49 (although this provision was repealed in 2011).
[168] Art 52(1).
[169] Art 53.

order amend the definition of whisky in paragraph (2)'. How can a whisky seller or distiller predict the legal effect of their actions when the definition of whisky is unpredictable? This power has never been exercised, so why was it inserted in the first place?

There is an increasingly common practice in legislation to include a power to make further consequential provision by subordinate legislation. An Act will typically make all necessary consequential amendments to other legislation. However, the new practice is to insert an additional power to make further amendments in future as a consequence of the legislation. Take as an example section 48 of the Pension Schemes Act (Northern Ireland) 2016:

> Power to make consequential amendments
>
> 48. – (1) The Department may by regulations make provision that is consequential on any provision made by this Act.
>
> (2) Regulations under this section may amend, repeal, revoke or otherwise modify any statutory provision (whenever passed or made).

This is a general power inserted just in case the legislators have missed something. This makes legislation very unpredictable. Previously a person could read the amending Act and know (from reading the schedule of consequential amendments) all changes that were being made. Now, the person is uncertain, not knowing what future consequential changes will be made. This kind of super-enabling clause is considered in more detail in chapter six.

Third, we have legislation that is never commenced. The Easter Act 1928 included a power to fix the date of Easter. This legislation has never been commenced, yet it is still on the statute book, with the banner heading of 'prospective' (in the sense that this legislation may come into force at some point in the future). What is the user to think? This legislation is on the statute book, it was made 90 years ago and has never been repealed. But the law does not accord with reality, the words on the statute book do not correspond with what actually happens on the ground. Why on earth clutter up the statute book with material that will most likely will never actually be implemented?

Perhaps the most egregious example of real world inapplicability of the words on the statute book is contained in section 21A of and Schedule 4A to the Northern Ireland Act 1998. These provisions deal with the arrangements for the appointment of the Minister (or Ministers) of Justice in Northern Ireland. As it was unclear precisely what arrangements would be agreed between the parties, the legislation entered into not one, but four parallel universes of what would happen if a particular arrangement was adopted.

1. Minister appointed by First Minister and deputy First Minister, approved by resolution of the Assembly.[170]
2. Minister appointed following resolution of the Assembly.[171]

[170] s 21A(3).
[171] s 21A(3A).

3. Two Ministers acting jointly.[172]
4. Minister and junior Minister appointed, with these posts being rotated.[173]

This was further complicated by Schedule 4A setting out a further 20 pages of just in case provisions relating to each of the four options. There was a pressing political reason for this inclusion of all this material in the statute book – it was needed to keep political parties committed to an evolving negotiation. However, as legislation, it promotes unpredictability. The only message the reader receives is confusion.

4.6.10. Legislative Provisions that are Intended to be Obeyed, but are Not Planned to be Enforced

The final category of laws that aren't properly applied in the real world are those legislative provisions that the state does want us to obey, for which there are enforcement mechanisms, but for which there is no appetite on the part of the state to actually enforce in practice. This sets up a legal fiction – the law is there, we are told we have to obey it, but the state takes no active steps to actually do anything with the law. This turns law from being something that has legal effect, to law as performance art – that it is there to be seen, not to be done.

A good example of this kind of provision was given by Kit Malthouse MP, Minister of State in a discussion on Fixed Penalty Notices (FPN).

> Much of the notion behind FPNs is almost a psychological game. We put up dog fouling notices everywhere that say someone will be issued with an FPN, but in fact, if you look at boroughs across the UK, hardly any of them ever issue one of these things. They just never get issued. It is a psychological game that is being played.[174]

Psychological games may be an appropriate tool in the overall regulatory toolbox of government. However, they should not be a tool used as part of legislation as to do so undermines the Rule of Law. Predictability means that if we see a law in black and white, we expect it to be applied and enforced. The moment we treat it as a game of poker where we consider calling the government's bluff and seeing if they will actually enforce a law, is the moment when we lose respect for the law and treat it as a negotiable request, rather than a fixed and certain command.

4.7. Implementability

The legal effect of one's conduct can only be predicted by reference to legislation if that legislation is actually implemented. Implementation requires

[172] s 21A(4).
[173] s 21A(5).
[174] At set out in para 50 in Justice Committee, 'COVID-19 and the Criminal Law: Fourth Report of Session 2021–22' (House of Commons 2021) HC 71 <https://committees.parliament.uk/publications/7439/documents/77794/default/>.

two things, first a willingness for the state to implement the legislation on the ground. Second, processes and procedures within the legislation that allow for it to be implemented. Peter Weir, a Northern Ireland politician has spoken of the trap of thinking that once legislation is passed, the matter is closed, saying that 'it is actually about implementation'.[175] Complimenting the Autism (Amendment) Bill he went on to say 'It is all about ensuring that best practice and best implementation actually happens. Ensuring that it happens is one of the major reasons why it is a good Bill.'[176] There is both a quantitative and a qualitative aspect to implementation mechanisms in legislation. The quantitative one is that the implementation method exists, the qualitative one is that the implementation method is effective.

One current example of failure to implement a law relates to abortion rights in Northern Ireland. Abortion is lawful in England, Wales and Scotland by virtue of the Abortion Act 1967, but that Act did not extend to Northern Ireland.[177] Despite political pressure within Northern Ireland, no legislation was proposed to change this in the Northern Ireland Assembly. However, the Westminster Parliament stepped in in 2019, and in a constitutionally odd provision, made abortion lawful and directed the Secretary of State

> … to ensure that the recommendations in paragraphs 85 and 86 of the CEDAW report are implemented in respect of Northern Ireland …
>
> … by regulations make whatever other changes to the law of Northern Ireland appear to the Secretary of State to be necessary or appropriate for the purpose of complying with subsection (1) …[178]

But this law remains unimplemented. Despite an Act of Parliament making abortion lawful, there is still no abortion in Northern Ireland. Law on the page is of little value if it is not law that has been implemented.

Benedetto draws a distinction between a substantive norm (the thing that must be done) and the consequential norm (the consequence of failing to do the thing), and she sees this as the difference between obedience and enforcement.[179] These two things are clearly conceptually different. However, they must both be present if the law is to be implementable.

So, as a general principle, if a law imposes a duty upon a person to do a thing, there ought to be a clear understanding of what will happen if the person doesn't do the thing. This is most obvious in the criminal law where the duty and the consequence of failure to comply are wrapped up together – if you commit the criminal act, you are subject to the criminal penalty. In other areas of law this link is not

[175] Peter Weir MLA, Official Report 21 September 2021, Northern Ireland Assembly.
[176] ibid.
[177] s 7(3) Abortion Act 1967.
[178] Northern Ireland (Executive Formation etc) Act 2019, ss 9(1) and (4).
[179] M de Benedetto, 'Why Do We Need Effective Law?' (Conference: Effective Law and Regulation, Institute of Advanced Legal Studies, 7 July 2017).

always as obvious and sometimes needs to be implied. A good example is a time limit for a person to do a particular thing. If the person doesn't do the particular thing within the time, what is the effect? If a provision is mandatory, it means that if the thing isn't done in the required way, the thing is not regarded as having being validly done. If a provision is directory, it means that even if the thing isn't done in the required way, it is still regarded as having been validly done.[180] The distinction between a mandatory and directory provision is not easy to discern. According to Thornton

> if the drafter makes no specific provision, the intention of the legislation will be ascertained, not according to any general rule of formula, but by construing the statute as a whole and considering the provision which has been disobeyed in its context in relation to the general object to be secured.[181]

The necessity for a general inquiry into the nature of the legislation is a strong indication of a failure of legislation. The answer to the question 'what is the consequence if I fail to execute this obligation?' should be set out next to the obligation, or easily findable from the obligation. It should not require a close analysis of the legislation as a whole in order to discern the outcome from the general thrust of the legislative intent. So, rather than saying 'A notice must be served upon the Department within 28 days', it is better to say 'A notice is not valid unless it is served upon the Department within 28 days'. In the second formulation, the consequence of failure to comply is explicit, whereas in the first formulation, we know that there is a duty, but we are unclear what happens if there is a breach of that duty.

Contrast the obligations in the following two statutory provisions:

> Enforcement notice: safety measures
>
> 71. – (1) This section applies in relation to a controlled reservoir where it appears to the Department that the reservoir manager has failed to comply with—
>
> (a) the manager's duty under section 36(1) (to ensure compliance with a direction in an inspection report or a pre-commencement safety recommendation),
>
> (b) the manager's duty under section 46(1) (to ensure compliance with a direction in a safety report).
>
> (2) The Department may by notice served on the reservoir manager require the manager to comply with the duty before the end of the period specified in the notice.[182]

The preceding provisions of this Act set out obligations in relation to safety measures. Section 71 then goes on to make (I haven't quoted all the subsections) detailed provisions about what happens if a reservoir manager doesn't comply

[180] See Thornton and Xanthaki (n 34) 275 for a discussion of mandatory versus directory provisions.
[181] ibid.
[182] Reservoirs Act (Northern Ireland) 2015.

with those obligations. This is an example of excellent legislation. The duty is clearly spelt out. Then consequences of failure are clearly spelt out. Contrast this with the following:

> Formation of the Opposition
>
> 2. – (1) Standing orders must make provision for the formation of an Opposition in accordance with this section.[183]

There is nothing to state what will happen if standing orders don't do this. There is no time frame in which the duty must be complied with. If the correct thing is done, there will not be a problem. But if the legislation isn't obeyed then we cannot predict the effect of a failure to implement. This makes for bad legislation.

The standing orders example flags up one additional difficulty with specifying the consequences of a failure to comply with a duty – the identity of the person with the obligation. If a duty applies to a person, then it is reasonable to indicate the consequences of non-compliance. But if the duty applies to a minister (or other emanation of the state) then this becomes more problematic. The general custom in UK statutes is that only the duty is specified for the state, not the enforcement mechanism for failure to comply. The assumption underlying this is that the state respects the Rule of Law and will comply with its legal obligations. It is a matter of constitutional etiquette – the state respects the law and obeys it, and the law respects the state and doesn't threaten it with sanctions. In my view, this represents a reasonable compromise. First, the statute book isn't cluttered up with provisions for enforcement of legal obligations on ministers. Second, the very act of enacting an enforcement clause for a minister opens up the possibility to the minister that they can refuse to comply with a legal obligation. Third, the fact that no enforcement is specified in the legislation doesn't mean that there is no enforcement as the field of constitutional and public law gives many remedies for where the state fails to act lawfully. Fourth, it is reasonable (or at least historically it has been reasonable) to assume in the UK that the state will not wantonly disregard a direct legal obligation.

Unfortunately, Northern Ireland provides an example that undermines the assumption that the state will comply with a law. Legislation included a requirement for the state to make regulations concerning the rights of victims of certain crimes to compensation.[184] When the state didn't do this, they were taken to court, and the court was unequivocal:

> the Executive Office seeks to persuade the Court that it is legitimate for the Executive Office to deliberately refuse to comply with a legal requirement set out in a legislative scheme promulgated by the Westminster Parliament in order to force changes to that

[183] Assembly and Executive Reform (Assembly Opposition) Act (Northern Ireland) 2016.
[184] Northern Ireland (Executive Formation etc) Act 2019.

> legislative scheme. This is a truly shocking proposition. It demonstrates either wilful disregard for the rule of law or abject ignorance of what the rule of law means in a democratic society.[185]

Precisely the same problem arose in another case from Northern Ireland, again involving ministers failing to comply with their statutory duties. *Re Napier* concerned refusal of certain ministers to comply with the requirement set out in the Northern Ireland Act 1998 to attend meetings of the North-South Ministerial Council.[186] The legislation did not set out the consequences of failure to attend the meetings. This placed the court in an unenviable situation. It was happy to declare the actions of the ministers unlawful, but unwilling to delve into political controversy by ordering attendance, leading me to ask the question, what should courts do when ministers break the law?[187]

Voermans talks about implementation as being the Achilles heel of European integration.[188] He is speaking in the context of European legislation being implemented into domestic law. However, his point is the same as the point being made here – the system is failing if legislation isn't being implemented.

The qualitative aspect of implementation means that the particular enforcement mechanism will genuinely lead to the law being properly applied. Take the regulation of car emissions by the EU as a bad example. Car emissions are governed by a plethora of EU Regulations.[189] These set out the manner in which car emissions are to be measured. Unfortunately, these are to be assessed in a laboratory under artificial conditions. The headlines in car trade magazines and blogs indicate how unrealistic these tests are: 'How Emissions Tests Work, And Why They're Stupidly Unrealistic',[190] '"Unrealistic" Emissions Tests Could Make Some Diesel Models "Unaffordable", Say European Carmakers',[191] 'VW Scandal Highlights Unrealistic Lab Tests'.[192] The European Commission eventually

[185] *McNern and Turley* [2020] NIQB 57.

[186] *Re Napier* [2021] NIQB 86, *Re Napier* [2021] NIQB 120. These were two separate cases on the same point, with the same end result.

[187] R Cormacain, 'What Should Courts Do When Ministers Flout the Law?' (*UK Constitutional Law Association*, 22 December 2021) <https://ukconstitutionallaw.org/2021/12/22/ronan-cormacain-what-should-courts-do-when-ministers-flout-the-law%ef%bf%bc/>.

[188] W Voermans, 'Implementation: The Achilles Heel of European Integration' (2014) 2 *Theory and Practice of Legislation* 343.

[189] Commission Regulation (EC) No 692/2008 on emissions from light passenger and commercial vehicles (Euro 5 and Euro 6) and on access to vehicle repair and maintenance information. The Regulations go all the way back to Euro 1.

[190] 'How Emissions Tests Work, And Why They're Stupidly Unrealistic' (*Car Throttle*) <www.carthrottle.com/post/how-emissions-tests-work-and-why-theyre-stupidly-unrealistic/> accessed 21 January 2016.

[191] '"Unrealistic" Emissions Tests Could Make Some Diesel Models "Unaffordable", Say European Carmakers' (*International Fleetworld*) <http://internationalfleetworld.co.uk/news/article.cfm?clk=0444&article_id=021978&urltitle=8216Unrealistic8217-emissions-tests-could-make-some-diesel-models-8216unaffordable8217-say-European-carmakers>.

[192] 'VW Scandal Highlights Unrealistic Lab Tests | Fleetcare' <www.fleetcare.com.au/news-info/fleet-beat-blog/october-2015/vw-scandal-highlights-unrealistic-lab-tests>.

responded and at time of writing is talking about 'robust testing methods' and a Real Driving Emissions test.[193] If the law requires car emissions of a certain level, then people will reasonably expect that the implementation of these measures results in emissions of a certain level. But if the implementation measures are not realistic then we cannot rely upon the words of the legislation as reflecting what actually happens.

The final point on implementation is a specific one regarding implementation by means of subordinate legislation. The standard position is that primary legislation sets out the main principles of the law (the powers and duties etc), leaving some of the minor details to be filled in by subordinate legislation (time periods, notices, forms – some of the administrative machinery of the law). But, what if the legislation can't be fully implemented unless the subordinate legislation is made? For example, if an application under an Act must be made on a form, but the form is to be prescribed in regulations made under the Act – if the form isn't prescribed, the application can't be made. The usual approach is that Departments are given discretionary powers to make subordinate legislation 'the Minister may, by regulations …'. However, necessary implementing provisions shouldn't be a matter of power, they should be a duty. So, in order for the law to be implemented, the legislation ought to impose a duty upon a Department to make necessary implementing regulations.

This point was addressed by the Supreme Court in *RM(AP)*.[194] At issue was the Mental Health (Care and Treatment) (Scotland) Act 2003 that gave rights to mental health patients that could in part be exercised via an application to a Tribunal. However, before this right could be exercised, it required the Scottish ministers to make regulations setting out the necessary administrative machinery. The Scottish ministers had failed to make these regulations before the Act came into force. The Supreme Court ruled that this failure was unlawful – essentially that they had an obligation to implement an Act of the Scottish Parliament that had been commenced.

Conclusion

The Rule of Law requires fixed, clear and certain law – that the legal consequences of our actions ought to be predictable. This means that legislation can be used as a reliable tool to guide our actions.

Predictability requires determinacy, that is certainty of outcomes based upon the text of the legislation. So legislation ought to be unambiguous and precise.

[193] European Commission, 'Press Release: Commission Welcomes Member States' Agreement on Robust Testing of Air Pollution Emissions by Cars' (28 October 2015) https://ec.europa.eu/commission/presscorner/detail/en/IP_15_5945.

[194] *RM(AP) v The Scottish Ministers* [2012] UKSC 58.

Legislation also ought to be relatively stable, although not unchanging. It is inevitable that the law will change over time, but care must be taken over too frequent, or too radical a change. If frequent or radical change is required, then there are steps that can be taken to mitigate the shocks this creates in the legal system.

Predictability is also enhanced if the legislation clearly states when the period to which it applies. This requires a clear commencement date and clear information about when it ends. Consistency is another tool to aid predictability. If similar things are done in similar ways, then the reader can have confidence in predicting the outcome. As with stability, this is not an absolute value, and does not require adherence to outdated or suboptimal forms of legislation.

Legislation also needs to be realistic, that is, it should be capable of being applied in the real world, and intended to be applied in the real world. Legislation should not be conceived of as something simply to pass through a legislature, but something to take effect in society. Provisions should only be included if they are intended to be applied. Related to this is implementability, that is that legislation ought to contain mechanisms within it that allow for it to be fully implemented.

5

Intelligibility

Introduction

The Rule of Law requires that legislation ought to be intelligible and clear. Intelligible means able to be understood, to be comprehensible. Clear means that something is easy to understand or interpret. These two words are not the same, but they are similar. The difference between them is the degree of understandability, 'clear' indicating a higher degree (or greater ease) of understandability. To avoid long-windedness, in this chapter I will mainly use the term 'intelligibility' as the Rule of Law concept to mean making legislation easier to understand. This ties quite neatly in with Fuller's morality of aspiration concept, of striving to make legislation easier to understand, rather than a binary distinction between intelligible and unintelligible legislation. I do not undertake an epistemological analysis of the concept of a person 'understanding' legislation as this would be beyond the scope of this work. I am content with the bald statement that intelligible legislation is easier to understand. This principle can hardly be said to be new, the Latin phrase *leges ab omnibus intelligi debent* (laws should be understood by everyone) stems back to antiquity.

Part 1 looks at the theory of intelligibility from the perspective of the Rule of Law. It also inquires into why legislation is sometimes not intelligible, either in an unthinking way, or deliberately so.

Part 2 is the main part of the chapter and derives form of legislation principles from the Rule of Law requirement of intelligibility. These are that intelligibility should focus on the user, that amending legislation should be intelligible, avoiding excessive interconnectedness, using plain language, easification, good writing and using examples.

Part 1: The Theory of Intelligibility

5.1. The Importance of Intelligibility

Bingham said that laws must be, so far as possible, intelligible and clear.[1] This mirrors Xanthaki's argument (albeit from the perspective of effectiveness of

[1] T Bingham, *The Rule of Law* (London, Penguin UK, 2011) 37.

legislation rather than the Rule of Law) that good quality legislation ought to be clear.[2] Bingham's reasons for this are the same as the reasons for making law accessible and predictable, he didn't deconstruct these elements into their constituent parts. To recap (from previous chapters) laws should be intelligible so that individuals can easily know what the law is. This is for three reasons. The first is to do with effectiveness of the law – if we can't understand what the law is, we can't obey it. The second is related, if we don't understand the law, we cannot take advantage of its provisions. The third is a commercial one, that commerce is improved if it is regulated by rules that are clear and easy to understand for commercial actors.

Two key reports make it clear that intelligibility of legislation is a fundamental requirement of the Rule of Law. First, the Venice Commission on the Rule of Law stated that legislation must be clear and precise.[3] Second, Lord Simon in the Renton Report stated that 'a society whose regulations are incomprehensible lives with the Rule of Lottery, not of Law'.[4] Dickson recognised the importance of Bingham's definition and his short-hand way of describing the qualities of the Rule of Law was that it was accessible and understandable.[5] Voermans expressly links intelligibility to the Rule of Law.[6]

Raz prefigured Bingham by stating in his principle 1 that law ought to be clear. His reason was that if law wasn't clear, it can't guide people. Therefore, law should not be obscure. This is a practical reason, which he develops further – that if a particular law is to succeed, people need to be capable of following it. And if they can't understand it, they can't follow it. Implicitly following Raz, Hashim, a legislative drafter from Malaysia directly considers the necessity of having clear law and adds that 'the most important reason is the rule of law'.[7] Baratta introduces a small twist to this, not only is it important that the law is intelligible to individuals, it must also be intelligible to the officials charged with implementing it, particularly in the context of domestic officials implementing EU law.[8]

Fuller's desideratum 4 is clarity of laws. Surprisingly he didn't go into great detail about what he meant by clarity, although he does talk about the opposite, 'obscure and incoherent legislation can make legality unobtainable by anyone'.[9] We can gain further insight from his exposition on eight ways to make bad law, where the fourth way is a failure to make rules understandable. This exposition puts him in conformity with Bingham's requirement for intelligibility.

[2] H Xanthaki, *Drafting Legislation: Art and Technology of Rules for Regulation* 1st edn (Oxford, Hart Publishing, 2014).

[3] Venice Commission, 'Report on the Rule of Law' (2011). See para 46.

[4] 'Report of the Renton Committee on the Preparation of Legislation' (1975) Cmnd 6053 133.

[5] B Dickson, *Law in Northern Ireland* 2nd edn (Oxford, Hart Publishing, 2013) 20.

[6] W Voermans, 'Legislation and Regulation', in *Legislation in Europe: A Comprehensive Guide for Scholars and Practitioners* (Oxford, Hart, 2017) 24.

[7] NA Hashim, 'Plain Language: Give It a Try!' (2013) 39 *Commonwealth Law Bulletin* 423, 425.

[8] R Baratta, 'Complexity of EU Law in the Domestic Implementing Process' (2014) 2 *Theory and Practice of Legislation* 293.

[9] LL Fuller, *The Morality of Law: Revised Edition* (Revised, New Haven, Yale University Press, 1969) 63.

As may be expected from someone whose writing on legislation was voluminous, Jeremy Bentham had much to say on the subject of intelligibility in statute law. His preferred solution was a Pannomion – 'a complete body of proposed law, in the form of statute law'.[10] One goal of the Pannomion was cognoscibility, meaning that the law is capable of being known. As he explained to US President James Madison, this meant that individuals would know what they are meant to do, or not meant to do. His Pannomion would be 'a written, and visible, and intelligible, and cognoscible rule of action'.[11]

Bentham developed his theory of cognoscibility in further letters to US states in 1817 (Madison had politely rejected Bentham's proposal to draft the entire US federal code). The properties desirable in a body of laws as set out in these letters include notoriety 'only in so far as it is present to the mind can any idea be productive of any effect'.[12] Another property was clearness of language.[13] In Letter VIII he prefigured the plain language movement by nearly 200 years calling for legislation that was 'all plain reading'.[14]

Underpinning all these criteria is the goal that 'every man should be his own lawyer'[15] and they can only do that if they can understand the law. The Lex scripta of the Isle of Man makes the same argument 'the laws are plain, simple, summary – to all capacities intelligible … that the door of justice is open to the poor and the rich'.[16] This was precisely the root of the objection of a Canadian court to unintelligible tax law,

> while there is little danger that the Act will ever become user-friendly or self-explanatory, it is of particular importance in a self-assessment tax system to promote an interpretation of provisions, where possible, that is comprehensible to the taxpayers themselves.[17]

Bentham was particularly dismissive of lawyers in his own time 'say that a lawyer has no interest in the uncertainty of the law, as well might you say, that a gunpowder maker has no interest in war, or a glazier in the breaking of windows'.[18] Although not writing directly from the perspective of the Rule of Law, Bentham was adamant that legislation ought to be capable of being known by the people it was directed at.

[10] Letter to James Madison, October 1861, quoted in J Bentham, *Legislator of the World: Writings on Codification, Law, and Education* (Oxford, Clarendon Press and Oxford University Press, 1998) 5. Bentham was fond of these grand, sweeping institutions, his ideal jail was a Panopticon, a prison where one warder could see all the inmates.

[11] ibid 18.

[12] Letter III ibid 119.

[13] Letter II ibid.

[14] Letter VIII ibid 163.

[15] ibid 123.

[16] L Marsh-Smith and G Wright, 'Information Technology on a Budget: A Giant Leap for the Isle of Man' ('Winds of Change', The Commonwealth Association of Legisaltive Counsel conference, Cape Town, April 2013) 12.

[17] *Will-Kare Paving and Contracting v Canada* [2000] 1 SCR 915, 948.

[18] ibid 153.

5.1.1. The Qualifier: So Far as Possible

As with predictability, intelligibility isn't an absolute value. It isn't something to be achieved at all costs, just 'so far as possible' according to Bingham. So, for Gower although it is good that legislation is readily intelligible, this isn't to be achieved at the cost of sacrificing certainty.[19] As I set out below, there are sometimes good reasons why legislation is not as intelligible as it could be.

5.2. Why is Legislation Sometimes Not Intelligible?

There is unanimity across the spectrum of academics[20] and practitioners[21] writing on legislation and the Rule of Law that legislation ought to be intelligible. I have not found a single writer seriously arguing that legislation ought to be hard to understand. However, there is also widespread exasperation that legislation is frequently unintelligible. This comes from:

- Journalists who speak of legislation which is 'torturous and laborious even by the standards of statute-speak'.[22]
- Judges who speak of 'drafting quagmires'.[23]
- Parliamentarians who state that 'we have simply no right to legislate in a manner which is incomprehensible to the people to whom the legislation is addressed'.[24]
- Legislative drafters who give examples of unintelligible legislation.[25]

Why is there this paradox? All those involved in the legislative process want intelligible law, but they are the ones who don't produce it. I suggest that there are five reasons for this. Although there is overlap between these reasons, there are enough differences to warrant division into different categories.

[19] E Gowers, *The Complete Plain Words* (HMSO, 1986) 7.

[20] Xanthaki and Thornton both devote chapters to clarity in their works, Xanthaki (n 2); GC Thornton and H Xanthaki, *Thornton's Legislative Drafting* (London, Bloomsbury Professional, 2013).

[21] Office of the Parliamentary Counsel, 'When Laws Become Too Complex – Inside Government' (March 2013) <www.gov.uk/government/publications/when-laws-become-too-complex/when-laws-become-too-complex>. Para 3.4 states that a criteria of quality in law is clear. In virtually every issue of *The Loophole*, there is an article extoling the benefits of clarity in legislation.

[22] John Lanchester, 'The Snowden files: why the British public should be worried about GCHQ' *The Guardian* (3 October 2013).

[23] Rt Hon the Lord Brightman, 'Drafting Quagmires' (2002) 23 *Statute Law Review* 1. See also the comments of judges on unintelligible statutes quoted in the appendix to 'Report of the Renton Committee on the Preparation of Legislation' (n 4).

[24] Lord Simon of Glaisdale (26 June 1997) 581 HL debs Col 1648.

[25] R Carter, 'Statutory Interpretation and the Rectification of Drafting Errors' [2012] *New Zealand Law Review* 207.

5.2.1. Exhaustiveness/Comprehensiveness

A law can be short and intelligible if it covers a single proposition that governs the vast majority of the populace. However, 'the vast majority' is not 'all' and so sometimes, for the purposes of certainty and predictability, it is necessary to go into more detail to cover all eventualities, not simply the most common ones. The difficulty is that this level of detail can obscure the main point and thus make the legislation less intelligible, or as John put it 'the detailed rules aim to achieve legal certainty, which in turn leads to over particularisation and incomprehensible regulation'.[26]

Take as an example legislation on a social security payment in Northern Ireland known as a welfare supplementary payment (WSP). There are a large number of different types of WSP which a person is entitled to if they (or their partner) meet certain criteria.[27] The legislation exhaustively sets out all these different criteria. But it then goes on to provide for what happens if a couple separate and what impact this has on entitlement. Furthermore, it makes provision for what happens if a person who is entitled to WSP in their own right subsequently forms a couple with another person who may also be entitled to a different type of WSP. This leads to the following 'challenging' provision:

> (5) Where case 1 or 2 applies, the amount of welfare supplementary payment to which A is entitled is reduced to the amount of welfare supplementary payment to which A would have been entitled under Part 3 if A had satisfied the conditions for payment on loss of carer premium on transition from disability living allowance to personal inde pendence payment.[28]

The need for predictability necessitates a comprehensive provision, as people on benefits will get married and separate, and they need to know how that changes their entitlement to benefit. This is so even though the exhaustive nature of the provisions as a whole makes the law less intelligible.

But there is not always a need for exhaustiveness. I previously stated that

> Drafting practice in common law countries (particularly the UK) is to set out both the principles and the details. There is a noble desire for the law to cover every possible eventuality, but this sometimes means that the basics of the law become obscured. In civil law systems, the detail is usually not included.[29]

[26] J Ubena, *How to Regulate Information and Communications Technology: A Jurisprudential Inquiry into Legislative and Regulatory Techniques* (Stockholm, Jure, 2015) 99.

[27] See for example the Welfare Supplementary Payment (Amendment) Regulations (Northern Ireland) 2017.

[28] Regulation 22C, Welfare Supplementary Payment (Loss of Carer Payments) Regulations (Northern Ireland) 2016.

[29] R Cormacain, 'Have the Renton Committee's Recommendations on Electronic Access to Legislation Been Fulfilled?' (2013) 19 *Web Journal of Current Legal Issues*.

The civil law system has much to recommend it in this respect. We don't need to expressly state every possible combination and permutation, nor state things which are common sense or which a reasonable reader would apply anyway. Take another example of a draft Bill on special measures for vulnerable witnesses giving evidence. Clause 3 begins

> (1) A witness is eligible for assistance in giving evidence if the court considers that the quality of evidence given by the witness is likely to be diminished by reason of fear or distress in connection with testifying in the proceedings.[30]

This is tolerably clear. However, the rest of the clause then continues with a long list of factors that the judge must consider when deciding whether a witness should have the benefit of a special measure in giving evidence.[31]

Does the long list of factors to consider really assist either the court or the reader? In my view it is reasonable to expect a judge to have a modicum of intelligence and discernment. Although it may be helpful to have a list of factors to consider, these are surely things which any reasonable judge turning her mind to the question, would consider anyway. The overly prescriptive list is not necessary here, and tends to make the legislation less intelligible. The Renton report supports this move away from detail to towards principles in favour of intelligibility. However, in reviewing the impact of Renton ten years on, Lord Simon stated that 'these recommendations have been completely disregarded; and statutes are still drafted in elaborate and incomprehensible detail to deal with every foreseeable combination of circumstances which might arise'.[32]

It is hard to be dogmatic on what level of prescriptive detail a statute should contain. If it renders the statute unintelligible, that would indicate removing it. If it isn't strictly necessary for the purposes of precision, that also indicates

[30] Civil Evidence (Witnesses) Bill in Northern Ireland Law Commission, 'Vulnerable Witnesses in Civil Proceedings' (2011) NILC 10.

[31] Those factors are:

(a) the nature and alleged circumstances of the matter to which the proceedings relate,
(b) the nature of the evidence the witness is likely to give,
(c) the age of the witness,
(d) any relationship between the witness and any party to the proceedings,
(e) the behaviour towards the witness of-
    (i) any party,
    (ii) family members or associates of any party,
    (iii) any other person who is likely to be a party or a witness, and
(f) any views expressed by the witness.

The judge must then consider:

(a) the racial group of the witness,
(b) the domestic and employment circumstances of the witness,
(c) any religious beliefs or political opinions of the witness,
(d) the sexual orientation of the witness, and
(e) any other matter that the court considers relevant.

[32] Lord Simon, 'Renton Report – Ten Years on, The' (1985) 1985 *Statute Law Review* 133, 135.

removing it. Following Orwell's suggestion, if text isn't strictly necessary, cut it out.[33] John reaches the same conclusion, that detailed law should only be used where necessary.[34]

5.2.2. Complex Policy

It is possible to work backwards from unintelligible legislation that is caused by the complexity of the law, which is caused in turn by the complexity of the legal policy behind the law. This is similar to unintelligibility arising through exhaustiveness, but it is more of a policy choice to have different rules applying in different situations. Complex policy is about creating policy distinctions between different cases when the law would work (from a legal perspective) without those different policy distinctions. An exhaustive law seeks to cover all eventualities, whereas a complex law will seek to introduce different rules for different circumstances.

An example may make things clearer. A simple policy is that the Ombudsman may investigate maladministration in public bodies.[35] However, the actual policy is more complicated, and so we need to have different rules for how the Ombudsman may investigate health and social care bodies,[36] general health care providers,[37] independent providers of health and social care[38] and universities.[39]

The decision to have a complex policy isn't a legal decision, it is a political one. Complexity leads to reduced intelligibility and therefore those involved in the legislative process should ask if there is a need for this amount of complexity. Although it is possible to express complex things simply, this is difficult. This is borne out by the official findings of the Office of the Parliamentary Counsel report on complexity in legislation. One of the headings of that report is 'mapping the causes of unnecessary complexity'.[40] The clear implication is that there is such a thing as 'necessary complexity'. However, we should be clear here that the necessity is a political one, not a legal imperative. The House of Commons recognised the limits of drafting skill to make complex law more intelligible:

> However, while the tax profession has welcomed the [Tax Law Rewrite]'s outputs and made positive comment on the usability of the legislation it has produced, it has certainly not made the underlying tax law appreciably easier for the layman to navigate. Nor, as the Institute of Directors pointed out, has it clarified the underlying tax policy.[41]

[33] G Orwell, *Politics and the English Language* (London, Penguin, 2013).
[34] Ubena (n 26) 99.
[35] s 14 Public Services Ombudsman (Northern Ireland) 2016.
[36] ibid s 15.
[37] ibid s 16.
[38] ibid s 17.
[39] ibid s 18.
[40] Office of the Parliamentary Counsel (n 21).
[41] House of Commons, Treasury Committee, Principles of tax policy, Eighth Report of Session 2010–11 para 45.

5.2.3. Complexity Masking a Lack of Direction

Complex (and unintelligible) legislation can sometimes mask a lack of understanding and certainty about what the law and policy are meant to be. It is hard to hide ignorance in an intelligible provision, much easier to do so in a long, meandering and incomprehensible one. Orwell was critical of this style of writing where 'the slovenliness of our language makes it easier for us to have foolish thoughts'[42] and 'the writer either has a meaning and cannot express it, or he inadvertently says something else, or he is almost indifferent as to whether his words mean anything or not'.[43]

The OPC report on complexity in legislation bears witness to this. It notes one reason for 'unnecessary complexity' as being a dysfunctional relationship between policy and legislation, which can be caused by imprecise policy objectives, rushed instructions, public or media pressure, political contingencies and a failure to think things through.[44] A drafter can't weave straw into gold. If the policy is incoherent then the resulting legislation will be unintelligible.

5.2.4. Desire for Solemnity

Which is more impressive: Moses comes down from the mountain with a stone tablet declaiming 'thou shalt not kill', or a drafting committee producing a piece of paper which says 'It is an offence to kill'? There is a human desire for majesty and solemnity in our legislation – that not only must it be law, but it must look and feel like law. Greenberg has found a desire for 'legalese' in legislation so that people (individuals, legislators) will be impressed by it, that they will accord it a higher status because of its weighty form.[45] This is perhaps one reason why the enacting words in UK statutes are rather grandiose ('Be it enacted by the Queen's most Excellent Majesty …'). Bennion gives an example where his draft included the more intelligible 'tried his best' rather than the less intelligible 'used his best endeavours'. Rather than welcoming the plainer words, parliamentarians lamented it as 'amateurish'.[46]

The desire for solemnity can sometimes morph into a desire for pomposity and ponderous language. Greenberg argued that in reality, people like a bit of pomposity in law.[47] But legalese can be unclear.[48] This can lead to unintelligible and archaic phrases 'as aforesaid', 'hereinafter' etc. This is rather like the wizard in the Wizard

[42] Orwell (n 33) 1.
[43] ibid 2.
[44] Office of the Parliamentary Counsel (n 21). See para 4.2.
[45] D Greenberg, *Laying down the Law: A Discussion of the People, Processes and Problems That Shape Acts of Parliament* (London, Sweet & Maxwell, 2011) 219.
[46] F Bennion, *Bennion on Statute Law* (London, Longman, 1990) 38.
[47] D Greenberg, 'The Three Myths of Plain English Drafting' [2011] *The Loophole* 103.
[48] D Mellinkoff, *The Language of the Law* (Searcy, Resource Publications, 2004) 24.

of Oz making himself sound impressive by the use of smoke and mirrors. However, there is a sense in which the desire for solemnity is well-placed. If the Rule of Law means we are all subject to the law, we should enact law which is more likely to be respected and obeyed, and if legislation is phrased in too casual a manner, it is less likely to engender respect. Intelligibility shouldn't be sacrificed for solemnity, but neither should the use of demotic language dilute respect for legislation.

5.2.5. The Nature of Legislation

The nature of legislation itself is a barrier to intelligibility. Legislation is law enacted by Parliament and it must conform to the requirements of the medium. The various techniques available to other forms of communication are not available to it. For example, it cannot repeat itself, it cannot include unnecessary material, it cannot use an informal style. One particular limitation is the use of direct speech or the second person 'you must have a licence' rather than 'a person must have a licence'. According to Stefanou, the idea of drafting in the second person has not been well received in the UK and has not been used.[49] Having searched through the UK statute law database the only 'you' in it is in tax law (PAYE or pay as you earn) and in forms which are directed to members of the public. As Pearce says 'the legislative drafter is obliged to follow a form that enables the bill as drafted to be debated in accordance with the standing orders of the parliament that is to consider it'.[50]

Part 2: Promoting Intelligibility in the Form of Legislation

5.3. Characteristics of the User

So far, I have spoken about intelligibility without any qualification. But intelligibility does not exist in a vacuum, it has at least two dimensions:

- The statute to be understood
- The person who is to understand it

So, a general principle that legislation ought to be intelligible is too unfocused. Instead, the principle is that a particular piece of legislation ought to be intelligible by the particular persons who will use it.

[49] He cites evidence from the Tax Law Rewrite in the UK, see C Stefanou, *Drafting Legislation: A Modern Approach* 1st edn (H Xanthaki ed, London, Routledge, 2008).

[50] DC Pearce and RS Geddes, *Statutory Interpretation in Australia* 5th edn (London, LexisNexis, 2001) 3.

5.3.1. Conception of Legislation and Relationship with Human Autonomy

To whom is legislation (or a particular piece of legislation) directed? Before answering this in a practical way, it is necessary to consider the theoretical and philosophical conception of legislation. One view is quite paternalistic, that legislation is bestowed upon the populace by the legislature and then applied to them by the government. This conception of law and state sees the citizen as the object of the legislation – the thing to which law is applied. Under this view, the citizen is the passive recipient of law. Bennion stated that 'It may be positively dangerous to encourage non-lawyers to think they can understand legal texts unaided by expert advice.'[51] The other perspective sees the citizen as more of an active participant in law. The citizen is the subject of the law, the citizen reads it, interprets it and then applies the law. The citizen has autonomy and volition such that the citizen is the end user of the law rather than the state.

If the citizen is the object, then the target audience of the legislation (ie the user) will be the various state actors (civil servants, ministers, judges, police etc). It isn't necessary that the law be intelligible to the citizen, what is important is that the government actors who are actually applying and enforcing the law understand it. But if the citizen is the subject, then the legislation needs to be intelligible to the citizen, it is the citizen who the legislator must have in mind when enacting legislation.

Most people would eschew the first conception of legislation as being the property of the state. Instead, they would value human autonomy and conceive of legislation which is to be directed at citizens and thus intelligible by them. So, at a high theoretical level, we can say that legislation ought to be intelligible by the citizen, although as will be seen below, we can sometimes subdivide this, and we can sometimes consider the user as the state.

5.3.2. Target Audience: The Individuals Using the Legislation

Some laws are very broad and general in their application such that it is reasonable to assume that the populace as a whole will use them. For example, we all might be users of the criminal law on assault, or on driving a car. We could summarise this approach as *legislation must be intelligible to all individuals.*

The orthodox view is that criminal law and tax law applies to all individuals, and so must be drafted in a way that renders it understandable to them.[52]

[51] F Bennion, Letter to *The Times*, 24 January 1995, 'Don't put the law into public hands.'

[52] For example, in a parliamentary debate as long ago as 1853, the Chancellor was urged to make tax law intelligible to everyone, quoted in a chapter on tax simplification in R Chote and others, *The IFS Green Budget: January 2008* (IFS 2008) <www.ifs.org.uk/publications/4112>. In recommending

But the position is not as straightforward as this, as much of the criminal and tax law will be irrelevant to most of the population. For example, the person on the street doesn't need to be able to understand the offences relating to registration and authorisation for radioactive substances.[53] Only those working (in the main) in the nuclear industry need to be able to understand this. Taking another example, a small shopkeeper should be able to understand the provisions of income tax legislation which apply to them, but they don't need to know (taking a random provision from the tax legislation) the tax treatment of the expenses of management investment companies.[54]

Then there is legislation that clearly does not apply to the entirety of the populace. So, the law on the duties of company directors only needs to be intelligible to company directors (and perhaps a small number of others who use companies law).[55] So, if a piece of legislation is addressed to a particular user group, it is only necessary that it be intelligible by that user group, not by the population as a whole. On rare occasions there has been research to identify the user group of a particular piece of legislation, with consequences for how that legislation is to be drafted.[56] Bertlin notes the findings of some key empirical research on who are the users of legislation in the UK, and this has implications for how we draft specific pieces of law.[57] This approach could be summarised as: *specific legislation must be intelligible to the specific individual to whom it applies.*

The Business Tenancies (Northern Ireland) 1996 Order is a specific law with a reasonably discrete group of users: landlords, business tenants and their advisers.[58] Do they form a semiotic community? They form such a community if they share a common understanding of words and phrases that the larger community do not share. Taking another example, there is a semiotic community of oil producers who understand the definition of 'light oil' within the meaning of the Hydrocarbon Oil Duties Act 1979. The technical definition ('not less than 90 per cent by volume distils at a temperature not exceeding 210C') is probably meaningless for most people, but meaningful for them.

The key point is that the person who will use a particular statutory provision needs to be able to understand that provision. This requires a level of granularity or particularisation in the intelligibility of the legislation. A blanket exhortation that everyone must understand all the law, (or even all of the criminal or tax law)

codification of the criminal law, the Law Commission spoke of criminal law as being a 'particularly public and visible part of the law … should not be undermined by perceptions that it is intelligible only to experts', Law Commission for England and Wales, *Criminal Law: A Criminal Code for England and Wales*, vol 1 (HMSO 1989) 6.

[53] Radioactive Substances Act 1993.

[54] s 75 Income and Corporation Taxes Act 1988.

[55] Part 10, Chapter 2, Companies Act 2006.

[56] Northern Ireland Law Commission, 'Consultation Paper: Business Tenancies' (2010) NILC 5.

[57] A Bertlin, 'What Works Best for the Reader? A Study on Drafting and Presenting Legislation' [2014] *The Loophole* 25.

[58] I discussed this previously in R Cormacain, 'A Plain Language Case Study: Business Tenancies (Northern Ireland) Order 1996' [2012] *The Loophole* 33.

is unnecessary and unrealistic. What is needed is focused intelligibility, that the person to whom the law applies needs to be able to understand it. This should be widened slightly, as users won't simply look at the single provision which applies to them, in searching for it, they will look at the provisions around it. So, the provision that applies to an individual, as well as the provisions surrounding it (or the provisions set in their context), should be intelligible by the user of the legislation.

The danger though is that the legislator only considers *one* user group when enacting legislation, not the whole *panoply* of potential users. So, one might consider that the law on financial regulation only needs to be intelligible by those working in the finance sector.[59] But if a financial services provider becomes insolvent, there is a mechanism by which ordinary investors can claim compensation.[60] Those provisions could be used by ordinary investors, so it is important that it is intelligible to them.

One useful rule of thumb is that any provision that states that a person must (or may) do a particular thing ought to be intelligible by any person who could reasonably be considered to be subject to it. So an obligation on a person in relation to the storage of nuclear waste should be written so as to be intelligible by a person who is storing nuclear waste. But an obligation on a person in relation to driving a car should be written so as to be intelligible by a person who is likely to be driving a car.

5.3.3. Target Audience: State-Focused Legislation

Despite disagreeing with the general conception of legislation as being bestowed upon individuals who are passive recipients of it, there are some instances where it is proper to consider the target audience as being the state. Some statutes are directed at the administration of the state. So if a statute sets up a new quango, the provisions of the statute regulating the constitution of that quango are really only of interest to the quango itself.[61] If legislation restructures the health service or the education service, then it only needs to be intelligible to those governmental officials actually implementing this change, or as the EU suggests 'texts may include technical requirements whose implementation falls to specialised officials in that field'.[62]

However, this is subject to a rather large caveat. Although the users of this legislation may be state officials, many ordinary individuals will have an interest in the policy choices and the impact upon them as individuals. So, intelligibility

[59] Financial Services and Markets Act 2000.

[60] ibid Part 15.

[61] See for example Schedule 1 of the Equality Act 2006 setting out the constitution of the Equality Commission.

[62] European Union, 'Joint Practical Guide for the Drafting of Community Legislation' (Office for Official Publications of the European Communities 2003) 13.

of the legislation as it passes through parliament is important as it helps voters in their efforts to lobby for changes in that legislation, or to hold their elected representatives to account. Complex administrative provisions may be fine for officials in the newly established Office for Environmental Protection, but not much use to NGOs and parliamentarians trying to figure out if the new office is sufficiently independent of the government.[63]

This becomes truly problematic if the interests of those charged with the administration of the legislation take priority over those who the legislation affects. The Supreme Court considered immigration rules in *Mandalia v Secretary of State for the Home Department*.[64] It considered the audience of immigrants to whom the rules applied and stated 'it is difficult for the applicants, for many of whom English is not even their first language, to navigate their way around the requirements. It may be, however, that, *as intended, the system is not difficult for caseworkers to administer*'.[65] The idea that legislation is drafted for the benefit of the state rather than the individual is anathema to basic notions of fairness.

5.3.4. Target Audience: Special Cases – Those with a Particular Difficulty in Understanding Legislation

The principle set out so far is that legislation should be intelligible by its users. But there are some circumstances where it would be unreasonable to expect the end user to understand the legislation. Two prime examples are legislation governing children and legislation governing those who lack mental capacity. So, section 1 of the Children Act 1989 states that 'the child's welfare shall be the court's paramount consideration'. These words are vital as they set out what is called the welfare principle, that the child comes first. But the phrase 'paramount consideration' is unlikely to be understood by a child, particularly a young child. Equally, depending upon the mental capacity (or lack of mental capacity) it may not be reasonable to expect a person to understand the Mental Capacity Act 2005. In special cases like these, it may simply not be possible to make the legislation intelligible to the end user.

5.3.5. Target Audience: Those Who Will Always have an Interest in the Legislation

There are some groups who will always be users of the legislation, no matter what the legislation is. Legislators always need to be able to understand the

[63] R Cormacain, 'Environment Bill – Office for Environmental Protection: A Rule of Law Analysis' (Bingham Centre for the Rule of Law 2021).

[64] [2015] UKSC 59.

[65] ibid para 2, my emphasis.

legislation they are enacting, otherwise there is a substantial loss of legitimacy of that legislation. Therefore, legislation needs to be intelligible to them. However, notwithstanding the criticism of intermediaries set out below, it is reasonable to expect legislators to be briefed on legislation and to be assisted in scrutinising that legislation by experts.

Judges, and others involved in the legal system, also need to be able to understand legislation. This specific user group can be assumed to have a high level of legal ability, so a requirement that legislation be intelligible to them will most likely be subsumed that the legislation is intelligible by the rest of the target audience. The reverse is also true, if a piece of legislation is unintelligible to a trained judge, what chance does the lay user have? For the sake of completeness, it is also reasonable to expect that juries may sometimes be end users of legislation. However, it is reasonable to expect that they will have substantial assistance from a judge in the form of directions when it comes to them understanding the law.

5.3.6. Intelligibility and Law as a Method of Communication

Legislation performs at least two functions. The most obvious function is to make new law, in the sense that it brings law into being. But another function, as Crabbe points out, is to communicate that new law.[66] Stefanou develops this concept stating that 'law is a form of communication where legal relations are comprehended and appreciated through a communicative process'.[67] Roebuck goes further and argues that language is a code, and the purpose of it is to transmit a message.[68]

So one text both does the thing and explains the thing. It is this second function to which intelligibility is more relevant. The first function is satisfied if the legislation is certain and precise, even if it very difficult to understand. It is only in conveying the information to the end user that intelligibility becomes important (or in Stefanou's analysis transmitting the message to the receiver). But this sets up an internal tension, because things which tend to make the legislation more communicable are not always conducive with making the law. Consider the following two statements on the obligation to have car insurance.

- A person in charge of a motor vehicle must be in possession of a valid certificate of motor insurance.
- Drivers, it is absolutely vital, and I cannot stress this enough, that your car is insured.

[66] VCRAC Crabbe, *Legislative Drafting Vol I: V. 1* (London, Routledge-Cavendish, 1993) 27.

[67] C Stefanou, 'Is Legislative Drafting a Form of Communication?' (2011) 37 *Commonwealth Law Bulletin* 407, 408.

[68] D Roebuck, 'Plain, Clear and Something More? Criteria for Communication in Legal Language' (2014) 16 *European Journal of Law Reform* 633.

The first statement makes the law, the second statement communicates it. They are both effective within their own paradigm, but not so effective when considering the other paradigm. Statement 1 is a definite statement of law, but doesn't perhaps convey the gravity of the command. Statement 2 conveys the importance, and is directed at the end user, but its use of repetition means it doesn't work as a legal obligation. But legislation doesn't have the luxury of containing two statements, it only has one. And so that one statement must seek to do both, making the law and communicating the law.[69]

In moving towards intelligibility for the purposes of communication, it is therefore vital not to lose sight of the fact that legislation is first and foremost the way of making law. As I previously stated, 'the primary purpose of a statute is not educative, it is to effect a change in the law'.[70] Repetition, tmesis, underlining, rhetoric and many other devices that aid communication are incompatible with a document which makes law. So the principle of intelligibility is constrained by the function of legislation as a tool for making law. Methods that promote intelligibility within those constraints are to be welcomed, methods that break those constraints are unacceptable.

Pennisi goes further than this and argues that for specialised discourses (including legislation), there is in fact a need for two separate texts, one for specialists and one for the lay person.[71] The communicative purpose of the lay text is informative. This could be seen as the logical extension of what I have argued above, that communicating information to the lay person is not the primary purpose of legislation. However, I think Pennisi's argument goes too far as it provides an excuse for a retreat back into unintelligibility, safe in the knowledge that a second text will communicate the law to users. Although there is much that is admirable about government providing additional material to help explain the law to lay readers, this does not take away from the obligation to make the legislation itself intelligible to lay users.

Having argued that intelligibility shouldn't lead to certainty being subverted, it is also necessary to argue in the other direction – just because legislation is there to make law, doesn't mean that we should ignore its communicative dimension. Ilahi points out that some critics of the plain language movement 'deny any communicative role of the legislation and are of the view that the legislation is only meant to change and contain (not explain) the command of the law'.[72] This is a wilfully blind view as it completely ignores the fact that legislation is also about communication.

[69] Although explanatory notes attached to legislation may perform this other function.

[70] Cormacain, 'A Plain Language Case Study: Business Tenancies (Northern Ireland) Order 1996' (n 58) 41.

[71] Giulia Pennisi, 'Legislative Provisions in Context: A Linguistic Approach' (2016) 37 *Statute Law Review* 101.

[72] M Ilahi, 'Plain Language Movement: A Case Study of the Islamic Republic of Pakistan' (PhD Thesis, University of London, Institute of Advanced Legal Studies, 2012) 31.

5.3.7. Role of Intermediaries

So far, my argument has been that legislation ought to be intelligible by its users. However, is this a realistic requirement to impose upon the makers of a statute? For many people, legislation is not consumed directly, but it is interacted with by way of an intermediary – someone who mediates between the law and the individual. The most obvious intermediary is the lawyer who advises the client on the client's legal rights and responsibilities under the legislation. But there are other intermediaries: the accountant who advises on tax law, the Citizen's Advice Bureau worker who advises a client on social security benefits, the campaigning charity who advises members on the impact of a proposed new law. The government itself can act as an intermediary, advising individuals on the changes made by a new law by producing guidance notes. This approach can be summarised as: *legislation must be intelligible to intermediaries, who must then produce guidance that is intelligible to users.*

What are the consequences of this for intelligibility? If the legislator knows that the individual will be making use of an intermediary, then all that is necessary is for the legislation to intelligible to that intermediary, not the end user. This is precisely what Bennion argued for.[73] Legislation will be the primary source of information, but the individual will use the secondary source provided by the intermediary. Developing Stefanou's theory on legislation as communication, it is the effectiveness of this secondary source as a means of communication that is important. The mediated information doesn't have to fulfil the function of 'making the law', only of 'communicating the law', so it can take advantage of those communicative techniques which are prohibited to the drafter of the legislation.

There are four broad objections to the argument that legislation only needs to be intelligible to the intermediary. The first is the practical one, that the secondary source (the information provided by the mediator) may not accurately reflect the actual content of the law. In processing and transmitting the legislation, the intermediary may simply get it wrong. There is always the risk that in transcribing the information, the transcriber will make an error. So, it is much better for the legislation itself to be intelligible so that it doesn't need to be mediated.

The second objection is that the use of intermediaries sets up a self-fulfilling loop which justifies unintelligibility of legislation. The loop works like this: legislation is unintelligible, so we need an intermediary to render it intelligible to the layperson, if the layperson is using an intermediary then the legislation only needs to be intelligible to the intermediary. So the use of intermediaries justifies setting low standards of intelligibility in legislation.

The third objection relates back to the Rule of Law and the conception of legislation as something which is made for us and which we are subject to.

[73] Bennion (n 51).

Sullivan is scathing in her criticism of what she terms as law being oracle rather than canon.

> The statute book as oracle, however, invites a different kind of response. Messages sent through oracles call for interpretation; they have to be deciphered to be understood. The words of an oracle are pregnant with meaning, but the meaning is obscure and incomplete. They may provide a fixed basis for law, a stable entry point, but they say different things to different people. For this reason, official interpreters are needed to establish privileged readings of the text that can, when necessary, displace the vulgar readings of the uninitiated.[74]

Law as oracle as Sullivan describes it (or law through intermediaries as I describe it) divorces the citizens in whose name the law is made from the law itself. It reframes them once again as passive recipients of the law, who can't be trusted to interpret and apply it themselves. There is an interesting historical parallel here. Before the Reformation in Europe, the Christian religion was seen as something 'owned' by the religious classes who then instructed the laity on their obligations. The Bible was in Latin, and its message was mediated by the clergy. However, one of the fundamental changes made by the Reformation was the move to the vernacular Bible and the removal of the priest as the mediator between the person and God.[75] The individual was trusted to find their own route to salvation via their own reading of the Bible (although still within the limits set out by the wise masters!).

It is fundamentally undemocratic and antithetical to the Rule of Law if the persons who will use legislation cannot be expected to understand it, and must employ others to explain it to them. Legislation isn't quantum physics which is intrinsically complex and hard to understand by its very nature.[76] Legislation is a human construct so it must be susceptible to human reasoning. It infantilises individuals to say that they are much too stupid to even attempt to comprehend the law, that they must be spoon-fed it via a lawyer. Legislation is not there for lawyers, it is there for the individual.[77] Barnes considers both sides of this argument, but doesn't come down on one side or the other.[78]

The fourth objection is another practical one – how is the legislator to know what legislation will be consumed directly by the individual and what will be mediated? Or alternatively, when is it reasonable to assume that intelligibility needs only to be directed at the intermediary? With the rise of smart phones, and

[74] R Sullivan, 'Some Implications of Plain Language Drafting' (2001) 22 *Statute Law Review* 145, 156.

[75] Article 24 of the Augsburg Confession of Faith (1530) states that 'Paul commanded to use in the church a language understood by the people'.

[76] It was said in 1919 'that only three persons in the world can understand [Einstein's theory of] relativity'. See further J Eisenstaedt, *The Curious History of Relativity: How Einstein's Theory of Gravity Was Lost and Found* (Princeton, Princeton University Press, 2006).

[77] House of Representatives Standing Committee on Legal and Constitutional Affairs, 'Clearer Commonwealth Law: Report of the Inquiry into Legislative Drafting by the Commonwealth' (Parliament of the Commonwealth of Australia 1993). See para 6.12.

[78] J Barnes, 'The Continuing Debate about "Plain Language Legislation": A Law Reform Conundrum' (2006) 27 *Statute Law Review* 83.

the drop in legal aid, it is becoming more and more common that individuals use search engines and legislation.gov.uk to find the answers to their legal questions online. Even if some individuals will eventually pay a solicitor for legal advice, most will use the official database of legislation as their first port of call. Relying upon intermediaries to explain complex legislation is not always feasible.

However, even if intermediaries are used, intelligibility can help those intermediaries as well as helping the lay reader. Some empirical research has shown that lawyers can struggle with intelligibility as much as non-lawyers.[79]

5.3.8. The Consequences for Intelligibility in Considering the User

Proceeding from the conclusion that law ought to be intelligible to the person who is using it, what are the consequences for the form of legislation? The main consequence is that the language used must be appropriate to the target audience. So if the target audience is the populace at large, the legislation must be intelligible to them. This doesn't mean reducing the language to the lowest common denominator in terms of simplicity, but it does mean using language that most ordinary people could reasonably expect to understand. It doesn't mean using the wrong word merely because the wrong word is easier or more common-place. Provided that the user could readily identify the meaning of the uncommon (but correct) word, then that word should be preferred.

I previously discussed this in relation to the legislation on tenancies and a definition that included the phrase 'the effluxion of time'.[80] This is not a common phrase in regular English usage. The *Shorter Oxford English Dictionary on Historical Principles* defines it as 'the action or process of flowing out: an outflow'.[81] Aiyar includes effluxion of time within a legal dictionary and defines it, with reference to tenancies as

> the conclusion or expiration of an agreed term of years specified in the deed or writing, or expiration arising in the natural course of events, in contradistinction to the determination of the term by the acts of parties or by some unexpected or unusual incident or other sudden event.[82]

The requirement of intelligibility would suggest substituting a simpler synonym for effluxion, such as 'passage of time', or 'expiry of time'. Both of these phrases are more intelligible to readers and neither of them requires the use of a dictionary for the reader of average intelligence. Neither 'expiry' nor 'passage' captures the

[79] Bertlin (n 57) 47.

[80] Cormacain, 'A Plain Language Case Study: Business Tenancies (Northern Ireland) Order 1996' (n 58). Some of the following text appeared in this article.

[81] CT Onions (ed), *Shorter Oxford English Dictionary on Historical Principles* 3rd edn (Oxford, Oxford University Press, 1955).

[82] P Ramanatha Aiyar, *The Law Lexicon* (New Delhi, Wadhwa Nagpur, 2007).

precise meaning which effluxion conveys. If time effluxes, it runs out. It conveys the notion that there was a fixed quantity of time and now that time has naturally flowed out – there is none left. The passage of time or the expiry of time do not give that same sense of the fixed quantity running out by a natural process. Effluxion may not be as readily understandable but it is the more precise term. So effluxion is the more accurate word to use, even though we lose some intelligibility.

It is when we come to consider legislation to be used by a specific group that there are more important consequences for the form of legislation. If legislation is to be used by a particular group, then it is reasonable to use language and concepts that are readily intelligible by that group, even though these may not be intelligible by the populace as a whole. So technical language, or even jargon, might be acceptable for that legislation as it would be intelligible by that audience. So, the ordinary reader may struggle to know what an ampoule is (a small sealed capsule containing a liquid), but for vets it is perfectly acceptable for legislation to talk about storing a batch of donors in the same ampoule.[83]

5.3.9. The Reality of Individuals Using Legislation

Much of what I have argued above is predicated on the right of individuals to understand legislation which affects them. But what actually happens in practice? There is little point in expending time and effort on making legislation intelligible to people if people don't actually read it. Bingham acknowledged this point when he joked that criminals don't check out the legislation before they decide to rob a bank. Hunt in particular has been critical of the desire to make legislation intelligible to a public who don't read legislation. In fact, he went so far as to call it an unwise assumption 'that members of the public are interested in reading raw legislation'.[84]

At the level of high theory, we are all treated as if we knew the law – it remains a legal maxim that ignorance of the law is no defence. Contrary to what Hunt originally asserted, there is now empirical evidence on the readership of legislation. A major study was carried out by the National Archives and the Office of the Parliamentary Counsel.[85] That research made for very interesting reading. The official UK legislation website has two million separate visitors each month. About 60 per cent of the visitors were found to be non-lawyers who used legislation for work (the examples given were police officers, human resources professionals or council officials). Then there were members of the public seeking to use law to enforce their rights. The final user group was lawyers of all kinds.

The results of this research give empirical weight to the central argument of this Chapter that legislation ought to be intelligible to the user. There are huge

[83] The Bovine Embryo (Collection, Production and Transfer) Regulations 1995, Schedule 7, para 18.
[84] B Hunt, 'Plain Language in Legislative Drafting: An Achievable Objective or Laudable Ideal?' (2003) 24 *Statute Law Review* 112, 115.
[85] Bertlin (n 57) 25.

numbers of non-lawyers using legislation. Legislation ought to be enacted in a way which is intelligible to them. Although bank-robbers might not read up on the Theft Act 1978, substantial numbers of people do read legislation. Ilahi prefigured the UK research when he argued in 2012 that even though the public at large may not read the entirety of the statute book, they will be interested in that portion of it which affects them.[86] Furthermore, he went on to argue that even if not everyone reads the law this 'does not absolve the State of her responsibilities to strive for making the laws easier to understand'.[87]

5.4. Intelligibility of Amending Legislation and of the Legislation as Amended

The thing to be understood is the legislation. In a simple world with a simple statute book this statement is straightforward and without nuance. But the world and the statute book are not simple. One complication is that a law rarely stands alone, complete in itself. Instead, it is woven into an existing tapestry of laws. Most legislation is amending legislation in that it amends existing legislation. There are therefore two potential targets for intelligibility:

1. The amending legislation (the most recent law which changes the existing law)
2. The legislation as amended (the existing law, taking into account those changes)

Although the distinction may seem Jesuitical, there is a crucial difference between the amending legislation and the legislation as amended. The first is the change itself, the second, the thing changed. For example, the Children and Social Work Act 2017 works in part by making multiple amendments to the Children Act 2004. So, is the goal to make the 2017 Act intelligible, or the 2004 Act intelligible? Or are they both important, or is one more important than the other? Is this akin to Heisenberg's Uncertainty Principle (the more precise your knowledge about an object's speed, the less precise you are about its location) – the more you know about the change, the less you know about the object being changed? Before addressing this, it is important to first set out *how* amending legislation works.

5.4.1. How Amending Legislation Works

Amendments normally work in one of two ways: textual amendments or non-textual amendments. A textual amendment makes a direct change to the text

[86] Ilahi (n 72) 35.
[87] ibid.

of the old law.[88] Thornton refers to this as 'direct and textual'.[89] The following is a direct textual amendment from the Children and Social Work Act 2017

> 29. In section 66(3) of the Children Act 2004 (regulations subject to affirmative procedure), after '12B(1)(b)' insert ', 16B (whether alone or with regulations under section 16F), 16E(3)'.

The 2017 Act delves into the text of the 2004 Act and inserts new material into it.[90]

A non-textual amendment makes an indirect change to the existing law, not by changing the text of the existing law, but by requiring it to be read in a different way.[91] The key point is that there is nothing on the face of the existing law indicating that it is to be read in this particular way. Thornton refers to this as 'indirect, referential and cumulative'.[92] I think that 'cumulative' is slightly misleading here as textual amendments are also cumulative in the sense that they build on top of each other. A non-textual amendment doesn't always refer directly and specifically to all the law that it amends, it can instead make a general or global reference. For example, the Department for Employment and Learning Act (Northern Ireland) 2001 changed the name of the government department. Instead of going through the statute book, identifying each instance where the old name was used and changing it, it instead stated that all references to the old name were to be read as references to the new name. This kind of non-textual amendment is very common, particularly when there are a very large number of 'cosmetic' changes to the law being made.

5.4.2. Different Users, Different Needs

When it comes to intelligibility of amending legislation versus legislation as amended, different users have different needs. Parliamentarians need to understand the law in front of them (the amending law) as they need to understand what they are enacting. Professionals working in the field will most likely know the existing law, and only need to know what the changes are. Lay persons most likely don't need to know the minutiae of when various amendments are made, they just need to know what the law as amended is.

In my view, textual amendments are most in accordance with the Rule of Law. This is because it is more important for individuals to know what the law actually is, rather than how the law has changed. The textual amendment makes it easier to read and understand the law as amended. The non-textual amendment is more difficult to find as it isn't part of the text of the existing law. Furthermore, the

[88] Crabbe (n 66) 137.
[89] GC Thornton, *Legislative Drafting* (London, Butterworths, 1996) 405.
[90] See also chapter two and the difference between the law as enacted and the law as amended.
[91] Crabbe (n 66) 137.
[92] Thornton (n 88).

non-textual amendment requires the reader to jump through the difficult intellectual hoop of reading a text 'as if' it actually said something else.

Ilbert was of the view that non-textual amendments were good for legislators 'for parliamentary purposes [non-textual amendment] is the most convenient, because under it every member of Parliament who knows anything of the subject learns at once the nature of the amendment proposed'.[93] But although legislators are an important user group of legislation, legislation is not made for their benefit, but for the benefit of society as a whole. It is more important for ordinary people to understand the law through its lifespan than it is for legislators to understand it at its birth.

The preponderance of views in the drafting community agrees with the argument that textual amendments are generally to be preferred. For Samuels 'textual amendment, substitution of a new section for the old section, is desirable in principle'.[94] Berry[95] and Thornton agree.[96] Textual amendments are far more common, both in the UK and around the Commonwealth. Non-textual amendments may be easier for drafters (less statutes to check and cross refer to) but they do not assist understanding where it is most needed.

As ever though, it is wise not to be dogmatic. Sometimes a non-textual amendment can be made with little loss of intelligibility but large gains in other directions. Going back to the departmental renaming legislation example. If we required textual amendments each time a departmental name changed, the statute book would quickly be littered with thousands of pointless cosmetic changes. If a textual amendment doesn't cause problems with intelligibility, its use can be justified.

But even if a non-textual amendment can be intelligible, it can cause uncertainty, precisely because the impact of the non-textual change hasn't been considered in every single place where it will be applied. Let's say there is a Dogs Act which regulates dogs, and let's say we now want to regulate cats. We could make textual amendments to the Dogs Act, by adding 'or cat' after every single 'dog'. We could draft an entirely new Cats Act which replicates the Dogs Act. Or we could make a non-textual amendment that in the Dogs Act a reference to a dog shall be taken to include a reference to a cat. If we do the job right and make a new Act, or make textual amendments to the Dogs Act, we will see that parts of it don't work for cats – for example a lead for a dog may make sense, but not for a cat, or there may not be dangerous breeds of cat in the same way that there are dangerous breeds of dog. But with non-textual amendments, we don't check those things, we simply make a global change without looking at the detail and consequence of what that change means in all circumstances.

[93] C Ilbert, *Legislative Methods and Forms* (Oxford, Clarendon Press, 1901) 259.

[94] A Samuels, 'The Courts and Legal Services Act 1990: An Exercise in Drafting' (1991) 12 *Statute Law Review* 76, 77.

[95] D Berry, 'Keeping the Statute Book up to Date: A Personal View' (2010) 36 *Commonwealth Law Bulletin* 79, 98.

[96] Thornton (n 88) 407.

The key point is what actually works, not an automatic rule that textual is good and non-textual bad. Generally, textual makes legislation more intelligible, as well as more certain. In some circumstances, where the application of the law is tightly constrained, a non-textual amendment will be both intelligible and certain.

5.4.3. Form of Legislation Solutions to Dealing with Amendments

I previously set out some thoughts on tools to enhance clarity in amending legislation.[97] In this section, I expand upon and develop that list. The following can assist intelligibility both of the law as amended, and of the amending legislation.

Access to the Law as Amended

In chapter two I argued that accessibility included a requirement for access to the law as amended. If this is done, then the fact of an amendment, in itself, causes zero intelligibility problems. This can be done via a statute law database, or (as Samuels[98] and Lord Simon[99] argued) via reprints of the law as amended. If the reprint or database is by the state, then it will be quasi-authoritative, even if it doesn't have the authority of an actual Act of Parliament. Beatson saw the value of this in Scotland where an unofficial version of the law as amended was reprinted 'because without it the new law was utterly incomprehensible'.[100] Teasdale is also of the view that the reprints (along with consolidations etc.) where valuable tools for improving the quality of the statute book.[101] The same conclusion was reached by the Renton Committee.[102]

Bare Textual Amendments

A bare textual amendment makes the amendment in the smallest possible number of words. So, if an amending statute changes the penalty for an offence from two to three years, the amendment is 'In section 6(2), for "2" substitute "3"'. A bare amendment has the benefit of brevity, but gives the reader of the amending statute very little idea about the nature of the change being made.

[97] R Cormacain, 'Keeling Schedules and Clarity in Amending Legislation' (2013) 15 *European Journal of Law Reform* 96.
[98] A Samuels, 'Consolidation: A Plea' (2005) 26 *Statute Law Review* 56.
[99] Lord Simon, 'Statute Consolidation: Interim Techniques' [1985] *Public Law* 352.
[100] J Beatson, 'Common Law, Statute Law and Constitutional Law' (2006) 27 *Statute Law Review* 1, 4.
[101] J Teasdale, 'Statute Law Revision: Repeal, Consolidation or Something More?' (2009) 11 *European Journal of Law Reform* 157.
[102] 'Report of the Renton Committee on the Preparation of Legislation' (n 4).

Expansive Textual Amendment

An expansive textual amendment develops the idea of a bare textual amendment. But instead of amending the one or two words which are actually changing, it sets out the whole provision in its amended form. So, the amendment is 'For section 6(2) substitute "A person guilty of an offence under this section is liable to imprisonment for a term not exceeding 3 years"'.

The only thing which is actually changing is the number 2 to 3, but the amendment restates the entirety of the subsection, letting the reader at least know what the nature of the amendment is. The EU suggests this as the best way to proceed: 'preference shall be given to replacing whole provisions (articles or subdivisions of articles) rather than inserting or deleting individual sentences, phrases or words'.[103] This is at least intelligible. The reader can understand what is in front of her, although the exact nature of the change may not be clear.

Consolidation with Amendments

A consolidation repeals all the previous legislation on the point, and re-enacts it with the amendments included within it. Lord Simon thought it the best way to deal with legislation which has been amended multiple times.[104] His fellow judge, Lord Hailsham, had the same view – 'statute law revision and consolidations are both valuable ways of improving the statute book'.[105] Consolidation is a statutory duty of the Northern Ireland Law Commission[106] and the Law Commissions and England and Wales and Scotland.[107] The value of them is reflected in the fact that special parliamentary procedures exist to make consolidation acts easier to pass through Parliament.[108]

Consolidation helps the reader to see what the law as amended is. However, it isn't particularly good at showing what the changes being made to the law are. This is because the changes aren't flagged up in any way, all that a consolidation does is set out the new law.

Repeal and Restatement

Repeal and restatement is consolidation but at a smaller level. Instead of repealing the entirety of the old law and passing a new consolidated act, only the old provision

[103] 'Interinstitutional Agreement of 22 December 1998 on Common Guidelines for the Quality of Drafting of Community Legislation' 1999/C 73/01. Guideline 18. This point is reiterated in European Union (n 62). Robinson points out that this isn't binding though, W Robinson, 'Manuals for Drafting European Union Legislation' (2010) 4 *Legisprudence* 129.

[104] Lord Simon (n 98).

[105] Lord Hailsham, 'Addressing the Statute Law' (1985) 6 *Statute Law Review* 4, 7.

[106] Justice (Northern Ireland) Act 2002, s 51(1).

[107] Law Commissions Act 1965, s 3(1)(d).

[108] Consolidation of Enactments (Procedure) Act 1949, Standing Orders of the House of Commons, Standing Order 58.

is repealed and restated in a new law. The courts have in the past expressed a preference for this 'where possible, statutes, or complete parts of statutes, should not be amended but re-enacted in an amended form so that those concerned can read the rules in a single document'.[109] This approach also finds favour with Lovgren.[110] As with consolidations though, this renders the amending law less intelligible, as it is hard to know what exactly is being changed. An up to date statute law database would render repeal and restatement unnecessary.

Textual Amendment with Explanatory Material

A textual amendment with explanatory material builds upon a bare textual amendment, but uses explanatory material (within the text of the amending legislation) to give a narrative to what is happening. So the amendment is 'In section 6(2) (penalty for offence of burglary) for "2 years" substitute "3 years"'.

Material in parenthesis can be used to describe the section that is being amended, and slightly more expansive amendments can be made than are strictly necessary. The reader can have a reasonably good idea of the subject matter of the amendment, and also the nature of the change being made. As I previously argued 'the drafter might amend more words than are strictly necessary, but the nature of the amendment will be more intelligible to the reader'.[111] The amending legislation is intelligible, and if that amendment is updated into the statute law database, the law as amended will also be intelligible.

Official/Unofficial Guidance

The state can also issue official or unofficial guidance on the law as amended. This can be a version of a consolidation, although without actually being legislation. In fact, the existence of such guidance was cited as a reason why there was no formal consolidation in the Social Security Fraud Bill 2000/01.[112] Although this may make the law as amended intelligible, it is a poor substitute for actual legislation. Although guidance can be a useful adjunct to legislation, if used instead of legislation, it attacks the Rule of Law – it is rule of pamphlet, not Rule of Law. As the Society of Public Teachers of Law said 'We view with considerable misgiving the widespread practice of government by circular, with no legal force. Legislation is so complex that administrators … use circulars instead of text'.[113]

[109] *Merkur Island Shipping Corporation v Laughton* [1983] 2 AC 570, 595.
[110] AC Lovgren, 'The Location of Textual Amendments in Bills' (1988) 9 *Statute Law Review* 27.
[111] Cormacain, 'Keeling Schedules and Clarity in Amending Legislation' (n 96) 103.
[112] (28 March 2001) 624 HL debs col 264.
[113] Society of Public Teachers of Law, 'Preparation of Legislation' (1974) 13 *Journal of the Society of Public Teachers of Law* 96, 99.

Brightman made a similar criticism, although he extended this to the output of commercial organisations as well.[114] The point he was making was that although these sources may be useful, they didn't have the authority of an actual Act of Parliament.

The use (and abuse) of guidance during the coronavirus pandemic in the UK is a reminder of the perils of reliance upon guidance. All too often, as noted by the police,[115] and multiple reports,[116] guidance was issued masquerading as law.

Keeling Schedules

A Keeling schedule is a schedule in amending legislation that sets out the legislation as amended. So, the London Local Authorities Act 2012 amended the City of Westminster Act 1999 by way of textual amendments in the body of the 2012 Act. Then, in a schedule to the 2012 Act it set out the 1999 Act as amended (including both all the amendments made before 2012 as well as the amendments made by the 2012 Act). So, in one statute, the reader can see the changes as well as the thing being changed. The amendments are done by way of textual amendment, and the schedule is essentially a restatement, or consolidation of the law. But the schedule, as part of a statute, is as authoritative as any other statute.

The Keeling schedule is a little known legal device in the UK.[117] It was named after Edward Keeling, the MP who first used it and its use was endorsed by the Prime Minister in 1938.[118] It is used very rarely, on average once a year since 1938. However, practically everyone who has considered it has recommended it: the Renton Committee,[119] the Statute Law Society,[120] Bates,[121] Brightman,[122] Beatson,[123] Samuels,[124] Hand,[125] Berry[126] and Simon.[127] Zander said it was

[114] Brightman (n 23) 6.

[115] 'Policing in the Pandemic: The Police Response to the Coronavirus Pandemic during 2020' (Her Majesty's Inspectorate of Constabulary and Fire and Rescue Services 2021).

[116] K Lines, 'Government Messaging on Exercising during Lockdown – A Rule of Law Analysis' (Bingham Centre for the Rule of Law) <https://binghamcentre.biicl.org/publications/government-messaging-on-exercising-during-lockdown-a-rule-of-law-analysis>.

[117] Crabbe gives nine lines to it in a 300-page book on drafting Crabbe (n 66). Thornton doesn't mention it at all (n 88).

[118] HC Debs 26 July 1938 Vol 338 col 2919.

[119] 'Report of the Renton Committee on the Preparation of Legislation' (n 4).

[120] Statute Law Society, 'Statute Law: The Key to Clarity' (1972). See para 31. Statute Law Society, 'Statute Law: Radical Simplification' (1974). See paras 101 to 120.

[121] T Bates, 'Monitoring of Current Legislation by the Statute Law Society' (1981) 1 *Statute Law Review* 39.

[122] Brightman (n 23).

[123] Beatson (n 99).

[124] Samuels, 'Consolidation: A Plea' (n 97); Samuels, 'The Courts and Legal Services Act 1990: An Exercise in Drafting' (n 93).

[125] C Hand, 'Drafting with the User in Mind – a Look at Legislation' (1983) 4 *Statute Law Review* 166.

[126] Berry (n 94).

[127] Lord Simon (n 98).

a 'simple and attractive idea'.[128] Carr said it would improve the statute book.[129] Hailsham 'will always do what I can to encourage … a Keeling schedule'.[130]

In the absence of a properly accessible statute book that contains the law as amended, Keeling schedules perform a vital role. In addition, they are particularly useful when amending legislation is passing through Parliament – the legislators can see both the amending law, and what the law will look like after they enact the changes. There are a number of problems with them, however. First, as Bennion argues, they can 'uselessly clutter up the statute book'[131] as all they do is collate (and then repeat) material already in the statute book. Second, they take up important parliamentary and drafting resources – instead of just adding a textual amendment, the drafter must manually update the legislation, and parliament must debate and pass a bill containing the law as amended.[132] Third, they give rise to the possibility of re-opening a contentious point which has already been resolved by the legislature – an amendment may deal only with a non-controversial point, but in passing a Keeling schedule on the entire legislation, parliament may then have a chance to debate afresh one of the contentious points contained within it. Fourth, if a statute is continually amended, the Keeling schedule will either itself have to be continually revised, or it will swiftly become out of date.

In my view, Keeling schedules can improve intelligibility of the law as amended. However, they are very much second best when compared to a proper statute law database containing all the law as amended. Technology should render them obsolete, and with that technology the calls for their use (despite what I have previously argued)[133] have less strength.

5.5. Excessive Interconnectedness of Legislation

Legislation is interconnected if one provision refers to another provision, either within the same statute or in a different statute. Legislation suffers from excessive interconnectedness if the number and density of interconnections makes the legislation harder to understand. So, if a reader can only understand section 10 of the Companies Act by also looking at section 50 and section 60, and section 100 of the Insolvency Act and section 52 of the Directors Act, then there are too many jumps, too many connections. Excessive interconnectedness requires a reader to read multiple provisions simultaneously, to have multiple books open at once, or on screen to have multiple windows up. Legislation by its very nature

[128] M Zander, *The Law-Making Process* 6th edn (Cambridge, Cambridge University Press, 2004) 29.
[129] C Carr, 'British Isles: Legislation' (1949) 31 *Journal of Comparative Legislation and International Law* 1.
[130] Lord Hailsham (n 104) 8.
[131] Bennion (n 46).
[132] Bates (n 120).
[133] Cormacain, 'Keeling Schedules and Clarity in Amending Legislation' (n 96).

is interconnected – none of it works in a vacuum. What I am arguing here, is that excessive interconnectedness is bad because it restricts the ability of the reader to understand a law.

There are three broad ways in which legislation can be interconnected:

1. Legislation which amends other legislation;
2. Legislation which contains (internal and external) signposts (see further chapter two);
3. Legislation which refers to other provisions within it (internal cross-references) or to provisions in other legislation (external cross-references).

5.5.1. Excessive Interconnectedness and Amending Legislation

The orthodox view is that multiple layers of amendments make legislation unintelligible. I have previously pointed to Article 48 of the Police and Criminal Evidence (Northern Ireland) Order 1989 as an example of bad legislation because it has been amended so many times.[134] This is not a recent criticism, Parliament stated in 1875 that

> A reference to parts of several Acts of Parliament, some of which are repealed, some amended, and others kept alive, subject to the provisions contained in the amending Bill … makes the Statute so ambiguous, so obscure, and so difficult of comprehension that the judges themselves can hardly assign a meaning to it.[135]

The problem goes back even further. Sir Francis Bacon in 1616 wanted to reform a situation where we had 'statutes heaped one upon another'.[136] Whether textual or non-textual, the argument has been that continually amending a statute make it less and less intelligible. Cross references can be 'a boon to the drafter but a bane to the reader'[137] and Spencer sees over-referential drafting as contributing to the impenetrability of the statute book.[138]

However, subject to two caveats, I no longer see multiple amendments as posing a problem for intelligibility. The first caveat is that the amending legislation is clear, perhaps by using the techniques set out above in section 5.4.3. The second caveat is that the legislation is truly accessible, as set out in chapter two, so that the reader can easily see the statute as amended. If this is the case, then it doesn't really matter

[134] ibid.

[135] 'Report from the Select Committee on Acts of Parliament' (1875). See page iv.

[136] Quoted in Berry (n 94).

[137] R Martineau and M Salernon, *Legal, Legislative and Rule Drafting in Plain English* (Toronto, Thomson West, 2005) 73.

[138] JR Spencer, 'Criminal Justice Legislation That Everyone Can Understand: A Flying Pig or a Realistic Aspiration' (Institute of Advanced Legal Studies, 25 January 2016).

that a section has been amended two times or 20 times, so long as the reader can read it with all those amendments contained within it. Multiple amendments do not, of themselves, make legislation unintelligible. It doesn't really matter what the provenance of each particular provision is, as long as the reader can read it easily.

5.5.2. Excessive Interconnectedness and Signposts/ Cross References

The more cross references that are needed to understand a provision, the more jumps that are necessary across the statute book, the less intelligible (and navigable) that statute is. This point applies equally whether the interconnection is a direct reference (for example 'director has the meaning given in the Directors Act') or a signpost (for example 'see the Directors Act for further information on the duties of directors'). A cross reference is necessary in order to give legal certainty to a provision, a sign post is inserted to make the legislation more intelligible. But once these start to mount up, then we start to lose intelligibility. The reader is placed in a spinning roundabout, trying to take in information from 360 degrees, and getting dizzier and dizzier with each revolution.

There are three form of legislation solutions to this. First, we can reduce the number of cross references. A sign post should only be used if it will make the legislation easier to understand. It should be a helpful aid to direct the reader to further information if the reader feels they need to know that other information. It should not be compulsory in order for the reader to understand the legislation in front of her. A cross reference should only be used if necessary. It will often be easier for the reader for a definition to be repeated in a statute rather than require the reader to go to another statute to read the definition. Rather than require the reader to go to the Directors Act for the definition of director, it may be better to instead copy out that definition and repeat it in the current Act.

But even this simple drafting solution is subject to exceptions. A short definition may be repeated instead of referred to. But a long definition, or a provision which is to be applied to the current Act may stretch over several pages. A short cross reference here may be better than adding several pages of text to the current Act. Furthermore, there may be definitions of general importance, where it is important that the same definition applies across the statute book. If we want to update that definition, it is easier if we only have to update it in one place, rather than in multiple places. For example, if company is defined only in the Companies Act, then if we want to extend that definition by adding single member companies to it, we only need to make one amendment. But if company is defined in the Companies Act, Insolvency Act, Directors Act etc, then if we want to update it, we need to amend the definition in three different places. This opens up the possibility of making mistakes where some definitions are updated but others aren't.

Second, we can avoid circular references – 'a reference to another provision which itself refers back to the provision which referred to it'.[139] This kind of cross reference traps the reader in a referential circle, going round and round in a loop to try to understand a provision.

Third, we can avoid serial references – 'a reference to another provision, which itself refers to a third provision and so on'.[140] This also sets the reader on a wild goose chase, chasing down cross references in more and more different statutes before eventually being able to understand the original statute.

5.6. Plain Language

5.6.1. What is Plain Language?

According to Eagleson

> Plain English is clear, straightforward expression, using only as many words as are necessary. It is language that avoids obscurity, inflated vocabulary and convoluted sentence construction. It is not baby talk, nor is it a simplified version of the English language. Writers of plain English let their audience concentrate on the message instead of being distracted by complicated language.[141]

In the context of legislation, 'plain language is language which is direct and straightforward. It is designed to deliver its message to its intended readers clearly, effectively and without fuss'.[142] Kimble[143] and Thomas[144] both advocate its use in legislation. Gashabizi, another drafter, agrees 'plain language is an approach to organising and writing documents which makes materials clear and understandable to the user while making use of everyday language'.[145] Xanthaki includes plain language as one of the elements in achieving high quality legislation.[146] Although it is possible to find arguments against the effectiveness of plain language drafting,[147] there is unanimity on the question of what plain language is, and what it strives to achieve.[148] According to Tanner, the use of plain language in legislation can

[139] European Union (n 62) 53.
[140] ibid.
[141] R Eagleson, *Writing in Plain English* (Commonwealth of Australia, 1990) 4.
[142] Office of the Scottish Parliamentary Counsel, 'Plain Language and Legislation' (2006) 2.
[143] J Kimble, 'Answering the Critics of Plain Language' (1994) 5 *The Scribes Journal of Legal Writing* 51.
[144] R Thomas, 'Plain English and the Law' [1985] *Statute Law Review* 139.
[145] AS Gashabizi, 'In Pursuit of Clarity: How Far Should the Drafter Go?' (2013) 39 *Commonwealth Law Bulletin* 415, 419.
[146] Xanthaki (n 2).
[147] Greenberg (n 47); A Samuels, 'Thou Shalt Not Steal' (1999) 20 *Statute Law Review* 95; Hunt (n 83); P Butt, 'Modern Legal Drafting' (2002) 23 *Statute Law Review* 12.
[148] J Bennett and C Balmford, 'The International Plain Language Movement: A Business Plan' (1994) 31 *Clarity (Journal of the International Association of Plain Legal Language)* 37.

be demonstrated to improve its intelligibility.[149] For Karpen legislation should be 'formulated in a clear, plain language'.[150]

The term I use here is plain language, rather than plain English. This is for two reasons. First, taking into account the Welsh statute book, the UK as a whole comprises at least one bilingual jurisdiction,[151] so 'English' by itself is not accurate. Second, I take a broad approach to language as covering not simply the words on the page, but structure, formatting, layout and numbering.[152]

Thornton becomes almost poetic in describing the problems that plain language seeks to overcome, referring to legislation as 'a veritable cobweb of words and in the forest of their verbosity, the reader dare not enter, or, if he enters, he is apt to get lost in no time'.[153] If there was a competition for the most vivid description of unintelligible legislation, it would go to Lord Harman who spoke of

> Wading through a monstrous legislative morass, staggering from stone to stone and ignoring the marsh gas ... A Slough of Despond through which the court would never drag its feet, but I have, by leaping from tussock to tussock as best I might, eventually, pale and exhausted, reached the other side.[154]

There are three broad criticisms of plain language. These are relatively minor or 'quibbles' as Dorsey puts it.[155] They are not arguments in favour of unintelligibility, merely criticisms of plain language as a tool to achieving intelligibility.

The first criticism, made by Greenberg, is that plain language gives a false sense of knowledge to the reader.[156] The argument is that, since the language is plain and the words simple, the meaning is therefore clear to the lay reader. But this may be false because the meaning of a word may not be in accordance with the plain language meaning, or a word or phrase may be freighted with legal meaning which places a different complexion on how it should be interpreted. Greenberg's example is the use of the word 'person' in legislation. Citizens may automatically assume that this is a human being, not being aware that it can extend to legal persons (corporations with a legal personality) as well as to unincorporated associations.[157] If a statute is only to extend to human beings, then the word used in the statute will

[149] E Tanner, 'Legislating to Communicate: Trends in Drafting Commonwealth Legislation' (2002) 24 *Sydney Law Review* 529.

[150] U Karpen and H Xanthaki (eds), *Legislation in Europe: A Comprehensive Guide for Scholars and Practitioners* (Oxford, Hart Publishing, 2017) 13.

[151] In Northern Ireland, the Administration of Justice (Language) Act (Ireland) 1737 still applies and this requires statutes to be in English. However, there have long been proposals for an Irish Language Act which would change this.

[152] This broad approach is expressly used by the Scottish drafters, Office of the Scottish Parliamentary Counsel (n 141).

[153] Thornton and Xanthaki (n 20) 53.

[154] *Davy v Leeds Corpn* [1964] 3 All ER 390, 394.

[155] T Dorsey, *Legislative Drafter's Deskbook: A Practical Guide* (Alexandria, The CapitolNet, 2006) 187.

[156] Greenberg (n 47).

[157] By virtue of the Interpretation Act 1978 in England, Wales and Scotland, and by virtue of the Interpretation Act (Northern Ireland) 1954 in Northern Ireland.

be 'individuals'. It is better, according to Greenberg, that the language is obscure so the reader knows they don't understand it, rather than being plain so that the reader thinks they understand it, when in truth they actually misunderstand it. Or in Donald Rumsfeld's phrase, it should be a known unknown – something we know that we don't know.[158]

There is some weight to this argument, even though it seems counter-intuitive. I don't attempt brain surgery because I know I am ignorant of the subject, but an amateur who 'thinks' he knows could cause irreparable brain damage. However, to my mind there are four counter-arguments which displace the notion that plain language is not helpful in improving the quality of legislation.

First, don't use words where the plain and ordinary meaning of the word is different from the meaning you intend it to have. This isn't simply ambiguous, it is downright misleading. In the EU, there is a list of 'faux amis', words which have one meaning in one language, but a different meaning in another language.[159] Using a word which normally means one thing to mean another thing is a deliberate faux ami, but without the excuse of a different language. In fact, the EU recognise this very drafting problem, stating that 'if a word has one meaning in everyday or technical language, but a different meaning in legal language, the phrase must be formulated in such a way as to avoid any ambiguity'.[160]

Second, it isn't critical if there isn't 100 per cent congruence between the ordinary meaning of the word and the technical meaning of the word, so long as the lay reader will get the gist of the word. So the lay reader will know that 'person' includes them, even though they may be ignorant that the penumbra of meaning also extends to bodies corporate and unincorporated associations.

Third, don't attempt to simplify language by using an ordinary word that is inaccurate and could ultimately mislead. Instead, use the precise legal word, even if that will hinder intelligibility. So, in the legislation setting out how land will be assessed for rates (local land tax), a unit liable to rating is called a hereditament.[161] If the legislation eschewed 'hereditament' for an ordinary English word like land, or building, then Greenberg's criticism would be correct, and the user would have a false sense of understanding. Better then to use the proper word rather than use an imprecise word. As Eagleson said, plain language isn't about dumbing down, and it doesn't require precision to be sacrificed.

Fourth, we can go beyond the third argument by clever use of definitions. We can use the ordinary and plain word throughout the text, the word that readers will generally understand. But then we can define that word using the correct and technical legal language. So, in the hereditament example above, we could use the word 'property' throughout the legislation when we are talking about what is liable to rates. Then at the end, we can define property to mean a hereditament, with

[158] Donald Rumsfeld, Press Briefing, 12 February 2002.
[159] European Commission, 'How to Write Clearly' (2011).
[160] European Union (n 62) 21.
[161] Rates (Northern Ireland) Order 1977.

the full technical meaning of hereditament. This is one working example of what Xanthaki calls the 'layered' approach, where different layers of complexity exist in the legislation. The ordinary reader will gain sufficient understanding at the first layer when they read the word 'property', and the technical reader will gain sufficient understanding at a subsequent layer when they read the definition of property.

The second criticism, made by Dorsey, is that plain language elevates intelligibility over certainty. In fact, he states that we should 'beware' plain language.[162] As I have already pointed out, there is a tension between intelligibility and certainty, but this does not mean they are diametrically opposed to each other. Legislation should strive to achieve both. Dorsey goes rather too far when he argues that 'precise but unclear might be exactly what the client wanted. Your duty as a drafter is to give effect – with 100% faithfulness – to what the client wants'.[163] Although it is true that the legislative drafter owes a duty to the client, this does not override the obligation to the Rule of Law. In my counter argument to the first criticism above, I pointed out that plain language does not require imprecision, and that the correct legal word can still be used. Both proponents and opponents of plain language are correct here – there is no point in being precise if you are unclear, but equally there is no point in being clear if you are imprecise.

The third criticism, noted by Xanthaki,[164] is that it is too simplistic a solution to merely require all legislation to be in plain language. It can certainly help with intelligibility, but it is not a panacea. As noted above, sometimes complexity cannot be removed from legislation. This ties in with one of Greenberg's complaints – that there is nothing innovative about the desire to use plain language. One only has to look at Thring, writing 150 years ago and telling legislative drafters that 'clarity is the main object to be aimed at in the drafting of Acts of Parliament'.[165] Plain language is a tool, which used correctly can promote intelligibility. The automatic or mechanical application of it though, without considering clarity and precision more generally, will not always promote the Rule of Law.

5.6.2. Plain Language Techniques

What follows are some specific plain language techniques, tools which are aimed at improving intelligibility in legislation. For a more in-depth consideration of these techniques, see Thornton[166] and Turnbull.[167]

[162] Dorsey (n 154) 186.
[163] ibid 187.
[164] Thornton and Xanthaki (n 20).
[165] H Thring, *Practical Legislation: The Composition and Language of Acts of Parliament* 3rd edn (M MacKenzie ed, London, Luathe Press, 2015) 73.
[166] Thornton and Xanthaki (n 20).
[167] M Turnbull, 'Clear Legislative Drafting: New Approaches in Australia' (1990) 11 *Statute Law Review* 161.

Short Sentences

According to Thornton, 'studies in linguistics show that a sentence of above 15–20 words is incomprehensible'.[168] The EU states that 'unnecessarily long sentences are a serious obstacle to clarity in European Commission documents'[169] and suggest an average sentence length of 20 words (although this advice is consistently ignored if one reads any preamble to any EU legislation). A sentence which rambles on over several lines is difficult to understand, because by the time the reader has reached the end, they may have forgotten the start. Brevity, by which I mean expressing legislation in short sentences, does lend itself to intelligibility, 'clarity is helped by the use of short sentences'.[170] Oscar Wilde can write a sentence 119 words long,[171] legislators cannot.

Uncomplicated Sentences

But brevity by itself is insufficient in sentence construction. We also need to make sentences less complicated by reducing the number of concepts contained within them. A sentence is complicated (and hence more difficult to understand) if it contains multiple rules, conditions, provisos, persons, exceptions etc. This harks back to Thring's statement that 'enactment in its simplest form consists of legal subject and legal predicate',[172] that is to say

1. A person
2. Must do (or not do) a thing

To this we can add the condition, case or circumstance in which the rule applies:

1. A person
2. Must do (or not do) a thing
3. In a particular case/circumstance

If subject, predicate and condition are simple, then all three can be expressed in a single, uncomplicated sentence. For example

> The members shall be appointed by the Department.[173]
>
> The court must refuse to hear an application under a provision listed in subsection (2) if it considers that the applicant does not have a sufficient interest in relation to the missing person's property or financial affairs.[174]

[168] Thornton and Xanthaki (n 20) 60.
[169] European Commission (n 158).
[170] Office of the Parliamentary Counsel, 'Drafting Guidance' (Office of the Parliamentary Counsel, UK, 2020) 2.
[171] O Wilde, *The Picture of Dorian Gray* (New York, Modern Library, 2006).
[172] Thring (n 164) 73.
[173] s 6(3) Charities Act (Northern Ireland) 2008.
[174] s 19(1) Guardianship (Missing Persons) Act 2017.

However, once these categories start filling up, it becomes increasingly difficult to understand a single sentence which still contains them all. Mackinlay refers to this as 'syntactic discontinuity' if there is too much of separation of two elements of the same phrase by the insertion of another element.[175] So, if there are multiple legal subjects, predicates or cases, then it can be better to separate these out into different sentences. We can then have the outline framework at the start, followed by further sentences which explain the details. For example

- A person, as defined in subsection (2)
- Must do the thing described in subsection (3)
- In the circumstances set out in subsection (4)

There is no hard and fast rule about how many concepts are 'too many' for a single sentence. But at some point, intelligibility will decrease the more concepts are packed in, and it will be better to chop a long sentence up into smaller sentences. Paradoxically, this can mean that a longer section is more intelligible than a shorter section as instead of one long provision, we have several shorter ones. As Blaise Pascal is reputed to have said: 'I'm sorry for writing such a long letter, I didn't have time to write a shorter one'.

Division into Paragraphs

This flows on from the above point and follows Thornton's advice on paragraphing.[176] Division of a provision into paragraphs allows for a more logical structure for that provision. It allows the reader, at a glance, to see the division into the different elements of subject, predicate and case. For example:

> 4 (1) A person is entitled to welfare supplementary payment under this Part if the person meets –
> (a) the IS entitlement condition,
> (b) the disability-related premium entitlement condition,
> (c) the PIP refusal condition, and
> (d) the termination of disability-related premium condition.[177]

The reader sees at a glance that there are four conditions that must be satisfied, and the following paragraphs then set out in greater detail what each of these conditions are. However, if a list is short, it may be better to keep it all together rather than unnecessarily break it into paragraphs.

[175] J Mackinlay, 'Syntactic Discontinuity in the Language of the UK and EU Legislation' <www.esp-world.info/Articles_7/Syntactic%20DiscontLegal.htm>.
[176] Thornton and Xanthaki (n 20) 66.
[177] Regulation 4(1) Welfare Supplementary Payment (Loss of Disability-related Premiums) Regulations (Northern Ireland) 2016.

Active Not Passive Voice

In general terms, writing is more intelligible if it is in the active voice rather than the passive voice.[178] When it comes to legislation, it is imperative that individuals know what duties fall upon them: 'the thing must be done' is unclear compared to 'the person must do the thing'. As a bad example, in relation to consumer credit agreements 'All the contracting parties shall receive a copy of the credit agreement'.[179] Is the government to send out the agreements, or the creditor, or the consumer or a credit intermediary?

Of course, context can provide the identity of the person upon whom the duty does fall, particularly if this is set up by what comes before. So, if a person must make an application for a licence, it is acceptable for the following provision to refer to application requirements in the passive voice, as it is clear that the person making the application must comply with them.

Main Point First

The main point ought to come first, both at the level of an individual section, and at the level of the Act itself. Law isn't poetry, open to nuance and a multitude of subjective opinions, nor is it an adventure novel where there can be a twist at the end of the story. It is an instruction to individuals with consequences for failure to comply, so it must get its message across from the start. Starting with the main point first allows the reader to understand the legislation from the outset, rather than struggling through minor points of detail without knowing where they are going. So, if a section is going to ban cars from the city centre, it should begin with this bold statement, rather than by starting with definitions of cars and city centres.

It can be more difficult to do this at the level of the Act itself, as often Acts will have several main points. But the more important the provision, the closer it should go to the start, particularly with single purpose Acts. For example, the main purpose of an Act was to ban criminals from acting as special advisers to government ministers, so in the second section, the first line reads: 'Subject to subsection (2) and section 3, a person is not eligible for appointment as a special adviser if the person has a serious criminal conviction'.[180]

Use of Negatives (and Double Negatives)

Legislation is easier to understand if it is expressed in the positive rather than the negative.[181] 'An application must be in writing' is better than 'an application will

[178] Thornton and Xanthaki (n 20) 64.
[179] Art 10 Consumer Credit Directive, Directive 2008/48/EC.
[180] s 2(1) Civil Service (Special Advisers) Act (Northern Ireland) 2013.
[181] Thornton and Xanthaki (n 20) 65.

not be accepted unless it is in writing'. Double (or triple or more) negatives are a barrier to understanding as the reader must first jump an intellectual hurdle before understanding a provision: 'please untick this box if you do not want to receive marketing material' is not as good as 'tick here to receive marketing material'.

Front-loading of Sentences with Conditions

Watson-Brown counsels against front-loading sentences with conditions.[182] This is a specific outworking of the general advice for uncomplicated sentences. Front-loading means that the conditions for application of the rule appear in a long list before the rule itself appears. I previously argued that 'it is difficult for readers to link the first part of the sentence to the last part of the sentence if they have to push their way through four conditions in the interim'.[183]

Formatting and Numbering

As with paragraphing, formatting and numbering can help to visually organise sentences.

> (1) An indentation can indicate how a provision only relates,
>
> > (a) to certain cases, or
> >
> > (b) to other cases.
>
> (2) Before a return to the more general proposition.

Formatting can break up 'a large slab of unbroken text'[184] and white space on a page allows for a separation of concepts on the page, which leads to greater intelligibility.

Structure

A logical structure makes legislation more intelligible. This is dealt with in chapter two.

Jargon, and Archaic, Technical and Foreign Words

Thornton recommends avoiding archaic words, legalese and foreign words.[185] Classic examples, often favoured by lawyers, are hereby, as aforesaid etc. Thornton's

[182] A Watson-Brown, 'Defining "Plain English" as an Aid to Legal Drafting' (2009) 30 *Statute Law Review* 85.

[183] Cormacain, 'A Plain Language Case Study: Business Tenancies (Northern Ireland) Order 1996' (n 58) 40.

[184] Office of the Parliamentary Counsel (n 169) 20.

[185] Thornton and Xanthaki (n 20) 77.

advice is sound, although sometimes the precise word may be a foreign one, such as ultra vires (a Latin phrase literally meaning outside the power, or beyond the power). A phrase such as ultra vires has a very particular meaning, built up through case law, and so it can be risky to jettison it for an English concept such as 'beyond the powers'. As stated previously, depending upon the target audience, a technical word, or even a word that is jargon can be acceptable, if it is intelligible to those who will be using the legislation.

Visual Aids, Supplementary Aids

Legislation doesn't have to be just words. We can use maps, diagrams, formula, tables, flow charts etc. Research in the UK has found that users find it easy to understand mathematical calculations if they are written out as a formula rather than written out longhand in words.[186] To describe Pythagoras' Theorem we could say:

> The square of the hypotenuse is equal to the sum of the squares of the other two sides.

Or we could draw and label a triangle and then say:

$$a^2 = b^2 + c^2$$

Use of Present Tense

Legislation should be in the present tense. Legislation always speaks, meaning that we should write the law as if it will be applied right now.

Splitting the Verb

The greater the distance between the person and the thing they are to do, the more unintelligible the legislation. Xanthaki suggests that we shouldn't split the verb.[187] This is another outworking of the basic plain language technique of avoiding complicated sentences.

Avoid Nominalisations

If there is a simple verb, use it, rather than turning it into a noun and adding another verb.[188] So, it is simpler to say that 'a constable may investigate' rather than 'a constable may carry out an investigation'.

[186] Bertlin (n 57).
[187] Thornton and Xanthaki (n 20) 65.
[188] ibid 70.

Separate Out Provisos

A proviso is an additional qualification or restriction at the end of a provision which colours how that provision is to be applied. Thring cautioned against their misuse,[189] Coode spoke strongly against them,[190] as did Driedger[191] and Thornton.[192] There are certainly times when they can be used, but if they are used, they should be separated out and stand alone, rather than appear at the end of a long sentence. Considering the following example, which deals with several plain language techniques. First, we have the original provision from 1996:

> 2. Action which is or may be investigated by the Attorney General with a view to the institution of proceedings under section 31 or 46(9) of the Local Government Act (Northern Ireland) 1972.
>
> Provided that, if, after the Attorney General has decided not to proceed with such an investigation into such action or not to institute such proceedings in respect of it, or after the final determination of any such proceedings in respect of such action, a person aggrieved complains that such action resulted in his sustaining injustice in consequence of maladministration and that such injustice has not been remedied, the Commissioner may, if satisfied that there are reasonable grounds for that complaint investigate such action, notwithstanding any limitation of time imposed by Article 10(6).[193]

Then we have the new version from 2016, restated in plain language, using several of the techniques discussed in this part.

> 4. (1) Action which is or may be investigated by the Attorney General with a view to the institution of proceedings under section 31 or 46(9) of the Local Government Act (Northern Ireland) 1972.
>
> (2) But the Ombudsman may investigate that action, notwithstanding any limitation of time imposed by section 26, if conditions 1 and 2 are satisfied.
>
> (3) Condition 1 is that—
>
> (a) the Attorney General has decided not to proceed with an investigation,
> (b) the Attorney General has decided not to institute proceedings, or
> (c) there has been a final determination of those proceedings.
>
> (4) Condition 2 is that—
>
> (a) a person aggrieved complains that the action resulted in the person aggrieved sustaining injustice in consequence of maladministration and that such injustice has not been remedied, and
> (b) the Ombudsman is satisfied that there are reasonable grounds for that complaint.[194]

[189] Thring (n 164) 83.
[190] G Coode, *Legislative Expression* (London, William Benning and Co, 1845).
[191] E Driedger, *The Composition of Legislation: Legislative Forms and Precedents* 2nd edn (Department of Justice, 1976).
[192] Thornton and Xanthaki (n 20) 86.
[193] Para 2, Schedule 3, Commissioner for Complaints (Northern Ireland) Order 1996.
[194] Para 4, Schedule 5, Public Services Ombudsman Act (Northern Ireland) 2016.

5.7. Easification

Easification is a linguistic tool designed to make legal text more accessible, readable and easier to understand.[195] It provides the perspective of linguists on the Rule of Law requirement of intelligibility. It comes from a different professional background, but the end goal is the same. Therefore, it can be used as a form of legislation principle derived from the Rule of Law. For Pennisi, 'linguistics can provide a method by which drafters can assess the effectiveness of their draft'.[196]

Easification analyses legal discourse – the construction and organisation of language. It needs to be distinguished from simplification – which is a separate linguistic tool that produces an additional (and simpler) form of the text. Simplification is therefore not relevant to the form of legislation, although it is relevant to the production of explanatory material which may accompany the legislation. Easification makes legislation more intelligible, simplification allows for the creation of additional material to shed light upon the legislation.

For Bhatia, there is an implicit criticism of the form of legislation where it is 'considered advantageous to condense all the necessary information into a single sentence'.[197] This produces difficulties with cognitive structuring – the ability of the brain to process many different concepts at the same time. The solution is good cognitive structuring which is about 'facilitating the cognitive and syntactic processing of long sentences with multiple qualifications inserted at various points often adding excessive information load at various points in the syntactic arrangement of legislative provisions'.[198]

Pennisi expands upon this and gives practical examples about how legislation can be improved by these techniques.[199] This involves parsing sentences by reference to their different components: case, condition, sub-condition, legal subject, legal action. Where one of these components splits into binomials or multinomials, then that split can either be removed and placed elsewhere, or the text can be reformatted to show that split as a clear and logical sub-clause. So, if a long line of text has multiple conditions, and multiple references, it can be re-organised into a clearer format of:

IF

X or Y applies

THEN a person must

Do A or B

[195] PDKL Bhatia, *Textbook on Legal Language and Legal Writing* (New Delhi, Universal Law Publishing, 2010) 56.

[196] Pennisi (n 71) 101.

[197] PDKL Bhatia, 'Drafting Legislative Provisions: Challenges and Opportunities' [2010] *The Loophole* 5, 11.

[198] PDKL Bhatia, 'Linguistic and Socio-Pragmatic Considerations in Legislative Drafting' (2014) 2 *Theory and Practice of Legislation* 169, 179.

[199] Pennisi (n 71).

Easification gives academic weight to what is often done in practice – to write out all the elements that are to go into a provision, and if there are too many elements, to split them into different provisions, or use formatting and numbering to show divisions and sub-divisions. Pennisi also sees the value of focusing on the core regulatory message as soon as possible, and using other devices already discussed in relation to plain language, such as active not passive voice. Easification represents a more formal and empirically grounded form of plain language techniques and is a useful additional tool in enhancing intelligibility.

5.8. Good Writing

Paul Romer, former Chief Economist at the World Bank, stated that 'if a document is well written, anyone with a copy can read it and convert the codified knowledge stored in text back into human capital'.[200] Legislation is more likely to be understood if it is well written. The concept of good writing isn't one applying just to legislation, it is to all writing. A detailed inquiry into good writing is beyond the scope of this book. However, we can take one of the best proponents of good writing in the English language and examine his findings on the issue.

George Orwell, the author of (among other things) *1984* and *Animal Farm*, was a writer rather than a legislator. But his first two questions for a writer are: what am I trying to say and what words will express it?[201] Bowman, former First Parliamentary Counsel in the UK set out his approach to legislative drafting.[202] He summed up his drafting philosophy very simply: first decide what you want to say, second, say it. This is uncannily similar to Orwell's command. Therefore, we can see if Orwell's solutions correspond to form of legislation principles.

Orwell's rules for good writing are:

- Avoid tired metaphors.
- Never use a long word where a short one will do.
- If it is possible to cut a word out, always cut it out.
- Never use the passive where you can use the active.
- Never use a foreign phrase, a scientific word or a jargon word if you can think of an everyday English equivalent.
- Break any of these rules sooner than say anything outright barbarous.[203]

His first rule would not be popular with legislative drafters, particularly those who rely heavily upon precedents in their drafts. Unlike most writers, drafters are under

[200] P Romer, 'Writing' <http://wb-ce.org/writing.html>.
[201] George Orwell, *Politics and the English Language* (London, Penguin, 2013) 12–13.
[202] G Bowman, 'The Art of Legislative Drafting' (2005) 7 *European Journal of Law Reform* 3.
[203] Orwell (n 33) 19.

no pressure to say something novel, in fact the reverse pressure usually applies – to use the same words which have been proven to have worked in the past. However, the rest of Orwell's rules can find direct analogues in form of legislation principles – even down to the exhortation that the rules should be broken if necessary.

5.9. Examples

The dictionary definition of an example is a thing characteristic of its type, or an illustration of a general rule. The preponderance of views in the legislative drafting community is that examples make legislation more intelligible. Greenberg stated that 'there is possibly no innovation that could do more to help the readers of legislation and bring additional clarity to the statute book'.[204] Barnes likes them because they give a concrete illustration of the rule.[205] Piper is a fan because they help readers understand a general principle.[206] For Flesch 'whenever you write about a general principle, show its application in a specific case; … tell a pointed anecdote. These dashes of colour are what the reader will take away with him'.[207] Dorsey is unusual in opposing examples.[208]

5.9.1. Different Ways of Including an Example

Examples can be included in several ways. The most obvious is to say 'for example'.

> A local authority may meet an adult's needs under subsection (3) where, for example, the adult is terminally ill.[209]

This is a relatively new way (in the UK) to give an example. Much more commonplace is the 'inclusionary example' technique. Under this technique the general rule is given, followed by a few specific things that the rule is expressly stated to include. This is an example, even though the phrase 'for example' isn't used.

> the results of the ballot, including in particular—
> (i) the total number of votes cast,
> (ii) the number of persons who voted in favour of the imposition of the BRS,
> (iii) the number of persons who voted against its imposition …[210]

[204] Greenberg (n 45) 237.
[205] J Barnes, 'Shining Examples' [2004] *The Loophole* 8.
[206] B Piper, 'What, How, When and Why – Making Laws Easier to Understand by Using Examples and Notes' [2007] *The Loophole* 74.
[207] R Flesch, *The Art of Readable Writing* (Springfield, Collier Books, 1962) 38.
[208] Dorsey (n 154) 187.
[209] s 19(4) Care Act 2014.
[210] Schedule 1, para 20, Business Rate Supplements Act 2009.

There are two variations (at least) on this inclusionary example. The first is to give the rule, and then follow it by 'without prejudice to the generality of the foregoing, this includes …'. The second is slightly shorter, after the rule is stated it is followed by 'including, without limitation …'. The purpose of these two variations is to make it clear that the use of an example is not intended to limit the general application of the rule, so that if something falls outside the example, it may still fall within the rule.

5.9.2. Appropriate Cases Where Examples Can be Used

Examples do help the reader to understand legislation and ought to be used. The following are cases where it is appropriate to do so.

First, where the rule must be expressed in a precise (perhaps even technical way), but we need also to convey meaning to the user. In this case, we can give an example of the most common circumstance where the rule will be used. The rule may cause the casual reader to scratch their head, but the example will make it clear.

> Optical instruments for capturing or storing images (for example a camera) are prohibited inside a prison.

The rule may be expressed in a broad and technical way, in order to capture many different devices, but the reader may not understand what we are talking about here. However, when we give the example, the reader straight away gets the gist of the provision. The example is short, it allows for a precise rule, but also for an illustration to make the rule intelligible.

Second, where we want to give an indication to the reader the various kinds of activities or circumstances that it is envisaged the rule will cover, in order for them to better understand how the law may be used.

Persons must be compensated if they are abused in a care home, and abuse includes

1. Physical abuse
2. Sexual abuse
3. Emotional abuse

Abuse is a wide term, by giving examples, we are setting out the different sorts of circumstances we envisage where compensation will be paid. This can be useful especially when we are making a provision which empowers a public authority, or gives rights to individuals as it helps them to be aware of the breadth of the rule. A rule which allows a local council to take measures to help children with special needs at school sounds useful. But it is more illuminating if the rule then says 'this may include setting up additional facilities for those children, or employing an additional teacher or assistant to help in the classroom'.

Third, where there is a particularly contentious or problematic case which may crop up often, and we want to ensure that if falls within the rule. If we don't include an example, there could be arguments about whether the case is included within the rule

> The notice must be in writing (including by way of a text message).

Legislation must be as clear as possible, so there is no doubt whatsoever about what it covers. So, if there is a question mark over whether text messages can constitute a notice, then the legislation isn't working. Better then to make it absolutely crystal clear that text messages are included so that there is no confusion. However, this particular use of an example is a little problematic as it can allow for shoddy legislation in the first place, on the basis that any shoddiness will be remedied by the example. This is a common ground to attack the use of examples in legislation which is explored more below.

5.9.3. Difficulties with Examples

These above cases are all what Piper would call a 'textual example'.[211] He contrasts this with 'narrative examples'. Unfortunately, although he gives 'examples' of these, he doesn't actually define them. I would tentatively put forward the distinction between these two. A textual example is a brief statement of a case to which the rule applies. A narrative example is a longer, narrative statement illustrating how the rule will apply in detail. The following is a textual example:

> A vehicle, for example a car, must not be allowed into a park.

The following is a narrative example:

> A vehicle must not be allowed into a park.
>
> So, if Fred is driving a car and approaches the gates to the park, he must stop at the gates and is not allowed to go any further.

In my view, a narrative example goes beyond illustration and becomes an exposition and explanation of the legislation. Although such exposition can be useful, and does have a place (possibly in explanatory notes, or official guidance) that place is not in legislation as it is not making law, merely describing the effect of that law. In mathematics, this would be called a 'worked example' as it follows through all the steps of the formula (or rule) to show how we reach the end result. But the legislation ought to be clear enough without the need for a worked example, the rule should be clear in itself without needing to be repeated with some sample facts thrown in to show how it will apply. A narrative example doesn't illustrate a case to which the law applies, it is an explanation or restatement of the rule itself.

The second difficulty with an example is where the example conflicts with the rule itself. This sets up a clear tension or ambiguity in the legislation, should the

[211] Piper (n 205).

rule be followed or the example? In the UK, whatever is contained in the text of the legislation is part of the legislation. This obviously creates huge problems for the interpreter if two different parts of the legislation conflict. This is the height of bad legislation, far from being an aid to intelligibility, it creates confusion. If the legislator is faced with this situation, then the legislator needs to either revise the way the rule is expressed, or delete the example.

The third difficulty is related to the second, and it is where the particularisation of the example may colour how the rule will be used in practice. Barnes thought that this would be a good thing 'while in theory an example does not close off a discretion but merely illustrates it, the example may provide a strong message that it is a desirable, or at least a safe course'.[212] Although this is not wrong, it is problematic. The rule is there to prescribe or proscribe a general course of action, but if the example is too specific, it may influence users into thinking that only the example, or things like the example, are the things that are prescribed or proscribed.

Take a hypothetical case where we want a broad new offence 'it is an offence to obstruct the administration of justice'. Let's say we add to that 'for example by bribing a judge'. This example may start readers thinking along the lines of courts and judges, and not thinking about other types of obstruction, for example threatening witnesses or lying to police officers. This is linked to the principle of statutory interpretation known as *ejusdem generis*.[213] That principle means that the scope of general words in legislation may be limited in their application by reference to specific words which follow them. Bennion's example is 'having in possession or conveying in any manner', where the normal broad meaning of possession is limited in its sense by the narrowing concept of conveying.[214]

The fourth difficulty is where an example isn't used just as an illustration of a rule, but is instead (or additionally) used to help justify or explain the rule. Barnes argued that an example 'can illustrate the reason for the general rule'.[215] I think that this is wrong, as it politicises the law. It is of course important that law is justified, but that justification should take place at the time it is made, and amongst those debating the law. If we start including reasons/arguments/justification for law within the law itself, we are clogging up the law with propaganda. Take a bad example from the EU:

> Member states shall specify a time period of at least seven days during which the consumer will have sufficient time to compare offers, assess their implications and make an informed decision.[216]

[212] Barnes (n 204) 17.
[213] O Jones, *Bennion on Statutory Interpretation* 6th revised edn (London, Butterworths Law, 2013) 1231.
[214] ibid.
[215] Barnes (n 204) 19.
[216] Art 14, Mortgage Credit Directive 2014/17/EU.

The law is that the consumer has a seven-day time period before a mortgage agreement is concluded. The reason behind that is to give the consumer time to think through the offer and look at alternatives. But the use of this example above conflates law and justification in a confusing way. Do consumers break the law if they don't compare offers?

Conclusion

Legislation ought to be intelligible, meaning that it must be clear and easy to understand. If we can't understand what our obligations are, we can't be expected to comply with them and it would be unfair to penalise us under them. The Rule of Law principle of intelligibility is therefore underpinned by notions of practicality and fairness.

Intelligibility should not be considered in the abstract, that laws in general are intelligible. Rather it should focus on the characteristics of the user, so that a particular law ought to be intelligible to the particular person likely to use that law. So the characteristics of the target audience should be considered when designing a piece of legislation in order that it will be intelligible to that audience.

By its nature most legislation is layered on top of older legislation. Therefore, the form of legislation ought to consider intelligibility in two dimensions: intelligibility of the old law after it is amended by the new law, and intelligibility of the new law which is doing the amending. Different users will have different needs, some will want to see the changes that are being made, others will simply want to know what the law now is. Intelligibility needs to address both these needs. Another characteristic inherent in legislation is its interconnectedness, that nothing truly stands in isolation, but only makes sense when connected to other statutes. Excessive, or unnecessary interconnectedness can be reduced, and where there is a value in connectedness, signposts can be used to assist users in navigating around a particular statute, and the statute book in general.

Plain language is a linguistic tool, developed outside the world of legislation, which can help improve intelligibility. There can sometimes be a tension between over-simplifying things for the sake of intelligibility and over-complicating things for the sake of certainty and precision. But most of the time, the twin goals of certainty and clarity can work together. A clear law which is wrong is as bad as an unclear law which is correct. There are many individual plain language techniques (short sentences, good use of paragraphs, active not passive voice, etc.) which can improve intelligibility in legislation. Easification represents a development of the ideas behind the plain language movement. It provides more techniques to 'easify' or make more simple, a piece of text. It too can improve the form of legislation.

Although George Orwell was a dedicated writer in the field of politics, he also gave general advice on good writing. That advice is mirrored in the advice often given to legislative drafters. Although legislation is not known for its aesthetically pleasing qualities, it is possible to write well, using some of Orwell's suggestions. He preferred simple words to complicated ones, the active voice over the passive one, and breaking these rules rather than saying anything barbarous.

The final form of legislation technique for improving intelligibility is the example. Examples can help to illustrate the point for readers, and give a concrete out-working of what the legislation is intended to do. Provided that they are illustrative and not limiting, examples can make legislation easier to understand.

6

Constraints on Discretion

Introduction

The Rule of Law requires that we are governed in accordance with clear and established law, not governed in accordance with the personal preferences of individual ministers or officials. Tom Bingham summed up this Rule of Law requirement as law not discretion.[1] In terms of principles for the form of legislation, this means that legislation ought to contain constraints on the exercise of discretion by ministers and officials. The law not discretion principle is a shorthand way of saying that there must be uniform and rational decision-making by reference to fixed and clear rules. By contrast, unfettered discretion has the potential for arbitrary, capricious or whimsical decision-making. As the European Court of Human Rights said

> In matters affecting fundamental rights it would be contrary to the rule of law, one of the basic principles in a democratic society enshrined in the Convention, for a legal discretion granted to the executive to be expressed in terms of an unfettered power.[2]

In Part 1, I examine the theory behind this idea of law not discretion.

In Part 2 I derive form of legislation principles to give effect to this Rule of Law principle. These are as follows. There ought to be a clear demarcation in legislation between what is a straightforward application of legal criteria to a situation, and when a decision allows for the exercise of discretion. There are six different dimensions in which discretion can be constrained: the purpose of the power; the hurdle that must be cleared before discretion can be exercised; how precisely specified is the extent of the discretionary power; additional factors to be considered by the decision-maker; proportionality between the purpose of the discretion and its exercise; and external codes to be borne in mind before exercising discretion. Ouster clauses ought to be rejected. Powers that grant officials the power to disapply legislation ought to be curtailed. Purpose clauses can be used to help constrain discretion. There are then specific issues to consider when legislation grants discretion in how secondary legislation is made. Super-enabling clauses ought to be rejected. Framework legislation ought to have particular restrictions on how it is to be used. Finally, Henry VIII clauses ought to be rejected.

[1] T Bingham, *The Rule of Law* (London, Penguin UK, 2011) ch 4.
[2] *Beghal v United Kingdom* App no 4755/16 28 February 2019.

Part 1: The Theory of Constraints on Discretion

6.1. Law Not Discretion

Bingham stated that 'Questions of legal right and liability should ordinarily be resolved by application of the law and not the exercise of discretion'.[3] This issue can arise in a large variety of circumstances, but most commonly when an organ of state (a minister, an administrative agency, an official, a judge etc) comes to exercise a function or make a decision. The way in which that function is exercised or that decision taken should be within boundaries or limits set out in law, or by reference to criteria set out in law, rather than being simply a matter of personal choice. The Rule of Law means we are ruled by law, not by the exercise of individual preferences of individual officials. If a person seeks planning permission for a new house, the decision shouldn't be taken on a whim by the planning official who likes the look of the house, or who thinks the applicant is a jolly good chap. Instead, there should be detailed rules setting out who can apply for planning permission, on what grounds, for what purposes, and detailed criteria to guide the decision-maker through the process. This means that there will be, by and large, a common and uniform approach across the country. As the Supreme Court in *Catt* stated, this 'ensures that the law is not so wide or indefinite as to permit interference with the right on an arbitrary or abusive basis'.[4] In Bingham's own example, it doesn't matter if Mrs Smith in Durham or Mrs Brown in Newcastle applies for funding from the government, if they are both in the same position, they should both get the same outcome from different officials.

This is one facet of the principle of legality, that everything must be done in accordance with the law. Taking Fuller's example of King Rex, there is no proper legal system if Rex can simply do anything he wants.[5] Translating this to a liberal democracy, the Prime Minister is not an omnipotent being who simply issues commands in all spheres that must be obeyed. The Supreme Court in *Miller (No 2)* put paid to over-reaching Prime Ministerial hubris, ruling that the Prime Minister couldn't simply dismiss Parliament because it suited him to do so.[6] In the Venice Commission checklist of the Rule of Law it states that 'unlimited powers of the executive are, de jure or de facto, a central feature of absolutist and dictatorial systems'.[7] The Prime Minister can only do that which is authorised by law. But the law not discretion principle goes further than this. It is also a point about the substance of the law authorising things to be done. The substance of the law must itself require decisions to be taken, and functions exercised, in a rational, legal way, by reference to established criteria.

[3] Bingham (n 1) 48.
[4] *Catt v Commissioner of Metropolitan Police* [2015] UKSC 9, para 11.
[5] LL Fuller, *The Morality of Law: Revised Edition* (Revised, New Haven, Yale University Press, 1969).
[6] [2019] UKSC 41.
[7] Venice Commission, 'Report on the Rule of Law' (2011).

Both the following systems would equally infringe the Rule of Law:

1. Rex as king can do whatever he wants, and
2. Parliament passes legislation to say that the Prime Minister can do whatever she wants.

The second system will have the veneer of legitimacy in that it is 'authorised' by law, but it would still allow all decisions to be made by way of untrammelled discretion, rather than by law. This was reason why the Supreme Court in *Gallagher* rejected a 'discretion so broad that its scope is in practice dependent on the will of those who apply it, rather than on the law itself'.[8] Legislation is not just a rubber stamp that allows everything done under it to be valid. The Rule of Law also requires that the things done under the legislation are in accordance with the 'law not discretion' principle.

The principle of legality is satisfied by legislation authorising a thing to be done. But the principle of law not discretion is only satisfied if the legislation authorising the thing to be done has itself substantial constraints on *how* the thing may be done. Therefore, the over-arching form of legislation principle here is that the legislation ought to set out constraints on the exercise of discretion. For Emon, 'the possibility of government action based on will as opposed to reason or reasoned deliberation is a keystone that reveals the undercurrent of rule of law debates'.[9] The courts have warned that:

> The public must not be vulnerable to interference by public officials acting on any personal whim, caprice, malice, predilection or purpose other than that for which the power was conferred. This is what, in this context, is meant by arbitrariness, which is the antithesis of legality.[10]

In the phrase 'law not discretion', law means more than simply 'authorised by law'. It is a shorthand way of saying that decisions must be in accordance with clear, rational criteria, set out in law that constrain the way in which the decision may be made and implemented. In human rights jurisprudence the term used is 'in accordance with law' or 'prescribed by law', and this term encapsulates these points about law not discretion.[11] This human rights jurisprudence should not be seen as separate to the Rule of Law point, as Bingham himself said, speaking in a judicial capacity, 'the lawfulness requirement in the Convention addresses supremely important features of the rule of law'.[12] The human rights case law on the 'in accordance with the law'/'prescribed by law' requirement explicitly says that this test is used to ensure that restrictions on rights comply with the rule of law. For example, in *Malone v United Kingdom* the European Court of Human Rights said that the 'in accordance with the law' test 'does not merely refer back to

[8] *In the matter of an application by Gallagher* [2019] UKSC 3, para 17.

[9] A Emon, 'On Statutory Interpretation and the (Canadian) Rule of Law: Interpretive Presumptions as Boundary Setting' (2015) 3 *Theory and Practice of Legislation* 45, 48.

[10] *Gillan v Commissioner of Police* [2006] UKHL 12, para 34.

[11] M Amos, *Human Rights Law* 3rd edn (Oxford, Hart, 2021) 103.

[12] *Gillan v Commissioner of Police* [2006] UKHL 12, para 34.

domestic law but also relates to the quality of the law, requiring it to be compatible with the rule of law'.[13] Therefore, where legislation sets out a discretion for an official, it must also set out constraints, limitations or restrictions on that that discretion is to be exercised.

6.1.1. Link to Predictability and Certainty

Although law not discretion is a Rule of Law element in its own right, it also links in with the elements of predictability and certainty. If there is too wide a discretion, there is no predictability about the way in which that discretion will be exercised, and as a consequence there is no certainty in the law. An untrammelled discretion for an official to do whatever the official wants prevents individuals from planning their affairs in accordance with a fixed and stable law. The Supreme Court specifically linked this to the application of rules being 'reasonably predictable'.[14] Lady Hale in *Gallagher* stated that 'law will not be sufficiently predictable if it is too broad, too imprecise or confers an unfettered discretion on those in power'.[15]

6.1.2. Discretion and Corruption

A negative aspect of discretion is that it leaves open greater possibilities for corruption in interactions between citizens and officials. An automatic rule 'if the person does X, then the official must do Y' makes less space for corrupt decision-making. But a discretionary power 'if the person does X, then the official may do Y' opens up space for subjective decision-making influenced by corruption. Bratanovskiy and Zelenov argue that 'discretionary powers become a factor, provoking the improper behaviour (including the cases of bribery) of an official, when its limits are not clearly defined, or the criteria of its application are absent'.[16] The causes for corruption are manifold and just because there is discretion it does not necessarily follow that there will be corruption. However, reducing the scope for officials to exercise discretion in simple administrative functions does reduce the opportunity for those officials to take a bribe. This was one of the driving factors in the 'one-stop-shop' initiative in Azerbaijan, whereby many common interactions with officials were replaced with an automated process with fixed criteria. The new system was found by the Blavatnik School of Government to have achieved the aim of reducing corruption.[17]

[13] *Malone v United Kingdom* (1984) 7 EHRR 14 at para 67.
[14] *Catt* (n 4) para 11.
[15] *Gallagher* (n 8) para 73.
[16] SN Bratanovskiy and MF Zelenov, 'Discretionary Powers as a Corruption Factor within the System of Executive Authorities' [2016] *Administrative and Municipal Law* 311.
[17] 'Curbing Corruption in Azerbaijan: The Case of ASAN' (Blavatnik School of Government, University of Oxford 2017).

6.1.3. Exercise of Discretion by the State

To be clear, this is not about how private individuals may make choices, it is instead about the exercise of discretion by an emanation of the state. The archetypal exercise of discretion is where a minister has a particular power to do something. But it can extend to all organs of the state: civil servants, judges, police officers, administrative agencies etc. If the official is exercising a function that affects the rights of individuals, then that decision ought to be in accordance with the 'law not discretion' principle, that is to say, that there ought to be constraints on that discretion.

6.2. But Not All Law and No Discretion

There have been those who have argued that this principle means that everything should be done by way of law, and that there ought to be no discretion on the part of organs of the state when exercising their official functions. Dicey was opposed to discretion and thought it anathema to the Rule of Law.[18] Hewart had a similar view, arguing that if ministers could simply do what they thought fit, there was no proper Rule of Law at all.[19]

However, there has been a justified backlash against the view that any kind of discretion is bad for the Rule of Law.[20] A certain amount of discretion is necessary for the effective administration of the modern state. Discretion gives flexibility. In fact, human rights jurisprudence cautions against the blanket application of automatic rules without the possibility of individual circumstances being taken into account.[21] Turpin states that

> we have today a better understanding of the necessity and value of discretionary power in many branches of public administration, in order that varying circumstances as well as the needs of justice in individual cases can properly inform the making of decisions.[22]

Davis calls for 'a proper balance between rule and discretion'.[23] In considering powers to take measures in response to coronavirus, the courts have recognised the degree of discretion that must be afforded to ministers.[24] In particular, in deciding upon the furlough scheme and financial package for workers, there is a wide degree of discretion for ministers to set up schemes.[25]

[18] AV Dicey, *An Introduction to the Study of the Law of the Constitution* (1885).
[19] Lord Hewart, *The New Despotism* (London, Ernest Benn, 1929).
[20] Gavin Drewry, 'Public Law' (1995) 73 *Public Administration* 41, 46.
[21] *Thlimmenos v Greece* Application no 34369/97 (2000).
[22] C Turpin and A Tomkins, *British Government and the Constitution* 6th edn (Cambridge, Cambridge University Press, 2007) 94.
[23] KC Davis, *Discretionary Justice: Preliminary Inquiry* 5th printing edn (Champaign, University of Illinois Press, 1971) 42.
[24] *Dolan v Secretary of State for Health and Social Care* [2020] EWHC 1786 (Admin).
[25] *Adiatu v HM Treasury* [2020] EWHC 1554 (Admin).

There is no simple and universal answer to the question over whether it is better to have fixed rules, or better to have discretion. Looked at in another way, one person's flexibility may be another person's unwarranted discretion. Unfettered discretion, or discretion without limits is generally wrong, but some amount of flexibility in decision-making is necessary. I do not seek to answer the difficult question of what level of discretion is appropriate, but in Part 2 of this chapter I set out form of legislation principles to help place limits on discretion.

Part 2: Form of Legislation Principles for Constraining Discretion

6.3. Clear Demarcation between Law and Discretion

The simplest and most obvious form of legislation principle is to clearly demarcate law from discretion. Law means duty and uses the language of obligation – an official *must* do a thing. Discretion connotes power or choice and uses the language of permissiveness – an official *may* do a thing. In legislative language, an Act 'confers a power' or 'imposes a duty'.[26] Conferring a power upon the official means the official may do the thing, there is discretion or a choice to be made. Imposing a duty upon an official means the official must do the thing, there is no discretion involved, simply that if the legislative criteria are met, the official has to do the thing. See Table 6 below setting out an example of the difference between a duty and a power.

In Northern Ireland, the choice of language is made even more explicit in its interpretation legislation.

> Construction of 'shall' and 'may'
>
> In an enactment passed or made after the commencement of this Act, the expression 'shall' shall be construed as imperative and the expression 'may' as permissive and empowering.[27]

Table 6 Duties and Powers

Duty (automatic outcome)	Power (discretionary outcome)
If a person fills in the form the Department must grant the licence.	If a person fills in the form, the Department may grant the licence.

There has been a long (and to outsiders rather dreary) debate within the legislative drafting community about the difference between 'shall' and 'must'. It is enough to say that both indicate duty rather than power. 'Shall' is arguably more limited in scope as it can sometimes have the sense of 'is to be X', rather than 'obligation

[26] See for example s 12(1) Interpretation Act 1978.
[27] s 38 Interpretation Act (Northern Ireland) 1954.

to bring about X'. So the Fairy Godmother tells Cinderella that she 'shall go to the Ball', which means that she will go to the Ball in the future, rather than she has an obligation to go to the Ball. For this reason 'must' is preferrable to indicate obligation, even though 'shall' has more religious and imperative resonance for historical reasons ('thou shalt not steal').[28] Having said that, 'shall' can also be useful at times, for example bringing a new body into existence – 'there shall be a body corporate to be known as the Northern Ireland Human Rights Commission'.[29]

6.4. The Different Dimensions in Which Discretion Can be Constrained

Proceeding on the basis that discretion ought to be placed within limits, how then can we structure those limits? I contend that there are at least six different dimensions, or six different directions in which these constraints can be framed. These dimensions are not mutually exclusive and can be layered on top of each other as desired. The term 'safeguards' appeared in the Supreme Court judgment in *Beghal* 21 times in the context of the exercise of official discretion.[30] The dimensions set out in this section are all about ensuring there are adequate safeguards on how power is exercised.

To illustrate these different dimensions of constraints, I use a hypothetical legislative power that:

> The minister may do the thing.

6.4.1. Dimension 1: The Purpose for Which the Power May be Exercised

Requiring that a power can only be exercised for a particular purpose is the first dimension for constraining the exercise of discretion.

> The minister may do the thing for the purposes of X.

Sometimes there will no specific criteria to be satisfied before the power will be exercised, merely that the minister may do the thing. This makes for the easiest kind of discretion to be exercised. More commonly, there will be a specific purpose for which the power may be exercised. So, in the Police and Criminal Evidence Act 1984, a court may exclude evidence if it would have 'an adverse effect on the fairness of the proceedings'.[31] In the Bail Bill, a court has discretion to refuse bail

[28] The seventh of the Ten Commandments in the Christian and Jewish faiths.
[29] s 68 Northern Ireland Act 1998.
[30] *Beghal v DPP* [2015] UKSC 49.
[31] s 78(1).

on the grounds that the defendant would fail to surrender to custody, commit an offence on bail, or interfere with witnesses.[32]

The more specific the purpose, the more the discretion is constrained. The broader the purpose, the less that discretion is constrained. Some purposes are so broad that they could cover practically anything. For example, the standard grant of legislative powers to British colonies was that they could 'make laws for peace, order and good government'.[33] A narrower purpose is that an official 'may, for the purposes of this Act [exercise the power]'.[34] Even this could still be too broad, and it can be better to specifically list a particular purpose in the Act for which the power may be exercised, for example 'for the purpose of bringing the matters contained in [a notice] to the attention of persons likely to be affected by them'.[35] Coronavirus has seen a resurgence in broadly framed purposes of 'preventing danger to public health as a result of the spread of infection or contamination'.[36] But even though this could be framed in a broad way, most of the interpretative provisions in coronavirus legislation state that 'any reference to infection or contamination is a reference to infection or contamination with coronavirus which presents or could present significant harm to human health'.[37] Whichever way the purpose is framed, if the power can only be exercised for a particular purpose, then this limits discretion.

6.4.2. Dimension 2: The Height of the Hurdle

The second dimension is that there is some level that must first be reached before the power can be exercised. To put this another way, there is a hurdle to clear before the power can be exercised.

> The minister may, if it is reasonable, do the thing.

There is a sliding scale for how easy it is to exercise discretion in a particular case. At the bottom of the scale, there is no hurdle at all, merely that 'the official may do the thing'. The scale then proceeds upwards until there is a very high hurdle to be overcome 'the official may do the thing in exceptional circumstances'. Table 7 below sets out this scale in a non-exhaustive way. The exact ranking on the scale is subjective.

[32] Clause 3(1) in Northern Ireland Law Commission, 'Bail in Criminal Proceedings' (Northern Ireland Law Commission 2012) NILC 14.
[33] The Canadian example is s 91 British North America Act 1867.
[34] Schedule 2, para 9, Crossrail Act 2008.
[35] Art 4(6), Water and Sewerage Services (Northern Ireland) Order 2006.
[36] One example among many of this kind of purpose is set out in regulation 34(3)(b) of the Health Protection (Coronavirus, International Travel) Regulations (Northern Ireland) 2021.
[37] ibid reg 2(3).

Table 7 Ease/Difficulty of Exercising Discretion

Height of hurdle	Legislative provision
low	The official may do X
↓	The official may, if she thinks fit, do X
	The official may, if appropriate, do X
	The official may, if convenient, do X
	The official may, if reasonable do X
	The official may, if just, do X
	The official may, if necessary, do X
	The official may, in special circumstances, do X
high	The official may, in exceptional circumstances, do X

This hurdle can be further constrained by requiring there to be an objective rather than subjective test to overcome. A subjective test would be 'the minister may do X if the minister considers it reasonable'. This places the responsibility with the minister, and allows the decision to be their subjective decision about what is reasonable. An objective test is 'the minister may do X if it is reasonable'. This creates a higher standard, and won't provide an excuse for the minister who exercises poor judgement. For Kouroutakis, 'appropriate is a more subjective term which leaves room for discretion to ministers, while the term necessary is more objective and limits the options only to what was required'.[38]

6.4.3. Dimension 3: Specificity of the Thing that May be Done

An official can be given a broad power to do virtually anything, but discretion is constrained if there is a narrow and very specific list of things that the official can do. Contrast the following two formulations:

> The minister may take any measures necessary, in order to fight crime

OR

> The minister may impound the vehicle of a person who has been convicted of an offence related to the importation of illegal drugs, in order to fight crime.

Discretion is better constrained when an official is given a specific thing, or list of things that the official can do. Discretion is less constrained when the official is given the broad power to do anything that they want in order to achieve

[38] A Kouroutakis, 'The Henry VIII Powers in the Brexit Process: Justification Subject to Political and Legal Safeguards' (2021) 9 *Theory and Practice of Legislation* 97, 110.

a particular goal. The worrisome National Security Law that China imposed on Hong Kong contains the following provision:

> The Government of the Hong Kong Special Administrative Region shall *take necessary measures* to strengthen public communication, guidance, supervision and regulation over matters concerning national security, including those relating to schools, universities, social organisations, the media, and the internet.[39]

This is a duty rather than a power, but the point remains the same – that 'necessary measures' is worryingly broad and does not in any way constrain actions that the official may desire to take. Fowler complained about 'broad Ministerial powers used inappropriately' in the context of powers to make coronavirus regulations.[40] Although it can sometimes be appropriate to grant broad powers, it is better, particularly when the rights of the individual are being negatively affected, to enumerate a specific list of things that the official can do. In general terms, a power to do X, Y and Z, is better than a power to do anything necessary.

6.4.4. Dimension 4: Adding Additional Factors to Consider before the Exercise of Discretion

Discretion is constrained if the decision-maker is given a list of additional matters that must be taken into account before that discretion is exercised.

> Before doing the thing, the minister must first consider A, B and C.

The legislation may sometimes state what factors the decision-maker must take into account in exercising discretion. When these are present, then the decision-maker must consider these factors and this thus acts as a constraint on the exercise of discretion. A bland requirement to 'take all relevant factors into consideration' is unhelpful – if it wasn't there, would we expect the decision-maker to take irrelevant factors into consideration? However, these factors can often be helpful in guiding the decision-maker to the decision. The more detailed they are, the more predictable the exercise of the discretion. The factors can be exhaustive (only the factors listed in the legislation) or non-exhaustive (decision-maker can consider any other factors not listed that are thought relevant). For example:

> (3) In determining for the purposes of this section whether procedures for self-regulation are effective OFCOM must consider, in particular—
>
> (a) whether those procedures are administered by a person who is sufficiently independent of the persons who may be subjected to the procedures; and

[39] Art 9, The Law of the People's Republic of China on Safeguarding National Security in the Hong Kong Special Administrative Region, 2020, my emphasis.

[40] B Fowler, 'The Care Home Covid Vaccination Regulations: A Case Study in Problems with the Delegated Legislation System' (*Hansard Society*) <www.hansardsociety.org.uk/blog/the-care-home-covid-vaccination-regulations-a-case-study-in-problems-with>.

(b) whether adequate arrangements are in force for funding the activities of that person in relation to those procedures.[41]

Instead of being given carte blanche to exercise discretion, the official is given a detailed set of criteria to consider before exercising that discretion.

6.4.5. Dimension 5: Proportionality/Link between the Thing to be Done and the Purpose of the Legislation

Discretion is constrained if the decision-maker is obliged to have some sort of causal link, nexus or proportionality between the exercise of that discretion and the legislative purpose of that discretion.

> The minister may do the thing if it is proportionate to the purposes of the Act.

Even if this is not explicit, administrative law will generally imply some sort of constraint along these lines. A bald power to do something in legislation will not be interpreted in a bald way by the courts. Instead, it will be subject to a host of criteria implied by administrative law. So, it will be implied that this discretion is not to be exercised capriciously, but must be exercised for reasons, that those reasons are rational, that the decision-maker has considered all relevant factors and ignored irrelevant ones etc. These rules are sometimes summarised as 'procedural impropriety'[42] or the 'rules of natural justice'.[43] The House of Lords considered this point in relation to the discretion of the Home Secretary to release prisoners serving a mandatory life sentence.[44] Lord Steyn stated that

> Parliament does not legislate in a vacuum. Parliament legislates for a European liberal democracy founded on the principles and traditions of the common law. And the courts may approach legislation on this initial assumption.

So, in that case even though the statutory discretion was worded in very broad terms, concepts of reasonableness, legality and non-retrospectivity were read into it. In the *Unison* case, the Supreme Court went even further with implying certain fundamental values into the power to make delegated legislation. It held that the power to set court fees by way of delegated legislation did not include the power to set fees at such a level that they would restrict access to justice.[45] For John Laws this was based on the 'surely conventional principle that access to justice is not to be denied without very specific statutory authority'.[46]

[41] s 6(3) Communications Act 2003.
[42] See for example Lord Diplock in *Council of Civil Service Unions v Minister for the Civil Service* [1985] AC 374.
[43] See for example *Al-Mehdawi v Secretary of State for the Home Department* [1989] UKHL 7.
[44] *R v Secretary of State for the Home Department ex p Pierson* [1998] AC 539.
[45] *R (Unison) v Lord Chancellor* [2017] UKSC 51.
[46] J Laws, *The Constitutional Balance* (Oxford, Hart, 2021) 20.

However, even better than implied restrictions are express restrictions. So the legislation can itself state that there has to be some sort of nexus between the thing to be done and the reason for doing the thing. This overlaps with the imposition of a purpose dimension of constraints on discretion. The most common constraint of this type is the obligation that the exercise of power is proportionate to the end sought. For example

> (5) A notice under subsection (1) must state why the Welsh Ministers consider that the issuing of the notice is an appropriate and proportionate action in all the circumstances relating to the incidence or transmission of coronavirus.[47]

Proportionality, or a nexus between the exercise of the power and its purpose, is a way of constraining a discretionary power, rendering its exercise more uniform and predictable.

6.4.6. Dimension 6: Additional Codes and Guidance

Discretion is constrained if the decision-maker is obliged to bear in mind additional requirements set out in official guidance.

> Before doing the thing, the minister must have regard to guidance issued by the Department.

The legislation can also point to additional external requirements that have to be obeyed in the course of exercising a discretion. These could be obligatory requirements in a statutory form, for example a Code of Practice issued as a statutory instrument. Or they could be non-obligatory and non-statutory, for example official guidance issued by a government department. The most common approach is to require the official to 'have regard to' or 'consider' an extra-statutory document before exercising discretion. One point in favour of the legality of the discretion considered by the court in *Catt* is that there was a Code of Practice that 'leaves room for discretionary judgment by the police within specified limits'.[48] Although statutory guides are more immediately obvious, even a non-statutory guide will act so as to place limits on discretion.

6.4.7. How Tightly Does the Discretion have to be Constrained?

This section has set out different ways in which discretion can be structured in legislation. A tightly constrained discretion would have:

1. A specific purpose for which the power can be exercised.
2. A high hurdle before the power can be exercised.

[47] s 33, Coronavirus Act 2020.
[48] *Catt* (n 4) para 13.

3. A specific thing which can be done.
4. Lots of factors to be considered before the thing can be done.
5. An express requirement for proportionality between the thing to be done and the purpose of the power.
6. A requirement to have regard to a code of practice before exercising the power.

A loose discretion would have exactly the opposite. But on what basis should the legislator decide to have a tight or a loose discretion? It isn't automatically the case that discretion should always be tightly constrained, there may be circumstances where maximum flexibility (and discretion) would be beneficial. As with so much to do with principles for the form of legislation, there is no right or wrong answer. But in this subsection, I will set out some principles that may assist in determining the appropriateness of constraints on discretion.

Consequences of Exercise of Discretion

The more serious the effects on the individual of the exercise of the discretion, the more tightly the discretion ought to be constrained. So, the decision to release a life sentence prisoner has a serious impact upon the liberty of the prisoner, so that discretion should be tightly constrained. A decision to award a bursary for education has less serious consequences and can be less constrained. This point was made expressly by the Supreme Court in considering powers to detain at a port, 'the need for safeguards is measured by the quality of intrusion into individual liberty and the risk of arbitrary misuse of the power'.[49] Parliament itself has recognised this principle with the Delegated Powers and Regulatory Reform Committee arguing that where ministers are granted the power to define the elements of a criminal offence, the Committee would expect a compelling justification before this would be authorised.[50]

Nature of the Decision-Maker

In determining the nature of the discretion, consider the integrity and skills of the decision-maker. The more trust reposes in the decision-maker, the less constrained the discretion needs to be. So, a judge may be given a broad discretion in reliance upon judicial integrity, training, experience and high standards of ethics and probity. Thus the rules of procedure for the Inquiry into Historical Institutional Abuse are 'to be such as the chairperson may direct'.[51] This is because the chairperson has to be a high court judge. But if the decision-maker doesn't have the same

[49] *Beghal* (n 30) para 45.

[50] Delegated Powers and Regulatory Reform Committee, 7th Report of Session 2014–15 Special Report: Quality of Delegated Powers Memoranda (HL Paper 39) p 48.

[51] s 6(1) Inquiry into Historical Institutional Abuse Act (Northern Ireland) 2013.

professional standards to adhere to, or has less training or experience, it may be more appropriate to more tightly constrain their discretion.

Review Mechanisms

Consider also the existence of complaint or review mechanisms. The more prevalent these are, and the easier they are to access, the less constraint need be placed on the exercise of discretion as any defects in that exercise can be remedied by the complaint or review mechanism.

Example: Discretionary Powers of a Judge in Accepting Late Applications

A practical example may illustrate the exercise of these principles. The Inquiry into Historical Institutional Abuse has already been mentioned. The rules of the Inquiry are to be formulated by the Chairperson. He made a rule on late applications, ruling that they could only be accepted in 'truly exceptional cases'.[52] So there is a high hurdle for the exercise of discretion. Then the Chairperson had to have regard to the amount of time people already had to submit applications, and other ways in which people could present testimony to the Inquiry. So there are additional factors to consider. There isn't a blanket rule, and the Chairperson, as a judge, would have regard to all relevant factors. This approach was validated by the court when the exercise of this discretion was challenged by a person refused permission to apply out of time.[53] Dealing specifically with the amount of discretion, the court stated that 'In relation to the conduct of proceedings before the Inquiry, significant discretion must be afforded to the Inquiry'.[54]

6.5. Rejecting Ouster Clauses

6.5.1. Definition

An ouster clause is a clause in legislation that seeks to oust the jurisdiction of the courts. It means that the subject matter of the ouster clause cannot be challenged in the courts, in other words that it is non-justiciable. This means that the decision or action of an official in relation to that subject matter is final, and cannot be challenged legally. An older formulation of an ouster clause is contained in the Foreign Compensation Act 1950: 'The determination by the Commission of any

[52] A Hart, 'Remarks at Third Public Session of HIA Inquiry' (Historical Institutional Abuse Inquiry, 4 September 2013) <www.hiainquiry.org/index/chairman_s_address_130904_low_res.pdf> 3.
[53] *In the matter of an application by DR for leave to apply for judicial review* MAG 9875 8/1/2016.
[54] ibid [9].

application made to them under this Act shall not be called into question in any court of law'.[55]

A slightly more modern formulation is contained in the Regulation of Investigatory Powers Act 2000

> Except to such extent as the Secretary of State may by order otherwise provide, determinations, awards and other decisions of the Tribunal (including decisions as to whether they have jurisdiction) shall not be subject to appeal or be liable to be questioned in any court.[56]

Their nadir was the full-frontal attack on the ability of the courts to question anything done in pursuance of powers set out in the United Kingdom Internal Market Bill, as that Bill was introduced in the House of Lords. Clause 47 originally provided that

> (1) The following have effect notwithstanding any relevant international or domestic law with which they may be incompatible or inconsistent-
>
> (a) section 44,
>
> (b) any regulations made under section 44(1), …
>
> (2) Accordingly (among other things)-
>
> (a) regulations under section 44(1) or 45(1) are not to be regarded as unlawful on the grounds of any incompatibility or inconsistency with relevant international or domestic law …
>
> (d) any other provision or rule of domestic law that is relevant international or domestic law ceases to have effect so far and for as long as it is incompatible or inconsistent
>
> (4) No court or tribunal may entertain any proceedings for questioning the validity or lawfulness of regulations under section 44(1) or 45(1) other than proceedings on a relevant claim or application.

The scope of this purported ousting of the jurisdiction of the courts was breathtaking, leading me to previously refer to it as the mother of all ouster clauses.[57] The provision purported to prevent the courts from hearing any case about regulations made under these provisions. Furthermore, even if they did hear such a claim, it would deem those regulations to be lawful, despite them being inconsistent with any other provision of international or domestic law. Thankfully, this extreme provision was rejected by Parliament and did not make it into the statute book.[58]

[55] s 4(4) Foreign Compensation Act 1950.

[56] s 67(8) Regulation of Investigatory Powers Act 2000, as originally enacted.

[57] 'United Kingdom Internal Market Bill: House of Lords Committee Stage: A Rule of Law Analysis of Clauses 44–47' (Bingham Centre for the Rule of Law 2020). See also R Cormacain, 'The UK Internal Market Bill and the Mother of All Ouster Clauses – Ronan Cormacain' (*UK Human Rights Blog*, 15 October 2020) <https://ukhumanrightsblog.com/2020/10/15/the-uk-internal-market-bill-mother-of-all-ouster-clauses-ronan-cormacain/>.

[58] See Part 5 of the United Kingdom Internal Market Act 2020 that does not contain any of these provisions seeking to oust jurisdiction of the courts.

There is a difference between a clause that seeks to oust the jurisdiction of the courts completely, and a clause that merely reallocates the jurisdiction of the courts to resolve certain points. For example, a provision that states that the Investigatory Powers Tribunal is the only appropriate tribunal for hearing certain matters[59] was held by the Supreme Court to be lawful. It didn't oust the jurisdictions of the courts, it merely meant that a different court held jurisdiction.[60]

Likewise, there is a difference between an ouster clause, and a clause that restricts the ability of a person to bring a claim before the courts. For example, a strict time limit of three months for the bringing of a judicial review may limit the ability of a person to bring a claim, but it does not oust the jurisdiction of the courts.[61]

6.5.2. Problems with Ouster Clauses

Ouster clauses undermine the Rule of Law. The application of an ouster clause is in direct contradiction to the principle of legality that everyone is subject to the law and the principle that we are all entitled to have our rights vindicated by a court. The state isn't subject to law, and there is no access to justice as there is no way for an individual to enforce their legal rights. In a very practical way, it is also the antithesis of the law not discretion principle as there is no impediment to the state ignoring the law and instead simply exercising unfettered discretion.

The objections to ouster clauses within Parliament have been made clear. For example, in the Justice and Security (Northern Ireland) Bill, the Constitution Committee of the House of Lords objected to an ouster clause, stating that 'the Rule of Law is diminished if an aggrieved citizen is barred from challenging an allegedly unlawful decision taken by a public authority'.[62] In debating the ouster clause contained in the Judicial Review and Courts Bill, Lord Marks stated that ouster clauses 'hand power to the Executive to act contrary to law and outside the limits of what the law permits the Executive to do. In that way, they are inimical to the rule of law'.[63]

Writing extra-judicially, Lord Hewart criticised the following legislative example:

> The expression 'land likely to be used for building purposes' shall include any land likely to be used as, or for the purpose of providing, open spaces, roads, streets, parks, pleasure or recreation grounds, … and the decision of the Minister whether land is likely to be used for building purposes or not, shall be final and conclusive.[64]

[59] s 65(2)(a) Regulation of Investigatory Powers Act 2000.

[60] *R (on the application of A) v Director of Establishments of the Security Service* [2009] UKSC 12.

[61] Order 54.5, Civil Procedure Rules, Rules and Directions.

[62] Constitution Committee, 'Justice and Security (Northern Ireland) Bill, 4th Report of Session 2006–07' (2007) HL Paper 54 3.

[63] Hansard, House of Lords, Vol 819, 21 February 2022 Col 111.

[64] s 1(3) Town Planning Act 1925.

This example is a negation of the Rule of Law as it allows the minister to do whatever he wants. He could designate any land to be land for building purposes and that designation could not be called into question.

6.5.3. Judicial Attitudes to Ouster Clauses

It is reasonable to say that the courts do not like ouster clauses. The orthodox view is that they will give effect to them, provided that the statutory language introducing them is clear. So they have said that

> It is a principle not by any means to be whittled down that the subject's recourse to Her Majesty's courts for the determination of his rights is not to be excluded except by clear words.[65]

The difficulty, from the legislature's perspective, is that even when they do use clear words to oust the jurisdiction of the courts, the courts construe those clear words in a way that prevents them having that effect. In *Anisminic* the court ruled that an ouster clause that clearly said that a 'determination' could not be questioned in a court, actually meant that a 'lawful determination' could not be called into question in a court.[66] So, if a determination had no basis in law, it was not actually a determination, and therefore could be reviewed. With the ouster clause in the Regulation of Investigatory Powers Act 2000, the legislature went further, extending the ouster to decisions about whether the Tribunal had jurisdiction. The Supreme Court in *Privacy International* ruled that this still didn't oust cases where the determination of the Tribunal had no basis in law.[67] Essentially the Supreme Court ruled that if Parliament really, *really* wanted to oust jurisdiction, they should have said there was no power of the courts to review 'a determination *or a purported determination*'. In terms of protecting the Rule of Law and preventing bad or unlawful decisions from being unreviewable, the Supreme Court took the correct course. But in doing so, they strained the plain meaning of the words in the statute to breaking point.

This argument strays even deeper into the constitutional question of whether Parliament could ever decide by itself to remove the right of judicial review. Lord Carnwath in *Privacy International* suggested that it could not.[68] Much better to not put judges in this awkward position of having to choose between respecting the intention of parliament, and protecting the Rule of Law.

[65] *Pyx Granite Co v Ministry of Housing and Local Government*[1960] AC 260, 286.
[66] *Anisminic v Foreign Compensation Commission* [1969] 2 AC 147.
[67] *Privacy International v Investigatory Powers Tribunal* [2019] UKSC 22.
[68] ibid, para 131.

6.5.4. Current Proposed Reforms to Ouster Clauses

These should not be seen as one-off instances, but instead a long-term dialogue (putting it politely) between the executive, which wants to insulate itself from judicial oversight in certain cases, and the judiciary, which wants to ensure access to the courts. It is not a dialogue between two parties who have diametrically opposed views. On some occasions, Parliament has acted to restrict the use of ouster clauses. For example, in the Tribunals and Inquiries Act 1992, it passed a law that said that

> Any provision in an Act passed before 1st August 1958 that any order or determination shall not be called into question in any court …
>
> Shall not have effect so as to prevent the removal of proceedings into the High Court …[69]

On the other side of the coin, Lord Sumption (dissenting) in *Privacy International* argued that the ouster cause was effective and that the judicial character of the Tribunal was sufficient vindication of the Rule of Law. This was so even if the Tribunal had made an error of law.

This dialogue was reinvigorated in July 2020 with the Government launching the Independent Review of Administrative Law. This followed a manifesto commitment from the Conservative Party to 'update … administrative law … We will ensure that judicial review is available to protect the rights of the individual against an overbearing state, while ensuring that it is not abused to conduct politics by another means'.[70] Contrary to some expectations, the Independent Panel carrying out this Review did not recommend a wholesale acceptance of ouster clauses. Instead they stated that 'the Panel considers that there should be highly cogent reasons for taking such an exceptional course'.[71] In response, the Government accepted that there should be no general framework for ouster clauses, but that the need for them should be considered separately in each individual piece of legislation.[72] It drew a distinction between three situations: (1) there is an excess of jurisdiction of a body; (2) there is an abuse of that jurisdiction, for example a breach of the rules of natural justice; and (3) some other error of law. The suggestion is that it would be legitimate, in highly unusual circumstances, to enact an ouster clause. Although not explicit, the Government response implies that ousting jurisdiction in circumstance (3) is more legitimate than in the other circumstances.

When it came to enacting legislation to give effect to these policies, the Government have (at time of writing) introduced the Judicial Review and Courts Bill.[73] The concrete legislative proposals are modest and they only make provision

[69] s 12(1), Tribunals and Inquiries Act 1992.

[70] 'Get Brexit Done: Unleash Britain's Potential. The Conservative and Unionist Party Manifesto 2019'.

[71] 'The Independent Review of Administrative Law' (2021) CP 407.

[72] 'Judicial Review Reform Consultation – The Government Response' (Ministry of Justice 2021) CP 477.

[73] Introduced into the House of Commons, July 2021.

in relation to one particular right of appeal from one tribunal. Clause 2 of that Bill states that

> (2) The decision is final, and not liable to be questioned or set aside in any other court.
>
> (3) In particular—
>
> (a) the Upper Tribunal is not to be regarded as having exceeded its powers by reason of any error made in reaching the decision;
>
> (b) the supervisory jurisdiction does not extend to, and no application or petition for judicial review may be made or brought in relation to, the decision.

This is a classic ouster clause. In the definition subsection, it goes on to state that '"decision" includes any purported decision …'.

This addresses the *Anisminic* and *Privacy International* strategy of saying that only lawful decisions cannot be questioned by a court. At first glance, this ouster clause therefore has the potential of being fully 'judge-proof' in that there is no interpretative approach that allows the courts to question the decision. However, there are significant exceptions to this ouster clause, set out in the Bill, which weaken its ability to oust the jurisdiction of the courts. So, clause 2 continues

> (4) Subsections (2) and (3) do not apply so far as the decision involves or gives rise to any question as to whether—
>
> (a) the Upper Tribunal has or had a valid application before it under section 11(4)(b),
>
> (b) the Upper Tribunal is or was properly constituted for the purpose of dealing with the application, or
>
> (c) the Upper Tribunal is acting or has acted—
>
> (i) in bad faith, or
>
> (ii) in fundamental breach of the principles of natural justice.

Although this would appear to be a legislatively effective ouster clause, in the sense that there is no wriggle room for judges to claim that their jurisdiction is not ousted, the actual scope of the ouster has been cut down. Judicial review is only really ousted if there has been an error of law by the Upper Tribunal. But if the Upper Tribunal has made a mistake about its jurisdiction, has acted in bad faith, or has fundamentally breached the principles of natural justice, the courts can still hear an appeal relating to its decision. So on the one hand, this clause seeks to establish a cast iron ouster of jurisdiction of the courts, but on the other hand, to state that this ouster only applies in certain circumstances.

6.5.5. Rejecting Ouster Clauses

It is hard, if not impossible, to reconcile an ouster clause with the Rule of Law. Law not discretion, right of access to courts and the principle of legality are fundamental aspects of the Rule of Law that are negated by an ouster clause. Enacting legislation that makes a particular decision immune from legal scrutiny undermines the Rule of Law. As Lord Sales said in *Privacy International* in the Court of Appeal, 'If an individual cannot get before a court or tribunal to determine a complaint that a public authority has engaged in unlawful conduct, the rule of law will be defeated. The law will not be applied as it should be.'[74] Although it is conceivable that there are some issues that ought to be non-justiciable, it should be left to the courts to develop that jurisprudence, not for the legislature and the government itself to enact laws setting out no-go legal areas. As a form of legislation principle, ouster clauses should be rejected.

6.5.6. The Little Sister of Ouster Clauses: Clauses Restricting Remedies

If the UK Internal Market Bill contained the 'mother of all ouster clauses', then the Environment Act 2021 contains the 'little sister of ouster clauses'. This is a provision that does not seek to oust the jurisdiction of the courts, but instead restricts the remedies a court may grant if an official acts unlawfully. The response in the vast majority of cases to an official acting unlawfully is for a court to make an order remedying that unlawful act, for example by awarding damages, by ordering the act to cease, or quashing an unlawful statutory instrument etc.[75] A provision in legislation that prevents the court from awarding that remedy clearly undermines the principle of legality and the right of access to a court, as a law that cannot be vindicated and enforced does not have much value as a law.[76] Furthermore, such a provision also acts like an ouster clause to embolden officials to act with unfettered discretion rather than in accordance with law – if a court won't issue a remedy against their unlawful action, there is less incentive to act lawfully.

Those provisions in the Environment Act 2021 are as follows:

> (8) Where the court makes a statement of non-compliance it may grant any remedy that could be granted by it on a judicial review other than damages, but only if Condition A or Condition B is met.
>
> (9) Condition A is that the court is satisfied that granting the remedy would not—
>
> (a) be likely to cause substantial hardship to, or substantially prejudice the rights of, any person other than the authority, or
>
> (b) be detrimental to good administration.
>
> (10) Condition B is that Condition A is not met but the court is satisfied that—
>
> (a) granting the remedy is necessary in order to prevent or mitigate serious damage to the natural environment or to human health, and
>
> (b) there is an exceptional public interest reason to grant it.[77]

[74] *Privacy International v Investigatory Powers Tribunal* [2017] EWCA Civ 1868 at [19].

[75] J King, 'Miller/Cherry and Remedies for Ultra Vires Delegated Legislation' (*UK Constitutional Law Association*, 19 September 2019) <https://ukconstitutionallaw.org/2019/09/19/jeff-king-miller-cherry-and-remedies-for-ultra-vires-delegated-legislation/>.

[76] R Cormacain, 'Environment Bill – Office for Environmental Protection: A Rule of Law Analysis' (Bingham Centre for the Rule of Law 2021).

[77] s 38, Environment Act 2021.

In effect, this section makes it much harder for a court to grant an effective remedy, even if an official has acted unlawfully. These types of clauses should generally be avoided as they make it more likely that decisions will be made in accordance with the discretion of an official, rather than in accordance with the law.

6.6. Curtailing Powers for Officials to Create Exemptions from the Law

It is common for legislation to have exceptions, or conditions that must be met before the rules apply. Normally those exceptions are set out in the legislation that contains the rules. For example, the Offensive Weapons Act 2019 makes it an offence to sell a corrosive product to a person under the age of 18.[78] But a person is not liable if they satisfy the conditions of the defence to remote sale set out in the Act.[79]

But sometimes, the detail of that exception or condition will not be set out in the legislation, but will instead be delegated to an official to determine. This is a statutory power, granted to an official, for the law not to apply to particular persons or in particular circumstances. The details of the exception are not set out in law, instead the official is simply granted a power to disapply the law. This is akin to, but much less extreme than, an ouster clause. But they both operate on the same continuum in that there is a power, granted by legislation, which allows an official the discretion to disapply or ignore a particular provision of that law. Summarising the criticisms of Hewart, Bingham said that 'particularly objectionable to him were the practices of authorising ministers to amend or disapply an Act of Parliament'.[80]

This is a specific instance of a legislative grant of power that gives too much unfettered discretion to an official and that undermines the law not discretion principle. How can we speak of fixed, certain and rational law, when the minister has the power, by administrative action, to set aside that law? There is a distinction to be made here, between a minister exercising a function to determine whether a particular circumstance falls within an exemption, and the minister having the power to create an exemption. The distinction is easy to set out in the abstract, but difficult sometimes to ascertain in practice.

A concrete example may help to explain. Under coronavirus regulations, a person is obliged to self-isolate if they test positive for coronavirus.[81] The Regulations contain lots of exemptions, for example attending a funeral, seeking medical assistance etc. Regulation 2(2) sets out a long list of these exemptions. There is a further exemption from the requirements to self-isolate where an

[78] s 1 Offensive Weapons Act 2019.
[79] s 2, ibid.
[80] Bingham (n 1) 48.
[81] Health Protection (Coronavirus, Restrictions) (Self-Isolation) (England) Regulations 2020.

individual is participating in what is called a 'testing scheme'. A testing scheme is defined as follows:

> 'testing scheme' means a scheme—
> (a) under which participants take a test for the detection of coronavirus at such intervals as are specified in the scheme for a period specified in the scheme, and at a place and in a manner specified in the scheme, and
> (b) which is approved by, or on behalf of, the Secretary of State.[82]

This provision gives the Secretary of State the power to exempt people from the law, without very much in the way of constraints on that discretion. Although the scheme must specify where and when the testing must be done, there are no criteria setting out when the testing scheme can be set up, or what its purpose is. It gives a large degree of flexibility/discretion to a minister to exempt people from the law without any formalities about how this is to be done, publicised or recorded. It is a classic example of Hewart's criticism of legislation that empowers ministers to disapply the law.

The reason for constraining discretion is to stop the abuse of official power. This abuse was manifested in the self-isolation exemption when the Prime Minister and Chancellor of the Exchequer were required to self-isolate in accordance with the Regulations. They stated that they were actually taking part in a workplace testing pilot (eg a testing scheme within the meaning of the Regulations) and would therefore not have to follow the rules.[83] Although exempting themselves under the 'testing scheme' was subject to one of the fastest U-turns in recent political history, it shows precisely why ministers ought not to be given the discretion to disapply the law.

Another questionable use of a discretionary power to disapply a legal obligation comes from another coronavirus regulation (emergency laws seem to be the most popular instance of the Rule of Law being abused). This time, it was the prohibition on large gatherings.[84] The Secretary of State was given an express power to disapply any relevant restriction or requirement.[85] On this occasion, it could only be done for the specific purpose of 'a research programme to evidence the potential transmission of coronavirus in controlled environments'.[86] The Secretary of State was first required to consult with the Chief Medical Officer.[87] The direction to disapply was required to be published online and then published, as soon as reasonably practicable, in the *London Gazette*.[88]

[82] Reg 2D(6), ibid.
[83] K Lines, 'The Contact Tracing Self-Isolation Regime in England: A Rule of Law Analysis' (Bingham Centre for the Rule of Law, October 2021).
[84] Health Protection (Coronavirus, Restrictions) (Steps) (England) Regulations 2021.
[85] Reg 9(1), ibid.
[86] Reg 9(2), ibid.
[87] Reg 9(4), ibid.
[88] Reg 9(5), ibid.

This power was exercised at some point in June 2021 and the event specified was the 2020 UEFA football matches at Wembley stadium on 22 and 26 June 2021. There are a number of problems with the exercise of this discretionary power of a minister to disapply the law. First, a search of the *Gazette* does not reveal any notice published on it. Second, the online version of the notice does not state the date on which it was made. Third, although it was announced before the matches, a careful search online after the announcement did not reveal any evidence of this 'research programme' being published.[89] These are minor and procedural failings. But the main flaw is that it appears that this was not a genuine research programme, but more of a populist political decision. The Secretary of State, on 14 July 2021 referred to these as 'events pilots' and said that 'It is fantastic to see the crowds at Wembley. We are making progress, and these freedoms have returned'.[90] Scott Benton MP, commenting upon the opening, said 'Thanks to the brilliant events research programme, thousands of people have been able to enjoy events including the FA cup final and Euro 2020 fixtures at Wembley.'[91] Nigel Huddleston MP, the Minister, in reply said

> That is precisely why we conducted the programme. Despite the cynicism we have heard from Opposition Members, the events research programme is important not just for its scientific learnings but in helping to lift the mood of the nation. The fact that we have been able to watch football with crowds in stadiums again has been fantastic. We will shortly see other events such as Wimbledon, with centre court again at full capacity. Life is getting back to normal, and that is something we should be celebrating.[92]

It is stretching credulity to believe that this was a genuine research programme designed to test transmission rates. It has all the hallmarks of a popular political gesture. There is nothing wrong with popular political gestures, but ministers should not have the discretion to disapply the law to make themselves popular.

Statutory authority granting discretionary powers to disapply the law can sometimes be legitimate and helpful for the efficient functioning of government. These powers should not automatically be rejected. But their use should be curtailed. In addition to the five dimensions for constraining discretion set out above, the need for them ought to be demonstrated before they are included in the legislation. Furthermore, each individual exercise of these powers ought to be both justified and publicised.

[89] The notice was eventually published online at https://assets.publishing.service.gov.uk/government/uploads/system/uploads/attachment_data/file/995296/ERP_Directions_EUROS_Pilots_22nd_and_26th_June_2021.pdf.

[90] Hansard Vol 697 Col 81, Monday 14 June 2021.

[91] Hansard Vol 697 Col 768 22 June 2021.

[92] ibid.

6.7. Purpose Clauses

Lord Reid in *Padfield* explained that

> Parliament must have conferred the discretion with the intention that it should be used to promote the policies and objects of the Act; the policy and objects must be determined by construing the Act as a whole.[93]

If discretion is to be constrained by reference to the purposes of legislation, it is helpful if those purposes are made explicit, rather than left to be teased out of an Act. This is one benefit of a purpose clause. The purpose clause is a provision in legislation, usually at the start, which expressly states the purposes of the legislation. Their point is to explain *why* the legislation is being made, not *what* it contains. For example 'The purpose of this Act is to promote access to innovative medical treatments …'[94]

Provisions that are not expressly called purpose clauses can still have that effect. For example, in section 1 of the Children Act 1989 it states that when a court is determining an issue with respect to a child 'the child's welfare shall be the court's paramount consideration'.[95]

Purpose clauses are rare in UK legislation. Their closest precursor is the long-disused preamble, or a recital of the wrongs that the legislation was introduced to address. Most famously, the Statute of Charitable Uses 1601[96] commences with a long list of social wrongs of the Elizabethan era which that Statute sought to remedy. It begins: 'The relief of aged, impotent and poor people; the maintenance of sick and maimed soldiers and mariners, schools of learning, free schools and scholars of universities; the repair of bridges …' In Ireland, its near contemporary, the Statute of Pious Uses 1634 contains a similar list in its preamble.[97]

As well as being an aid to interpretation, the purpose clause (or the older preambles) can have the effect of constraining discretion by expressly listing the purposes for which that discretion ought to be exercised. Berry noted the 'important function of purpose sections is to define the limits of discretion conferred by legislation'.[98]

Purpose clauses are not favoured because of the risk that they could conflict with the substantive provisions of an Act. This is a valid concern and led the Renton Committee to recommend that they only be used sparingly.[99] Xanthaki

[93] *Padfield v Minister of Agriculture, Fisheries and Food* [1968] AC 997.

[94] s 1, Access to Medical Treatments (Innovation) Act 2016.

[95] s 1(1), Children Act 1989.

[96] Statute of 43 Eliz. 1 Cap. 4.

[97] 10 Car. 1 Sess. 3 Cap. 1. For a consideration of the effect of differences between these two statutes, see K O'Halloran and R Cormacain, *Charity Law in Northern Ireland* (Dublin, Round Hall Ltd, 2001).

[98] D Berry, 'Purpose Sections: Why They Are a Good Idea for Drafters and Users' (2011) 2 *The Loophole* 49, 51.

[99] 'Report of the Renton Committee on the Preparation of Legislation' (1975) Cmnd 6053. See also the discussion in the House of Commons Political and Constitutional Reform Committee, First Report of Session 2013–14, para 68.

points out another valid concern, that they could be used to shoehorn emotive or political statements into what should be a neutral statement of the law.[100]

Although uncommon in the UK, purpose clauses are common in Australia and New Zealand[101] (where they are sometimes called objects clauses). There is even official guidance on their use in New Zealand from the Legislation Design and Advisory Committee.[102] That guidance is explicit in stating that one function of the purpose clause is 'to form a basis for statutory criteria or tests for discretions under a regime'.

Although they should never be mandatory, a purpose clause can be a helpful form of legislation principle to ensure that the law not discretion principle is maintained.

6.8. Constraining the Power to Make Secondary Legislation

So far, this chapter has considered general grants of powers to officials and argued that those grants ought to contain constraints on how they should be exercised. There is an important sub-category of the grant of a power. This is the power, delegated to an official or a minister, to make secondary legislation. This is a particularly important power as it is the power to make rules that bind society as a whole. In this section and the following sections I consider how the power to make legislation ought also to contain constraints on how that power is exercised. In the same way that a general power ought to be constrained, so too should the specific power to make secondary legislation be constrained.

An enabling power is the power granted by primary legislation for an official to make secondary legislation. That official will normally be named as the minister, although in practice it may be senior civil servants who take some of the decisions. But the power may also be granted to other organs of the state. For example, a department, a rule-making committee or some sort of administrative agency.

Even though statutory instruments are self-evidently legislation, the decision on what they contain is largely the result of an exercise of discretion by ministers and officials. It is they who decide upon the content of statutory instruments. There are two democratic checks on this process. First, the enabling legislation

[100] H Xanthaki, *Drafting Legislation: Art and Technology of Rules for Regulation* 1st edn (Oxford, Hart Publishing, 2014) 186.

[101] R Carter, *Burrows and Carter: Statute Law in New Zealand* (5th edn, Lexisnexis 2015) 263. For a general review of countries that use them, see Berry (n 98).

[102] See information on Designing purpose provisions and statements of principle available at http://ldac.org.nz/.

must authorise the grant of the power to make secondary legislation. Second, the secondary legislation must itself pass through some form of legislative scrutiny in the legislature, for example, it may require the active assent of the legislature, or the legislature may have the power to reject it. In remarking upon the efficacy of this second democratic check, the Secondary Legislation Scrutiny Committee noted the rarity of Parliament actually rejecting a statutory instrument.[103]

Notwithstanding these democratic checks on the process, the official retains considerable power in deciding upon the substance of secondary legislation. This means that the grant of the power to make statutory instruments should not be unfettered, but should also contain constraints on its exercise. In analysing how Parliament carried out its scrutiny functions on delegated legislation, Simson Caird drew the conclusion that

> the normative framework applied by parliamentary committees when scrutinising delegated powers and delegated legislation is principally concerned with [among other things] limiting the government's legal discretion to legislate.[104]

Ideas around controlling the making of secondary legislation are normally framed in terms of constitutionality,[105] good law-making processes,[106] democratic legitimacy[107] or the separation of powers.[108] This makes it quite difficult to separate out what are Rule of Law constraints from other constraints. For the purposes of my analysis, secondary law-making can also be considered as an exercise in constraining discretion. The Venice Commission go so far as to consider the law-making power of the executive, and constraints on this, to be a separate element in the Rule of Law. Their taxonomy is different from mine, but it arrives at the same conclusion when they ask in Benchmark A4 of their Rule of Law checklist: 'When legislative power is delegated by Parliament to the executive, are the objectives, contents, and scope of the delegation of power explicitly defined in the legislative act?'[109]

Secondary legislation is a very useful way of making law, particularly when there is a need for detailed or technical provisions that would otherwise clog up

[103] Secondary Legislation Scrutiny Committee 'Government by Diktat: A call to return power to Parliament' HL Paper 105 (November 2021), see para 18.

[104] J Simson Caird and E Patterson, 'Brexit, Delegated Powers and Delegated Legislation: A Rule of Law Analysis of Parliamentary Scrutiny' (Bingham Centre for the Rule of Law 2020).

[105] J Simson Caird, R Hazell and D Oliver, *The Constitutional Standards of the House of Lords Select Committee on the Constitution* (London, University College London, 2014).

[106] Xanthaki (n 100) 257–75.

[107] Hermann Pünder, 'Democratic Legitimation of Delegated Legislation – a Comparative View of the American, British and German Law' (2009) 58 *International & Comparative Law Quarterly* 353.

[108] William D Neighbors, 'Presidential Legislation by Executive Order' (1964) 37 *University of Colorado Law Review* 105. See also the work of Dam questioning the use of the power of the President to make legislation without the legislature, Shubhankar Dam, *Presidential Legislation in India: The Law and Practice of Ordinances* (Cambridge, Cambridge University Press, 2014).

[109] Venice Commission (n 7).

an Act of Parliament. There is nothing wrong with secondary legislation in itself, my point here is that it should, as with other exercises of discretion, be set within limits.

6.8.1. Form of Legislation Principles for Grant of Power to Make Secondary Legislation

The six dimensions of constraining discretion set out above all apply. There are then specific principles, derived from the starting point of law not discretion. Some of these principles have been taken from the excellent synthesis made by Simson Caird and Patterson[110] of the legisprudence of the following Parliamentary committees: the Delegated Powers and Regulatory Reform Committee, the House of Lords Constitution Committee, the Joint Committee on Statutory Instruments, the European Statutory Instruments Committee and the Secondary Legislation Scrutiny Committee. Although the original justification for these constraints may have included democratic accountability, they also serve the law not discretion principle.

Power to Make Secondary Legislation No Wider than Necessary

The power to make secondary legislation should be no wider than is necessary for the purposes of the primary legislation. Each individual power in the enabling Act to make secondary legislation should be separately identified and justified.

Clarity of Scope of Enabling Power

The scope of the enabling power should be clear and well defined. This means that the extent of the power to make legislation should be precise and obvious. This means that there is (a) no doubt for legislators in what they are enabling and (b) no doubt for officials in what they can cover in the delegated legislation.

Important Provisions Should Not be Delegated

The important provisions should be set out in the primary legislation, not left to delegated legislation. For example, key definitions, criminal offences, politically sensitive matters – these are sufficiently important to warrant the collective decision of parliament, not the individual preference of the delegated rule-maker.

[110] Simson Caird and Patterson (n 104). See also the precursor to this work, dealing solely with the legisprudence of the Constitution Committee of the House of Lords, Simson Caird, Hazell and Oliver (n 105).

Matters connected to the devolution settlements between the central government and the Welsh, Scottish and Northern Irish bodies should not be delegated to secondary legislation. On this point, see further below in the discussion on framework legislation.

Minimal Not Maximal Approach to Delegation

Rather than asking 'what powers would make life easier for the department?', legislators should be asking 'what powers are actually necessary and will be used?'. This was the specific finding of the Delegated Powers and Regulatory Reform Committee in considering a Bill that contained a regulation making power in relation to the terms of office for elected mayors. The Committee ruled that

> It seems to us that any power to provide for those things in subordinate legislation should be limited so that it can only be exercised to the extent necessary to allow synchronisation with other elections, when the office of a mayor is first established.[111]

The locus of the enquiry ought to be what is actually necessary, rather than what does the rule-maker desire, or even worse, what does the rule-maker think they will get through the legislature.

Sunset Clauses

A sunset clause (a clause that states that a provision expires after a set period of time) is a way to reduce the time frame in which a discretionary power can be used. These can make broader powers seem more palatable as they won't apply in perpetuity. The sunset clause can appear in the primary legislation. For example, in the Civil Contingencies Act 2004, it states that regulations made under it lapse 30 days after they are made.[112] The sunset clause can also appear in the secondary legislation. For example, one of the many coronavirus regulations in Wales states on its face that it expires on 26 November 2021.[113]

Specifically Crafted Boundaries and Safeguards

The grant of legislative power should be circumscribed by boundaries or safeguards that are relevant to the circumstances of the particular grant. As well as the general constraints set out in this chapter, there ought to be specific constraints tailored to the particular subject matter of the rule-making power. For example, in exercising regulation-making power in relation to medicines where the regulations may have an impact on the safety of human medicines, 'the appropriate authority

[111] Delegated and Regulatory Reform Committee, First Report (2015).
[112] s 26, Civil Contingencies Act 2004.
[113] Regulation 3, Health Protection (Coronavirus Restrictions) (No 5) (Wales) Regulations 2020.

may make the regulations only if the authority considers that the benefits of doing so outweigh the risks'.[114] In addition to general constraints, specific constraints should be included that act as a safeguard against the abuse of discretion in relation to that specific power.

Example: Power to Amend Corporate Insolvency Legislation

A good example of constrained powers to make secondary legislation is set out in sections 20 to 27 of the Corporate Insolvency and Governance Act 2020. There is a general power to make regulations to amend the law on corporate insolvency.[115] But this is limited to the conditions that must be met before insolvency applies, or the way in which it applies. There are then a list of purposes for which the legislation can be made (although unfortunately there is a low hurdle that they can be made if the Secretary of State thinks it 'expedient').[116] There are several restrictions on making those regulations, for example the Secretary of State must consider interest groups, no criminal offences may be created, it wouldn't otherwise be practicable to achieve that result, and other restrictions.[117] There is a sunset clause so that the regulations themselves expire after six months, and furthermore, the power to make regulations also expires by April 2021.[118] Finally, there are detailed provisions about the procedure for making the regulations (although unfortunately some regulations can come into effect before they are laid before Parliament).[119] Although not ideal in all respects, the power to make regulations is constrained and thus discretion is fettered.

6.9. Constraining the Power to Make Secondary Legislation: Rejecting Super-Enabling Clauses

This section considers a particular form of the power to make secondary legislation. It has become very popular in recent years to include what I term a 'super-enabling clause' in primary legislation. An enabling clause grants a minister the power to make secondary legislation. A super-enabling clause is much broader and less specific, it grants a minister the power to make regulations to give full effect to an Act, or make further legislative changes consequential or incidental to an Act. In a way it acts like a sweeper clause, granting additional powers not already granted,

[114] s 2 Medicines and Medical Devices Act 2021.
[115] s 21 Corporate Insolvency and Governance Act 2020.
[116] s 22, ibid.
[117] s 23, ibid.
[118] s 24, ibid.
[119] s 26, ibid.

or a fall-back clause granting general powers to cover points not already set out in one of the specific powers.

For example, in Wales

> (1) If the Welsh Ministers consider it necessary or expedient for the purposes of giving full effect to any provision of this Act, or in consequence of any such provision, they may by regulations make—
>
> (a) any supplementary, incidental or consequential provision, and
> (b) any transitional or saving provision.[120]

At Westminster

> (1) The Secretary of State may by regulations make provision that is consequential on any provision made by or under—
>
> (a) Parts 1 to 5.[121]

In Scotland

> (1) The Scottish Ministers may by regulations make any incidental, supplementary, consequential, transitional, transitory or saving provision they consider appropriate for the purposes of, or in connection with, or for giving full effect to this Act or any provision made under it.[122]

In Northern Ireland

> The Assembly Commission may by order make such supplementary, incidental, consequential or transitional provision as it considers necessary or expedient for the purposes of, or in consequence of, or for giving full effect to, any provision made by or under this Act.[123]

The super-enabling clause goes against the principles set out above as it is both broader than necessary, and does not have a clear scope. It is becoming ubiquitous in any large piece of legislation in the UK to include a super-enabling clause. It is certainly convenient for ministers and officials and those engaged in preparing the legislation. But it is lazy law-making, and grants too much discretion to the executive. It is lazy law-making because the consequential changes, and measures to give full effect to the law, should be prepared and enacted in the Act, not left to be done later. It grants too much discretion as it should be for Parliament to decide what the law ought to be, not for a minister to come along later and make that decision as a matter of individual choice.

Granting a department the power to make whatever legislative changes they consider necessary to give full effect to an Act is writing them a blank cheque. Referring to the dimensions set out above, dimension 1 (the purpose) is extremely

[120] Social Services and Well-being (Wales) Act 2014, s 198.
[121] Domestic Abuse Act 2021.
[122] Tied Pubs (Scotland) Act 2021.
[123] Public Services Ombudsman Act (Northern Ireland) 2016.

vague, 'the purposes of the Act'. For dimension 2 (height of the hurdle) the hurdle is very low, in the legislative examples cited above, necessary, appropriate or expedient. For dimension 3, there is no specificity, other than it is supplementary, incidental, consequential, transitional or transitory. For dimension 4 there are no additional factors to consider. For dimension 5, there is no proportionality requirement. And for dimension 6, there are no additional codes. As long as there is some vague connection to the Act, there is nothing structurally to stop this discretion being exercised in any way a department pleases.

Super-enabling clauses undermine the law not discretion principle. They grant far too much power to ministers and officials to make further legislative change, by way of secondary legislation, with very little in the way of adequate parliamentary oversight. Although enabling clauses perform a valuable function, super-enabling clauses undermine the Rule of Law.

6.10. Constraining the Power to Make Secondary Legislation: Curtailing Framework Legislation

This section considers another particular form of the power to make secondary legislation – framework legislation. As with super-enabling clauses, these breach many of the general principles for curtailing discretion in the making of secondary legislation.

6.10.1. Definition

Framework legislation, also referred to as skeleton legislation, is a particular type of primary legislation. Framework legislation sets out the framework of the law, but then leaves the detail of the law to be determined by secondary legislation. As with super-enabling clauses, this makes it another area where there is wide discretion, contained in primary legislation, for officials and ministers to set the rules in secondary legislation. Van Gestel defines framework laws as 'laws with open target-oriented rules leaving much room for the delegation of policy decisions to the executive, administrative agencies or private rule-makers'.[124] A more critical definition comes from Hynes who calls them 'a sketchy outline of laws that are subsequently filled out by delegated legislation not subject to the same level of parliamentary scrutiny as the primary legislation'.[125] For Heidegren framework

[124] R van Gestel, 'The "Deparliamentarisation" of Legislation: Framework Laws and the Primacy of the Legislature' (2013) 9 *Utrecht Law Review* 106, 106.

[125] S Hynes, 'Parliamentary Scrutiny of Our Legislation Is Being Lost to Misused Executive …' (*Legal Action Group*, June 2017) <www.lag.org.uk/article/201782/parliamentary-scrutiny-of-our-legislation-is-being-lost-to-misused-executive-power>.

legislation is an example of the downward delegation of authority, where the decisions are taken not by Parliament but by administrative bodies, private bodies, ministers or officials.[126] The House of Lords has been less complimentary, describing framework bills as 'a legislative blank cheque'.[127] Framework legislation is the more neutral term, whereas skeleton legislation connotes distaste for it. This is not a formal category of legislation as set out in parliamentary rules, but more of an informal description of what happens in practice. The key elements are that framework legislation sets out principles, objectives, targets or goals, in a relatively short Act, and leaves the details to be filled in by the subsequent secondary legislation made under the enabling powers contained in the Act. The substance of the regulation, the actual rules will be contained in that subsequent secondary legislation. The open-textured nature of framework legislation gives adaptability and flexibility in the making of the secondary legislation.

Framework legislation is similar in many ways to goal legislation. Westerman describes goal legislation as legislation that sets out the goal to be achieved, but then delegates to others the decision on how to reach that goal.[128] Goal legislation doesn't contain rules, instead it has the targets. It is for the delegated legislation, or the administrative agencies in their executive functions, to achieve those targets. As with framework legislation, 'goal legislation shifts the centre of gravity of rule-making from the legislative process to a regulation process'.[129]

6.10.2. Why is it Used?

Framework legislation is not new. Lord Hewart was criticising it in the 1920s, even using the phrase 'legislation passed in skeleton form'.[130] Van Gestel notes extensive administration discretion in law-making in the Netherlands in the nineteenth century.[131] It is not that common, but it does seem to be on the rise in the present era in the UK, with Lord Judge making trenchant criticism of it recently in his capacity as a parliamentarian.[132] The Secondary Legislation Scrutiny Committee in the House of Lords also see this as being on the rise, and as can be seen in the

[126] Carl-Göran Heidegren, 'Social Acceleration, Motorized Legislation and Framework Laws', in *The Contemporary Relevance of Carl Schmitt* (Abingdon, Routledge, 2015).

[127] Secondary Legislation Scrutiny Committee 'Government by Diktat: A call to return power to Parliament' HL Paper 105 (November 2021), para 30.

[128] P Westerman, *Outsourcing the Law: A Philosophical Perspective on Regulation* (Cheltenham, Edward Elgar Publishing, 2018).

[129] Anna Louise Elisabeth Enequist, 'From Abstract Goals to Concrete Rules – Regulating Nursing Home Care in Sweden and the Netherlands' (Social Science Research Network 2015) SSRN Scholarly Paper ID 3803177 27 <https://papers.ssrn.com/abstract=3803177> accessed 20 August 2021.

[130] Hewart (n 19) 14.

[131] van Gestel (n 124).

[132] Lord Igor Judge, 'A Judge's View on the Rule of Law' (Annual Bingham Lecture, 3 May 2017) <www.biicl.org/documents/1637_2017_05_11transcript_of_lord_judges_speech_3.pdf?showdocument=1>.

title of their recent report, see it as part of a trend of 'Government by Diktat'.[133] One reason for the rise in its use is that it is seen to be particularly helpful in modern states in dealing with certain policy areas. Ebbesson makes a strong argument that primary legislation is too slow and too unwieldly to deal with certain areas of law, for example, laws for environmental protection. He speaks of the need for 'flexibility in social systems and institutions to deal with changes'.[134] Environmental law in particular needs to be able to change rapidly, and administrators need flexibility to achieve environmental ends, or as Ebbesson calls it, achieving environmental resilience.

As well as the speed necessary to respond to environmental or other changes, there is also the complexity and detail of regulation required in the modern state. Pünder argues that in an interventionist or welfare state, the legislature simply can't legislate all the rules themselves, that the detail has to be left to the administrative agencies.[135] There is a limit on the time available in parliament to debate everything, so inevitably some matters will be prioritised. There can also be political pressures to be seen to be taking fast and decisive action. Speaking from direct personal experience of drafting social security statutory instruments, I agree that it would be unfeasible for Parliament to itself directly enact the huge mass of them that are made each year.

6.10.3. Problems with Framework Legislation

The Constitution Committee of the House of Lords was scathing of framework legislation, recommending that 'skeleton bills inhibit parliamentary scrutiny and we find it difficult to envisage any circumstances in which their use is acceptable'.[136] Hewart, writing nearly 100 years ago was particularly critical

> The bureaucratic expert 'clothes himself with despotic' power since he can (a) get legislation passed in skeleton form; (b) fill up the gaps with his own rules, orders and regulations; (c) make it difficult or impossible for Parliament to check said rules, order and regulations; (d) secure for them the force of statute.[137]

These problems can be categorised as follows. First, there is the lack of scrutiny. When a framework Bill passes through a Parliament, it is difficult to scrutinise because there is nothing there to scrutinise. As the Delegated Powers and Regulatory Reform Committee described a particular Bill, it was 'an enabling

[133] Secondary Legislation Scrutiny Committee 'Government by Diktat: A call to return power to Parliament' HL Paper 105 (November 2021).

[134] Jonas Ebbesson, 'The Rule of Law in Governance of Complex Socio-Ecological Changes' (2010) 20 *Global Environmental Change* 414.

[135] Pünder (n 107).

[136] Constitution Committee, 'The Legislative Process: The Delegation of Powers' (House of Lords) 16th Report of Session 2017–2019.

[137] Hewart (n 19) 14. Hewart has more items in his list of criticisms, but these will suffice for now!

Bill in that it primarily confers delegated powers rather than containing operative provisions'.[138] Without operative provisions there is nothing to scrutinise. The ability to scrutinise only then arises when the secondary legislation made under the framework legislation comes before the legislature, and the degree of scrutiny of secondary legislation is poor compared with primary legislation. Lord Judge put it thus: 'no scrutiny during the enactment process, because there is nothing to scrutinise, and as we shall see, effectively no scrutiny when the regulation making powers are exercised'.[139]

Second, there is the loss of democratic legitimacy when important matters are left to administrative decision-making rather than parliamentary debate. Legitimacy is enhanced when legislation is made by the legislature, not by the executive and certainly not by unelected officials. The Dutch Council of State disliked framework laws for this reason, that they don't protect individuals from the Government because they lack substance.[140] The corollary is that the public are more likely to accept a restriction on liberty if it is done by an Act of Parliament rather than by an official sitting at their desk. Third, it diminishes the sovereignty of Parliament and leads to what has been called the 'deparliamentarisation' of legislation.[141] That is to say, parliament being removed from the process of making legislation. Hynes argues for a new constitutional settlement that re-establishes the pre-eminence of Parliament as the sovereign law-making body.[142]

Fourth, there is the lack of legal certainty, in that the individual won't know, from the passage of the framework legislation, what will be the actual content of the secondary legislation. Ebbesson does accept that this conflicts with our notions of the Rule of Law, but is prepared to accept this as a worthwhile trade-off in achieving the goals of a modern and interventionist state.[143] I disagree, there doesn't need to be a trade-off, and the need for flexibility doesn't trump the need for legal certainty.

Fifth, there is the lack of quality in legislation that inevitably happens when there is less time and less scrutiny. Primary legislation goes through line-by-line debate, with time for every possible mistake, every possible loophole to be exposed and then amended. With secondary legislation, that degree of attention to detail is simply not possible. Even worse, there is no process for amending secondary legislation when it is brought to parliament for authorisation, simply a binary option of accept it as a whole, or reject it as a whole.

[138] Delegated and Regulatory Reform Committee, First Report (2015).
[139] Judge (n 132).
[140] Council of State, 'Annual Report' (Council of State 2006). Translated from the Dutch by van Gestel in van Gestel (n 120).
[141] Van Gestel attributes this term to P Kirchhof, 'Entparlamentarisierung Der Demokratie?' in A Kaiser and T Zittel (eds), *Demokratietheorie Und Demokratieentwicklung – Festschrift Für Peter Graf Kielmansegg* (Wiesbaden, Springer, 2004).
[142] Hynes (n 125).
[143] Ebbesson (n 134).

Sixth, and crucially for this chapter on the use of law not discretion, framework legislation delegates too many important decisions and grants too much discretion to officials. As the Delegated Powers and Regulatory Reform Committee recently said, skeleton legislation 'leaves the real operation of legislation to be decided by ministers'.[144] There is most definitely a place for secondary legislation, setting out the details, the technical aspects or the mundane provisions that give effect to what has already been determined by Parliament. But this should not extend to the major policy decisions. Framework legislation has the risk of mis-categorising these as administrative or technical points, with rule-making on these portrayed as merely a bureaucratic exercise, not requiring any discretion. But in practice this can mask important policy questions that should be decided in accordance with the law passed by the legislature, not by the individual and unfettered preferences of an official. Lord Judge criticised 'skeleton bills, in which important policy questions are being left to delegated legislation'.[145]

One particular aspect of this wide discretion is the difficulty then faced by officials in deciding between competing policy aims. An Act of Parliament should make the difficult choices between goals that are in opposition to each other, but with framework legislation, that difficult choice is pushed down the decision chain to officials. Enequist's hypothesis is that 'these goals are concretised by civil servants, without real co-ordination between the different goals, and the norm-addressee has to balance the different interests and goals against each other'.[146] Within the context of framework legislation in the European Union, Weiß makes the same point, that the content of framework laws – 'require immediate democratic legitimation as they imply wide discretion, in particular, the need for political choices and value judgments that weigh conflicting policy aims and interests'.[147]

6.10.4. The European Union Dimension

It is impossible to ignore the European Union dimension in all this. First, at the EU level, much legislation is framework legislation – setting out the broad principles at the level of Regulations and leaving it to delegating and implementing acts to fill out the detail. The Animal Health Law is a good example of this, with the Regulation setting out the general approach, but requiring lots of other legislation to do the heavy lifting of rule-making.[148] Second, at the domestic level in the UK, in many cases Brexit is being implemented by way of framework legislation. Broadly

[144] Delegated Powers and Regulatory Reform Committee 'Democracy denied? The urgent need to rebalance power between Parliament and the Executive' HL Paper 106 (November 2021), para 66.

[145] Judge (n 132).

[146] AW Enequist, 'Framework Legislation in the Welfare State' (Thesis, University of Groningen, 2008).

[147] W Weiß, 'The Future of EU Executive Rulemaking' (2019) 44 *European Law Review* 337, 346.

[148] Regulation (EU) 2016/429.

drafted Bills are enacted granting considerable powers to ministers to make delegated legislation covering what was previously dealt with at the EU level.[149] Third, the arrangements for Brexit include the Northern Ireland Protocol, by which EU framework legislation still needs to be implemented in Northern Ireland.

6.10.5. Ameliorating the Negative Aspects of Framework Legislation

There are a number of form of legislation principles that can ameliorate those aspects of framework laws that undermine the Rule of Law. The following should be seen as supplementing the general form of legislation principles for secondary legislation.

Content of the Framework Legislation

The framework legislation should contain all the important aspects of the regulatory regime within it. The key policy decisions should be taken during the enactment of the framework legislation and those decisions should be explicitly and unequivocally reflected in the framework legislation. If there is to be any scope for making policy decisions in the delegated legislation, that scope should be tightly circumscribed in the framework legislation.[150] This principle is part of the legisprudence of the European Union

> 1. A legislative act may delegate to the Commission the power to adopt non-legislative acts of general application to supplement or amend certain non-essential elements of the legislative act.
>
> The objectives, content, scope and duration of the delegation of power shall be explicitly defined in the legislative acts. The essential elements of an area shall be reserved for the legislative act and accordingly shall not be the subject of a delegation of power.[151]

In the language of the EU, the 'essential elements' of the law should be set out in the primary legislation, leaving the 'non-essential elements' to be set out in the delegated legislation. In the language used in the UK, the 'important' matters should not be left to delegated legislation.[152] Enequist urges legislatures to balance the need for freedom for the executive with control over important points.[153] The decision on what is essential/important will inevitably involve some subjective distinctions. But points that infringe upon fundamental rights and freedoms

[149] Simson Caird and Patterson (n 104).
[150] Constitution Committee 9th Report (HL Paper 69) para 184.
[151] Article 290 Treaty on the Functioning of the European Union.
[152] Judge (n 132).
[153] Enequist (n 129).

should not be delegated, whereas technical or administrative details can be. For example creating new criminal offences should not be left to the secondary legislation, whereas setting the detailed scientific limits for emissions of noxious gases can be. Where fundamental rights are taken away by delegated legislation without this being expressly authorised in the primary legislation, the courts are prepared to strike down that secondary legislation.[154]

This extends to making the policy choices between competing aims. Rather than leaving this to the unfettered discretion of the maker of the secondary legislation, that choice should be made in the primary legislation. For example, there is an ongoing debate in the UK about the merits of airport expansion. On the one hand, it does seem to promote economic growth. But on the other hand, it has a negative effect on climate change. It is clearly an important question to answer, with competing interests and goals. If there is to be framework legislation on this point, then that framework legislation should be clear on the priority of goals, or actually make the decision on whether or not there should be airport expansion. Simply leaving it to a framework law that says 'the minister may by regulations take steps to promote economic growth' and 'the minister may by regulations take steps to prevent climate change' is unacceptable because it is the abdication of decision-making rather than the taking of a decision. Furthermore, having competing goals for the exercise of discretion makes that discretion more rather than less unfettered.

Justification of the Need for Framework Legislation

The need for framework legislation in general, and for each individual enabling provision within it needs to be justified before legislators should enact it. It is unsatisfactory to simply introduce framework legislation into a parliament with the excuse that 'we need it'. That need ought to be evidenced and proven. According to the Delegated Powers and Regulatory Reform Committee

> If a bill is, in effect, a skeleton bill (so that the real operation of the Act would be entirely by the regulations, or orders made under it), or if part of a bill is, in effect, a skeleton part of a bill, the Committee will expect a full justification for the decision to adopt that structure of powers.[155]

The Committee also criticised a 'widely drafted power' and recommended rejecting it unless the Government could provide 'a full and convincing justification as to why is both necessary and appropriate'.[156] 'Flexibility' on its own is not a sufficient justification, there needs to be shown why there is a need for flexibility,

[154] *General Mediterranean Holdings SA v Ramanbhai Manibhai Patel, Kirit Kumar Ramanbhai Patel* [1999] EWHC J0719.
[155] Delegated Powers and Regulatory Reform Committee, 7th Report of Session 2014–15 Special Report: Quality of Delegated Powers Memoranda (HL Paper 39) at para 47.
[156] Delegated Powers and Regulatory Reform Committee, 6th Report (HL Paper 29) at para 51.

for example dealing with rapid technological change or adhering to international treaty obligations.

The Delegated Powers Memorandum, which is meant to accompany any Bill containing the power to make delegated legislation, is a useful vehicle for setting out this information, as well as the information required under the next point. The Cabinet Office mention the importance of this memorandum in their Guide to Making Legislation.[157] The Committee's guidance supplements this and requires the memorandum to identify and explain all instances of delegated powers in primary legislation.[158]

Detailed Extra-statutory Information on How Discretion is Proposed to be Exercised

As well as setting out the justification for framework legislation, those introducing it into the legislature should give detailed information on how it is proposed to use those powers. The more detailed this information is then (a) the more legislators know what they are voting for and (b) the greater the constraints on the exercise of discretion in making the secondary legislation. The same point made in chapter four applies here – if something is important it should be contained in the actual legislation, rather than being extra-statutory.

Greater Scrutiny Procedures for the Secondary Legislation (Legislature)

There should be a greater than normal level of scrutiny of the secondary legislation made under framework legislation than under ordinary legislation. There are two aspects of this. First, there is the structural point, that the framework legislation should set out enhanced scrutiny requirements. For example, rather than the secondary legislation being subject to negative resolution (it becomes law unless the legislature passes a resolution against it), it is subject to affirmative resolution (it becomes law only if the legislature passes a resolution in favour of it). Second, there is the way it is scrutinised in practice. Greater attention should be paid to secondary legislation made under a framework law than would otherwise be the case. Even proponents of framework legislation like Ebbesson argue that there should be greater public participation and more review mechanisms as a safeguard for greater flexibility and adaptability.[159] In the EU context, Weiß argues that we should 'strengthen parliamentary control over executive rulemaking'.[160]

[157] Cabinet Office, *Guide to Making Legislation* (2013).
[158] Delegated Powers and Regulatory Reform Committee, 'Guidance for Departments on the Role and Requirements of the Committee' (House of Lords 2014).
[159] Ebbesson (n 134).
[160] Weiß (n 147) 338.

Unfortunately, arguing in favour of greater scrutiny of secondary legislation is like arguing in favour of measures to restrict climate change – everyone is for it, but no-one really seems to do anything about it.

Greater Scrutiny Procedures for the Secondary Legislation (Judicial)

Judges can and do rule against secondary legislation that is outside the scope of the enabling power. In *R (Public Law Project) v Lord Chancellor* the Supreme Court ruled that the substance of a particular order was nothing to do with the purpose for which the order making power was granted. The court therefore ruled that it was *ultra vires*.[161]

This is not really a form of legislation principle, but secondary legislation made under framework laws ought to be more closely scrutinised by judges than ordinary secondary legislation. Judicial deference towards executive law-making is an entirely separate subject.[162] But as van Gestel argues, judges should be particularly open to scrutinising framework laws. With less control by the legislature over them, there ought to be the counterbalance of more control by the judiciary. This is not a clear-cut point and there are well rehearsed arguments on both sides about judicial deference to executive decisions versus judicial interference with what Justice Whipple called 'a political decision … not a matter for lawyers'.[163]

6.10.6. Example: Fisheries Act 2020

Sections 36 to 42 of the Fisheries Act 2020 are an example of framework legislation. The Secretary of State is granted very broad powers to make secondary legislation for the purposes of implementing international obligations, for a conservation purpose, for a fish industry purpose, or for preventing aquatic animal diseases. This power to make secondary legislation includes:

- Henry VIII powers (see the next section).
- Power to create criminal offences, although not offences for which the sentence is imprisonment.
- Power to impose fees.

The Explanatory Notes describe these as powers 'to make provision on technical matters currently regulated by the EU under the [Common Fisheries Policy]'.[164]

[161] *R (Public Law Project) v Lord Chancellor* [2016] UKSC 39.

[162] For an introduction, see Roland Ismer and Klaus Meßerschmidt, 'Evidence-Based Judicial Review of Legislation: Some Introductory Remarks' (2016) 4 *The Theory and Practice of Legislation* 91.

[163] *Re (on the application of the Motherhood Plan) v HM Treasury* [2021] EWHC 309 (Admin) para 82.

[164] Explanatory Notes, page 28.

The Government prepared a detailed memorandum for the Delegated Powers and Regulatory Reform Committee that explains the use of delegated powers in the Act. It recognised that the Act 'contains a number of broad delegated powers',[165] and has 'sought to balance the need for powers broad enough to allow us to react quickly to changes in the international fisheries management regime and to scientific advice against the need for effective Parliamentary oversight'.[166] An additional reason for dealing with many of these matters in secondary legislation rather than primary legislation is because they are 'highly technical and in the Department's view they are best dealt with in future secondary legislation'.[167]

There are many legislative changes envisaged as being necessary to fisheries law, based on the current rate of legislative change. The government envisages that many of these changes will arise from keeping up to date with new EU law developments (implying that the UK will follow many of these). The volume and pace of legislative change is cited by government as another reason why there needs to be this broad power to make secondary legislation.

Sections 36 to 42 are skeleton provisions – they don't make the law, rather they set out a framework under which the law can be made by secondary legislation. Or, as Lord Hannay put it more eloquently in the Second Reading of the Act

> I suggest that the Fisheries Bill to which we are giving a Second Reading today is no more than a picture frame without a picture. What that picture will be – the detailed shape of Britain's new post-Brexit fisheries policies – remains as shrouded in mystery as ever.[168]

These provisions are of a concern as they may be in breach of the Rule of Law, in particular because of their breadth and because they contain a Henry VIII power. However, the government did make considerable efforts and are to be commended for setting out a highly detailed memorandum explaining and justifying these powers. Although still not an ideal way to legislate, this approach did at least ameliorate some of the negative consequences of framework legislation.

6.11. Constraining the Power to Make Secondary Legislation: Rejecting Henry VIII Clauses

This section considers another particular form of the power to make secondary legislation – the Henry VIII clause. A Henry VIII clause is an enabling clause in primary legislation that grants the power to amend primary legislation by way of secondary legislation. It is a remarkable provision that goes against the normal

[165] Fisheries Bill: Memorandum from the Department for Environment, Food and Rural Affairs to the Delegated Powers and Regulatory Reform Committee, page 5.

[166] ibid.

[167] ibid.

[168] Lord Hannay of Chiswick, HL Deb 11 February 2020 Vol 801 col 1276.

conception of the separation of powers. Only the legislature can make primary legislation, but a Henry VIII clause allows the Executive to usurp this power and make primary legislation itself. For example, Regulations made under the Childcare Act 2016 may 'amend, repeal or revoke any provision made by or under an Act (whenever passed or made)'.[169]

The Henry VIII is named after King Henry VIII who sought the power to make laws as if he himself were Parliament. In his Statute of Proclamations 1539 it states:

> Be it therefore enacted … that always the king for the time being, with the advice of his honourable council, whose names hereafter followeth, or with the advice of the more part of them, may set forth at all times by authority of this act his proclamations, under such penalties and pains and of such sort as to his highness and his said honourable council or the more part of them shall see[m] necessary and requisite; and that those same shall be obeyed, observed, and kept as though they were made by act of parliament.[170]

Henry VIII sought to rule by way of proclamations, which were to have the same effect as an Act of Parliament.

As well as being objectionable for undermining the sovereignty of Parliament, they are objectionable from a Rule of Law perspective because they are the opposite of law not discretion. They literally give an official the discretion to rewrite the law. They are the subject of criticism by the Hansard Society,[171] legislators[172] and judges, with Lord Judge describing them as 'extraordinary'.[173]

Henry VIII clauses are becoming more and more common. They are often included alongside, or incorporated into, framework legislation and super-enabling powers. This can give rise to a Frankenstein's monster of a super-enabling power, in framework legislation, which allows an official to rewrite current and future Acts of Parliament. Kouroutakis cites their use in connection with Brexit and argues that in extra-ordinary situations such as this, there use is justified, provided that there are adequate safeguards.[174]

The argument is sometimes made that Henry VIII clauses are necessary in order to make the necessary amendments that are consequential upon a new Act. So, if a new Act requires lots of technical and non-contentious changes to the rest of the statute book, the argument goes that a 'sweeper' Henry VIII clause should be inserted to make sure all those necessary changes are made subsequent to the passing of the Act. As a general principle, this is wrong. If consequential amendments are necessary, they should be included when the Act is made, for example

[169] s 4(2)(d) Childcare Act 2016.

[170] Statute of Proclamations, Henry 8, c.8

[171] R Fox and J Blackwell, 'The Devil Is in the Detail: Parliament and Delegated Legislation' (Hansard Society 2013).

[172] Many parliamentary words are devoted to objecting to them, as recorded in Simson Caird, Hazell and Oliver (n 105); Simson Caird and Patterson (n 104).

[173] Judge (n 132).

[174] Kouroutakis (n 38).

in a schedule of consequential amendments. If those consequential amendments have not all been prepared, then the Act is not ready to be enacted and should be delayed until all the consequential amendments have been drafted. This has been the historical practice, to prepare a detailed list of consequential amendments that are part of the Act, and which can then take effect by way of primary legislation.

It is conceivable that in extreme cases, there would be a need for a Henry VIII clause, as a 'just in case' precaution to catch some overlooked consequential amendments. Perhaps a good example of this is in the Civil Partnership Act 2004. That was the Act that established a new legal form of relationship for same-sex couples known as the civil partnership. There was a huge amount of consequential legislative change necessary, essentially to add 'or civil partnership' to every entry in the statute book referring to 'marriage', together with more detailed provisions to ensure that civil partners were treated in the same way as marriage partners. That Act contained a stupendous number of consequential amendments in a number of schedules to it. But it also contained a Henry VIII clause allowing a minister to make further provision (including supplementary, incidental or consequential provisions), and that provision could amend primary legislation passed before the end of the session in which the Civil Partnership Act was passed.[175] Given the huge volume of consequential amendments necessary, and the consequences of failing to pick one up, it did make sense in those circumstances to have a back-up power to make further amendments.

Kouroutakis has argued that the use of Henry VIII clauses is justified, but ought to be subject to additional safeguards: the use of sunset clauses, greater parliamentary oversight, more searching judicial review, political safeguards and enhanced legal safeguards.[176] Although these would all be helpful, in my view the form of legislation principle here is that Henry VIII clauses should generally be rejected, save in exceptional circumstances. This was also the conclusion reached by the Constitution Committee of the House of Lords.[177]

Conclusion

Fixed, clear and certain rules are of less value if the way in which decision-makers apply these rules is unpredictable. This unpredictability can arise if there are no constraints on the exercise of discretion by these decision-makers, if they have the latitude to ignore rules, or to apply them in a capricious fashion. The Rule of Law requires that we are governed in accordance with law, not discretion. To put this another way, that rationality, proportionality and consistency are built-in to the process, rather than simply having a system where officials decide in accordance

[175] s 259, Civil Partnership Act 2004.
[176] Kouroutakis (n 38).
[177] Constitution Committee (n 136) 19.

with their personal preferences. This does not mean that there should be the absence of discretion – a degree of flexibility is necessary in a modern administrative system. But it does mean that there are safeguards or boundaries set out in that system.

The way in which legislation is framed can help set boundaries on this exercise of discretion. There ought to be a clear demarcation between what is a simple matter of application of criteria to an outcome, and when there is a degree of choice or discretion on the part of the official. This can be as simple as the law stating when an official *may* do something and when they *must* do something.

There are six different dimensions in which a discretion can be constrained. First, there is the purpose for which a power can be exercised (rather than simply an unconstrained power to do something). Second, there is the height of the hurdle to be overcome before a power can be exercised, that is, how difficult it is for an official to exercise a discretionary power. Third, the specificity of the things that may be done. So instead of a broad power to do anything, there is a granular power to do specified and enumerated things. Fourth, there are additional factors or criteria that the decision-maker must consider before exercising discretion. Fifth, there can be a requirement for proportionality or some causal connection between the power and the purpose for which it must be exercised. Sixth, there can be established additional non-statutory guides or constraints that guide the exercise of that power.

There are then certain specific types of clauses that can be included (or excluded) from legislation in order to promote law not discretion. The most obvious candidate for exclusion is the ouster clause – a clause which ousts the jurisdiction of the courts. If the decision of an official cannot be questioned in a court, it substantially increases the chances of that decision being exercised in a capricious way. It is difficult to see situations in which ouster clauses are in accordance with the Rule of Law. Similar to the ouster clause, but of less concern from a Rule of Law perspective, are clauses in legislation that grant officials the powers to create exemptions from the law. There is less certainty in rules if an official can use a statutory power to create an exemption from those rules. This risks being an unwarranted extension of discretion and is open to abuse.

Purpose clauses, on the other hand, are clauses that can promote the Rule of Law as they give legislative authority to limiting the purposes for which powers may be exercised. A purpose clause sets out the purpose of a particular piece of legislation, and in doing so act as a constraint on how powers set out in that legislation may be exercised.

The final area in which the form of legislation can enhance the law not discretion principle is when it comes to the power to make secondary legislation. The power to make secondary legislation is itself in the nature of a discretionary power. Even the most ardent supporters of government would accept that parliamentary scrutiny of secondary legislation is not always detailed or considered enough. In order to promote the Rule of Law, powers to make secondary legislation ought to contain constraints, boundaries and limitations of the kind that apply to other official powers. Narrow powers, for particular purposes, and subject to specific restrictions are to be preferred over broad and general powers to make secondary legislation. One particularly worrisome practice is the super-enabling clause. This is now regularly inserted into legislation as a kind of sweeper clause, granting ministers the power to make regulations to 'give effect' to an Act. This grants huge legislative discretion to the minister, rather than actually setting out the details of the law in the Act. The other worrying development is framework legislation, where an Act will not set out the details, but merely a framework, leaving it to subsequent secondary legislation to fill in those details. The use of framework legislation ought to be curtailed as it too undermines the Rule of Law. Saving the worst for last is the Henry VIII clause, which gives ministers the power, by way of secondary legislation, to amend or repeal primary legislation. This literally gives ministers the power to get rid of the law. Their use is anathema to law not discretion as a Rule of Law principle.

7

Equality before the Law

Introduction

The Rule of Law requires that we are all treated equally before the law. This means that no one should be discriminated against on the basis of their background, and that we all have equal access to legal rights and protections. Legislation has a mixed relationship with the equality principle. Historically, legislation was used as an instrument of inequality, with legally imposed restrictions on certain classes of people. This has changed, with legislation increasingly being used to ban discrimination and promote equality of opportunity.

In Part 1 I briefly examine the theory of equality before the law as a Rule of Law concept. In Part 2 I derive form of legislation principles to give effect to equality before the law. One of the most obvious and long-running issues is how the language of law treats women. Equality before the law requires the use of non-gendered legislation, that is that legislation must not be written solely in terms of the male gender. This leads on to the more general point that offensive or discriminatory language is not acceptable in legislation, even where it is an historical throwback. In terms of the processes for making legislation, equality impact assessments or gender impact assessments are one tool for ensuring equality in the content of legislation. Vindicability means that rights contained within the law are capable of being used by all sections of society. Intelligibility is a form of legislation principle in its own right, but under the rubric of equality, intelligibility also includes the requirement that all should equally be able to understand the law. I then consider two particular sub-types of legislation that give rise to specific issues around equality before the law: legislation that affects the Crown and legislation that affects the armed forces.

Part 1: The Theory of Equality before the Law

7.1. The Meaning of Equality before the Law

Tom Bingham stated that 'The laws of the land should apply equally to all, save to the extent that objective differences justify differentiation'.[1] This is summed up in

[1] T Bingham, *The Rule of Law* (Penguin UK 2011) 55.

the Rule of Law principle that we are all equal under the law, or that there is equality before the law. This flows from the principle of legality, that prescribes that we are all subject to the law. For Dicey

> it means, again, equality before the law, or the equal subjection of all classes to the ordinary law of the land administered by the ordinary law courts; the 'rule of law' in this sense excludes the idea of any exemption of official or others from the duty of obedience to the law which governs other citizens or from the jurisdiction of the ordinary tribunals.[2]

It means that, in law, there is no hierarchy between citizens from different backgrounds, but that we should all be treated the same, from the highest in the land to the lowest, from the richest to the poorest. Equality means that we treat similar situations in the same way, and different situations differently.[3] Interestingly, although equality could be seen as implicit in Fuller's argument for laws that apply generally, it is not explicit in his desiderata of good law. As a writer with a 'thin' conception of the Rule of Law, Raz does not include equality as a component of the Rule of Law. However, the Venice Commission includes equality before the law and non-discrimination in four separate Rule of Law benchmarks.[4]

This ought to be an uncontroversial principle in a modern society. Equality ought to be a bedrock principle that no-one is born 'better' than anyone else. But sadly, if we look around the world, this does not hold true. Some theocratic regimes simply do not accept that women are the equal of men. The rise of the Taliban in Afghanistan demonstrates a mindset that deems it acceptable to force women from the public sphere. Rampant and officially supported homophobia in some European countries demonstrates the same disdain for equality.[5] Most countries around the world will have a discriminated-against minority group who are not treated on a par with the majority. Lest we think the United Kingdom is blameless in this regard, in the last century we created a state in Northern Ireland where Lord Craigavon, its first Prime Minister after saying that he treated all citizens equally, also felt free to say 'all I boast is that we are a Protestant Parliament and a Protestant state'.[6]

Having said that, the historical trajectory in the United Kingdom is towards equality. Although discrimination clearly still happens, it is no longer lawful. Huge strides have been made towards securing legislative equality between men and women, for people of different sexual orientation, religious and ethnic backgrounds, for people with disabilities etc. The open and blatant discrimination that used to exist is no longer in accordance with the law in the UK. There is still some distance to go, but law and society, in general, accept the principle of equality.

[2] AV Dicey, *An Introduction to the Study of the Law of the Constitution* (1885).

[3] Venice Commission, 'Report on the Rule of Law' (2011) 31.

[4] ibid.

[5] 'EU LGBTI Survey II A Long Way to Go for LGBTI Equality: Country Data – Hungary' (European Union Agency for Fundamental Rights 2020) <https://fra.europa.eu/sites/default/files/fra_uploads/lgbti-survey-country-data_hungary.pdf>.

[6] Official Report of Debates, Parliament of Northern Ireland, Volume 16, (1933–1934) Col 1095.

7.1.1. Direct and Indirect Discrimination

Without seeking to open a semantic can of worms, discrimination can be seen as the opposite of equality. To discriminate is to not treat someone equally. Discrimination can be direct, where two people in the same position are treated differently. For example, there are two candidates for a job, but the Muslim candidate is rejected on the basis of their religion. Discrimination can also be indirect, where there is a failure to treat differently persons whose situation is different. For example, a job requirement apparently applies equally to all applicants, but women will find the requirement significantly more difficult to comply with than men.

7.1.2. Objective Justification for Differential Treatment

Equality before the law does not demand that everyone always be treated in the same way. Differential treatment is acceptable if there is objective justification for it. So the general rule is that no-one should be put in prison. But if a person commits a crime, then there is an objective justification for treating that person differently from the general populace and jailing them. Everyone is entitled to vote, but there is objective justification for not letting children vote as they may not have the political maturity or capacity to understand the consequences of their vote. The question of what is an objective justification for differential treatment is a vast one and beyond the scope of this book. The very briefest summary is that this objective justification exists if there is a legitimate aim for pursuing differential treatment, and the means employed to achieve that aim are proportionate.[7]

7.2. The Chequered History of Legislation and Equality

As the focus of this book is on the form of legislation, it is appropriate to look at the interaction of legislation with the equality principle. It is a chequered history. Three distinct but overlapping phases can be discerned.

7.2.1. Legislation Permitting and Entrenching Inequality

Historically, legislation was used as an instrument of state to perpetuate and entrench inequality. In Ireland, the penal laws were enacted to prevent Roman Catholics from voting, standing for election, becoming members of the legal profession, buying land on a lease of more than 31 years, along with many other

[7] *Ghaidan v Godin-Mendoza* [2004] UKHL 30.

prohibitions.[8] Similar bans and prohibitions were imposed upon Presbyterians. In England, legislation was used to discriminate against Jews,[9] leading eventually to the Edict of Expulsion 1290 by which all Jews were expelled from England. Electoral legislation was used to ensure that only property holding men were allowed to vote. Even the advances made by the Great Reform Act 1832 discriminated blatantly against both women and non-property owners in terms of the right to vote:

> Be it enacted, that every male person of full age … who shall be seised at law or in equity of any lands … of the clear yearly value of not less than ten pounds … shall be entitled to vote …[10]

Even when legislation, such as the Solicitors Act 1843, ostensibly applied equally to men and women, it was held by the courts that this legislation did not remove the 'general disability' of women that prevented them from being solicitors.[11]

The key point in this phase is that law and legislation were used to actively promote discrimination and inequality. Discrimination against women, the poor, religious groups, ethnic minorities etc. was legitimised by being done through the instrument of law. This is a classic example of rule by law, rather than the Rule of Law.

7.2.2. Legislation Prohibiting Discrimination

The second phase is when legislation begins to be used as a tool for ending discrimination, and removing the historic restrictions and prohibitions faced by certain classes of person. The Roman Catholic Relief Act 1829 removed most of the legal restrictions on Catholics holding certain jobs, or being elected to parliament. The Jews Relief Act 1858 did the same for Jews (although Cromwell had centuries earlier repealed the Edict of Expulsion and welcomed Jews back to England).

Interestingly, some of the prohibitions contained in these Acts from the first phase are still in force. There is still a law on the statute books that no Roman Catholic may 'hold or exercise the office of guardians and justices of the United Kingdom, or of regent of the United Kingdom … the office of lord high chancellor, lord keeper or lord commissioner of the great seal of Great Britain'.[12] There has been doubt over the effectiveness of this provision.[13] That provision has now

[8] J Bardon, *A History of Ulster* (Newtownards, The Blackstaff Press, 2001) 168. It is difficult to track down all the legislation doing this as it has now all been repealed, but for example see Education Act 1695, Banishment Act 1697, Popery Act 1704.

[9] Statute of Jewry 1253.

[10] s XIX, Representation of the People Act 1832.

[11] *Bebb v Law Society* [1913] EWHC 1.

[12] s 12 Roman Catholic Relief Act 1829.

[13] Hansard HL Deb 11 June 1974 Vol 353 col 415 to 433.

been superseded (although not repealed) by the Lord Chancellor (Tenure of Office and Discharge of Ecclesiastical Functions) Act 1974. Section 1 of that Act states that, for the avoidance of doubt, Roman Catholics can hold the office of Lord Chancellor. As Rozenberg has pointed out, it is still the law that no Roman Catholic can advise on appointment to offices in the Church of England or Church of Scotland.[14] It also remains a crime for a Jew to advise the Crown, directly or indirectly, on appointment to offices in the Church of England or the Church of Scotland.[15] If a Cabinet Minister were to do this, they would, by law, be 'disabled for ever from holding any office, civil or military, under the Crown'.[16]

Although the Great Reform Act 1832 cited above did discriminate against women and the poor, it did at least widen the franchise and granted many more people the right to vote than was previously the case. Subsequent pieces of electoral law widened the franchise and ended its clearly discriminatory terms so that the universal right to vote was eventually granted. The Slavery Abolition Act 1833 abolished slavery in no uncertain terms, 'and slavery shall be and is hereby utterly and for ever abolished and declared unlawful throughout the British colonies, plantations and possessions abroad'.[17]

In the modern era, there are a plethora of statutes all banning discrimination on various grounds. The Race Relations Act 1965 was enacted to 'prohibit discrimination on racial grounds in places of public resort, to prevent the enforcement or imposition on racial grounds of restrictions on the transfer of tenancies'.[18] And this was followed by further legislation widening the prohibition on discrimination.[19] The Sex Discrimination Act 1975 made certain kinds of discrimination on the grounds of sex unlawful. The Disability Discrimination Act 1995 made similar provision in relation to discrimination on the grounds of disability. These individual statutes against discrimination were rolled up into the Equality Acts 2006 and 2010. Those Acts sought to harmonise the treatment of discrimination at law, covering what are now regarded as the standard 'protected characteristics' of age, disability, gender, marital status, race, religion or belief, sex and sexual orientation.[20]

Northern Ireland is a particularly interesting case study for the use of legislation to promote equality. Historically, it had high levels of religious and political discrimination. Legislation has been the tool of choice to redress these issues and

[14] Joshua Rozenberg, 'Boris Can No Longer Pick Bishops' (*A Lawyer Writes*, 30 May 2021) <https://rozenberg.substack.com/p/boris-can-no-longer-pick-bishops>. See also s 18, Roman Catholic Relief Act 1829.

[15] s 4, Jews Relief Act 1858.

[16] s 4, ibid.

[17] s 12, Slavery Abolition Act 1833. The courts had previously declared that slavery was not known to the law in England, *Somersett* (1772) 20 State Tr 1.

[18] Long title, Race Relations Act 1965.

[19] Race Relations Act 1968, Race Relations Act 1976.

[20] Part 2, Equality Act 2010.

achieve equality.[21] Equality in political structures was effected by the Northern Ireland Act 1998 and its power-sharing structures for government. Discrimination in the electoral system was outlawed by several pieces of legislation modifying electoral law. Diversity in policing was sought by temporarily amending the Police (Northern Ireland) Act 2000. The proposed method of ending discrimination against the Irish language, and promoting the Ulster Scots language is an Irish Language Bill (not yet introduced). Discrimination on the basis of religion and political belief in the employment context followed the UK model in various pieces of Fair Employment legislation, for example the Fair Employment and Treatment (Northern Ireland) Order 1998.

The key point in this phase is that legislation is used as a tool to prohibit individual acts of discrimination across a range of fields. To discriminate is to act unlawfully.

7.2.3. Legislation Promoting and Advancing Equality

The third phase of legislative intervention in respect of equality moves from prohibiting individuals from discriminating, to imposing a positive duty upon the state to actively promote equality. Rather than seeing discrimination as a problem caused by individuals, it instead sees it as more of a systemic or institutional problem that requires active engagement by the state. Instead of reacting and prohibiting discrimination, there is instead a positive duty for state institutions to proactively do something in order to achieve full equality for all sections of the community. This approach avoids the problems that Olatokun diagnoses with construing discrimination as 'agentic decisions by malignant individuals, emphasising the moral responsibility of outliers, rather than looking at the collective burden of discrimination'.[22]

This new statutory approach can best be seen in what has become known as the Public Sector Equality Duty. That duty states that

> (1) A public authority must, in the exercise of its functions, have due regard to the need to—
>
> (a) eliminate discrimination, harassment, victimisation and any other conduct that is prohibited by or under this Act;
>
> (b) advance equality of opportunity between persons who share a relevant protected characteristic and persons who do not share it;
>
> (c) foster good relations between persons who share a relevant protected characteristic and persons who do not share it.[23]

[21] R Cormacain, 'Promoting (Religious and Political) Diversity through Legislation in Northern Ireland' (2021) 9 *Theory and Practice of Legislation* 59.

[22] M Olatokun, 'Does the Law Think That Black Lives Matter? A Reflection upon the Role of the Public Sector Equality Duty in Promoting Racial Equality before the Law' (2021) 9 *Theory and Practice of Legislation* 83.

[23] s 149(1), Equality Act 2010.

With its special circumstances, it should be no surprise that Northern Ireland led the way with this obligation to promote equality of opportunity. From a key law in 1998:

> (1) A public authority shall in carrying out its functions relating to Northern Ireland have due regard to the need to promote equality of opportunity—
> (a) between persons of different religious belief, political opinion, racial group, age, marital status or sexual orientation;
> (b) between men and women generally;
> (c) between persons with a disability and persons without; and
> (d) between persons with dependants and persons without.[24]

Olatokun was clear that this new approach of promoting equality worked – 'a duty imposed by legislation upon public authorities was having a concrete effect in changing outcomes'.[25] There is however a difference between the obligation to 'have regard to' a particular aim, and the obligation to 'achieve' that aim.[26] The goal of equality is but one goal for the decision maker to weigh up in making a decision.[27] This distinction led Olatokun to call it a moderate step in the right direction.[28]

This phase encapsulates both the state having positive obligations with regards to its own activities and a positive duty to intervene in the private sector. Vuković argues for a 'proactive, state-led approach' when it comes to the imposition of gender quotas in corporate decision-making bodies.[29]

The key point here is that legislation creates a positive duty to do something, rather than a negative duty to avoid doing something.

Part 2: Form of Legislation Principles for Equality before the Law

7.3. Non-gendered Legislation

Do women exist? And if they do exist, are they persons? The answers to these questions are so self-evidently both 'yes', that it seems almost like trolling to ask them. However, the historic answer to both these questions is 'well, sort of, it depends'. Thus Blackstone was able to write, in 1765 that

> By marriage, the husband and wife are one person in law: that is, the very being or legal existence of the woman is suspended during the marriage, or at least is incorporated and consolidated into that of the husband.[30]

[24] s 75(1), Northern Ireland Act 1998.
[25] Olatokun (n 22) 88.
[26] *Baker v Secretary of State for Communities* [2008] EWCA Civ 141.
[27] *R (Bracking) v Secretary of State for Work and Pensions* [2013] EWCA Civ 1345.
[28] Olatokun (n 22) 92.
[29] A Horvat Vuković, 'Gender Quotas in Corporate Decision-Making Bodies – Regulatory Promotion of Equality of Results in the EU' (2021) 9 *Theory and Practice of Legislation* 3.
[30] W Blackstone, *Commentaries on the Laws of England in Four Books* (1765).

Gendered legislation, as will be seen, can lead to both direct and indirect discrimination against women. If the female gender does not exist in law, it means that no account need to be taken of women in legislation.

7.3.1. The Problems with Gendered Legislation

Historically, legislation referred only to the male gender. Pronouns were nearly always male pronouns. For example,

> (3) It shall be a defence for a person charged with an offence under subsection (1) or (2) above to prove that *he* had good reason or lawful authority for having the article or weapon with *him* on the premises in question.[31]

Williams shows that sexist language 'based upon the premise that the norm of humanity is male' has been around for 150 years in English language legislation.[32] Up until around the start of the twenty-first century, the form of legislation was structured around the male gender. Human beings were referred to as 'persons' but beyond this, all pronouns were male only (he/him/his/himself) and gendered nouns were used (chairman[33]/policeman[34]/medical man[35]). It was as if there was no female gender, women didn't exist in law, and legislation was constructed with only men in mind.

Grabham explains how this way of writing statutes both draws on, and creates, powerful sex and gender norms.[36] Mary Beard has written very eloquently about the consequences of the absence of half the population from the public sphere, saying that 'if women aren't perceived to be within the structures of power, isn't it power that we need to redefine?'.[37] Applying this to law, Hill argued that it was 'intellectually dishonest to pretend of aspirations to include all members of a society as equal participants absent the use of language that eliminates inappropriate gender implications'.[38] Focusing specifically on gendered legislation, the Attorney General of Australia said that it 'implies that personality is really a male attribute, and that women are a sub-species'.[39]

Even when legislation was expressed in non-gendered language, for example using 'persons', the courts still did not always respect the equality principle. Perhaps

[31] s 139A, Criminal Justice Act 1988, my emphasis.

[32] C Williams, 'The End of the "Masculine Rule"? Gender-Neutral Legislative Drafting in the United Kingdom and Ireland' (2008) 29 *Statute Law Review* 139, 139.

[33] s 3, Local Government Act 1972.

[34] Reg A18(1), Police Pensions Regulations 1987.

[35] s 26, Regulation of Railways Act 1868.

[36] E Grabham, 'Exploring the Textual Alchemy of Legal Gender: Experimental Statutes and the Message in the Medium' (2020) 10 *feminists@law*.

[37] M Beard, *Women & Power: A Manifesto* (Main edition, London, Profile Books, 2017).

[38] W Hill, 'A Need for Non-Sexist Language in the Courts' (1992) 49 *Washington and Lee Law Review* 275, 276.

[39] Commentary, 'Avoidance of Sexist Language in Legislation' (1985) 11 *Commonwealth Law Bulletin* 590.

most famous was the case of Ms Bebb who wished to become a solicitor and in 1913 informed the Law Society that she would present herself for the exam. She was told this was not possible as she was a woman. Despite the Solicitors Act 1843 stating that a person could become a solicitor, and despite its interpretation section saying that references to the masculine were to also include references to the feminine, the court in *Bebb v Law Society* ruled she was not eligible to become a solicitor.[40] Although the judgment could be charitably viewed in terms of judges not wanting to change the law without the express assent of Parliament, the bottom line was still that a woman was not to be regarded as a person for the purposes of the Solicitors Act.

7.3.2. Interpretation Act Approaches

There are at least four different approaches in interpretation legislation dealing with the issue of gender, as identified by Petersson.[41]

Masculine Rule

The masculine rule states that a reference in legislation to the male gender includes a reference to the female gender. Thus, in the Interpretation Act (Northern Ireland) 1954:

> (1) Words in an enactment importing (whether in relation to an offence or otherwise) persons or male persons shall include male and female persons, corporations (whether aggregate or sole) and unincorporated bodies of persons.[42]

This at least makes it clear that women are subject to the rights and duties set out in legislation to the same extent as men. In theory, this at least makes the law nominally equal as it does apply to both men and women. However, in terms of the form of legislation, it is unequal as the female gender is completely absent from legislation. Legislation is conceived and constructed as a male only space.

Two Way Rule

References to male include references to female, and references to female include references to male. Thus, in England and Wales, in the Interpretation Act 1978

> In any Act, unless the contrary intention appears,—
> (a) words importing the masculine gender include the feminine;
> (b) words importing the feminine gender include the masculine …[43]

[40] *Bebb v Law Society* [1913] EWHC 1.
[41] S Petersson, 'Gender Neutral Drafting: Recent Commonwealth Developments' (1990) 20 *Statute Law Review* 35; S Petersson, 'Gender Neutral Drafting: Historical Perspective' (1998) 19 *Statute Law Review* 93.
[42] s 37, Interpretation Act (NI) 1954.
[43] s 6, Interpretation Act 1978 (applying in England and Wales).

This is, on the face of it, a better approach to equality. In theory men and women are being treated the same as a reference to one will be construed as a reference to the other. However, this is legislative window-dressing. I am not aware of any UK legislation that uses the female gender as a way to include the male gender. This approach is ornamental – legislation is still framed solely by reference to the male gender.

All Gender Rule

Under this approach, any word that connotes gender includes all genders. This rule avoids specifying any genders, so steps closer towards proper equality. In Australia

> In any Act:
> (a) words importing a gender include every other gender …[44]

Wales has stepped further than England and Northern Ireland in this regard in its interpretation provisions:

> In an Act of Senedd Cymru or a Welsh subordinate instrument, words denoting persons of a particular gender are not to be read as limited to persons of that gender.[45]

The Welsh example is even more inclusive as it is wide enough to cover not just 'every other gender' but those who do not wish to identify as having a gender. The explanatory notes to the Welsh Act make a point of noting that this goes beyond male and female genders.

Although this is helpful, it can still lead to gendered legislation referring to men and using male pronouns only. In practice, the pronouns can still be male only and the commitment to equality only skin deep. What matters more than a single interpretation act is how legislation generally deals with references to gender.

No Gender Rule

The most radical approach is the opposite of all the above approaches. It is the no gender rule. This rule states that

> In any Act
> (a) words importing the masculine gender do not include the feminine gender,
> (b) words importing the feminine gender do not include the masculine gender …

If this rule were adopted, it would mean that any legislative provision that used male pronouns would only apply to males. It is very much a nuclear option, but it would force the adoption of gender neutral drafting.

[44] s 23, Acts Interpretation Act 1901 (Commonwealth Consolidated Acts).
[45] s 8, Legislation (Wales) Act 2019.

7.3.3. Gender Neutral Drafting

Gendered legislation, by which I mean legislation that is expressed solely in terms of the male gender, undermines the equality principle. Gendered legislation creates an ontology based upon the male actor, or the male legal being. The solution is gender neutral drafting – legislation that applies in form as well as in substance, to all genders. Using gender neutral language creates an additional layer on top of legislation, communicating something else than just the subject matter of that legislation. As such it is a meta-concept – as well as saying that a person must not do X, it also at the same time says that a woman is also a person. Meta-messages in law should not be seen as revolutionary – the old meta-message was that only men had legal personality.

There are many different techniques of gender neutral drafting, as set out below. Some are more elegant than others. The key principle is simple – to use gender neutral language, that is, to avoid specifying a particular gender.

Person, Not Man

Instead of referring to 'a man' or 'men', refer to 'person' or 'persons', or just avoid the use of male words. Even *Star Trek* managed to change its opening voice over from 'to boldly go where no man has gone before' (original *Star Trek* series) to 'to boldly go where no one has gone before' (*Star Trek: The Next Generation*). Glossing over the split infinitive, this is a good example of gender neutral language. Thankfully, the use of 'person' rather than 'man' has long been prevalent in UK legislation. The reason is probably more utility than gender neutral awareness – 'person' can include legal entities such as corporations as well as human beings. But the net result still favours equality.

Double Up Pronouns

Instead of just 'he' use 'he or she'. For example, 'Where a person does X, he or she is guilty of an offence'. This can however become quite long-winded if the pronoun has to be repeated multiple times. It is cumbersome and is best avoided. Probably the only time that this is justified is with reflexive pronouns (for example, himself). It is difficult to make a reflexive pronoun gender neutral without simply doubling up that pronoun. For example, 'a person who is 16 or over lacks capacity in relation to a matter if, at the material time, the person is unable to make a decision for himself or herself about the matter'.[46] As the point is about the person's ability to make decisions in relation to the person, one of the only ways to make it gender neutral is to double up with himself or herself.

[46] s 3(1), Mental Capacity Act (Northern Ireland) 2016.

Repeat the Noun

Instead of using a gendered pronoun, simply repeat the noun. For example, instead of a member resigning his office, 'A member of the Tribunal may resign the office of member'. This can become unwieldy if the noun is a long one.

Create New, Shortened Noun

Replace the noun with a new shortened noun, or with a letter, and then repeat that shortened one. For example,

> (1) A person (D) commits an offence if—
>
> (a) D holds any person in slavery or servitude and the circumstances are such that D knows or ought to know that the person is so held ...[47]

This can be helpful if the noun is a long or complicated one. So, if the noun was 'the director of an insolvent company', it would actually shorten the provision to use D rather than repeat that entire phrase. Shortened nouns are also helpful if there are multiple persons referred to in a provision. These can be shortened to A and B, rather than 'the first person' and 'the second person'.

Use Plurals

If a plural is used, the pronoun will be automatically gender neutral. In English, they, their and themselves are all gender neutral. For example,

> (1) Members of the public seeking to attend proceedings of the Assembly shall be permitted in such places reserved for them by the Speaker save that –
>
> (a) they are not permitted in the Public Gallery during Prayers ...[48]

Using plurals can create uncertainty though, as it can sometimes imply that the condition only applies if multiple persons are doing it, rather than just a single person. For example, if 'persons are guilty of an offence if they do X', does this mean that the offence is only committed if two or more persons are doing X?

Singular Nouns, Plural Pronouns

The English language lacks a third person singular gender neutral pronoun (he or she). Only when it comes to third person plural do we have gender neutral pronouns (they). But like water finding its way downhill, language finds a way through. The lack of a second person plural pronoun (you) has not prevented people in Northern Ireland creating 'youse' or 'youse-uns' (you ones, meaning you

[47] s 71, Coroners and Justice Act 2009.
[48] Standing Order 66(1), Standing Orders of the Northern Ireland Assembly.

plural, other dialects may have produced similar solutions). The same evolution of language to match need can be seen in the common use of the third person plural 'they' when we are referring to a third person singular noun – 'I saw the person who did that, they went that way'.

On balance (and with apologies to linguists more fully engaged in this debate), it is probably grammatically wrong to combine a singular noun with a plural pronoun – 'a person' does not correlate with 'they'. In the past, I have railed against grammatically incorrect language in legislation, for example

> *A member* shall not be eligible for nomination as a chairperson of a standing committee if at the date of such nomination *they* are a chairperson of another standing committee or a statutory committee.[49]

I have now changed my mind. As Xanthaki has pointed out, grammar is a tool, not a chain.[50] What she means is that it is there as an aid to communication and to serve the values that the law seeks to transmit, not that it dictates exactly what is said in that law, or how it is framed. Revell and Vapnak argue that breaches of the rules of grammar 'pale in comparison with the harms done by non-inclusive language'.[51] Going back to Orwell's rules on writing – we should break any rule rather than say something barbarous.[52] Evidence from Grabham suggests that the drafting community are increasingly open to the use of 'they' as singular.[53] Provided that there is no risk of misunderstanding, grammatical infelicity is a price worth paying for promoting equality before the law.

Convert Noun to Verb Form

Rather than saying that a person may give his consent, say 'A person may consent'. This may require some re-ordering of the syntax of a sentence, but it is not particularly difficult to do, and shouldn't affect the meaning of the sentence if done carefully.

Use Non-gendered Nouns

There is no reason now to use gendered nouns like chairman or policeman when there are lots of acceptable alternatives like chairperson or police officer. Language ossifies if we demand the retention of existing terms and resist the introduction of new ones. Legislation has the power to force social change; in fact, the primary purpose of nearly all legislation is to effect some sort of legal or social change. So if legislation still requires the appointment of a chairman, then chairman will be the

[49] Standing Order 51(10), ibid.

[50] GC Thornton and H Xanthaki, *Thornton's Legislative Drafting* (London, Bloomsbury Professional, 2013).

[51] D Revell and J Vapnek, 'Gender-Silent Legislative Drafting in a Non-Binary World' (2020) 48 *Capital University Law Review* 103, 127.

[52] G Orwell, *Politics and the English Language* (London, Penguin, 2013).

[53] Grabham (n 36).

legally correct term. But if the legislation speaks of a chairperson, then that will be the legally correct term and there will be no justification for using outdated, sexist terms. Although there will inevitably be some inertia in dealing with the old term, the officially mandated new term will change social usage very quickly. Furthermore, there is the symbolic impact of the legislature's official recognition that chairman does not represent everyone.

Words in a foreign language may prove more challenging to change. For example, the Swedish word ombudsman is seen by some as being gender neutral, even though the etymology of the word indicates that it is a gendered term. When originally introduced into the Northern Ireland Assembly, one Bill was entitled the Public Services Ombudsperson Bill, before eventually being amended to Ombudsman during its passage through the Assembly.[54]

Use Relative Clauses

Wrap up a term into a relative clause, rather than separating it into two separate clauses. So instead of 'Where a person sells a house, he must not', use 'A person who sells a house must not'.

Use Definite/Indefinite Articles Instead of Personal Pronouns

The context will generally relate the noun to the person, without having to use a personal pronoun to relate it to the person. So instead of 'his firearm' use 'A/the firearm'.

Other Techniques

The Office of the Parliamentary Counsel have issued very sensible advice on gender neutral drafting that includes these techniques listed above as well as others.[55] Interestingly, they dislike the practice of replacing the noun with a letter, arguing that it does not reflect normal English usage, and that it should generally be avoided.

Dealing with Historic Gendered Legislation

Proceeding on the basis that gender neutral language ought to be used, how then are we to cope with a statute book that stretches back centuries and contains gendered language?

New legislation ought always to be gender neutral. A new amendment to existing legislation could set up problems of interpretation. Most of the gender neutral

[54] Public Services Ombudsman Act (Northern Ireland) 2016.

[55] Office of the Parliamentary Counsel, 'Drafting Guidance' (Office of the Parliamentary Counsel, UK, 2020).

techniques cited above can be used without any change to the meaning of an older statute. But what if an older statute refers to 'chairman' and there is a need for some unrelated amendments – should those amendments continue to use the old 'chairman' or should they change to 'chairperson'? It is generally very bad practice to use two different words to mean the same thing in legislation – the implication being that different words have different meaning. However, although it could cause momentary confusion, it is unlikely that there would be actual uncertainty if 'chairperson' appeared in the middle of a text speaking about 'chairman'. Any uncertainty that does exist would be balanced against the lack of equality in repeating an outmoded term.

This is a way to make incremental change – to revise the statute book one statute at a time whenever an older statute needs to be amended. However, what about a wholesale and systematic change to the entirety of the statute book to remove gendered language? Although such an approach would create benefits in terms of making a strong commitment to equality, it would be extremely resource intensive. When issuing reprints of legislation, the Chief Parliamentary Counsel of New Zealand does have the power to revise existing legislation to make it gender neutral.[56] No equivalent power exists in the UK. 'Waving a magic wand' to fix the whole statute book (as Grabham refers to it)[57] is not, in my view, feasible.

7.3.4. The Rise of Gender Neutral Drafting

A survey carried out by Revell and Vapnak in 2020 showed that gender neutral drafting is the norm in many countries.[58] Gender neutral drafting is now standard practice throughout the UK. In 2007, Jack Straw MP announced in the House of Commons that gender neutral drafting would be standard in all government legislation.[59] Even before that date, it was seen as best practice to be gender neutral. Watkin points out that from the onset of devolution in Wales in 1999, there was a commitment to gender neutrality in legislation.[60] Guidance issued for Westminster legislation by the Office of the Parliamentary Counsel repeats government policy that gender neutral language be used 'so far as it is practicable to do so'.[61] It is hard to envisage any circumstances when it will not be practicable to use gender neutral language. Even with challenging provisions like reflexive pronouns there are gender neutral options like doubling up the pronoun. No legislative drafter worth his (or her, or their!) salt should be stymied by an obligation to use gender neutral language in legislation. In fact, the Office of the Parliamentary Counsel together with the Government Legal Department have gone further and

[56] s 25(1)(a), Legislation Act 2021.
[57] Grabham (n 36).
[58] Revell and Vapnek (n 51).
[59] HC Deb 8 March 2007, col 146 WS.
[60] TG Watkin, 'Gender Neutrality: Description and Prescription' (2022) *Theory and Practice of Legislation* (forthcoming).
[61] Office of the Parliamentary Counsel (n 55).

written a guide on gender neutral language for use more generally in legal circles. They state that they are

> Proud to have this opportunity to share our approach to gender-neutral drafting with the wider legal profession responsible for private law agreements and other products. There is no reason why gender-neutral drafting cannot become the norm across the profession.[62]

7.3.5. Gender Silent Drafting

Astute readers will already have noticed that gender neutral drafting, and the preceding text, itself runs the risk of excluding certain people. Male and female are not the only two possible genders, and many people identify with different genders, or even no gender at all. Constructing legislation in a way that strait-jackets people into one of only two genders may itself be discriminatory.

Except in rare cases, it is unnecessary to specify gender at all in legislation. The better approach is therefore gender silent drafting where no gender is specified. 'He or she' may exclude those who consider themselves as neither he nor she. In order to avoid this kind of exclusion, it is necessary for legislation to be silent on gender, to not make any binary specifications on gender. This is the conclusion reached by Revell and Vapnek,[63] and it is hard to disagree with it save by spluttering that 'that isn't how we normally do things here'.

Thankfully, gender silent drafting is relatively easy within the gender neutral techniques outlined above, as nearly all of them are gender silent anyway. The only one to be avoided is the doubling up approach of saying 'man or woman' or 'he or she'. Revell and Vapnek's suggestions on gender silent drafting can be seen as a repetition of the Rule of Law principle of equality, including 'legislation should address all users equally' and 'the language of law should not offend'.[64]

7.4. Offensive or Discriminatory Language More Generally

Picking up on this last point made by Revell and Vapnek, the use of gendered or sexist language is but one instance of a broader problem of the use of language in legislation that is offensive or discriminatory in some way. It is very unlikely that an offensive term would be purposefully used, but its existence in legislation can arise in two ways. First, were the original sense or historical use of the term was not offensive. Second, where an historic term is used in the present without any real thought as to whether it ought to be changed.

[62] Office of the Parliamentary Counsel and Government Legal Department, *Guide to Gender-Neutral Drafting* (2019).
[63] Revell and Vapnek (n 51).
[64] ibid 134.

The statute book contains many terms that we would now consider offensive. The thirteenth century contains both a statute Concerning those born out of wedlock[65] and a statute Inheritance of Bastard.[66] The word bastard appears in the Defence Forces (Temporary Provisions) Act, 1923 (in Ireland) as well as in the Navy and Marines (Property of Deceased) Order 1956. We have the Trial of Lunatics Act 1883. Those words have long been seen as offensive and are no longer appropriate to be used in legislation.

There are more recent examples of language that can be seen as problematic. 'Disabled person' can be seen as offensive as it defines a person by reference to their disability first, or reduces them to just their disability. The Disability Discrimination Act 1995 used this phrase without malice when it was first enacted. The term was then defined to mean 'a person who has a disability'.[67] The difficulty of using the correct language is complicated further by the changing nature of language. So the Autism Act (Northern Ireland) 2011 refers to 'a person with autism' as that was seen as the most appropriate term at the time. However, there is now a move towards 'autistic person' by those who have autism, as they don't wish to deny or hide their autism.

The form of legislation principle here is to avoid discriminatory or offensive language in legislation. If a term is offensive or discriminates, then don't use that term. Rather than unthinkingly following an existing statutory precedent, consider if that precedent fits our present-day conceptions of equality. As with gendered text in historic legislation, it may not be feasible to trawl through the entirety of the statute book to fix older statutes, but when those statutes are being amended, it is a perfect time to rectify historic prejudices.

7.5. Gender Impact Assessments and Equality Impact Assessments

Following the gender neutral or gender silent techniques set out above will result in legislation that satisfies, in its form, equality. This is a necessary prerequisite for the Rule of Law requirement of equality before the law, but it is not in itself enough. Equality before the law requires equality of substance as well as equality of form. As Anatole France caustically remarked 'In its majestic equality, the law forbids rich and poor alike to sleep under bridges'.[68] A law that on its face applies to all will be an unequal law if it disproportionately affects certain sections of society.

How is a legislator to know if a proposed law will undermine equality? It is necessary to examine the content of legislation to assess what its actual impact will be on different sections of society. Everyone can be guilty of both conscious and unconscious bias, and institutions and procedures can perpetuate structural or systemic bias. We all view society through the prism of our own experiences

[65] 1237 21 Henry 3.
[66] 1238 22 Henry 3. Both now repealed by the Statute Law Revision Act, 1983 in Ireland.
[67] See s 1, Disability Discrimination Act 1995, now repealed.
[68] A France, *The Red Lily, Complete* (1894).

and character. As a white, middle-class, straight man, I may not even be aware of issues affecting other persons when it comes to considering legislative policies. To use some specific (and hypothetical examples) if a legislative assembly is all Christian, will they consider the needs of Muslims during Ramadan when passing laws on restaurants? If legislators are all able-bodied, will they see the need for ramps in laws regulating building control? Will a predominantly male legislature have a sufficient awareness around female biology to pass a law banning abortion from six weeks in a way that respects female autonomy?

These are all questions around the substance of legislation, and this is a book on form of legislation principles. Therefore, a discussion on the merits of individual legislative provisions is beyond its scope. However, there is one form of legislation principle that can assist, and that is the formal process for making legislation. Proper scrutiny of legislation during its passage through the legislature provides opportunities for spotting equality problems with that legislation. As Johnson observed 'the systematic application of parliamentary gender-sensitive legislative scrutiny by parliaments increases the chance that discriminatory provisions and opportunities to advance gender equality are uncovered and – importantly – remedied.'[69] Within the context of Regulatory Impact Assessments, two specific mechanisms exist which can assist with equality proofing of legislation: the equality impact assessment and the gender impact assessment.

A Regulatory Impact Assessment (generally shortened to RIA) is a 'systematic, comparative appraisal of how proposed primary and/or secondary legislation might affect stakeholders, society, economic sectors and the environment'.[70] Although regulatory impact assessments are part of good quality law making they are not, in themselves, a component of the Rule of Law. An equality impact assessment (or EIA) is probably best seen as a sub-species of RIA. They have been defined as 'An analysis of a proposed organisational policy, or change to an existing one, which assesses whether the policy has a disparate impact upon persons with protected characteristics'.[71]

An EIA is not limited to a legislative proposal, but it is a tool that can help to inform the content of legislation. A gender impact assessment is a specific form of EIA that looks at the impact of a proposal on issues around gender. A gender impact assessment will assist in gender mainstreaming, that is, pursuing 'the integration of the gender perspective into the design, preparation, implementation, monitoring and evaluation of policies, spending programmes and regulatory measures'.[72] In Choi's view, compulsory gender impact assessments for legislation in Korea improves equal protection under the law for women.[73]

[69] H Johnson, 'Legislating for change: gender-sensitive ex ante legislative scrutiny in practice' (2022) *Theory and Practice of Legislation* (forthcoming).

[70] S Naundorf and C Radaelli, 'Regulatory Evaluation Ex Ante and Ex Post: Best Practice, Guidance and Methods' in U Karpen and H Xanthaki (eds), *Legislation in Europe: A Comprehensive Guide for Scholars and Practioners* (Oxford, Hart Publishing, 2017).

[71] D Pyper, 'The Public Sector Equality Duty and Equality Impact Assessments' (House of Commons Library 2020).

[72] K Choi, 'Gender Equality and Legislative Evaluation of Gender-Based Laws in Korea' (2021) 9 *Theory and Practice of Legislation* 25.

[73] ibid.

The great Scots poet Robbie Burns wrote:

> O wad some Pow'r the giftie gie us:
> To see oursels as ithers see us![74]

(Oh, would some power give us the gift, to see ourselves as others see us). A gender impact assessment may not quite have the eloquence of Burns, but it allows us to see others as they see themselves.

The underlying justification for carrying out an EIA is the public sector equality duty (for England, Wales and Scotland)[75] and the section 75 equality duty (for Northern Ireland).[76] These duties were discussed above in Section 7.2.3. According to an exhaustive case law review by the House of Commons Library, it is not compulsory in the UK to carry out a formal EIA before making legislation, but some sort of consideration of equality concerns must be carried out.[77] This is also the practice in the making of Northern Ireland legislation, where reference will be made in a Bill's explanatory memorandum either to an EIA, or to a screening assessment that determined that there was no need for an EIA.

7.6. Vindicability

Vindicability means the capacity of a legal right to be vindicated. By this I mean, the ability of an individual to rely in practice upon a right granted to them by legislation, either by using or applying that right in practice, by having that right respected by the state, or by enforcing that right in a court. Vindicability is the flip side of implementability discussed in chapter four. Implementability means that the state is able to implement legislation. Vindicability means the individual is able to rely upon legislation. To put this in context, there is no point in having beautifully crafted and extensive rights set out in a piece of legislation, if the persons to whom they are directed can't take advantage of those rights. In considering access to employment tribunals, the Supreme Court said

> when Parliament passes laws creating employment rights, for example, it does so not merely in order to confer benefits on individual employees, but because it has decided that it is in the public interest that *those rights should be given effect*.[78]

Vindicability is important for the Rule of Law generally, but it has particular importance for the principle of equality before the law. This is because the rich and the powerful generally have the financial resources or social capital to enable them to vindicate their rights, but the poor or disadvantaged do not. If a legal right

[74] Robbie Burns, *To a Louse: On Seeing One on a Lady's Bonnet, at Church* (1786).
[75] s 149, Equality Act 2010.
[76] s 75, Northern Ireland Act 1998.
[77] Pyper (n 71).
[78] *R (UNISON) v Lord Chancellor* [2017] UKSC 51, para 72, my emphasis.

is something that can only be utilised by the privileged, then there is no equality before the law in practice. Vindicability is about equality in substance as well as in form. It means that in practice, all citizens are able to take advantage of their legal rights. There are several components to vindicability that ought to be considered when enacting any piece of legislation.

7.6.1. Knowable and Known

A legislative provision is only vindicable if it is both capable of being known, and actually known. The right of an unintentionally homeless person to accommodation[79] is useless unless that person knows about that right, and the local authority to whom they apply also knows about that right. The prerequisite for this is accessibility and intelligibility of legislation, as set out in chapters two and five. These principles make this right knowable, but the right still remains ineffective unless it is actually brought to the attention of the homeless person. Wagner-von Papp concluded that legislation ought to be 'known', but that this does not merely mean that it is published.[80] The Joint Committee on Statutory Instruments made particular reference to the ability to know the contents of legislation depending upon who you were

> the issue is more acute when the instrument is of general concern to members of the public as opposed to, say, only a small number of well-resourced commercial organisations who can be expected to have stayed abreast of legislative developments concerning them through correspondence with Government Departments or in other ways.[81]

If knowing legislation depends upon you being a well-resourced commercial organisation, then there is no equality before the law. In designing legislative provisions, the form of legislation principle is to consider how a particular right can be brought to the attention of the person who could be expected to have need of that right. Otherwise, that legislation is simply inconsequential words on a page. A good example of this in practice is contained in the Homelessness Reduction Act 2017, which sets out concrete steps for vindicating homelessness rights by bringing these rights to the attention of the homeless. Section 2 of that Act amended the Housing Act 1996 by inserting the following provision

> (1) Each local housing authority in England must provide or secure the provision of a service, available free of charge to any person in the authority's district, providing information and advice on—
>
> (a) preventing homelessness,
> (b) securing accommodation when homeless,

[79] s 189B, Housing Act 1996.

[80] F Wagner-von Papp, 'A Law and Economics Perspective on Effective Legislation' (Conference: Effective Law and Regulation, Institute of Advanced Legal Studies, 7 July 2017).

[81] Joint Committee on Statutory Instruments, *Transparency and Accountability in Secondary Legislation* (12 June 2018) para 4.12.

(c) the rights of persons who are homeless or threatened with homelessness, and the duties of the authority, under this Part,
(d) any help that is available from the authority or anyone else, whether under this Part or otherwise, for persons in the authority's district who are homeless or may become homeless (whether or not they are threatened with homelessness), and
(e) how to access that help.[82]

The requirement of vindicability can be implemented if legislation contains duties to inform and advise individuals and officials on the content of the rights set out in that legislation. This could include training requirements for civil servants and an information service for the users of public services.[83] It can also include a duty to provide information to the general public about particular legal provisions.[84]

7.6.2. Practical and Realistic

Legislative rights are only vindicable if the way they are meant to be applied in day to day life is practical and realistic. If the practical application contains unrealistic hurdles for those seeking to make use of legislation, then this makes the legislation of no actual benefit. The form of legislation principle here is to consider the end user and consider whether the method of application/utilisation of the legislation is feasible. For example, a right to claim asylum in the UK is a good right on paper. But if this right requires the immigrant to comply with certain procedures or formalities that are not feasible in practice, then the value of the right is reduced. In discussing the current Nationalities and Borders Bill provisions on asylum seekers, Raza Husain QC made this point:

> the principle that informs the Bill should be based upon need, but not on resettlement or legal routes that do not exist, or if they do exist may be inadequate or unsafe. The reality … is that refugees have very little choice as to how to get here.[85]

If a refugee is to be penalised for failing to use a 'legal route' that does not exist, then the legislation is divorced from reality and all that is left is a paper commitment to asylum rights, rather than an actual or practical commitment.

A non-legislative example of this also illustrates the point. Following the conviction of a serving police officer for the murder of Sarah Everard, there were understandable concerns about the safety of women when approached by a lone

[82] s 179, Housing Act 1996.
[83] See the model used in clause 2 of the Autism (Amendment) Bill currently before the Northern Ireland Assembly on information about autism.
[84] s 2, Human Tissue (Authorisation) (Scotland) Act 2019, and information about presumed consent for organ donation.
[85] Joint Committee on Human Rights, Oral Evidence: Legislative Scrutiny of the Nationalities and Borders Bill, HC 588, 8 September 2021.

plain-clothes, police officer. The advice given by the Metropolitan Police was that women in those circumstances should 'challenge' that officer, and demand to know the officer's identity and intentions.[86] However, it seems neither realistic nor feasible to expect a person accosted by the police to demand to see identification/dial 999/speak to the officer's supervisor.

7.6.3. Easy Routes to Enforcement

If a legislative right is denied to a citizen, that right is only vindicable if there is an easy route for that citizen to enforce that right. If the route to enforcement is only open to those with expensive lawyers, then there is no equality before the law. Section 37 of Magna Carta includes the famous words that 'we will sell to no man, we will not deny or defer to any man either justice or right'.[87] Lord Reed characterised these words as 'a guarantee of access to courts which administer justice promptly and fairly'.[88]

We do not live in a utopia where all rights of the citizen are respected by other citizens and by the state. We therefore need to have some way of achieving a remedy if rights are not respected. The precise route to be taken is not as important as is the existence of an easy route to achieve vindication of rights.

A good example is contained in the Family Homes and Domestic Violence (Northern Ireland) Order 1998. The Order sets up a regime for the protection of persons from domestic violence, in particular by the creation of two legal remedies: the non-molestation order[89] and the occupation order.[90] A non-molestation order prohibits a person from molesting another person. An occupation order enforces a person's right to remain in occupation of a dwelling-house. These are important rights that have the potential to be of great benefit in protecting victims of domestic violence. However, if they required a long and drawn-out court process to obtain, they would not be effective. Those who enacted this Order were clearly aware of this as they included a provision in the Order allowing for an *ex parte* order to be made 'even though the respondent has not been given such notice of the proceedings as would otherwise be required by rules of court'.[91] The *ex parte* route means that if a person is beaten up on Monday night, they can see their solicitor on Tuesday morning and get an order in place by Tuesday afternoon. There is no guarantee the order will prevent the abuse, but it does provide a formal and concrete measure of protection that is instantly available to the victim.

[86] 'Sarah Everard: Challenge Plain-Clothes Officers, Met Police Says' *BBC News* (1 October 2021) <www.bbc.com/news/uk-58757375>.

[87] Magna Carta 1215.

[88] *UNISON v Lord Chancellor* [2017] 3 WLR 409, para 74.

[89] Art 20, Family Homes and Domestic Violence (Northern Ireland) Order 1998.

[90] Art 11, ibid.

[91] Art 23, ibid.

7.6.4. Routes to Enforcement that are Financially Viable

One particularly important component of the requirement that there are easy routes to enforcement is that the route to enforcement is financially viable to the person seeking to vindicate their rights. If the route to enforcement leads through a court, then access to that court must be open to all in society, not just to the wealthy. Sandhurst has argued that 'every man is equal before the law, but he has got to get before the law before he can attain that equality'.[92] This is absolutely correct.

There are two aspects of this. First, court fees must be at a level that those who are to be expected to use that court can afford. Second, legal assistance is available at an affordable cost, to those who will need it.

The Supreme Court in *UNISON* considered this first point in great detail.[93] The narrow issue was whether setting court fees at a high level by secondary legislation was ultra vires the enabling Act. The broader issue was the constitutionally critical function of the citizen being able to vindicate their rights by way of an application to a court. The court was explicit, 'In order for the fees to be lawful, they have to be set at a level that everyone can afford'.[94] It went on to say

> Fees must therefore be affordable not in a theoretical sense, but in the sense that they can reasonably be afforded. Where households on low to middle incomes can only afford fees by sacrificing the ordinary and reasonable expenditure required to maintain what would generally be regarded as an acceptable standard of living, the fees cannot be regarded as affordable.[95]

The whole tenor of the judgement of the Supreme Court in that case was about 'the reality' or 'in practice'. The Rule of Law does not require abstract justice. It requires that the particular person, who has suffered a particular legal wrong, has a right to an actual remedy, which is achievable in practice. The route to vindication must not lie through court proceedings that are beyond the financial means of the persons who could be expected to have need of them.

The second point concerns legal aid, that is to say, the scheme whereby the state pays the legal fees of those in need of legal advice and assistance. Legal aid has been subject to a seemingly never-ending debate over the right level of the legal aid budget. Sir James Mumby, President of the Family Division has called the legal aid system as it applies in the family courts neither compassionate nor humane.[96] Sandhurst surveyed the field of legal aid and concluded

> the cuts to legal aid have had profound negative consequences, the relatively small saving in the civil and legal aid budget (c.£400m) being a large proportion (c. 34 per cent) of spend.

[92] Lord Sandhurst, 'Access to Justice in the 2020s: Recommendations for a Joined up Approach to Legal Aid, Funding and Procedural Reform in the Civil and Family Courts for the New Conservative Government' (Society of Conservative Lawyers 2020).

[93] *R (UNISON)* v *Lord Chancellor* [2017] UKSC 51.

[94] ibid, para 91.

[95] ibid, para 93.

[96] J Hyde, 'Munby: Legal Aid System "Not Humane"' *Law Gazette* <www.lawgazette.co.uk/law/munby-legal-aid-system-not-humane/5045849.article>.

> Unintended consequences, both financial and societal, have compounded that cost and have had a profound effect on the justice system and society as a whole … The promise of a property owning democracy rings hollow if citizens do not have the opportunity to defend their property rights through the courts.[97]

This does not just relate to property rights, but to family law, employment law, civil cases, public law and other fields of law. If a person, for want of financial means, cannot vindicate their rights in a court, then there is not equality before the law.

The form of legislation principle here is that legislation that is designed to be applied must contain provisions that allow citizens a meaningful route to enforcing its provisions.

7.7. Intelligibility and Equal Access to the Law

Intelligibility has already been considered as a Rule of Law value in its own right in chapter five. In this section, I consider intelligibility as one aspect of equality before the law.

Equality is enhanced if everyone has the same chance to read, understand and apply the law. Equality is diminished if some sections of society have an enhanced right to read, understand and apply the law that others do not possess. There are three ways in which this kind of inequality can be present.

The first and most obvious one is where the legislative text is so unintelligible that it needs legal assistance in order to understand it. This will place the person with the resources available to pay a lawyer at an advantage over the person without those resources. Legislation that only the wealthy are able to understand is not legislation that respects equality before the law.

The second way is where legislation is only intelligible to a select group of people who are 'in the know'. Those in the know are lawyers, judges and others who know about the arcane rules of statutory interpretation that are used to understand the 'true' meaning of the law. This is the argument that Murynka makes in pointing out that if only an elite group know the rules around how law is structured, then only they have the special knowledge necessary to properly understand the law.[98] This is an argument in favour of intelligible legislation and an approach to interpretation of that legislation that relies upon the words in the statute, rather than discerning a nebulous 'will of parliament' that lies behind those words. Murynka goes on to say that 'access to extrinsic interpretive aids such as legislative history creates a potential for clever lawyers to complicate otherwise simple interpretive matters'.[99]

[97] Lord Sandhurst (n 92).
[98] D Murynka, 'Some Problems with Killing the Legislator' (2015) 73 *University of Toronto Faculty of Law Review* 12.
[99] ibid.

Durcia concludes this line of thought by arguing that this makes legislation inaccessible to those without formal legal training.[100] He goes on to say that

> There is something unfair in a legal system where an ordinary citizen reads the law and makes a good faith effort to comply with that law but is nonetheless punished because they forgot to consider [various complex rules of statutory interpretation].[101]

This use of exclusive language need not be consciously planned, but as a result of background and training. It may lead to the outcome criticised by Pierre Bourdieu of elite groups entrenching power within the elite by the use of cultural practices and language that those outside of that elite may not be able to access or understand.[102]

The third way that unintelligible legislation can diminish equality before the law is if that legislation uses language that is familiar to some sections of society, but that excludes other sections of society. We are all guilty of viewing language through the prism of our background and using language accordingly. Most of those involved in the legislative process are likely to come from affluent backgrounds and enjoy the benefits of university education. This makes us familiar with a particular way of using language, which means that we craft legislation with a similar end-user in mind. Does legislation use overly-formal language that is intelligible to those familiar with such an approach, but unintelligible to those not familiar with these modes of speech?

The form of legislation solution to all these issues is the same – to use clear, plain and everyday language that everyone can understand.

7.8. Legislation and the Crown

This section considers one particular example of the interaction of the equality principle with the form of legislation – the relationship between the Crown and legislation.

The Crown occupies an interesting place in UK constitutional theory. The concept of the Crown is slightly nebulous as it can cover a range of meanings. It can mean the person and personal rights of the individual who is the monarch. But it can also mean the Executive, acting in the name of the Crown in theory, but in

[100] S Durcia, 'Rediscovering the Pole Star: A Close Look at Legislative Intent and Statutory Interpretation' [2021] *The Loophole* 16, 49.

[101] ibid.

[102] See for example the description of Bourdieu's work in M Maclean and C Harvey, 'Pierre Bourdieu and Elites' in SR Clegg and M Pina e Cunha (eds), *Management, Organizations and Contemporary Social Theory* (London, Routledge, 2019).

actual fact acting in its own right. In discussing the concept of Crown immunity, Bennion says that the concept

> extends to all bodies and persons acting as servants or agents of the Crown, whether in its private or public capacity. In particular the doctrine embraces all elements of the executive government, from ministers of the Crown downwards.[103]

This last element of the immunity (ministers of the Crown downwards) is open to the charge of soritical vagueness – we know that ministers are exempt, but at what point, or how far down the chain, does this immunity end?

Legislation is technically made not by Parliament, but by the monarch in Parliament. Ministers exercise prerogative powers, not because those powers inhere in them as ministers, but because those powers inhere in the Crown, and in exercising those powers they are acting in the name of the Crown. By some constitutional alchemy, political actions of ministers become solemn actions of the monarch.

The interaction of the Crown with legislation and the legislative process throws up two areas where there are form of legislation principles that can be derived from the Rule of Law: the rule on application of legislation to the Crown, and the practice of King's consent to legislation.

7.8.1. Application of Legislation to the Crown

One paradox within the UK constitution is on the application of legislation to the Crown. On the one hand, since at least Magna Carta in 1215, it has been solid legal doctrine that the Crown is subject to the law, meaning that it sits within the legal framework, not outside it. Dicey was very clear that everyone is bound by law, see Section 7.1 above. On the other hand, we have the doctrine of Crown immunity, which means that the Crown is not bound by legislation, unless that legislation expressly (or by necessary implication) states that it binds the Crown.

It is not easy to resolve this paradox. Diplock LJ said that 'laws are made by rulers for subjects'[104] but that does rather offend against the notion that we are all equal before the law, and all liable before the law. It is rather like claiming, as the pigs did in *Animal Farm*, that 'all animals are equal, but some animals are more equal than others'.[105] A partial resolution of this paradox is that if Parliament states that the Crown is bound, then the Crown is bound. But the paradox then re-emerges with the practice of King's consent, which means that the Crown must first consent to legislation that affects it.

[103] F Bennion, *Bennion on Statutory Interpretation* 5th edn (London, LexisNexis, 2008) 207.
[104] *BBC v Johns (Inspector of Taxes)* [1965] Ch 32, 78.
[105] G Orwell, *Animal Farm* (London, Secker and Warburg, 1945).

7.8.2. Application to the Crown in the UK: Regional Variations

There is no uniform rule across the UK in respect of the principle of Crown immunity when it comes to legislation. The orthodox position is expressly set out in Northern Ireland in its interpretation legislation.

> Crown not bound, unless named.
>
> No enactment passed or made after the commencement of this Act shall bind or affect in any manner whatsoever Her Majesty or Her Majesty's rights or prerogatives, unless it is stated therein that Her Majesty is bound thereby to the full extent authorised or permitted by the constitutional laws of Northern Ireland or to such less extent as is specified in the enactment.[106]

This language, and its references to 'Her Majesty' and 'her' rights suggest that this is discussing the personal rights of the Crown, rather than the rights of the executive acting on behalf of the Crown.

When it comes to Westminster legislation, the principle is not as easily identifiable. Bennion says that 'Since an Act is made by the Queen in Parliament for the regulation of subjects, it follows that, unless the contrary intention appears, the Act does not bind the Crown itself'.[107] However, although this is an accurate reflection of the common law position, the statutory formulation of this is more difficult to find. Rather than being an express provision, it is to be found as a Savings provision in the Crown Proceedings Act 1947, where it states that

> (2) Except as therein otherwise expressly provided, nothing in this Act shall:-
>
> …
>
> (f) affect any rules of evidence or any presumption relating to the extent to which the Crown is bound by any Act of Parliament …[108]

Although this is legally effective, it refers to Crown immunity obliquely rather than establishing it. Rather than saying 'the Crown is immune', it instead says that it doesn't affect any existing rules about immunity of the Crown from legislation. This then leads the reader into an inquiry about what were (in 1947) the existing rules about the application of legislation to the Crown.

Scotland and Wales have taken a different approach to their legislation, reversing the orthodox position by stating that the Crown is automatically bound by legislation, unless there is an express exception. Thus we have 'An Act of the

[106] s 7, Interpretation Act (Northern Ireland) 1954.
[107] Bennion (n 103) 206.
[108] s 40(2)(f), Crown Proceedings Act 1947.

Scottish Parliament or a Scottish instrument binds the Crown except in so far as the Act or instrument provides otherwise',[109] and

(1) An Act of Senedd Cymru binds the Crown.
(2) A Welsh subordinate instrument binds the Crown so far as it is made under an enactment which binds the Crown or confers a power to make provision binding the Crown.[110]

This combination of legislative provisions is all rather confusing to the reader. Rather than a simple rule on when the Crown is bound, it depends on what legislature passed the law, when it was passed, whether it expressly says that it binds the Crown or whether by necessary implication it binds the Crown.

7.8.3. Equality and Crown Immunity

The idea of a special status for one particular person or body undermines the principle of equality before the law. A default rule, either at common law or by legislation, which states that legislation doesn't apply to a particular person goes against the Rule of Law. It is arguable that, in some cases, there may be an objective justification for differential treatment. But the approach set out in Westminster and Northern Ireland legislation flips this on its head by stating that, by default, the Crown is in a privileged position by comparison with everyone else in the country. Objective justification for differential treatment requires that justification to be express, not left to a default assumption that differential treatment for a particular individual.

Consider the hypothetical example of a monarch being accused of serious sexual offences. The natural assumption would be that the monarch would be prosecuted. But not so fast. If one looks at the Sexual Offences Act 2003, there is no section in it that states 'this Act binds the Crown'. If a monarch drives so badly that they break the rules of the road, they cannot be prosecuted – the Road Traffic Offenders Act 1988 only directs that that Act applies to 'vehicles and persons in the public service of the Crown'.[111]

Less extreme examples than the criminal law abound. Bennion states that

> the doctrine of Crown immunity means that the Crown can claim to be exempt from any onerous enactment, for example one imposing taxation. The premises owned by the Crown were held not be subject to Rating Acts, the Rent Acts, or the Town and Country Planning Acts.[112]

A brief perusal of recent Acts of Parliament will reveal that many do not contain that key phrase 'this Act binds the Crown'. However, despite not being bound by

[109] s 20(1), Interpretation and Legislative Reform (Scotland) Act 2010.
[110] s 28, Legislation (Wales) Act 2019.
[111] s 92, Road Traffic Offenders Act 1988.
[112] Bennion (n 103) 208.

legislation unless specifically named, the Crown can take advantage of legislation even if not specifically named. The Crown Proceedings Act 1947 states that 'this Act shall not prejudice the right of the Crown to take advantage of the provisions of an Act of Parliament although not named therein'.[113] The position then is: one rule for the Crown and another for everyone else, unless a particular rule benefits the Crown, in which case the same rule for the Crown as for everyone else.

Tom Bingham's example was that it didn't matter if you were the Archbishop of Canterbury, the law still applies. That remains accurate, but it misses a blind spot when it comes to the Crown.

7.8.4. Special Modification of Laws in their Application to the Crown

As well as the long-standing rule of Crown immunity, there is a related long-standing practice of modifying legislation in its application to the Crown. The rule and the practice often go hand in hand. So a provision in an Act will state that the Act applies to the Crown, but with certain modifications. For example, the Heat Networks (Scotland) Act 2021, passed by the Scottish Parliament, states that it does apply in relation to Crown land, but that powers of entry are only exercisable with the permission of certain persons connected to the Crown.[114] Another example can be seen in section 30 of the Cultural Property (Armed Conflicts) Act 2017. That Act does bind the Crown,[115] but it goes on to say that the Crown cannot be criminally liable,[116] and that it does not affect Her Majesty in her private capacity.[117] Given the colonial legacy of the Crown, it would not be unreasonable to suppose that an Act that is about returning cultural property in the event of armed conflict will have less impact if it doesn't apply in respect of property in the possession of the Crown.

How do special rules for a particular individual (the monarch) or the Executive more generally square with a commitment to equality before the law? It is hard to see how they do. In the examples above, it is hard to see why permission is required before accessing Crown lands when no permission is necessary before accessing other private land. It is hard to see an objective justification why rules on stolen cultural property apply to everyone, except to the Crown.

In a series of articles, *The Guardian* newspaper have delved into the special relationship between the Crown and legislation.[118] One of their articles related

[113] s 31(1), Crown Proceedings Act 1947.
[114] ss 97 and 98, Heat Networks (Scotland) Act 2021.
[115] s 30(1), Cultural Property (Armed Conflicts) Act 2017.
[116] s 30(2), ibid.
[117] s 30(5), ibid.
[118] The series is entitled Queen's consent investigations, and has run throughout 2021. The articles are gathered together at www.theguardian.com/uk-news/series/queens-consent.

to the Heat Networks (Scotland) Act 2021 referred to above and in particular to the right of a licence holder to compulsorily acquire land that is required for the construction or operation of a heat network.[119] A power of compulsory purchase of land necessary for major infrastructure work is relatively common, and is usually accompanied by checks and balances to protect private property rights. However, when the Act was passing through the Scottish Parliament, an amendment was tabled by the energy Minister, Paul Wheelhouse MSP stating that

> (3) The Scottish Ministers must not authorise under subsection (1) any acquisition in relation to land which belongs to Her Majesty in right of Her private estates unless the appropriate authority consents to the acquisition.[120]

This amendment was passed. It essentially means that the Crown must itself consent to the compulsory purchase. No individual really wants the compulsory purchase of their land, even with the payment of compensation. But ordinary citizens simply have to accept it. Not so the Crown, which is placed in a privileged position. Opposing the amendment, Andy Wightman MSP said

> [the monarch] cannot, on the one hand, claim rights to private estates as a private citizen and, on the other hand, continue to be exempt from the rules that govern the affairs of all other private citizens who own land – most particularly, in this respect, the risk that, in the public interest, some of one's land might be subject to a compulsory purchase order.[121]

The Minister did not really offer any substantial reason for the different treatment of the Crown, merely saying that it was 'appropriate' and 'required to ensure the smooth passage of the Bill'.[122]

For another example, see coronavirus regulations as they apply in relation to Crown land.[123] The normal rule created a power for a council to impose a restriction on the use of public outdoor places. The modification in relation to Crown land stated that a restriction could not be imposed upon Crown land save with the consent of the Crown. In criticising this previously, I argued that it is 'an anti-democratic anachronism that two powerful individuals [the monarch and the Prince of Wales] have rights and privileges over public legislation that the rest of the public do not have'.[124]

This practice undermines the principle of equality before the law. If there is a genuine objective justification for treating the Crown differently, then it should be

[119] s 68, Heat Networks (Scotland) Act 2021.

[120] s 68(3), ibid. See the original amendment in the marshalled list of amendments at www.parliament.scot/-/media/files/legislation/bills/current-bills/heat-networks-scotland-bill/stage-3/marshalled-list-of-amendments-at-stage-3.pdf.

[121] Official Report, The Scottish Parliament, 23 February 2021.

[122] ibid.

[123] Regulation 8, the Health Protection (Coronavirus, Restrictions) (England) (No 3) Regulations 2020 (now revoked).

[124] R Cormacain, 'Queen's Consent and the Crown's Exemption from Lockdown Rules – Are We All in This Together?' (*UK Constitutional Law Association*, 15 February 2021) <https://ukconstitutionallaw.org/>.

clearly explained and evidenced. But the current practice is a deferential throwback to a different age and (as set out below) has more to do with the behind the scenes power of the Crown than it has to do with a legitimate aim for differential treatment.

7.8.5. King's Consent and Prince of Wales Consent

This is the second area of interaction between legislation and the Crown – the practice known as King's consent and Prince's consent. King's consent means that the King must consent to legislation that affects his interests before the legislation can proceed through Parliament. The consent of the Prince of Wales is likewise required when legislation affects his interests. According to Erskine May

> Bills affecting the prerogative (being powers exercisable by the Sovereign for the performance of constitutional duties) on the one hand, or hereditary revenues, personal property or interests of the Crown, the Duchy of Lancaster or the Duchy of Cornwall on the other, require the signification of Queen's consent in both Houses before they are passed.[125]

King's consent is now given at Third Reading of a Bill. If the consent is not given, then the Bill cannot proceed.[126] The requirement for King's consent is what opens the procedural door to legislation being modified in its application to the Crown. If it is not modified to the satisfaction of the monarch, then the Crown will not consent, and the legislation cannot be enacted. King's consent is not about whether the King agrees with the general thrust of legislation, it is about whether he agrees to be bound by it.

King's consent and Prince's consent should be distinguished from Royal Assent. Royal Assent is the formal process by which the monarch assents to an Act of Parliament – it is the outworking of the constitutional theory that legislation is made by the King in Parliament. Royal Assent is a formality and there is no suggestion that the monarch has any discretion to refuse to assent to an Act.

The Office of the Parliamentary Counsel have prepared detailed guidance on the operation and procedures connected with King's and Prince's consent.[127] Although both these sources deal with this as a mandatory requirement, they do not state the legislative or common law source of this obligation, save to say that it is longstanding.

In Scotland, there is an express obligation to obtain King's consent set out in the Scotland Act 1998.

> The standing orders shall include provision for ensuring that a Bill containing provisions which would, if the Bill were a Bill for an Act of Parliament, require the consent of

[125] Para 9.6, *Erskine May, Parliamentary Practice* 25th edn (London, Butterworths, 2019).
[126] Para 9.7, ibid.
[127] Office of the Parliamentary Counsel, 'Queen's or Prince's Consent' (2018).

> Her Majesty, the Prince and Steward of Scotland or the Duke of Cornwall shall not pass unless such consent has been signified to the Parliament.[128]

In Wales, there is a similar provision in the Government of Wales Act 2006.[129] In Northern Ireland, there is no such provision, although an early draft of the Northern Ireland Bill (as it then was) did contain a provision stating

> Crown interests
>
> 5. The standing orders shall include provision for ensuring that a Bill containing provisions which would, if the Bill were a Bill for an Act of Parliament, require the consent of Her Majesty shall not pass unless such consent has been signified to the Assembly.[130]

The deliberate choice to not include such a provision in the Northern Ireland Act 1998 is strong evidence that there is no obligation to seek King's consent for Acts of the Northern Ireland Assembly. The Standing Orders of the Northern Ireland Assembly do not contain any requirement that Bills before that Assembly must get King's consent.

The House of Commons undertook an inquiry into King's and Prince's Consent in 2014.[131] The consensus in its report was that consent was a matter of parliamentary procedure. There was no indication in that report that it had reached the level of a constitutional convention. Professor Adam Tucker, in giving evidence to that Committee, was very clear that King's consent did not have the necessary components to elevate it from a procedural matter into a constitutional convention.[132]

7.8.6. Equality and King's Consent

As with the doctrine of Crown immunity, it is hard to reconcile the parliamentary practice of King's consent with the principle of equality before the law. It is of course important that persons who are subject to the law have an opportunity to participate in the development and making of that law.[133] But there are two key differences between the good law-making practice of participation/consultation and the practice of King's consent. First, participation represents an opportunity to contribute to legislation, whereas King's consent is the power of veto. Second,

[128] Paragraph 7, Schedule 3 to the Scotland Act 1998.

[129] s 111(4), Government of Wales Act 2006.

[130] Northern Ireland Bill, Schedule 7, para 5, available at https://publications.parliament.uk/pa/cm199798/cmbills/cmbills/229/98229--r.htm.

[131] Political and Constitutional Reform Committee, 'The Impact of Queen's and Prince's Consent on the Legislative Process: Eleventh Report' (House of Commons 2014) <https://publications.parliament.uk/pa/cm201314/cmselect/cmpolcon/784/78402.htm>.

[132] A Tucker, 'The Impact of Queen's and Prince's Consent on the Legislative Process: Evidence' (Unpublished, 2014).

[133] F Uhlmann and C Konrath, 'Participation' in U Karpen and H Xanthaki (eds), *Legislation in Europe: A Comprehensive Guide for Scholars and Practitioners* (Oxford, Hart, 2017).

participation is a mechanism open to everyone, whereas King's consent is only open to two people (the King, and where appropriate, the Prince of Wales).

Tucker says that

> the Consent requirements are not merely redundant. They exceed the boundaries set by constitutional principle in terms of their range, their depth and their potential impact on the legislative process.[134]

I would go further and say that they undermine the principle that we are all equal before the law. A special right of the monarch to say that a particular law does not apply to her personally is not a right that others have. Other than deference, it is hard to see an objective justification and a legitimate aim for this differential treatment.

7.8.7. Form of Legislation Principles in Relation to the Crown

As is hopefully apparent from the above, there are three form of legislation principles here that respect the equality before the law principle as it applies to the Crown.

First, following the Scottish and Welsh provisions, all legislation should automatically apply to the Crown, unless there are express words to the contrary in a particular piece of legislation. Second, there should be no special modification of legislation in its application to the Crown, unless there is clear objective justification for this, and that justification is expressly set out. Third, the parliamentary practice of King's consent should end.

7.9. Legislation and the Armed Forces

This section considers another specific example of the equality principle in legislation – the way in which legislation treats the armed forces.

The underlying ethos of military law respects equality before the law. That ethos is that there is no special treatment for members of the armed forces, and that the ordinary law of the land applies to them. The modern restatement of this military law principle is set out in section 42 of the Armed Forces Act 2006.

> (1) A person subject to service law, or a civilian subject to service discipline, commits an offence under this section if he does any act that—
>
> (a) is punishable by the law of England and Wales; or
>
> (b) if done in England or Wales, would be so punishable.[135]

[134] Tucker (n 132).
[135] s 42(1), Armed Forces Act 2006.

The procedures for arrest, investigation and prosecution may be different, but the underlying requirement is that the armed forces are still subject to the same law as the rest of us. Members of the armed forces are

> bound by the criminal law of England and Wales wherever in the world they are serving. There is no special treatment or dispensation for Service personnel. If they break the criminal law, they can face the consequences in court just like any other citizen.[136]

Halsbury's Laws of England confirms this:

> It is one of the cardinal features of the law of England that a person does not, by enlisting in … the armed forces, thereby cease to be a citizen, so as to deprive him of his rights or exempt him from his liabilities under the ordinary law of the land.

When the House of Lords debated the chain of command, the importance of the point was reaffirmed from a political perspective:

> In a free country there is not and cannot be one law for soldiers and another for citizens. I believe that all noble and gallant Lords who have made such powerful speeches today would accept that basic point. Indeed, we frequently boast of the fact that our soldiers are citizens in uniform.[137]

Different procedures are in place for the way in which allegations of crimes against the military are investigated, but these can be objectively justified by reference to the circumstances and location in which these crimes are alleged to have occurred. However, the substantive criminal law applies, and thus equality before the law is respected.

7.9.1. Overseas Operations (Service Personnel and Veterans) Act 2021

This Act was passed in order to give greater legal protections to the armed forces and the Ministry of Defence. Part 1 introduced various restrictions on the prosecution of service personnel if the alleged conduct took place overseas and took place more than five years ago. There is a presumption against prosecution – prosecutions can only take place in exceptional circumstances.[138] There are a number of criteria to consider in deciding whether or not to prosecute, these criteria all being criteria that would persuade against prosecution.[139] Prosecution requires the prior consent of the Attorney General. Certain serious offences (for example war crimes, rape, torture) are excluded from these restrictions.[140]

[136] Evidence of Martin Hemming, former Government lawyer to the Ministry of Defence, UK Armed Forces Personnel and the Legal Framework For Future Operations, Written Evidence to Defence Select Committee, Session 2013–2014.
[137] Hansard House of Lords, 14 July 2005 Vol 673 Col 1251.
[138] s 2, Overseas Operations (Service Personnel and Veterans) Act 2021.
[139] s 3, ibid.
[140] Schedule 1 sets out the excluded offences.

Part 2 introduces restrictions on civil claims against service personnel and the Ministry of Defence. These restrictions all concern the time period within which those civil claims can be brought. Unlike other civil claims, there is now an absolute six-year time limit within which claims must be brought. There are further criteria to consider before allowing a claim after three years.

This Act undermined the equality principle in a number of ways. First, service personnel are now granted privileges that other members of society are not granted. There is no statute of limitations for ordinary citizens for serious crimes, but there is for service personnel. Second, the discretion that judges possess to extend the time in which civil claims may be brought does not apply if the defendants are in the privileged class of service personnel or the Ministry of Defence. There is no discretion where a civilian victim of military abuse brings an action out of time. Nor is there any discretion where a soldier suffers as a result of negligence of the Ministry of Defence. What matters is not the evidence or the strength of your case, but who you are.

7.9.2. Northern Ireland Legacy Proposals

In July 2021, the Secretary of State for Northern Ireland introduced the Government's proposals for dealing with the legacy of the armed conflict in Northern Ireland (referred to in the proposals as The Troubles).[141] Included in the paper are two proposals on the justice system. The first is a statute of limitations that would have the effect of immediately barring all prosecutions and investigations by both the police and the Police Ombudsman in respect of Troubles-related incidents. Although not given the name 'amnesty' this would effectively be an amnesty. The second is a complete statutory bar on all future and current civil cases and inquests arising out of the Troubles. Any existing judicial proceedings would immediately cease, and no future cases could be brought.

These proposals are fundamentally in opposition to the Rule of Law from many different perspectives. They undermine the principle of legality, that we are all subject to the law. They represent a gross breach of the separation of powers by the legislature stopping all existing court cases. They are the opposite of vindicability as they bar the ability of a person to vindicate a legal right.

For the purposes of this chapter, these proposals also undermine the principle of equality before the law as they place members of the armed forces in a privileged position. Although on the face of it, these proposals will apply equally to service personnel as well as paramilitaries, in practice there will be a differential effect. This is because, from 1970 to 1973, there was in force an arrangement that 'if an offence against the ordinary criminal law was alleged against military personnel in Northern Ireland the interviewing of military witnesses and of the alleged offender

[141] Addressing the Legacy of Northern Ireland's Past (CP 498, July 2021).

himself was conducted exclusively by military investigation'.[142] It has been held that this approach precluded an effective investigation of crimes alleged to have been committed by service personnel.[143] As argued in the case of *Burns and McCready*, this means that there is no equality before the law as soldiers will never have been the subject of an effective investigation simply because they are soldiers.[144]

Conclusion

If the Rule of Law requires that we are all treated equally before the law, then this informs some principles about how we should construct legislation.

Legislation has always reflected society, and if that society is unequal, then it follows that legislation will reflect that inequality. Although we are (hopefully) moving to a more equal society, legislation can be slow to remedy institutional or implicit discriminatory words or practices. One of the most obvious of these is law conceived of and presented as a male construct, in particular the practice of enacting law that refers solely to the male gender. There have been huge strides in the last few decades towards gender neutral drafting – ensuring that the way in which we write legislation is inclusive of males and females. This is classic territory for a technical, form of legislation response to a social wrong. Not only can the substance of the law give effect to gender equality, but so to can its very form. In fact, as society develops further, we can see that the next stage is not gender neutral legislation that reflects both genders, but gender silent legislation that does not exclude any gender. This leads on to a more general point about the type of language we use in legislation, in particular the use of terms that are now seen as outmoded, discriminatory or offensive against particular sections of society. Although consistency of language promotes the Rule of Law value of certainty and constancy, it is not a justification for continuing to use offensive language.

Turning next to the process of making legislation, there are ways that we can enhance the Rule of Law by including equality as one of the stages in legislative design. This is where gender impact assessments and equality impact assessments help. These are specifically created to combat the risk of discrimination (direct or indirect) in legislation. Building these into the process reduces the chances of discriminatory provisions.

The enactment of legislation ought not to be a paper exercise leading to a few words on the statute book. If legislation is to contain rights, then those rights must be capable of being vindicated by those who hold those rights. Vindicability means the property of legislation that it is able to be used in practice by those it is designed

[142] *R* v *Foxford* [1974] NI 181.
[143] *Mary Louise Thompson's Application* [2003] NIQB 80. See also judicial criticism of this lack of proper investigations in *R v Soldier A and Soldier C* [2021] NICC 3.
[144] *Re Burns and McCready* (High Court of Justice of Northern Ireland, 2021, unpublished).

to protect. If it can only be used by the wealthy or the powerful, then there is no equality in the effect of that legislation. The form of legislation principle here is to ensure that the rights it contains are capable of being effectively enjoyed by all, or vindicated by all in a court if there is a breach of them. This is connected to the principle of implementability as well as to the principle of intelligibility – these are all about everyone being able to read, understand and implement the law.

Finally, there are two specific examples of areas of law where there is not equality, or at least, the risk of inequality. First, there is the relationship between legislation and the Crown. There still exists a legislative culture of deference to the Crown in the UK, which means that legislation doesn't apply to the Crown in the way that it applies to everyone else. Either it won't apply at all unless it contains the formula 'this Act binds the Crown', or it will apply to the Crown, but with special modifications. Those modifications generally lessen the obligations upon the Crown and treat it more favourably than others. Additionally, there is the formal procedure of King's consent whereby permission is sought from the Crown before enacting legislation that could impact upon the rights of the Crown. There is not equality before the law if some individuals have rights that the rest of the population do not have.

The second area is the interaction of legislation with the regulation of the armed forces. The ordinary law of the armed forces is a very good example of equality before the law, as members of the armed forces are to be treated in the same way as civilians, save for sensible procedural modifications. However, this long-standing principle has been undermined recently. First, in the Overseas Operations (Service Personnel and Veterans) Act 2021, members of the armed forces are given limited immunity from prosecution, and the Ministry of Defence given special protections from civil claims. Second, the government currently propose to introduce a general amnesty to all military personnel for crimes committed during The Troubles in Northern Ireland. This would have the effect of placing military personnel in a privileged position under the law, enjoying legal protections that the ordinary person does not have.

8

Conclusion

8.1. The Rule of Law Matters …

The Rule of Law matters. It is one of the fundamental building blocks not just of the UK constitution, but of states around the world. Its simple premise is that everyone is subject to the law and that no-one is above the law. It is a premise that children at play will easily recognise – 'hey, that's cheating, you're not allowed to do that'. The exact same premise applies to Prime Ministers and Presidents – 'it's not one rule for you and a different rule for everyone else'.

Although the Rule of Law in itself is not enough to solve all our societal woes, its full implementation would do much to rectify them. In the USA, when the legal outcome of the election is not in any doubt, there is no right for the losing President to seek to be above that duly constituted result. In the UK, if a leader doesn't agree with the law, they should change it rather than pretending it doesn't apply to them personally. In China, the solution to political instability is not to treat Uighur Muslims as being undeserving of legal protections, of being outside the law's protection. There are clearly examples that could be found for virtually any country in the world. Proper application of the Rule of Law would go at least some way to resolving much of the injustice, and the unaccountability of wealth, privilege and power in our world.

The call for the Rule of Law rings as clear and true now as it rang millennia ago. Stretching back into antiquity, for the Babylonians, Hammurabi wrote out his Code 'to prevent the strong from oppressing the weak and to see that justice is done to widows and orphans'.[1] For the ancient Israelites, their 10 Commandments had a divine source,[2] but they represented laws that all must follow. Plato called for the government to be the slave to the law,[3] and Aristotle argued it was better for the law to rule than one of its citizens.[4] Jumping forwards considerably, the core point of Magna Carta 1215 was that the King could not be above the law. In the *Case of Prohibitions* (1607) 12 Co Rep 63, Coke quotes Bracton in stating that

[1] Epilogue, Hammurabi Code, approximately eighteenth century BCE.

[2] Exodus 20: 2–17.

[3] Plato, Laws, Book IV, 715d.

[4] J Warrington (tr), *Aristotle's Politics and the Athenian Constitution* (London, JM Dent, 1959) Book III, s 1287, p 97. Counter views did also exist in antiquity, for example the Roman maxim 'princeps legibus solutus' means that the prince is free of laws, see for example the discussion in G Post, 'Bracton on Kingship' (1967) 42 *Tulane Law Review* 519.

'the King ought not to be under any man, but under God and the law'. Coke ruled in that case that the King cannot sit in judgments in cases before the courts, but that cases ought to be judged according to the laws of England.

In the same era, James Harrington argued for an 'empire of laws, not of men'.[5] According to Corwin, Harrington himself ascribed the idea back to Aristotle.[6] The idea was picked up by the American revolutionaries. For example, the Declaration of the Rights of the Massachusetts Constitution 1780 includes references to a government of laws, not of men and according to Mason the concept is a fundamental part of the US constitutional structure.[7] This is what Thomas Paine meant when he said that in the US there was no king, but that the law was king.[8]

According to Zamboni 'practically all Western legal and political orders have adopted the rule of law'.[9] But is not simply a Western liberal democracy ideal. In the epilogue to his book, Bingham lists academics and leaders from around the world all subscribing to the Rule of Law.[10] Tamanaha sets out an even broader list:

> politicians, government officials, political and legal theorists, business leaders, development experts, the World Bank and IMF, and many others around the globe, from liberal and non-liberal societies, from developed countries and developing countries, promote the rule of law as offering worldwide benefit.[11]

The Rule of Law is not limited to the UK, or the USA. It is present in the German concept of *Rechsstaat* (the constitutional state), the French concept of *État de droit* (a state of law), the Italian concept of *Stato di diritto* (law-based state) and the Swedish one of *Rättsstaten* (state based on law). Linguistic ignorance precludes me from naming many non-European analogues. The Rule of Law is listed in Article 1 of the constitution of South Africa. It forms part of the preamble of the constitutions of Mali and Senegal. The constitutions of Algeria and Mauritius speak of the primacy of law. In Uzbekistan the constitutional reference is to the law-governed state, in Ukraine the law-based state, in the Lebanon the sovereignty of the law. Voermans cites these references and more on the importance of the Rule of Law in constitutional preambles, and notes the exponential rise in these references since the 1950s.[12] There is even a guide to the Rule of Law for politicians.[13]

[5] J Harrington, *The Prerogative of Popular Government* (1656).

[6] ES Corwin, 'The Higher Law Background of American Constitutional Law' (1928) 42 *Harvard Law Review* 149, 156.

[7] AT Mason, 'Ours – A Government of Laws and Not of Men' (1929) 13 *Constitutional Review* 197.

[8] T Paine, *Common Sense* (1776).

[9] M Zamboni, 'Legislating Politics: An Introduction' (2008) 2 *Legisprudence* 155, 156.

[10] T Bingham, *The Rule of Law* (London, Penguin UK, 2011) 171–73.

[11] B Tamanaha, *On The Rule of Law* (Cambridge, Cambridge University Press, 2004) 137.

[12] W Voermans, M Stremler and P Cliteur, *Constitutional Preambles: A Comparative Analysis* (Cheltenham, Edward Elgar Publishing, 2017) 34.

[13] Raoul Wallenberg Institute, *Rule of Law: A Guide for Politicians* (Raoul Wallenberg Institute 2012).

8.1.1. The Rule of Law in the UK

If we focus on the UK, there are a number of pieces of evidence to demonstrate the importance of the Rule of Law. First, the UK legislature has declared the importance of the rule of law. Part 1 of the Constitutional Reform Act 2005 is entitled the rule of law. Section 1 states that the Act does not affect the existing constitutional principle of the rule of law. Section 17 amends the Promissory Oaths Act 1868 so that the Lord Chancellor's oath includes a promise to 'respect the rule of law'. In a country without a codified constitution, these are important provisions.

It is true that this is the only place in the UK statute book with an express commitment to something called 'the Rule of Law'. However, many of the fundamental constitutional statutes in the UK give effect to some of the key precepts of the rule of law. Magna Carta 1215 is probably the single most important law on the UK statute book, and a key source of the rule of law.[14] The same basic principle, that citizens can only be punished in accordance with the law, is behind the Petition of Right 1628. Some key provisions of the Bill of Rights 1689 (Parliament's 'bargain' with the new King) were that there was no divine authority to overrule the law, that there was no power to suspend laws without the consent of Parliament and that there was no power to dispense with laws.

Second, judges have many times stressed the importance of the Rule of Law. Lord Neuberger, President of the Supreme Court, gave an interview warning of the dangers of governments ignoring judicial judgements.[15] The former Lord Chief Justice of Northern Ireland also speaking in an extra-judicial capacity, said that we were a 'society subject to the rule of law'.[16] Lord Steyn called the rule of law an 'overarching principle of constitutional law'.[17]

Judges also say the same when speaking in a judicial capacity. Lord Hope stated that 'the rule of law enforced by the courts is the ultimate controlling factor on which our constitution is based'[18] and the European Court of Justice agrees.[19] Lord Steyn ruled that 'unless there is the clearest provision to the contrary, Parliament must be presumed not to legislate contrary to the rule of law'.[20] The Supreme Court restated this when it stated that 'there is no principle more basic to our system of

[14] G Bindman, 'Magna Carta Lives' (2014) 164 *New Law Journal* 7.

[15] O Bowcott and legal affairs correspondent, 'Senior Judge Warns over Deportation of Terror Suspects to Torture States' *The Guardian* (5 March 2013) <www.guardian.co.uk/law/2013/mar/05/lord-neuberger-deportation-terror-suspects>.

[16] 'Law Chief: Informed Criticism Fine' *BBC* (2 May 2013) <www.bbc.co.uk/news/uk-northern-ireland-22389117>.

[17] Lord Steyn, 'Democracy through Law' [2002] *European Human Rights Law Review* 723, 727.

[18] *Axa General Insurance v Lord Advocate* [2011] UKSC 46, [51] and see also *Jackson v Attorney General* [2005] UKHL 56.

[19] *Kadi v Council of the European Union* [2009] 1 AC 1225.

[20] *R v Secretary of State for the Home Department ex p Pierson* [1998] AC 539, 591.

law than the maintenance of rule of law itself and the constitutional protection afforded by judicial review'.[21]

Third, politicians regularly cite the importance of the Rule of Law. Respect for the Rule of Law is part of the Pledge of Office of all Northern Ireland Ministers.[22] No Northern Ireland Minister can therefore be appointed unless they pledge to uphold the rule of law. Former Prime Minister David Cameron gave a speech to the Foreign Policy Centre. He was trying to describe the shared values of what it meant to be British and he said: 'We can do it in a single phrase, freedom under the rule of law'.[23] In debates on Bills in the Houses of Parliament, it is rare that a debate will pass without a reference to the Rule of Law.[24]

8.2. … and the Form of Legislation Can Promote it

Given the importance of the Rule of Law, how can we give effect to it? There are many practical ways to do this: obeying and implementing the law, respecting courts judgments, not undermining the independence of the judiciary, treating people equally. Some things can be done by legislation, for example including appeal rights in legislation, providing for the appointment of independent judges, not seeking immunity for breach of the law, obliging equal treatment under the law. These things are all to do with the *substance* of legislation – what it contains, its content. But there is another more subtle way that the Rule of Law can be vindicated – in the *form* of legislation. Not what we express, but how we express it. How we conceive of, structure and draft legislation and the processes that we go through whenever we are developing and enacting it. Although on the face of it, such an enquiry may seem dull and technical, its excavation exposes a rich seam of legisprudence – legal theory relating to legislation. Many interesting nuggets emerge, adding to our store of knowledge on both legislation and the Rule of Law.

The form of legislation offers huge scope to promote the Rule of Law. Legislation is our single most important source of law, regulating a vast sweep of our behaviour. If we enact legislation in accordance with the Rule of Law, we are delivering a meta-message that goes beyond the regulatory message of an individual statute. The meta-message is that we respect the Rule of Law, that we want law to apply equally, that we want citizens to be able to understand it, that we want it to be clear and certain and that we all agree to be subject to it. We can do much to promote the Rule of Law by adhering to some relatively modest and politically uncontroversial principles.

[21] *R (Cart) v Upper Tribunal* [2011] UKSC 2 at [122].

[22] Pledge of Office, 1.4(cd) and (ce).

[23] D Cameron, 'Speech to the Foreign Policy Centre' (Foreign Policy Centre, 24 August 2005). See further speech on Extremism, Individual Rights and the Rule of Law in Britain, 26/2/2008, Equality and Human Rights Commission.

[24] See various Reports of the Rule of Law Monitoring of Legislation Project, at the Bingham Centre for the Rule of Law, available at https://binghamcentre.biicl.org/.

8.2.1. The Particular Role of Legislative Drafters in Promoting the Rule of Law in the Form of Legislation

Although this book is directed at all those involved in the process of making law, legislative drafters have a very particular and important role. Legislative drafters (also referred to as legislative counsel, parliamentary counsel or law writers) are those whose job it is to actually draft or write the law.

Not only are drafters important to the process of making law, they also have a special responsibility for the content and integrity of the statute book. This is perhaps best summed up in the description of legislative drafters as 'guardians of the statute book'. Although it is unclear who first coined this phrase, it has been used by Bromley,[25] Burrows,[26] Levert,[27] Elliot[28] and Poloko.[29] In a similar vein, drafters have been called 'custodians of the statute book' by Donelan,[30] and Wolmarans.[31] Erasmus endorsed Bennion's use of the phrase 'keepers of the statute book'[32] as a description of drafters, 'what a lovely word that – keeper – with its echoes of custodian, preserver and protector'.[33] Erasmus makes the point that politicians come and go, but laws (and even drafters) are there for longer. Laws makes exactly the same point when he considers drafters as being advocates for the integrity of the statute book.[34] He argues that they are responsible for maintaining legislative language at a high standard so as not to debase the 'coinage of communication' between the legislature and the executive.[35] Wilson argues that drafters have a special responsibility for the coherence of the statute book.[36] Archer argues that responsibility to protect the statute book also belongs to the Law Officers, that is, the Attorney General and Solicitor General.[37] Daintith and Page consider this

[25] M Bromley, 'Whose Law Is It? – Accessibility Through LENZ: Opportunities for the New Zealand Public to Shape Law as It Is Made' [2009] *The Loophole* 16.

[26] J Burrows, 'Legislation: Primary, Secondary and Tertiary' (2011) 42 *Victoria University of Wellington Law Review* 65, 69.

[27] L Levert, 'Work Methods and Processes in a Drafting Environment' [2011] *The Loophole* 23, 36.

[28] D Elliot, 'What Is Plain English?' (1990) 11 *Statute Law Review* 237, 238.

[29] L Poloko, *Drafting of Legislation in Compliance with Model Laws* (Unpublished LLM thesis 2012) <http://sas-space.sas.ac.uk/4703/1/Lesedi_Poloko_LLM_ALS_Dissertation.pdf>.

[30] E Donelan, *Review of the Irish Statute Book: A Guide to Irish Legislation by Brian Hunt* (First Law Book Review 2008) <www.francisbennion.com/pdfs/non-fb/2008/2008-002-nfb-review-of-brian-hunt-book.pdf>.

[31] J Wolmarans, 'An Argument for Codification of Provincial Legislation and the Establishment of an Independent Legislative Services Agency for KwaZulu Natal' (August 2005).

[32] F Bennion, 'More on Godfrey Carter CBE Deceased' *The Times Register (Lives Remembered)* (9 September 2003) <www.francisbennion.com/pdfs/fb/2003/2003-017-lr006-more-godfrey-carter.pdf>.

[33] Janet Erasmus, 'Keepers of the Statute Book: Lessons from the Space-time Continuum' [2010] The Loophole 7. Elliot also endorsed Bennion's phrase, D Elliot, 'Access to Statute Law in New Zealand' (1990) 20 *Victoria University of Wellington Law Review* 131, 150.

[34] S Laws, 'Drawing the Line' in C Stefanou and H Xanthaki (eds), *Drafting Legislation: A Modern Approach* (Farnham, Ashgate, 2008).

[35] ibid 32.

[36] C Wilson, 'Managing Increasing Government Expectations with Respect to Legislation While Maintaining Quality' [2009] *The Loophole* 21.

[37] P Archer, *The Role of the Law Officers* (London, Fabian Society, 1978).

point in detail, describing drafters as custodians of legal values who have a duty 'to the law and the statute book'.[38]

As well as being regarded as guardians of the statute book, legislative drafters are also regarded as having a special obligation to the Rule of Law. Gashabizi, a Rwandan drafter, said that it is 'a cardinal principle of the rule of law that citizens should know in advance their rights and obligations under the law'.[39] His context was arguing in favour of clarity in legislation. Hashim, a Malaysian drafter, presents a case for adoption of plain language drafting.[40] She cites several reasons for this 'but to the writer the most important reason is the "rule of law"'.[41] Greenberg, a British drafter, said that 'a good Parliamentary drafter is … totally dedicated to the rule of law'.[42] Davies, a Welsh drafter, cites both Fuller and Bingham as evidence for his contention that legislation in Wales should be accessible in Welsh.[43] Seidman, an American drafter, said that a 'Third World drafter cannot avoid the obligation to draft to enhance the rule of law'.[44] Seidman puts the case particularly strongly, not only should the form of the legislation respect the Rule of Law, but it must be drafted in such a way that it maximises compliance with the Rule of Law on the ground. This requires the drafter to have a substantial policy input into legislation. One of Elliot's (a Canadian drafter) arguments in favour of high quality legislation is that it enhances respect for the Rule of Law.[45] Bartole concludes that 'the drafting of the legislative acts is strictly connected with the establishment of the rule of law'.[46] For Bartole, if the drafters aren't experts in the Rule of Law, then those experts must also be brought into the process of making legislation. For Lovric, an Australian drafter, if there is a loss of experienced legislative counsel this poses a risk not just to the drafting office, but to the Rule of Law itself.[47]

Laws, a former First Parliamentary Counsel in the UK, didn't expressly state that drafters should obey the Rule of Law. However, he has stated that the Rule of Law

[38] T Daintith and A Page, *The Executive in the Constitution: Structure, Autonomy and Internal Control* (Oxford, Oxford University Press, 1999) 254.

[39] Alain Songa Gashabizi, 'In Pursuit of Clarity: How Far Should the Drafter Go?' (2013) 39 *Commonwealth Law Bulletin* 415, 416.

[40] NA Hashim, 'Plain Language: Give It a Try!' (2013) 39 *Commonwealth Law Bulletin* 423.

[41] ibid 425.

[42] D Greenberg, *Laying Down the Law: A Discussion of the People, Processes and Problems That Shape Acts of Parliament* (London, Sweet & Maxwell, 2011) 31. He cites the importance of the rule of law again at 222, 271.

[43] D Hughes and Huw G Davies, 'Accessible Bilingual Legislation for Wales (Deddfwriaeth Hygyrch a Dwyieithog i Gymru)' (2012) 33 *Statute Law Review* 103. The job description for Welsh drafters states that 'we also seek to draft legislation in a way that is consistent with the government's responsibility to the rule of law', Welsh Government, 'Senior Legislative Counsel (Deputy Director) Welsh Government Job Description and Person Specification' (2013).

[44] R Seidman, 'Drafting for the Rule of Law: Maintaining Legality in Developing Countries' (1987) 12 *Yale Journal of International Law* 84, 86.

[45] D Elliot, 'Drafting Legislation: Challenges and Improving Ways' (Lebanon Parliament, 16 February 2012) <www.davidelliott.ca/legislativedrafting.htm>.

[46] S Bartole, 'Law-Making Principles under the Rule of Law' (2012) <www.venice.coe.int/WebForms/documents/?pdf=CDL%282013%29016-e> 64.

[47] D Lovric, 'A Strategic View of Drafting Training for Tomorrow's Needs' [2013] *The Loophole* 7, 15.

(in particular Fuller and Bingham) 'provide[s] a useful pragmatic guide to drafters on how to avoid producing legislation that cuts across the grain of the values of the law'.[48] Another former First Parliamentary Counsel has expressly referred not only to the rule of law but to Bingham's definition of the rule of law and then went on to say that 'For legislative drafters, and for the government's online publishers, this is a fundamental part of our mission'.[49] According to Feldman 'one of the tasks of lawyers in politics … to uphold respect for the values of the rule of law among ministers, civil servants and parliamentarians'.[50]

Daintith and Page set out a non-exhaustive list of the kind of things that drafters should object to.[51] Although this list isn't headed 'the Rule of Law' it contains many elements that form part of the Rule of Law. They go on to say that 'in the absence of a higher law by which a sovereign Parliament is bound, the concept of legal policy as interpreted by Parliamentary Counsel is as close as our system has traditionally come to a check on the "constitutionality" of legislation'.[52]

8.3. Principles for the Form of Legislation Derived from the Rule of Law

This book has derived a number of principles for the form of legislation from different elements of the Rule of Law. These principles are set out below, arranged by reference to their Rule of Law source.

8.3.1. Principles Derived from Accessibility

In chapter two I examined accessibility – that citizens must have access to legislation. Bingham, Fuller, Raz and Locke, along with others, spoke of the importance of accessibility. There are difficulties with access, in terms of the cost of it, the volume of legislation, its interconnectedness and the speed with which we make new legislation.

I derived three form of legislation principles. First, the text of the law must be *available* to citizens: this means both the law as enacted, and the law as it applies at any given point in time. In addition, citizens need to know what law applies in the

[48] S Laws, 'Legislation and Politics', in *Law in Politics, Politics in Law* (Oxford, Hart Publishing, 2015) 96.

[49] R Heaton, 'Making the Law Easier for Users: The Role of Statutes' (Institute of Advanced Legal Studies, 14 October 2013) <www.gov.uk/government/speeches/making-the-law-easier-for-users-the-role-of-statutes--2> accessed 20 January 2016.

[50] D Feldman, 'Looking Back and Moving On', in *Law in Politics, Politics in Law* (Oxford, Hart Publishing, 2015) 257.

[51] Daintith and Page (n 38) 254–56.

[52] ibid 254.

different parts of the UK. As well as the bald text of the legislation, the legislation must also be contextualised, by referring to other legislation (and non-legislative texts) that have a direct impact upon how the law will be used. Finally, legislation must be enacted to promote findability, to make it easier for the user to find the particular statutory provision that is relevant to them.

Second, legislation ought to be *navigable*. It must be well-mapped and signposted so that users can find their way around it as easily as possible. There are many specific forms of legislation techniques to enhance navigability: descriptive short titles of Acts, avoiding omnibus legislation, descriptive section headings, logical structure for Acts (including, where appropriate, parallel structures), signposting of other relevant provisions, sensible numbering and avoiding 'hidden' provisions.

Third, legislation must be *inclusive* of all important legal information. If something extraneous to the legislation will have a direct influence on it, the reader of the legislation will have a misleading impression of what the law does. This is particularly the case where a broad power is included in an Act, but a ministerial statement is made that, notwithstanding this broad formulation, the power will only be exercised in limited ways.

8.3.2. Principles Derived from Prospectivity

Chapter three covered prospectivity. Bingham stated that law must take effect generally in the future. Fuller and Raz both expressly stated that legislation must be prospective. Prospectivity means that law must take effect in the future and not go back in time to have a legal effect before it is made. I established a fresh taxonomy of Janus-faced legislation to highlight the different ways in which legislation can apply over time: retroactive legislation, retrospective legislation and legislation that affects existing rights.

The first form of legislation principle is that legislation must be *explicit about the period of time* to which it applies. This includes being explicit about the precise subset of Janus-faced legislation it contains. Second, *transitional and saving provisions* ought to be used to ameliorate the negative effects of legislation that contains Janus-faced components. Third, there is no absolute rule that legislation must always be prospective, what is necessary is a consideration in each individual case, by *reference to criteria* set out in common law and in the European Convention on Human Rights.

8.3.3. Principles Derived from Predictability

Chapter four was concerned with predictability – that users ought to know what the legal effect of their actions will be by reading the legislation. Bingham, Locke, Fuller and Raz all argued from this perspective. There are sometimes reasons why legislation is not predictable, for example if it is as a result of a political compromise that papers over ambiguities.

I derived six form of legislation principles. First, legislation must be *determinate*, it must be fixed and certain. In order to be determinate, it has to be unambiguous and precise. There is however a difficult line between being exhaustive enough to cover all circumstances, and being over-precise and burdening the legislation with too much detail. Second, legislation must be relatively *stable*, so that the law today is reasonably similar to the law tomorrow. This doesn't mean that the law should remain set in stone, but it does mean that there must be good reason for legal change. In addition, the destabilising effect of frequent or large legal change can be ameliorated by highlighting the change, advertising it or giving a long lead in time for it. Dealing with rapid technological change is a challenge for the stability of legislation, but this can be partially solved by legislating more in general principles and less in technical detail.

Third, legislation should have a *clear commencement*. The date the law comes into force should be immediately obvious to the reader without having to search for additional legislation setting out commencement dates. Fourth, legislation should be drafted in a *consistent* manner. So, words should mean the same thing in a statute, grammar should be applied consistently (and in accordance with normal grammatical rules), similar things should be done in similar ways, and the same issues should be addressed. But as with stability, this doesn't mean ossification, legislation can also innovate where that helps the user.

Fifth, the law on the statute book should be the same as the law *applied in the real world*. So, the law shouldn't be ignored, it shouldn't be foolish, impossible or Panglossian. There shouldn't be a disconnect between legislation and practice. Nor should there be things in the legislation that aren't intended to be applied in practice. Sixth, legislation should be capable of being *implemented*. So, the legislation must contain implementation mechanisms, it must contain sanctions. As well as saying what must happen, it ought to also say what is the outcome if the person fails to comply with a duty.

8.3.4. Principles Derived from Intelligibility

In chapter five I examined intelligibility and clarity, meaning that the law must be capable of being easily understood by users. Bingham, Raz and Fuller all argued that law must be intelligible, and Bentham argued that it must be cognoscible. There are some sound reasons that can make the law more complex and less intelligible, for example where the law seeks to be exhaustive, or where there is a complex policy.

There are seven form of legislation principles. First, legislation need not be intelligible in the abstract but must focus on the *characteristics of the user*. So, if a statute will be used by a specific user group, it must be intelligible to that user group. Although citizens will sometimes use intermediaries to understand legislation, it should always be enacted so that it is understandable by all readers, not just by intermediaries. Second, both the *legislation as amended and the amending legislation* need to be intelligible. So, users need to know both what the changes being made to the law are, as well as what the law will be like after those changes. It is possible to do this by creative use of textual amendment with explanatory material.

Third, we should avoid *excessive interconnectedness of legislation*. The more times a reader has to jump from provision to provision, from statute to statute, the less intelligible the legislation is. Fourth, legislators can make use of *plain language* techniques. Plain language is part of a broader movement to make writing easier to understand. There are many specific plain language techniques, such as shorter sentences, simpler words, active not passive voice etc.

Fifth, we can use *easification* techniques. These are specific linguistic tools that have been used by professionals in that field to make language easier to understand. Sixth, we can use *good writing* techniques. As with plain language, these are tools to make for a better quality of writing. Seventh, we can use *examples* in legislation to make things clearer for readers. Examples both set out specific matters that fall within or outside the law, as well as providing an illustration of how the law will be applied in practice.

8.3.5. Principles Derived from Constraints on the Exercise of Discretion

Chapter six examined the Rule of Law principle that there must be constraints on the exercise of discretion. This does not mean all discretion and no law, but equally, not all law and no discretion. I derived nine form of legislation principles.

First, there must be a clear *demarcation between law and discretion*. Legislation should set out areas where officials must to a particular thing, and areas where they have a power or a discretion to do a particular thing. The difference between these must be clear. Second, there are six different *dimensions in which discretion can be constrained*, six different general ways in which limits can be placed on the exercise of discretion. This is done by the way that the discretion is framed, and the different formal limits inserted into the legislation granting the discretion.

Third, *ouster clauses ought not to be included* in legislation. The power to oust the jurisdiction of the courts grants too much unfettered discretion to ministers and officials because it allows them to do things without the threat of a judicial check in the background. Fourth, and in a similar vein, we should *restrict the power of officials to create new exemptions*. Granting anyone the power to create an opt-out from the law allows too much discretion to that person. No-one should simply have the power to set aside the law. Fifth, *purpose clauses* can help to constrain discretion by expressly setting out the purposes for which the legislation is being made. This helps to frame the exercise of that discretion, by marking the boundaries, or the permitted reasons for official actions.

We then turn to constraining the exercise of discretion by way of the power to make secondary legislation. The sixth form of legislation principle is to *constrain the exercise of the power to make secondary legislation*. That power is too important to drop, but the way in which the power is framed can include important safeguards against its inappropriate exercise. As part of this, the seventh principle is to reject the use of *super-enabling clauses* – these clauses grant too much power to ministers to make legislation without proper parliamentary scrutiny. The eighth principle is to curtail the use of *framework legislation*. This legislation sets out the general theme of a statutory scheme, but leaves too much discretion to ministers to set out the detail by way of secondary legislation. Finally, *Henry VIII clauses should be avoided*. These clauses grant ministers the power to repeal or amend an Act of Parliament, but without usual attendant degree of parliamentary scrutiny.

8.3.6. Principles Derived from Equality before the Law

Finally, in chapter seven I examined the Rule of Law principle of equality before the law. Not only are we all subject to the law, but we all must be treated equally under the law. No-one has a special rank, or is a different class, which means that the ordinary rules don't apply to them. I derived four principles for the form of legislation from this.

First, *legislation should be non-gendered*, that is, it should apply in form and substance to all genders. The most obvious way that this can be done is by the use of gender neutral language. Going further, we can say that it should be gender silent, that is, rather than specifying male and female, it should be silent on issues of gender. This makes legislation satisfy equality by applying to all, not just to binary conceptions of gender. Following on from this, the second principle is that legislation should avoid and *remove discriminatory and offensive terms*. Even though these terms may have been appropriate in the past, if they now amount to a negative depiction of certain sections of society, their use should end. Third, the process for making legislation should include *equality and gender impact assessments*. This provides a formal mechanism for considering how legislation will affect all in society. This allows legislators to move away from pre-conceptions and the limitations of their own experience, to misquote Robbie Burns, they allow us to see others as they see themselves.

The fourth principle is *vindicability*. Vindicability means that the rights and obligations set out in legislation can be relied upon, used and vindicated by those for whose benefit they were enacted. This requires laws both known and knowable, laws that are practical and realistic, with routes to enforcement that are viable, both financially and otherwise.

I concluded chapter seven with two case studies demonstrating the challenges to equality before the law. The tangled and multi-layered relationship between the Crown and legislation shows us one institution that has rights and privileges in respect of legislation that the rest of us do not have. Recent legislation dealing with the armed forces displays an intention to place others in a privileged and unequal position under the law.

8.4. Justification: What Value Do these Principles Add to Society?

In a climate of populism with a predilection for authoritarian leaders, it is not enough to leave the argument with the conclusion that because doing X would promote the Rule of Law, then X is the right thing to do. It is not enough to assume that others share the view that the Rule of Law is a good thing, and therefore anything in conformity with the Rule of Law will be universally accepted. It is also necessary to justify it, to vindicate it, to show the benefit of the Rule of Law. In this section, I set out a range of values lying behind the Rule of Law that will be satisfied if we adopt form of legislation principles to give effect to the Rule of Law. This is not a moot point about legislative drafting styles, of interest only to those involved in the technical side of legisprudence. Instead, enacting legislation in accordance with the Rule of Law provides direct and tangible benefits to all of us.

8.4.1. Observance of Rules

One of the prime purposes of legislation is to regulate human conduct. One reason why we pass a law outlawing theft is to stop people stealing. But human conduct cannot be regulated by a law if humans don't know what the law is. This is at the root of Raz's theory of the rule of law – if we are to obey the law, we must know what the law is.[53] The vast majority of legislators want their laws to be obeyed, and the first prerequisite for this is that those laws are accessible. Austin changes the focus slightly on this point – accessible laws offer guidance and information for those who are bound to obey them.[54] This is essentially the same point though – we can't obey rules unless we know them.

If citizens can't understand the rules, then they can't obey them. Although rarely it is enough for legislation to simply be left on the page, by and large, legislation is made by governments in order to have effect.[55] If the function of legislation is to effect social change, to be observed by us, to be implemented by government, then this will be severely hindered unless the legislation is intelligible to those observing and implementing it. Sitting behind the Rule of Law is the pragmatic need for legislation to be observed.

[53] J Raz, 'The Rule of Law and Its Virtue', in *The Authority of Law: Essays on Law and Morality* (Oxford, Oxford University Press, 1979).

[54] J Austin and S Austin, *The Province of Jurisprudence Determined* (London, J Murray, 1861).

[55] H Xanthaki, *Drafting Legislation: Art and Technology of Rules for Regulation* 1st edn (Oxford, Hart Publishing, 2014) 2.

8.4.2. Fairness

If you are going to be held liable under a law, it is only fair if you know what that law is. The citizens of Fuller's Rex got very annoyed when they were expected to obey secret laws. In Kafka's *The Trial*, Joseph K is subjected to a travesty of justice when he is prosecuted under a law that is not disclosed to him.[56] Inaccessible, unpredictable or retroactive laws aren't fair because people have no opportunity to modify their behaviour to avoid the consequences of breaches of those laws. If you can predict the legal consequences of your actions, then it is fair to hold you to those consequences. However, if it is difficult for you to know what those consequences will be, it is unfair to hold you to them.

The *Haw* case provides a bad example of unpredictable legislation having an unfair effect upon an individual.[57] The legislation was section 132 of the Serious and Organised Crime and Police Act 2005 that made provision for regulating demonstrations in Parliament Square. A person would be guilty of an offence if they didn't do various things 'when the demonstration starts'. Unfortunately for the prosecutor, Mr Haw 'started' his demonstration long before the Act was made. Although the Divisional Court ruled that 'starts' meant 'starts',[58] the Court of Appeal ruled that 'starts' actually meant 'starts or continued'. He was therefore convicted of the offence.

The case is important for several reasons. For present purposes though, it is the lack of predictability that is problematic. An individual is entitled to read the law and be reasonably able to predict its effect. If an offence relates to conduct when a demonstration 'starts' then it is unfair that judges read this as meaning that it relates to conduct when a demonstration 'starts or continues'.

Particularly when it comes to criminal law, or tax law, it is unfair to suffer a detriment by virtue of law that is unintelligible. As Leith said 'a fundamental rule of law is that those governed by the law have the right to know what the law is'.[59] If I can't understand a law, it is unfair to hold me to account under it. This is perhaps the source of the various interpretative rules against doubtful penalisation set out by Bennion.[60]

Furthermore, fairness is enhanced by equality before the law. If there is an onerous law (for example restrictions on liberty due to the coronavirus pandemic) but everyone is subject to it, then people are more likely to follow it. But if they think that the Prime Minister and those in power are not subject to it, then their innate sense of unfairness will kick in and they will resent being forced to follow that law. The unfairness inherent in unequal treatment under the law has been encapsulated in the criticism meted out by the Labour Party in the UK – that it

[56] F Kafka, *The Trial* (Berlin, Verlag Die Schmiede, 1925).

[57] *Haw v Secretary of State for the Home Department* [2006] EWCA Civ 532.

[58] [2005] EWHC 2061 (Admin).

[59] P Leith and C Fellows, 'BAILII, Legal Education and Open Access to Law' (2013) 4 *European Journal of Law and Technology* <http://ejlt.org//article/view/209>.

[60] O Jones, *Bennion on Statutory Interpretation* 6th revised edn (London, Butterworths Law, 2013).

is one rule for them, and another for the rest of us. This criticism has now turned into a political slogan.[61]

8.4.3. Respect for Human Autonomy

Accessible law treats humans as rational beings who can make decisions about their conduct based upon correct information. Accessible law therefore respects the value of human autonomy and human freedom to choose. If we know what a law is, we can properly plan our activities. Bentham distinguishes us from 'brutes' because of our ability to plan for the future, and this is one reason for having a system of known laws.[62] For Waldron, part of the dignity of legislation is that people 'need to be able to plan around the law's demands in the autonomous organisation of their lives'.[63]

Predictable legislation means that we credit citizens with the ability to make up their own minds about their courses of action. It also means that we credit them with the ability to read and understand legislation. Predictable legislation respects human autonomy and treats us with respect.

8.4.4. Certainty

Predictability gives greater certainty to people about the content of the law. The desire for certainty reflects the core values set out above, in particular the possibility of planning your conduct. Bentham cites this as the principle of security that 'requires that events, so far as they depend upon laws, should conform to the expectations which the law itself has created'.[64] Certainty gives us security and peace of mind. It allows us to plan and to have a reasonable expectation that if we do a particular thing, then there will be a particular outcome.

It is for this reason that major legal reforms are not taken regularly. For example, the referendum on Scottish independence was (originally) seen as a 'once in a generation' activity.[65] Certainty has also been enshrined in legislation. For example, the Northern Ireland Act 1998 allows for a border poll to determine if the people of Northern Ireland want to remain in the UK or be part of the Republic of Ireland. However, the Act provides that there must be at least seven years between border polls.[66]

[61] See for example, BBC News, 12 January 2022 'Downing street party: "Why is it one rule for them, one rule for us?"' available at www.bbc.co.uk/news/av/uk-wales-politics-59974629.

[62] J Bentham, *Principles of the Civil Code* (J Bowring ed, Edinburgh, William Tait, 1843).

[63] J Waldron, *The Rule of Law and the Measure of Property* (Cambridge, Cambridge University Press, 2012) 53.

[64] Bentham (n 62).

[65] The Scottish Government, *Scotland's Future: Your Guide to an Independent Scotland* (The Scottish Government 2013).

[66] Paragraph 3 of Schedule 1 to the Northern Ireland Act 1998.

8.4.5. Economic Development

There is a subset of certainty that is particularly important – economic certainty. Predictable laws promote economic certainty that in turn promotes the economic wellbeing of a nation and its attractiveness to international investors. The English courts recognised this a long time ago 'In all mercantile transactions the great object should be certainty; and therefore, it is of more consequence that the rule should be certain, than whether the rule is established one way or the other'.[67]

Bingham himself stated 'the successful conduct of trade, investment and business generally is promoted by a body of accessible legal rules governing commercial rights and obligations'.[68] The World Bank measures how open a country is to business.[69] One criterion is that regulations are transparent, which it defines as regulations that are clear and accessible to anyone who needs to use them.[70] A jurisdiction may have fantastic intellectual property laws for example, but if no one can read them, no-one will register intellectual property rights there. In the Isle of Man, Marsh-Smith could not be more explicit about why they were creating an online database of legislation. 'For a sophisticated jurisdiction like the Isle of Man looking to attract outside investment it was clearly unacceptable that Manx legislation was obtainable only by subscription and a trip to the Tynwald library'.[71]

Predictable legislation allows for long-term planning. If a company knows that the long-term target is to reduce greenhouse gas emissions, then it can plan its energy policy accordingly.[72] If a retailer knows there is a legal obligation that goods must be of a satisfactory quality, it can arrange its production processes accordingly.[73]

Some of the strongest proponents for the Rule of Law are economists. Their view is that Rule of Law gives legal stability, certainty and promotes the protection of contractual and property rights.[74] These are preconditions to economic growth and law is a 'springboard to economic development'.[75] The *Economist* magazine published an article entitled 'Economics and the Rule of Law: Order in the Jungle' wherein it was argued that 'economists have repeatedly found that the better the rule of law, the richer the nation'.[76] Barron talks of the World Bank's 'discovery' of

[67] *Vallejo v Wheeler* (1774) 1 Cowp 143, 153.

[68] Bingham (n 10) 38.

[69] World Bank, *Doing Business 2013: Smarter Regulations for Small and Medium-Sized Enterprises* (World Bank and International Finance Corporation 2013).

[70] ibid.

[71] L Marsh-Smith and G Wright, 'Information Technology on a Budget: A Giant Leap for the Isle of Man' (winds of change-Calc conference, Cape Town, April 2013).

[72] Climate Change Act 2008.

[73] Consumer Rights Act 2015.

[74] Seidman (n 44) 88 (see footnote 15 of that page).

[75] S Holmes, 'Can Foreign Aid Promote the Rule of Law?' (1999) 8 *East European Constitutional Review* 68, 68.

[76] 'Economics and the Rule of Law: Order in the Jungle' [2008] *The Economist* <www.economist.com/node/10849115> accessed 12 May 2013.

the rule of law as a means to promote economic development.[77] Indeed, the World Bank has an index on its website where Rule of Law indicators can be compared to economic progress.[78] As Barro says 'the general idea of these indexes is to gauge the attractiveness of a country's investment climate by considering the effectiveness of law enforcement, the sanctity of contracts, and the state of other influences on the security of property rights'.[79] Carothers dampened this enthusiasm somewhat by pointing out that there was little empirical evidence that linked the rule of law with development.[80]

8.4.6. Constitutional Check on Power

If the rules are known by the ruled, it is more difficult for the rulers to break them. So, it can be said that knowable legislation is a check on state power. This is Locke's view[81] as well as Fuller's.[82] Ronald, in the context of executive legislation, viewed 'publicity as a safeguard for holding the rule-making officials in check'.[83] Carr said that laws should be published 'so that the public, in being informed of its ante-natal opportunity to criticise and the place where copies of the proposed rules can be obtained, is indirectly informed that legislation is impending'.[84] Although, Carr's argument is more about the value of consultations than the need for accessible legislation. More recently Irresberger and Jasiak see publication of legislation as providing a measure of 'democratic control' over the government.[85] For Shinar, the rule of law is 'first and foremost about tempering official power'.[86]

Our laws obtain their democratic legitimacy by being voted through by parliamentarians. If the parliamentarians don't understand what they are voting for, we lose a major part of that legitimacy. Furthermore, if the parliamentarians don't understand legislation, they cannot effectively scrutinise it. Intelligible legislation enhances democratic legitimacy.

[77] G Barron, 'The World Bank and Rule of Law Reforms' (London School of Economics and Political Science, Internationa Development Working Paper Series no 05-70, December 2005).

[78] http://info.worldbank.org/governance/wgi/index.asp.

[79] RJ Barro, 'Determinants of Democracy' (1999) 107 *Journal of Political Economy* S158, S173.

[80] T Carothers, *Promoting the Rule of Law Abroad: The Problem of Knowledge* (Washington DC, Carnegie Endowment for International Peace, 2003).

[81] J Locke, *Locke: Two Treatises of Government* (London, Awnsham Churchill, 1689).

[82] LL Fuller, *The Morality of Law: Revised Edition* (Revised, New Haven, Yale University Press, 1969).

[83] J Ronald, 'Publication of Federal Administrative Legislation' (1938) 7 *George Washington Law Review* 52.

[84] C Carr, *Delegated Legislation* (Cambridge, Cambridge University Press, 1921).

[85] K Irresberger and A Jasiak, 'Publication', in *Legislation in Europe: A Comprehensive Guide for Scholars and Practitioners* (Oxford, Hart Publishing, 2017).

[86] A Shinar, 'One Rule to Rule Them All? Rules of Law against the Rule of Law' (2017) 5 *The Theory and Practice of Legislation* 149.

8.4.7. Democratic Governance

If legislation is uncertain, then at some point, someone will have to decide on its actual meaning. The two key actors who will most commonly make this decision are the courts and the executive. So, if a word in a statute is vague and citizens are arguing over its meaning, the authoritative decision on meaning will generally be made by a court. Or if the command contained in a statute is imprecise, then the executive, in implementing that command, will reach its own decision on meaning. The problem with this is that there is a lack of democratic accountability. We vote for the legislature and they are meant to pass laws making the key decisions. And if we don't like those key decisions we can lobby to change the law, or vote out those legislators. But citizens don't have the same rights when it comes to judges or officials making key decisions. Unpredictable legislation creates a vacuum that can lead to a lack of democratic power, as VanSickle-Ward states 'policy-making by the bureaucracy and the courts poses a serious challenge for democratic governance'.[87]

8.5. The Why, What and How of Legislation

Any consideration of proposed legislation will come up with three interlinked and fundamental questions:

1. Why are we enacting this law?
2. What are we enacting?
3. How are we enacting it?

All three questions are important, but it is the first question that soaks up most of the political, public and academic debate. The why question is about the merits of the law, whether or not it is a good idea. The nature of this debate on this question is generally determined by party politics and political ideology: do we favour a big state or small state, free markets or government intervention, individual choices or communal responsibilities?

The second question is the detail of the legislation – what exactly is being enacted? Not just the headline policy (for example, to protect the environment) but the precise details (what type of emissions must be reduced, by what percentage, by reference to what baseline, in what time frame, with what sanctions for failure). The answers to the second question emerge in the policy development and legislative drafting phase of the legislation. On many occasions, it is only when draft legislation is being produced that there is the opportunity and capacity to fully consider all aspects of the policy. This second question does attract some light

[87] R VanSickle-Ward, *The Devil Is in the Details: Understanding the Causes of Policy Specificity and Ambiguity* (Albany, SUNY Press, 2014) 6.

and political focus, particularly by those who will be directly affected by a new law. It is partly a matter of political preference, but also partly about efficacy – will this particular provision produce the desired result?

The third question is the neglected bronze medal play-off match of the legislative world. Everyone wants to watch the gold/silver match, but there is much less interest in the fight for third and fourth place. But the how question is still fundamentally important. Once the why and the what arguments have been resolved, we are still left with the question of how to enact this sparkling new policy. What is the correct legislative vehicle? What form of words should be used? How should it be structured? In short, what form should the legislation take?

The how question, the form of legislation, is (hopefully) not a question to be resolved by reference to political ideology. It is hard to frame an argument that legislation should be uncertain, inaccessible or unintelligible. There already exist a core set of agreed-upon principles in the Rule of Law that can be used to inform the how. It ought not to be a partisan question to be resolved by partisan political preference. It should instead be a matter of deciding the most efficacious application of agreed-upon principles. Or in the language of Aristotle, it is phronesis – the practical application of wisdom. If we share an appreciation of the importance of the Rule of Law, then it becomes nearly a technical process of fully applying Rule of Law values to legislation.

My goal in this book has been to take the Rule of Law as my starting point and from it derive principles for better legislation. Taken individually, none of my form of legislation principles are startlingly innovative. But they are systematic, holistic and based upon sound Rule of Law foundations. They are also practical and capable of being implemented, as well as resonating with principles that other legisprudential scholars have advocated.

But, dear reader, what are you going to do with these form of legislation principles? If you are in government, will you ensure that legislation that you introduce is available and navigable? If you are a parliamentarian, will you enact legislation that is unintelligible to you? If you are a parliamentary official advising legislators, will you advise that a draft Bill ought to be prospective only, or at least ameliorate the impact of any backward-facing provisions? If you are a legislative drafter, will you accept a degree of vagueness of policy that makes the law indeterminate? If you are a civil servant developing policy, will you create policy so fiendishly complex, that not even Solomon, in all his wisdom, could understand the resulting legislation? If you are a judge, will you broadly or narrowly construe legislation granting excessive discretion to officials or ministers? If you are a lobbyist or member of an interest group trying to influence legislation, will you accept it if legislation has a discriminatory effect upon certain sections of society?

Finally, and most importantly. If you are a voter, will you put up with law-makers who enact too much law, too frequently, and that is impossible to understand?

BIBLIOGRAPHY

Adams, K, 'Behind the Scenes of the Comma Dispute' *Globe and Mail* (28 August 2007) <http://adamsdrafting.com/downloads/g-and-m-082807.pdf>

Adigun, M and others, 'Symbolic Legislation and the Regulation of Stroke Biobanking and Genomics Research in Sub-Saharan Africa' (2021) 9 *Theory and Practice of Legislation* 404

Agrast, M and Botero, J, *World Justice Report: Rule of Law Index 20122013* (World Justice Report, 2013)

Allan, T, 'The Rule of Law as the Rule of Reasons: Consent and Constitutionalism' (1999) 115 *Law Quarterly Review* 221

Allen, SCK, *Law in the Making* (Oxford, Clarendon Press, 1964)

Amos, M, *Human Rights Law* 3rd edn (Oxford, Hart Publishing, 2021)

Anthony, K, 'Public Access to Legislation Project: Served with Accompaniments' (2008) 16 *Australian Law Librarian* 21

Archer, P, *The Role of the Law Officers* (London, Fabian Society, 1978)

Asgeirsson, H, 'On Transferability of Legislative Solutions: The Functionality Test' in C Stefanou and H Xanthaki (eds), *Drafting Legislation: A Modern Approach* (Farnham, Ashgate, 2008)

—— 'Can Legal Practice Adjudicate between Theories of Vagueness?' (Social Science Research Network 2015) SSRN Scholarly Paper ID 2687091 <http://papers.ssrn.com/abstract=2687091>

Austin, J and Austin, S, *The Province of Jurisprudence Determined* (London, J Murray, 1861)

'Ban on New Petrol and Diesel Cars in UK from 2030 under PM's Green Plan' *BBC News* (18 November 2020) <www.bbc.com/news/science-environment-54981425>

Baratta, R, 'Complexity of EU Law in the Domestic Implementing Process' (2014) 2 *Theory and Practice of Legislation* 293

Bardon, J, *A History of Ulster* (Newtownards, The Blackstaff Press, 2001)

Barnes, J, 'Shining Examples' [2004] *The Loophole* 8

—— 'The Continuing Debate about "Plain Language Legislation": A Law Reform Conundrum' (2006) 27 *Statute Law Review* 83

Barrett Browning, E, 'How Do I Love Thee (Sonnet 43)'

Barro, R, 'Determinants of Democracy' (1999) 107 *Journal of Political Economy* S158

Barron, G, 'The World Bank and Rule of Law Reforms' (London School of Economics and Political Science, Internationa Development Working Paper Series no 05-70, December 2005)

Bar-Siman-Tov, I, 'The Puzzling Resistance to Judicial Review of the Legislative Process' (2011) 91 *Boston University Law Review* 1915

—— 'The Dual Meaning of Evidence-Based Judicial Review of Legislation' (Social Science Research Network 2016) SSRN Scholarly Paper ID 2818007 <https://papers.ssrn.com/abstract=2818007>

—— 'Temporary Legislation, Better Regulation and Experimentalist Governance: An Empirical Study' (2017) 11 *Regulation and Governance* 192

Bartole, S, 'Law-Making Principles under the Rule of Law' (2012) <www.venice.coe.int/WebForms/documents/?pdf=CDL%282013%29016-e>

Bates, T, 'Monitoring of Current Legislation by the Statute Law Society' (1981) 1 *Statute Law Review* 39

Beard, M, *Women & Power: A Manifesto* (Main edition, London, Profile Books 2017)

Beatson, J, 'Common Law, Statute Law and Constitutional Law' (2006) 27 *Statute Law Review* 1

Bennett, J and Balmford, C, 'The International Plain Language Movement: A Business Plan' (1994) 31 *Clarity (Journal of the International Association of Plain Legal Language)* 37

Bennion, F, 'Modern Royal Assent Procedure at Westminster' (1980) 2 *Statute Law Review* 133

—— *Bennion on Statute Law* (London, Longman, 1990)

—— 'The Readership of Legal Texts' (1993) 27 *Clarity* 1
—— 'More on Godfrey Carter CBE Deceased' *The Times Register (Lives Remembered)* (9 September 2003) <www.francisbennion.com/pdfs/fb/2003/2003-017-lr006-more-godfrey-carter.pdf>
—— *Bennion on Statutory Interpretation* (5th edn, New York, LexisNexis, 2008)
Bentham, J, *Principles of the Civil Code* (J Bowring ed, Edinburgh, William Tait, 1843)
—— *Theory of Legislation* (CK Ogden ed, London, Routledge, 1950)
—— *Legislator of the World: Writings on Codification, Law, and Education* (Oxford, Clarendon Press; Oxford University Press, 1998)
—— *An Introduction to the Principles and Morals of Legislation* (JH Burns and HLA Hart eds, Oxford, Clarendon Press, 1996)
Berry, D, 'Keeping the Statute Book up to Date: A Personal View' (2010) 36 *Commonwealth Law Bulletin* 79
—— 'Purpose Sections: Why They Are a Good Idea for Drafters and Users' (2011) 2 *The Loophole* 49
Bertlin, A, 'Clarity in Drafting: How Can We Know What Works Best for the Reader?' (Presentation Organised by Commonwealth Association of Legislative Counsel, Cape Town, April 2013)
—— 'What Works Best for the Reader? A Study on Drafting and Presenting Legislation' [2014] *The Loophole* 25
Bhatia, PDKL, 'Drafting Legislative Provisions: Challenges and Opportunities' [2010] The Loophole 5
—— *Textbook on Legal Language and Legal Writing* (New Delhi, Universal Law Publishing, 2010)
—— 'Linguistic and Socio-Pragmatic Considerations in Legislative Drafting' (2014) 2 *Theory and Practice of Legislation* 169
Bindman, G, 'Magna Carta Lives' (2014) 164 *New Law Journal* 7
Bing, J, 'Let There Be Lite: A Brief History of Legal Information Retrieval' (2010) 1 *European Journal of Law and Technology*
Bingham, T, 'The Case of Liversidge v Anderson: The Rule of Law Amid the Clash of Arms' (2009) 43 *The International Lawyer* 33
—— *The Rule of Law* (London, Penguin UK, 2011)
Blackstone, W, *Commentaries on the Laws of England in Four Books* (1765)
Bobbett, C, 'Retroactive or Retrospective? A Note on Terminology' (2006) 1 *British Tax Review* 15
Bowcott, O, 'Senior Judge Warns over Deportation of Terror Suspects to Torture States' *The Guardian* (5 March 2013) <www.guardian.co.uk/law/2013/mar/05/lord-neuberger-deportation-terror-suspects>
Bowman, G, 'The Art of Legislative Drafting' (2005) 7 *European Journal of Law Reform* 3
—— 'Why Is There a Parliamentary Counsel Office?' (2005) 26 *Statute Law Review* 69
Bradley, M, 'Ambulatory Approach at the Bottom of the Cliff: Can the Courts Correct Parliament's Failure to Update Legislation?' (2003) 9 *Canterbury Law Review* 1
Bratanovskiy, S and Zelenov, M, 'Discretionary Powers as a Corruption Factor within the System of Executive Authorities' [2016] *Administrative and Municipal Law* 311
Brightman, RH the L, 'Drafting Quagmires' (2002) 23 *Statute Law Review* 1
Bromley, M, 'Whose Law Is It? – Accessibility Through LENZ: Opportunities for the New Zealand Public to Shape Law as It Is Made' [2009] *The Loophole* 16
Brooke, LJ, 'Publishing the Courts: Judgements and Public Information on the Internet' (Commonwealth Law Conference, Melbourne, 15 April 2003)
Broring, HE, 'Administrative Rules in British Law' (1994) 1 *Maastricht Journal of European and Comparative Law* 273
Burgess, P, 'Why We Need to Abandon "The Rule of Law"' (*IACL-IADC Blog*, 21 September 2021) <https://blog-iacl-aidc.org/2021-posts/2021/9/21/why-we-need-to-abandon-the-rule-of-law>
Burrows, J, 'Legislation: Primary, Secondary and Tertiary' (2011) 42 *Victoria University of Wellington Law Review* 65
Burrows, J and Carter, R, *Statute Law in New Zealand* 4th edn (New York, LexisNexis, 2009)
Butt, P, 'Modern Legal Drafting' (2002) 23 *Statute Law Review* 12
Cabinet Office, *Guide to Making Legislation* (2013)
Calabresi, G, *A Common Law for the Age of Statutes* (Clark, The Lawbook Exchange Ltd, 1982)

Cameron, D, 'Speech to the Foreign Policy Centre' (Foreign Policy Centre, 24 August 2005)
Carothers, T, *Promoting the Rule of Law Abroad: The Problem of Knowledge* (Washington DC, Carnegie Endowment for International Peace, 2003)
Carr, C, *Delegated Legislation* (Cambridge, Cambridge University Press, 1921)
—— 'British Isles: Legislation' (1949) 31 *Journal of Comparative Legislation and International Law* 1
Carroll, L, *Through the Looking Glass* (London, Collector's Colour Library, 2011)
Carter, R, '"High Quality" Legislation – (How) Can Legislative Counsel Facilitate It?' [2011] *The Loophole* 41
—— 'Statutory Interpretation and the Rectification of Drafting Errors' [2012] *New Zealand Law Review* 207
—— *Burrows and Carter: Statute Law in New Zealand* 5th edn (New York, LexisNexis, 2015)
Carter, R and Green, M, 'The Act Is Self-Explanatory … or Is It? Explanatory Notes in New Zealand Legislation' (2007) 28 *Statute Law Review* 1
Cass, R, *The Rule of Law in America* (Baltimore, JHU Press, 2003)
Chaturvedi, K, 'Legislative Retrospectivity and Rule of Law' (2013) 34 *Statute Law Review* 207
Choi, K, 'Gender Equality and Legislative Evaluation of Gender-Based Laws in Korea' (2021) 9 *Theory and Practice of Legislation* 25
Chote, R and others, *The IFS Green Budget: January 2008* (IFS 2008) <www.ifs.org.uk/publications/4112>
Commentary, 'Avoidance of Sexist Language in Legislation' (1985) 11 *Commonwealth Law Bulletin* 590
'Common Legislative Solutions: A Guide to Tackling Recurring Policy Issues in Legislation' (Office of the Parliamentary Counsel)
Constitution Committee, 'Justice and Security (Northern Ireland) Bill, 4th Report of Session 2006–07' (2007) HL Paper 54
—— 'The Legislative Process: The Delegation of Powers' (House of Lords) 16th Report of Session 2017–2019
'Constitutional Law – Vagueness – Second Circuit Strikes Down the FCC's Indecency Policy as Void for Vagueness' (2011) 124 *Harvard Law Review* 835
Coode, G, *Legislative Expression* (London, William Benning and Co, 1845)
Cormacain, R, 'A Plain Language Case Study: Business Tenancies (Northern Ireland) Order 1996' [2012] *The Loophole* 33
—— 'Have the Renton Committee's Recommendations on Electronic Access to Legislation Been Fulfilled?' (2013) 19 *Web Journal of Current Legal Issues*
—— 'Keeling Schedules and Clarity in Amending Legislation' (2013) 15 *European Journal of Law Reform* 96
—— 'Prerogative Legislation as the Paradigm of Bad Law-Making: The Chagos Islands' (2013) 39 *Commonwealth Law Bulletin* 487
—— 'Retroactivity, Retrospectivity, and Legislative Competence in Northern Ireland: Determining the Validity of Janus-Faced Legislation' (2015) 36 *Statute Law Review* 134
—— 'Legislation, Legislative Drafting and the Rule of Law' (2017) 5 *The Theory and Practice of Legislation* 115
—— 'The UK Internal Market Bill and the Mother of All Ouster Clauses – Ronan Cormacain' (*UK Human Rights Blog*, 15 October 2020) <https://ukhumanrightsblog.com/2020/10/15/the-uk-internal-market-bill-mother-of-all-ouster-clauses-ronan-cormacain/>
—— 'Environment Bill – Office for Environmental Protection: A Rule of Law Analysis' (Bingham Centre for the Rule of Law 2021)
—— 'Promoting (Religious and Political) Diversity through Legislation in Northern Ireland' (2021) 9 *Theory and Practice of Legislation* 59
—— 'Protecting Veterans or Protecting the Ministry of Defence? Clarity in the Overseas Operations Bill' (*UK Constitutional Law Association*, 22 January 2021) <https://ukconstitutionallaw.org/2021/01/22/ronan-cormacain-protecting-veterans-or-protecting-the-ministry-of-defence-clarity-in-the-overseas-operations-bill/>

—— 'Queen's Consent and the Crown's Exemption from Lockdown Rules – Are We All in This Together?' (*UK Constitutional Law Association*, 15 February 2021) <https://ukconstitutionallaw.org/>
—— 'Environment Bill – Office for Environmental Protection: A Rule of Law Analysis' (Bingham Centre for the Rule of Law 2021)
—— 'Blue-Eyed Babies, Amnesties, Sovereignty of Parliament and the Rule of Law: The Northern Ireland Legacy Proposals' (*UK Constitutional Law Association*, 25 November 2021) <https://ukconstitutionallaw.org/>
—— 'What Should Courts Do When Ministers Flout the Law?' (*UK Constitutional Law Association*, 22 December 2021) <https://ukconstitutionallaw.org/2021/12/22/ronan-cormacain-what-should-courts-do-when-ministers-flout-the-law%ef%bf%bc/>
—— 'Coronavirus Bill: A Rule of Law Analysis (Supplementary Report – House of Lords)' (Bingham Centre for the Rule of Law) <https://binghamcentre.biicl.org/publications/coronavirus-bill-a-rule-of-law-analysis-supplementary-report-house-of-lords>
—— 'Coronavirus, Face Coverings on Public Transport Regulations: A Rule of Law Analysis' (Bingham Centre for the Rule of Law) <https://binghamcentre.biicl.org/publications/coronavirus-face-coverings-on-public-transport-regulations-a-rule-of-law-analysis>
Cormacain, R and Donovan, N, *Suspected War Criminals and Génocidaires in the UK: Proposals to Strengthen Our Laws* (Newtown, Aegis, 2009)
Cormacain, R and Garner, O, 'Schrödinger's Trafficking Directive and the Nationalities and Borders Bill: Simultaneously Law and Not Law' (*UK Constitutional Law Association*, 17 December 2021) <https://ukconstitutionallaw.org/2021/12/17/ronan-cormacain-and-oliver-garner-schrodingers-trafficking-directive-and-the-nationalities-and-borders-bill-simultaneously-law-and-not-law-%ef%bf%bc/>
Cormacain, R and Hunt, M, 'Terrorist Offenders (Restriction of Early Release) Bill A Rule of Law Analysis' (Bingham Centre for the Rule of Law 2020)
Corwin, E, 'The Higher Law Background of American Constitutional Law' (1928) 42 *Harvard Law Review* 149
Council of State, 'Annual Report' (Council of State 2006)
Crabbe, V, *Legislative Drafting Vol I: V. 1* (London, Routledge-Cavendish, 1993)
Crosskey, W, 'The True Meaning of the Constitutional Prohibition on Ex-Post-Facto Laws' (1947) 14 *University of Chicago Law Review* 539
Cryer, R and Mora, P, 'The Coroners and Justice Act 2009 and International Criminal Law: Backing into the Future?' (2010) 59 *International and Comparative Law Quarterly* 803
Cunnion, K, 'Earning a C for Rulemaking: The Ambiguity and Potential Impact of a Recent SEC Rule Governing Nationally Registered Statistical Rating Organizations' (2014) 93 *North Carolina Law Review Addendum* 150
'Curbing Corruption in Azerbaijan: The Case of ASAN' (Blavatnik School of Government, University of Oxford, 2017)
Daintith, T and Page, A, *The Executive in the Constitution: Structure, Autonomy and Internal Control* (Oxford, Oxford University Press, 1999)
Dam, S, *Presidential Legislation in India: The Law and Practice of Ordinances* (Cambridge, Cambridge University Press, 2014)
Davis, K, *Discretionary Justice: Preliminary Inquiry* 5th printing edition (Champaign, University of Illinois Press, 1971)
de Benedetto, M, 'Maintenance of Rules', in *Legislation in Europe: A Comprehensive Guide for Scholars and Practitioners* (Oxford, Hart Publishing, 2017)
—— 'Why Do We Need Effective Law?' (Conference: Effective Law and Regulation, Institute of Advanced Legal Studies, 7 July 2017)
de Paula, F, 'Does Brazil Have a Legislative Policy?' (2016) 5 *Theory and Practice of Legislation* 329
Delegated Powers and Regulatory Reform Committee, 'Guidance for Departments on the Role and Requirements of the Committee' (House of Lords 2014)

Dhavan, R, 'Legislative Simplicity and Interpretative Complexity – a Comment on the Renton Committee on "the Preparation of Legislation"' (1976) 5 *Anglo-American Law Review* 64
Dicey, A, *An Introduction to the Study of the Law of the Constitution* (1885)
Dickens, C, *Oliver Twist* New Ed edn (London, Penguin Classics, 2007)
Dickerson, R, 'The Diseases of Legislative Language' (1964) 1 *Harvard Journal on Legislation* 5
Dickson, B, *Law in Northern Ireland* 2nd edn (Oxford, Hart Publishing, 2013)
Directorate of Clerking and Reporting, *Guidance on Public Bills* 3rd edn (The Scottish Parliament, 2007)
Donelan, E, *Review of the Irish Statute Book: A Guide to Irish Legislation by Brian Hunt* (First Law Book Review 2008) <www.francisbennion.com/pdfs/non-fb/2008/2008-002-nfb-review-of-brian-hunt-book.pdf>
—— 'European Approaches to Improving Access to and Managing the Stock of Legislation' (2009) 30 *Statute Law Review* 147
Dorf, M, 'Legal Indeterminacy and Institutional Design' (2003) 78 *NYUL Review* 875
Dorsey, T, *Legislative Drafter's Deskbook: A Practical Guide* (Alexandria, The CapitolNet, 2006)
Drewry, G, 'Public Law' (1995) 73 *Public Administration* 41
Driedger, E, *The Composition of Legislation: Legislative Forms and Precedents* 2nd edn (Department of Justice, 1976)
—— 'Statutes: Retroactive Retrospective Reflections' (1978) 56 *Canadian Bar Review* 264
Drinóczi, T, 'Legislative Process', in *Legislation in Europe: A Comprehensive Guide for Scholars and Practitioners* (Oxford, Hart Publishing, 2017)
Duprat, J-P and Xanthaki, H, 'Legislative Drafting Techniques/Formal Legistics', in *Legislation in Europe: A Comprehensive Guide for Scholars and Practitioners* (Oxford, Hart Publishing, 2017)
Durcia, S, 'Rediscovering the Pole Star: A Close Look at Legislative Intent and Statutory Interpretation' [2021] *The Loophole* 16
Eagleson, R, *Writing in Plain English* (Commonwealth of Australia, 1990)
Ebbesson, J, 'The Rule of Law in Governance of Complex Socio-Ecological Changes' (2010) 20 *Global Environmental Change* 414
'Economics and the Rule of Law: Order in the Jungle' [2008] *The Economist* <www.economist.com/node/10849115>
Editorial, 'No Art to the Impossible' *New Scientist* (30 January 2016) 5
Eisenstaedt, J, *The Curious History of Relativity: How Einstein's Theory of Gravity Was Lost and Found* (Princeton, Princeton University Press, 2006)
Elliot, D, 'Access to Statute Law in New Zealand' (1990) 20 *Victoria University of Wellington Law Review* 131
—— 'What Is Plain English?' (1990) 11 *Statute Law Review* 237
—— 'Drafting Legislation: Challenges and Improving Ways' (Lebanon Parliament, 16 February 2012) <www.davidelliott.ca/legislativedrafting.htm>
Emon, A, 'On Statutory Interpretation and the (Canadian) Rule of Law: Interpretive Presumptions as Boundary Setting' (2015) 3 *Theory and Practice of Legislation* 45
Enequist, ALE, 'From Abstract Goals to Concrete Rules – Regulating Nursing Home Care in Sweden and the Netherlands' (Social Science Research Network 2015) SSRN Scholarly Paper ID 3803177 <https://papers.ssrn.com/abstract=3803177>
Enequist, A-W, 'Framework Legislation in the Welfare State' (Thesis, University of Groningen, 2008)
Energy and Climate Change Committee, 'Investor Confidence in the UK Energy Sector' (House of Commons 2016) Third Report of Session 2015–16
Engle, G, '"Bills Are Made to Pass as Razors Are Made to Sell": Practical Constraints in the Preparation of Legislation' (1983) 4 *Statute Law Review* 7
Enright, A, 'Antigone in Galway: Anne Enright on the Dishonoured Dead' *London Review of Books* (17 December 2015) 11

Erasmus, J, 'Keepers of the Statute Book: Lessons from the Space-Time Continuum' [2010] *The Loophole* 7

Erskine May, Parliamentary Practice (25th edn, Butterworths 2019)

'EU LGBTI Survey II A Long Way to Go for LGBTI Equality: Country Data – Hungary' (European Union Agency for Fundamental Rights 2020) <https://fra.europa.eu/sites/default/files/fra_uploads/lgbti-survey-country-data_hungary.pdf>

European Commission, 'How to Write Clearly' (2011)

—— 'Press Release: Commission Welcomes Member States' Agreement on Robust Testing of Air Pollution Emissions by Cars' (28 October 2015)

European Union, 'Joint Practical Guide for the Drafting of Community Legislation' (Office for Official Publications of the European Communities 2003)

Evans, J, *Statutory Interpretation: Problems of Communication* (Oxford, Oxford University Press, 1988)

Feldman, D (ed), *Law in Politics, Politics in Law* (Oxford, Hart Publishing, 2015)

—— 'Looking Back and Moving On', in *Law in Politics, Politics in Law* (Oxford, Hart Publishing, 2015)

—— 'Legislation as Aspiration: Statutory Expression of Policy Goals' (Institute of Advanced Legal Studies, 16 March 2015)

Fenwick, H, 'Anti-Terrorism, Crime and Security Act 2001: A Proportionate Response to 11 September, The' (2002) 65 *Modern Law Review* 724

Finnis, J, *Natural Law and Natural Rights* (Oxford, Oxford University Press, 1980)

Flesch, R, *The Art of Readable Writing* (Springfield, Collier Books, 1962)

Fowler, B, 'The Care Home Covid Vaccination Regulations: A Case Study in Problems with the Delegated Legislation System' (*Hansard Society*) <www.hansardsociety.org.uk/blog/the-care-home-covid-vaccination-regulations-a-case-study-in-problems-with>

Fox, R and Blackwell, J, 'The Devil Is in the Detail: Parliament and Delegated Legislation' (Hansard Society 2013)

France, A, *The Red Lily, Complete* (1894)

Freedman, J and Vella, J, *HMRC's Management of the UK Tax System: The Boundaries of Legitimate Discretion* (Oxford, Oxford University Centre for Business Taxation, 2010)

Fuller, L, *The Morality of Law: Revised Edition* (Revised, New Haven, Yale University Press, 1969)

Ganz, G, 'The War Crimes Act 1991 – Why No Constitutional Crisis?' (1992) 55 *Modern Law Review* 87

Garner, O and West, T, 'Freedoms' Risks and Opportunities? Certainty and Uncertainty in the Revision of Retained EU Law' (*UK Constitutional Law Association*, 17 February 2022) <https://ukconstitutionallaw.org/2022/02/17/oliver-garner-and-tom-west-brexit-freedoms-risks-and-opportunities-certainty-and-uncertainty-in-the-revision-of-retained-eu-law/>

Gashabizi, A, 'In Pursuit of Clarity: How Far Should the Drafter Go?' (2013) 39 *Commonwealth Law Bulletin* 415

Gee, D, 'Survey of Major Law Libraries around the World' (2013) 41 *International Journal of Legal Information* 108

—— 'SLS/BIALL Academic Law Library Survey 2012/2013' (2014) 14 *Legal Information Management* 215

Gestel, R van, 'Primacy of the European Legislature? Delegated Rule-Making and the Decline of the "Transmission Belt" Theory' (2014) 2 *The Theory and Practice of Legislation* 33

'Get Brexit Done: Unleash Britain's Potential. The Conservative and Unionist Party Manifesto 2019'

Gleeson, M, 'Courts and the Rule of Law' (2001) <www.hcourt.gov.au/assets/publications/speeches/former-justices/gleesoncj/cj_ruleoflaw.htm>

Gowers, E, *The Complete Plain Words* (HMSO, 1986)

Grabham, E, 'Exploring the Textual Alchemy of Legal Gender: Experimental Statutes and the Message in the Medium' (2020) 10 *feminists@law*

Greenberg, D, 'Nothing Will Come of Nothing' (2010) 160 *New Law Journal* 1084

—— *Laying down the Law: A Discussion of the People, Processes and Problems That Shape Acts of Parliament* (London, Sweet & Maxwell, 2011)

—— 'The Three Myths of Plain English Drafting' [2011] *The Loophole* 103

—— *Craies on Legislation* 10th edn (London, Sweet & Maxwell, 2012)

—— 'A Refreshing Decision; Or the Rule of Law in Action' (2012) 33 *Statute Law Review* 409

—— 'Gender Neutrality in the House of Lords (and Ladies)' (2014) 35 *Statute Law Review* v

—— 'Coping with Bad Legislation: Strategy No. 1 – Ignoring It' (2015) 36 *Statute Law Review* v

Hand, C, 'Drafting with the User in Mind – a Look at Legislation' (1983) 4 *Statute Law Review* 166

Harrington, J, *The Prerogative of Popular Government* (1656)

Hart, A, 'Remarks at Third Public Session of HIA Inquiry' (Historical Institutional Abuse Inquiry, 4 September 2013) <www.hiainquiry.org/index/chairman_s_address_130904_low_res.pdf>

Hashim, N, 'Plain Language: Give It a Try!' (2013) 39 *Commonwealth Law Bulletin* 423

Hayek, F, *The Road to Serfdom* (London, Routledge, 1944)

Heaton, R, 'Making the Law Easier for Users: The Role of Statutes' (Institute of Advanced Legal Studies, 14 October 2013) <www.gov.uk/government/speeches/making-the-law-easier-for-users-the-role-of-statutes--2>

—— 'Innovation and Continuity in Law-Making' (Institute of Advanced Legal Studies, 2014) <www.gov.uk/government/speeches/innovation-and-continuity-in-law-making>

Hedlund, D, Cederborg, A-C and Zamboni, M, 'The Art of the (Im)Possible: Legislators' Experiences of the Lawmaking Process When Reforming Migration Law' (2016) 4 *The Theory and Practice of Legislation* 45

Heidegren, C-G, 'Social Acceleration, Motorized Legislation and Framework Laws', in *The Contemporary Relevance of Carl Schmitt* (Abingdon, Routledge, 2015)

Hewart, Lord, *The New Despotism* (London, Ernest Benn, 1929)

Hicks, E, 'Implementing Legislation Systems – Considerations and Options' (CALC, Hyderabad, India, February 2011)

Hill, W, 'A Need for Non-Sexist Language in the Courts' (1992) 49 *Washington and Lee Law Review* 275

Hockman, S, 'Free the Law How the Australasian Legal Information Institute (AustLII) Achieved the Free Availability of Legal Information on the Internet' (2000) 1 *Journal of Information, Law and Technology*

Hogarth, R, 'The Government Must Draw a Clear Line between Law and Guidance during the Coronavirus Crisis' (*The Institute for Government*, 1 April 2020) <www.instituteforgovernment.org.uk/blog/government-law-and-guidance-coronavirus-crisis>

Holmes, S, 'Can Foreign Aid Promote the Rule of Law?' (1999) 8 *East European Constitutional Review* 68

Home Affairs Select Committee, 'Uncorrected Transcript of Oral Evidence' (House of Commons 2014) HC 231-vii <www.publications.parliament.uk/pa/cm201314/cmselect/cmhaff/uc231-vii/uc23101.htm>

Horvat Vuković, A, 'Gender Quotas in Corporate Decision-Making Bodies – Regulatory Promotion of Equality of Results in the EU' (2021) 9 *Theory and Practice of Legislation* 3

House of Representatives Standing Committee on Legal and Constitutional Affairs, 'Clearer Commonwealth Law: Report of the Inquiry into Legislative Drafting by the Commonwealth' (Parliament of the Commonwealth of Australia 1993)

'How Emissions Tests Work, And Why They're Stupidly Unrealistic' (*Car Throttle*) <www.carthrottle.com/post/how-emissions-tests-work-and-why-theyre-stupidly-unrealistic/>

Hughes, D and Davies, HG, 'Accessible Bilingual Legislation for Wales (Deddfwriaeth Hygyrch a Dwyieithog I Gymru)' (2012) 33 *Statute Law Review* 103

Hunt, B, 'Plain Language in Legislative Drafting: An Achievable Objective or Laudable Ideal?' (2003) 24 *Statute Law Review* 112

Hyde, J, 'Munby: Legal Aid System "Not Humane"' *Law Gazette* <www.lawgazette.co.uk/law/munby-legal-aid-system-not-humane/5045849.article>

Hynes, S, 'Parliamentary Scrutiny of Our Legislation Is Being Lost to Misused Executive …' (*Legal Action Group*, June 2017) <www.lag.org.uk/article/201782/parliamentary-scrutiny-of-our-legislation-is-being-lost-to-misused-executive-power>

Ilahi, M, 'Plain Language Movement: A Case Study of the Islamic Republic of Pakistan' (PhD Thesis, University of London, Institute of Advanced Legal Studies, 2012)

Ilbert, C, *Legislative Methods and Forms* (Oxford, Clarendon Press, 1901)
'Interinstitutional Agreement of 22 December 1998 on Common Guidelines for the Quality of Drafting of Community Legislation' 1999/C 73/01
Irresberger, K and Jasiak, A, 'Publication', in *Legislation in Europe: A Comprehensive Guide for Scholars and Practitioners* (Oxford, Hart Publishing, 2017)
Ismail, N, 'Legislative Drafters: Lawyers or Not?' (2013) 39 *Commonwealth Law Bulletin* 455
Ismer, R and Meßerschmidt, K, 'Evidence-Based Judicial Review of Legislation: Some Introductory Remarks' (2016) 4 *The Theory and Practice of Legislation* 91
Jack, M and others (eds), *Erskine May: Parliamentary Practice* 24th revised edition (London, Butterworths Law, 2011)
Jacobson, H, *Pussy* (London, Jonathan Cape, 2017)
Jamieson, N, 'Would a Parliamentary Counsel by Any Other Name Be More of a Law Draftsman' (1982) 3 *Statute Law Review* 13
Jones, B, 'Transatlantic Perspectives on Humanised Public Law Campaigns: Personalising and Depersonalising the Legislative Process' (2012) 6 *Legisprudence* 58
—— 'Manipulating Public Law Favorability: Is It Really This Easy?' (Social Science Research Network 2013) SSRN Scholarly Paper ID 2336895 <https://papers.ssrn.com/abstract=2336895>
Jones, O, *Bennion on Statutory Interpretation* 6th revised edition (London, Butterworths Law, 2013)
Jowell, J, 'The Global Economy and the Rule of Law' (Global Law Summit, London, 25 February 2015) <www.biicl.org/documents/504_sir_jeffrey_jowell_qc_-_global_law_summit_paper_25_feb_2015.pdf>
Judge, LI, 'A Judge's View on the Rule of Law' (Annual Bingham Lecture, 3 May 2017) <www.biicl.org/documents/1637_2017_05_11transcript_of_lord_judges_speech_3.pdf?showdocument=1>
'Judicial Review Reform Consultation – The Government Response' (Ministry of Justice 2021) CP 477
Justice Committee, 'COVID-19 and the Criminal Law: Fourth Report of Session 2021–22' (House of Commons 2021) HC 71 <https://committees.parliament.uk/publications/7439/documents/77794/default/>
Kafka, F, *The Trial* (Berlin, Verlag Die Schmiede, 1925)
Kaiser, A and Zittel, T (eds), *Demokratietheorie Und Demokratieentwicklung – Festschrift Für Peter Graf Kielmansegg* (Wiesbaden, Springer, 2004)
Karpen, U and Xanthaki, H (eds), *Legislation in Europe: A Comprehensive Guide for Scholars and Practitioners* (Oxford, Hart Publishing, 2017)
Kecskés, A, 'The Sarbanes-Oxley Act from a Legislative Viewpoint' (2015) 4 *Theory and Practice of Legislation* 27
Keyes, J, 'Perils of the Unknown – Fair Notice and the Promulgation of Legislation' (1993) 25 *Ottawa Law Review* 579
Kimble, J, 'Answering the Critics of Plain Language' (1994) 5 *The Scribes Journal of Legal Writing* 51
King, J, 'Miller/Cherry and Remedies for Ultra Vires Delegated Legislation' (*UK Constitutional Law Association*, 19 September 2019) <https://ukconstitutionallaw.org/2019/09/19/jeff-king-miller-cherry-and-remedies-for-ultra-vires-delegated-legislation/>
Kingsolver, B, *Poisonwood Bible* (New York, Harper Collins Publishing USA, 2012)
Kirchhof, P, 'Entparlamentarisierung Der Demokratie?' in A Kaiser and T Zittel (eds), *Demokratietheorie und Demokratieentwicklung* (Cham, VS Verlag für Sozialwissenschaften, 2004)
Kirkham, R, 'JR55, Judicial Review and the Limits of Textual Reasoning' [2017] *Public Law* 46
Knight, C, 'Taking an AXA to Acts of the Scottish Parliament' [2010] *JR* 163
Kouroutakis, A, 'The Henry VIII Powers in the Brexit Process: Justification Subject to Political and Legal Safeguards' (2021) 9 *Theory and Practice of Legislation* 97
Kryvoi, Y and Matos, S, 'Non-Retroactivity as a General Principle of Law' (2021) 17 *Utrecht Law Review* 46
Lampe, J, 'Retroactive Legislation: A Primer for Congress' [2019] *Congressional Research Service*
Lane, J-E, *Constitutions and Political Theory* (Manchester, Manchester University Press, 1996)
Lavery, U, 'The "Findability" of the Law' (1943) 27 *Journal of the American Judicature Society* 25

'Law Chief: Informed Criticism Fine' *BBC* (2 May 2013) <www.bbc.co.uk/news/uk-northern-ireland-22389117>

Law Commission, 'Post-Legislative Scrutiny' (2006) Law Com No 302

—— *Presentation of New Zealand Statute Law* (Law Commission 2008)

—— 'Form and Accessibility of the Law Applicable in Wales' (Law Commission 2015) Consultation Paper No 223

Law Commission for England and Wales, *Criminal Law: A Criminal Code for England and Wales*, vol 1 (HMSO 1989)

Lawn, G, 'Improving Public Access to Legislation: The New Zealand Experience so Far' (2004) 6 *University of Technology, Sydney Law Review* 49

Laws, J, *The Constitutional Balance* (Oxford, Hart Publishing, 2021)

Laws, S, 'Drawing the Line' in C Stefanou and H Xanthaki (eds), *Drafting Legislation: A Modern Approach* (Farnham, Ashgate, 2008)

—— 'Plus ca Change – Continuity and Change in UK Legislative Drafting Practice' (2009) 11 *European Journal of Law Reform* 139

—— 'Giving Effect to Policy in Legislation: How to Avoid Missing the Point' (2011) 32 *Statute Law Review* 1

—— 'Legislation and Politics', in *Law in Politics, Politics in Law* (Oxford, Hart Publishing, 2015)

Leigh, I, 'The Prerogative, Legislative Power, and the Democratic Deficit: The Fire Brigades Union Case' (1995) 3 *Web Journal of Current Legal Issues*

Leith, P and Fellows, C, 'BAILII, Legal Education and Open Access to Law' (2013) 4 *European Journal of Law and Technology* <http://ejlt.org//article/view/209>

Levert, L, 'Work Methods and Processes in a Drafting Environment' [2011] *The Loophole* 23

Lines, K, 'Government Messaging on Exercising during Lockdown – A Rule of Law Analysis' (Bingham Centre for the Rule of Law) <https://binghamcentre.biicl.org/publications/government-messaging-on-exercising-during-lockdown-a-rule-of-law-analysis>

Locke, J, *Locke: Two Treatises of Government* (London, Awnsham Churchill, 1689)

Lockwood, C, 'Defining Indefiniteness: Suggested Revisions to the Void for Vagueness Doctrine' (2009) 8 *Cardozo Public Law, Policy, and Ethics Journal* 255

Lord Hailsham, 'Addressing the Statute Law' (1985) 6 *Statute Law Review* 4

Lord Sandhurst, 'Access to Justice in the 2020s: Recommendations for a Joined up Approach to Legal Aid, Funding and Procedural Reform in the Civil and Family Courts for the New Conservative Government' (Society of Conservative Lawyers 2020)

Lord Simon, 'Statute Consolidation: Interim Techniques' [1985] *Public Law* 352

Lord Woolf, 'Access to Justice: Interim Report to the Lord Chancellor on the Civil Justice System in England and Wales' (Lord Chancellors Dept 1995)

Lovgren, A, 'The Location of Textual Amendments in Bills' (1988) 9 *Statute Law Review* 27

Lovric, D, 'A Strategic View of Drafting Training for Tomorrow's Needs' [2013] *The Loophole* 7

Mackinlay, J, 'Syntactic Discontinuity in the Language of the UK and EU Legislation' <www.esp-world.info/Articles_7/Syntactic%20DiscontLegal.htm>

Maclean, M and Harvey, C, 'Pierre Bourdieu and Elites' in SR Clegg and M Pina e Cunha (eds), *Management, Organizations and Contemporary Social Theory* (London, Routledge, 2019) 98–114

Magan, M, *32 Words for Field: Lost Words of the Irish Landscape* (Dublin, Gill Books, 2020)

Marmor, A (ed), *The Routledge Companion to Philosophy of Law* (Abingdon, Routledge, 2012)

'Marriage Bill Should Help Couples Remain Together' <www.newvision.co.ug/news/640738-marriage-bill-should-help-couples-remain-together.html>

Marsh-Smith, L and Wright, G, 'Information Technology on a Budget: A Giant Leap for the Isle of Man' ('Winds of Change', Commonwealth Association of Legislative Counsel conference, Cape Town, April 2013)

Martineau, R and Salernon, M, *Legal, Legislative and Rule Drafting in Plain English* (Toronto, Thomson West, 2005)

Mason, A, 'Ours – A Government of Laws and Not of Men' (1929) 13 *Constitutional Review* 197

Mellinkoff, D, *The Language of the Law* (Searcy, Resource Publications, 2004)

Mokhtar, A, 'Nullem Crimen, Nulla Poena Sine Lege' (2005) 26 *Statute Law Review* 41

Morville, P, *Ambient Findability: What We Find Changes Who We Become* (Sebastopol, O'Reilly, 2005)

Moses, L, 'Adapting the Law to Technological Change: A Comparison of Common Law and Legislation' (2003) 26 *University of New South Wales Law Journal* 417

—— 'Recurring Dilemmas: The Law's Race to Keep up with Technological Change' [2007] *University of Illinois Journal of Law, Technology and Policy* 239

Mousmouti, M, 'Making Legislative Effectiveness an Operational Concept' (Conference: Effective Law and Regulation, Institute of Advanced Legal Studies, 7 July 2017)

Murray, C, 'Vichy France and Vassalage: Hyperbole versus the Northern Ireland Protocol' (*UK Constitutional Law Blog*, 1 July 2021) <https://ukconstitutionallaw.org/>

Murynka, D, 'Some Problems with Killing the Legislator' (2015) 73 *University of Toronto Faculty of Law Review* 12

Naundorf, S and Radaelli, C, 'Regulatory Evaluation Ex Ante and Ex Post: Best Practice, Guidance and Methods' in U Karpen and H Xanthaki (eds), *Legislation in Europe: A Comprehensive Guide for Scholars and Practioners* (Oxford, Hart Publishing, 2017)

Negri, G, 'Nella Bozza Della Manovra Sospensione per Le Condanne Superiori a 20 Milioni. Vi Può Rientrare Il Lodo Mondadori' *Il Sole 24 Ore* (4 July 2011)

Nehushtan, Y and Davidson, M, 'Retrospective Rule Making and the Rule of Law: Between Fairness, Morality and Constitutionality' (2017) *2 Indian Journal of Constitutional and Administrative Law* 27

Neighbors, WD, 'Presidential Legislation by Executive Order' (1964) 37 *University of Colorado Law Review* 105

Northern Ireland Law Commission, 'Consultation Paper: Business Tenancies' (2010) 5

—— 'Vulnerable Witnesses in Civil Proceedings' (2011) 10

—— 'Bail in Criminal Proceedings' (2012) 14

O'Brien, P, 'Legislative Titles – What's in a Name?' [2012] *The Loophole* 17

'Obscene Publications: Legal Guidance: The Crown Prosecution Service' <www.cps.gov.uk/legal/l_to_o/obscene_publications/>

Office of the Leader of the House of Commons, 'Post-Legislative Scrutiny – the Government's Approach' (2008) Cm 7320

Office of the Parliamentary Counsel, 'When Laws Become Too Complex – Inside Government' (March 2013) <www.gov.uk/government/publications/when-laws-become-too-complex/when-laws-become-too-complex>

—— 'Queen's or Prince's Consent' (2018)

—— 'Drafting Guidance' (2020)

Office of the Parliamentary Counsel and Government Legal Department, *Guide to Gender-Neutral Drafting* (2019)

Office of the Scottish Parliamentary Counsel, 'Plain Language and Legislation' (2006)

O'Halloran, K and Cormacain, R, *Charity Law in Northern Ireland* (Dublin, Round Hall Ltd, 2001)

Oksanen, A and others, 'Semantic Finlex: Finnish Legislation and Case Law as a Linked Open Data Service', in *International Conference on Law via the Internet* (Joint project between Aalto University, HELDIG – Helsinki Centre for Digital Humanities, the Ministry of Justice, the Ministry of Finance, Edita Publishing Ltd, Tekes and Viestintäalan tutkimussäätiö 2018)

Olatokun, M, 'Does the Law Think That Black Lives Matter? A Reflection upon the Role of the Public Sector Equality Duty in Promoting Racial Equality before the Law' (2021) 9 *Theory and Practice of Legislation* 83

Onions, CT (ed), *Shorter Oxford English Dictionary on Historical Principles* 3rd edn (Oxford, Oxford University Press, 1955)

P Ramanatha Aiyar, *The Onoge, E, Structure of Legislation: A Paradigm for Accessibility and Effectiveness* (School of Advanced Studies, Unpublished LLM thesis, 2014)

Orr, G, 'Names without Frontiers: Legislative Titles and Sloganeering' (2000) 21 *Statute Law Review* 188

—— 'From Slogans to Puns: Australian Legislative Titling Revisited' (2001) 22 *Statute Law Review* 160
Orwell G, *Animal Farm* (London, Secker and Warburg, 1945)
—— *Politics and the English Language* (London, Penguin, 2013)
Paine, T, *Common Sense* (1776)
Parliamentary Counsel Office, 'Common Legislative Solutions: A Guide to Tackling Recurring Policy Issues in Legislation' (The Cabinet Office 2021)
Pearce, D and Geddes, R, *Statutory Interpretation in Australia* 5th edn (New York, LexisNexis, 2001)
Pennisi G, 'Legislative Provisions in Context: A Linguistic Approach' (2016) 37 *Statute Law Review* 101
Petersson S, 'Gender Neutral Drafting: Recent Commonwealth Developments' (1990) 20 *Statute Law Review* 35
—— 'Gender Neutral Drafting: Historical Perspective' (1998) 19 *Statute Law Review* 93
Piper B, 'What, How, When and Why – Making Laws Easier to Understand by Using Examples and Notes' [2007] *The Loophole* 74
'Policing in the Pandemic: The Police Response to the Coronavirus Pandemic during 2020' (Her Majesty's Inspectorate of Constabulary and Fire and Rescue Services 2021)
Political and Constitutional Reform Committee, 'Ensuring Standards in the Quality of Legislation' (House of Commons Political and Constitutional Reform Committee 2013) HC 85
—— 'The Impact of Queen's and Prince's Consent on the Legislative Process: Eleventh Report' (House of Commons 2014) <https://publications.parliament.uk/pa/cm201314/cmselect/cmpolcon/784/78402.htm>
Poloko, L, *Drafting of Legislation in Compliance with Model Laws* (School of Advanced Studies, Unpublished LLM thesis, 2012)
Popelier, P, 'Mosaics of Legal Provisions' (2005) 7 *European Journal of Law Reform* 47
Post, G, 'Bracton on Kingship' (1967) 42 *Tulane Law Review* 519
'Public Statement Relating to Decisions Not to Prosecute 24 Individuals Reported for Breaches of the Coronavirus Regulations in Connection with Attendance at the Funeral of Bobby Storey on 30 June 2020' (Public Prosecution Service (Northern Ireland) 2021) <www.ppsni.gov.uk/sites/ppsni/files/publications/PPS%20Public%20Statement%20on%20Covid%20funeral%2030%20March%202021_0.pdf>
Pünder, H, 'Democratic Legitimation of Delegated Legislation – a Comparative View of the American, British and German Law' (2009) 58 *International & Comparative Law Quarterly* 353
Pyper, D, 'The Public Sector Equality Duty and Equality Impact Assessments' (House of Commons Library 2020)
Ramanatha Aiyar, P, *The Law Lexicon* (New Delhi, Wadhwa Nagpur, 2007)
Ranchordas, S, *Constitutional Sunsets and Experimental Legislation: A Comparative Perspective* (Cheltenham, Edward Elgar Publishing, 2015)
Raoul Wallenberg Institute, *Rule of Law: A Guide for Politicians* (Lund, Raoul Wallenberg Institute, 2012)
Raz, J, 'The Rule of Law and Its Virtue', in *The Authority of Law: Essays on Law and Morality* (Oxford, Oxford University Press, 1979)
—— *Ethics in the Public Domain, Essays on the Morality of Law and Politics* (Oxford, Clarendon Press, 1994)
Renton, 'The Renton Report's Tenth Birthday' (1985) 6 *Statute Law Review* 60
'Report from the Select Committee on Acts of Parliament' (1875)
'Report of the Renton Committee on the Preparation of Legislation' (1975) Cmnd 6053
Revell, D and Vapnek, J, 'Gender-Silent Legislative Drafting in a Non-Binary World' (2020) 48 *Capital University Law Review* 103
Reynolds, S, '"You Have Committed a Great Offence and Have but a Weak Answer to Make for Yourself": When Clerks Make Mistakes' [2013] *The Table* 4
Robinson, W, 'Manuals for Drafting European Union Legislation' (2010) 4 *Legisprudence* 129
Rodgers, Lord, 'The Form and Language of Legislation' in D Feldman (ed), *Law in Politics, Politics in Law* (Oxford, Hart Publishing, 2015) 64

Roebuck, D, 'Plain, Clear and Something More? Criteria for Communication in Legal Language' (2014) 16 *European Journal of Law Reform* 633

Romer, P, 'Writing' <http://wb-ce.org/writing.html>

Ronald, J, 'Publication of Federal Administrative Legislation' (1938) 7 *George Washington Law Review* 52

Rozenberg, J, 'Boris Can No Longer Pick Bishops' (*A Lawyer Writes*, 30 May 2021) <https://rozenberg.substack.com/p/boris-can-no-longer-pick-bishops>

Roznai, Y, 'Access to Justice 2.0: Access to Legislation And Beyond' (2015) 3 *Theory and Practice of Legislation* 333

Rubin, E, 'Law and Legislation in the Administrative State' (1989) 89 *Columbia Law Review* 369

Russell, M and others, 'The Marginalisation of the House of Commons under Covid Has Been Shocking; a Year on, Parliament's Role Must Urgently Be Restored' (The Constitution Unit 2021) <https://constitution-unit.com/2021/04/21/covid-and-parliament-one-year-on/>

Salembier, J, 'Understanding Retroactivity: When the Past Just Ain't What It Used to Be' (2003) 33 *Hong Kong Law Journal* 106

Sampford, C, *Retrospectivity and the Rule of Law* (Oxford, Oxford University Press, 2006)

Samuels, A, 'The Courts and Legal Services Act 1990: An Exercise in Drafting' (1991) 12 *Statute Law Review* 76

—— 'Thou Shalt Not Steal' (1999) 20 *Statute Law Review* 95

—— 'Consolidation: A Plea' (2005) 26 *Statute Law Review* 56

'Sarah Everard: Challenge Plain-Clothes Officers, Met Police Says' *BBC News* (1 October 2021) <www.bbc.com/news/uk-58757375>

Sarat, A, 'Loose Talk Came Back to Haunt Trump in Judge's Travel Ban Ruling' *The Guardian* (16 March 2017) <www.theguardian.com/us-news/2017/mar/15/trump-travel-ban-muslims-hawaii-judge-power-words>

Schiemann, SK, 'The Advantages of Obscurity: The Drafting of EU Legislation and Judgements' (Institute of Advanced Legal Studies, 13 June 2013)

Schulz, F, *Principles of Roman Law* (Oxford, Clarendon Press, 1936)

Schweikart, D, 'Gender Neutral Pronoun Redefined' (1998) 20 *Women's Rights Law Report* 1

Seeley, J, *Introduction to Political Science: Two Series of Lectures* (London, Macmillan and Co, 1911)

Seidman, R, 'Drafting for the Rule of Law: Maintaining Legality in Developing Countries' (1987) 12 *Yale Journal of International Law* 84

Select Committee on European Scrutiny, 'Fifteenth Report' (House of Commons – European Scrutiny, 15th Report, Session 2002–03, printed 19 March 2003)

Shapiro, M, 'Is Bioethics Broke?: On the Idea of Ethics and Law "Catching Up" with Technology' (1999) 33 *Indiana Law Review* 17

Sheridan, J, 'People, Patterns and Data – the Story of Legislation.Gov.Uk People, Patterns and Data – the Story of Legislation.Gov.Uk' (*Social Tech Guide*, 2014) <www.socialtech.org.uk/blog/people-patterns-and-data-the-story-of-legislation-gov-uk/>

—— 'Using Data to Understand How the Statute Book Works' (2014) 14 *Legal Information Management* 244

Shinar, A, 'One Rule to Rule Them All? Rules of Law against the Rule of Law' (2017) 5 *The Theory and Practice of Legislation* 149

Shklar, J, 'Political Theory and the Rule of Law' in A Hutchinson and P Monahan (eds), *The Rule of Law: Ideal or Ideology* (Toronto, Carswell, 1987)

SIGMA, *Law Drafting and Regulatory Management in Central and Eastern Europe* (SIGMA Papers, No 18, OECD Publishing, Paris 1997)

Simamba, B, 'Should Marginal Notes Be Used in the Interpretation of Legislation' (2005) 26 *Statute Law Review* 125

Simon, Lord, 'Renton Report – Ten Years on, The' (1985) 6 *Statute Law Review* 133

Simson Caird, J, Hazell, R and Oliver, D, *The Constitutional Standards of the House of Lords Select Committee on the Constitution* (London, University College London, 2014)

Simson Caird, J and Patterson, E, 'Brexit, Delegated Powers and Delegated Legislation: A Rule of Law Analysis of Parliamentary Scrutiny' (London, Bingham Centre for the Rule of Law, 2020)

Smith, G, 'Future-Proofing the Investigatory Powers Bill' (BILETA, 11 April 2016) <www.slideshare.net/GrahamSmith9/futureproofing-the-ipbill-60769756>

Smyth, M, 'The Public Law of Commercial Regulation' (2009) 14 *Judicial Review* 197

Soames, S, 'Vagueness and the Law' in A Marmor (ed), *The Routledge Companion to Philosophy of Law* (Abingdon, Routledge, 2012) 95.

Society of Public Teachers of Law, 'Preparation of Legislation' (1974) 13 *Journal of the Society of Public Teachers of Law* 96

Spencer, J, 'Criminal Justice Legislation That Everyone Can Understand: A Flying Pig or a Realistic Aspiration' (Institute of Advanced Legal Studies, 25 January 2016)

Statute Law Society, 'Statute Law: The Key to Clarity' (Statute Law Society Reports, London, Sweet & Maxwell, 1972)

—— 'Statute Law: Radical Simplification' (Statete Law Society Reports, London, Sweet & Maxwell, 1974)

Statutory Publications Office, *Index to the Statutory Rules and Orders. Northern Ireland* (28th edn, The Stationery Office, 2007)

Stefanou, C, *Drafting Legislation: A Modern Approach* (H Xanthaki ed, 1st edn, Abingdon, Routledge, 2008)

—— 'Is Legislative Drafting a Form of Communication?' (2011) 37 *Commonwealth Law Bulletin* 407

Stevenson, K and Harris, C, 'Breaking the Thrall of Ambiguity: Simplification (of the Criminal Law) as an Emerging Human Rights Imperative' (2010) 74 *Journal of Criminal Law* 516

Steyn, Lord, 'Democracy through Law' [2002] *European Human Rights Law Review* 723

Strause, R and Bennett, A, 'How Federal Statutes Are Named' (2013) 105 *Law Library Journal* 7

Strauss, P, 'Legislative Theory and the Rule of Law: Some Comments on Rubin' (1989) 89 *Columbia Law Review* 427

Suetonius, *Lives of the 12 Caesars* (Alexander Thomson trans, 1883)

Sullivan, R, 'Some Implications of Plain Language Drafting' (2001) 22 *Statute Law Review* 145

—— *Sullivan and Driedger on the Construction of Statutes* 4th edn (London, Butterworths Law, 2002)

—— *Sullivan on the Construction of Statutes* 5th edn (Toronto, LexisNexis Canada, 2008)

Summers, J, 'The "Grandfather Clause"' (1914) 7 *Lawyer and Banker and Southern Bench and Bar Review* 39

Tamanaha, B, *On The Rule of Law* (Cambridge, Cambridge University Press, 2004)

Tanner, E, 'Legislating to Communicate: Trends in Drafting Commonwealth Legislation' (2002) 24 *Sydney Law Review* 529

Teasdale, J, 'Statute Law Revision: Repeal, Consolidation or Something More?' (2009) 11 *European Journal of Law Reform* 157

'The Independent Review of Administrative Law' (2021) *CP* 407

The Law Society Charity, 'Fiji: The Rule of Law Lost' (The Law Society Charity 2012)

The Scottish Government, *Scotland's Future: Your Guide to an Independent Scotland* (The Scottish Government, 2013)

Thomas, R, 'Plain English and the Law' (1985) 6 *Statute Law Review* 139

Thomas, T, 'Old Criminal Records Playing a Familiar Tune' (2012) 176 *Criminal Law and Justice Weekly* 539

Thornton, G, *Legislative Drafting* (London, Butterworths, 1996)

Thornton, G and Xanthaki, H, *Thornton's Legislative Drafting* (London, Bloomsbury Professional, 2013)

Thring, H, *Practical Legislation: The Composition and Language of Acts of Parliament* (London, HMSO, 1877)

—— *Practical Legislation: The Composition and Language of Acts of Parliament* 2nd edn (London, John Murray, 1902)
—— *Practical Legislation: The Composition and Language of Acts of Parliament* 3rd edn (M MacKenzie ed, London, Luathe Press, 2015)
Ticehurst, R, 'Retroactive Criminal Law' (1998) 9 *Kings College Law Journal* 88
Tomkins, A, 'Magna Carta, Crown and Colonies' [2001] *Public Law* 571
Truss, L, *Eats, Shoots and Leaves* (New York, Fourth Estate, 2009)
Tucker, A, 'The Impact of Queen's and Prince's Consent on the Legislative Process: Evidence' (House of Commons – Select Committee on Political and Constitutional Reofrm, 11th Report, 2014)
Turatsinze, E, 'The Pursuit of Clarity, Precision and Unambiguity in Drafting Retrospective Legislation' (Unpublished LLM thesis, 2012) <http://sas-space.sas.ac.uk/4711/>
Turnbull, M, 'Clear Legislative Drafting: New Approaches in Australia' (1990) 11 *Statute Law Review* 161
Turner, A, 'Steering the Ship of State – Functions of Parliament' (1980) 10 *Victoria University of Wellington Law Review* 209
Turpin, C and Tomkins, A, *British Government and the Constitution* 6th edn (Cambridge, Cambridge University Press, 2007)
Twining, W and Miers, D, *How to Do Things with Rules* 5th edn (Cambridge, Cambridge University Press, 2010)
Ubena, J, *How to Regulate Information and Communications Technology: A Jurisprudential Inquiry into Legislative and Regulatory Techniques* (Stockholm, Jure, 2015)
Uhlmann, F and Konrath, C, 'Participation' in U Karpen and H Xanthaki (eds), *Legislation in Europe: A Comprehensive Guide for Scholars and Practitioners* (Oxford, Hart Publishing, 2017)
UKCLA, 'R Cormacain: Instinct or Rules: Making Moral Decisions in the Cummings Scandal' (*UK Constitutional Law Association*, 28 May 2020) <https://ukconstitutionallaw.org/2020/05/28/ronan-cormacain-instinct-or-rules-making-moral-decisions-in-the-cummings-scandal/>
'United Kingdom Internal Market Bill: House of Lords Committee Stage: A Rule of Law Analysis of Clauses 44–47' (Bingham Centre for the Rule of Law 2020)
'"Unrealistic" Emissions Tests Could Make Some Diesel Models "Unaffordable", Say European Carmakers' (*International Fleetworld*) <http://internationalfleetworld.co.uk/news/article.cfm?clk=0444&article_id=021978&urltitle=8216Unrealistic8217-emissions-tests-could-make-some-diesel-models-8216unaffordable8217-say-European-carmakers>
Upham, F, *Mythmaking in the Rule of Law Orthodoxy* (Carnegie Endowment for International Peace 2002) <http://carnegieendowment.org/files/wp30.pdf>
van Gestel, R, 'The "Deparliamentarisation" of Legislation: Framework Laws and the Primacy of the Legislature' (2013) 9 *Utrecht Law Review* 106
—— 'Primacy of the European Legislature? Delegated Rule-Making and the Decline of the "Transmission Belt" Theory' (2014) 2 *The Theory and Practice of Legislation* 33
VanSickle-Ward, R, *The Devil Is in the Details: Understanding the Causes of Policy Specificity and Ambiguity* (Albany, SUNY Press, 2014)
Venice Commission, 'Report on the Rule of Law' (European Commission for Democracy Through Law – Rule of Law Checklist, published by the Venice Commission and the Council of Europe, 2011)
Voermans, W, 'Style of Legislation and Their Effects' (2011) 32 *Statute Law Review* 38
—— 'Implementation: The Achilles Heel of European Integration' (2014) 2 *Theory and Practice of Legislation* 343
—— 'Legislation and Regulation', in *Legislation in Europe: A Comprehensive Guide for Scholars and Practitioners* (Oxford, Hart Publishing, 2017)
Voermans, W, Stremler, M and Cliteur, P, *Constitutional Preambles: A Comparative Analysis* (Cheltenham, Edward Elgar Publishing, 2017)
Voermans, W, ten Napel, H-M and Passchier, R, 'Combining Efficiency and Transparency in Legislative Processes' (2015) 3 *Theory and Practice of Legislation* 279

'VW Scandal Highlights Unrealistic Lab Tests | Fleetcare' <www.fleetcare.com.au/news-info/fleet-beat-blog/october-2015/vw-scandal-highlights-unrealistic-lab-tests>
Wadhwa, V, 'Lawmakers Can't Keep Up with Technology' (*MIT Technology Review*) <www.technologyreview.com/view/526401/laws-and-ethics-cant-keep-pace-with-technology/>
Wagner-von Papp, F, 'A Law and Economics Perspective on Effective Legislation' (Conference: Effective Law and Regulation, Institute of Advanced Legal Studies, 7 July 2017)
Waldron, J, *The Dignity of Legislation* (Cambridge, Cambridge University Press, 1999)
—— 'Is the Rule of Law an Essentially Contested Concept (in Florida)?' in R Bellamy (ed), *The Rule of Law and Separation of Powers* (Farnham, Ashgate, 2005)
—— *The Rule of Law and the Measure of Property* (Cambridge, Cambridge University Press, 2012)
Warrington, J (tr), *Aristotle's Politics and the Athenian Constitution* (London, JM Dent, 1959)
Watkin, T, 'Consensus and the Constitution' [1994] *Ecclesiastical Journal* 232
—— 'Publication Review: Law and Theology in the Middle Ages' [2004] *Ecclesiastical Journal* 353
—— *The Legal History of Wales* 2nd edn (Cardiff, University of Wales Press, 2012)
—— 'Bilingual Legislation and the Law of England and Wales' (2014) 2 *Theory and Practice of Legislation* 229
—— 'Bilingual Legislation: Awareness, Ambiguity, and Attitudes' (2016) 37 *Statute Law Review* 116
Watson-Brown, A, 'Defining "Plain English" as an Aid to Legal Drafting' (2009) 30 *Statute Law Review* 85
Weiß, W, 'The Future of EU Executive Rulemaking' (2019) 44 *European Law Review* 337
Welsh Government, 'Senior Legislative Counsel (Deputy Director) Welsh Government Job Description and Person Specification' (2013)
Westerman, P, 'The Emergence of New Types of Norms' (Social Science Research Network 2006) SSRN Scholarly Paper ID 1609565 <https://papers.ssrn.com/sol3/papers.cfm?abstract_id=1609565>
—— *Outsourcing the Law: A Philosophical Perspective on Regulation* (Cheltenham, Edward Elgar Publishing, 2018)
What the Eye Says, 'The Shame of Britain's Binge Law Making' [2005] *Private Eye* 24
Whitley, E, 'On Technology Neutral Policies for E-Identity: A Critical Policy Based on UK Identity Policy' (2013) 8 *Journal of International Commercial Law and Technology* 134
Wilde, O, *The Picture of Dorian Gray* (New York, Modern Library, 2006)
Williams, C, 'The End of the "Masculine Rule"? Gender-Neutral Legislative Drafting in the United Kingdom and Ireland' (2008) 29 *Statute Law Review* 139
Williams, D, 'Extra-Statutory Concessions' [1979] *British Tax Review* 137
Wilson, C, 'Managing Increasing Government Expectations with Respect to Legislation While Maintaining Quality' [2009] *The Loophole* 21
Wolmarans, J, 'An Argument for Codification of Provincial Legislation and the Establishment of an Independent Legislative Services Agency for KwaZulu Natal' (August 2005)
World Bank, *Doing Business 2013: Smarter Regulations for Small and Medium-Sized Enterprises* (World Bank and International Finance Corporation, 2013)
Wyn-Jones, R, 'Let's All Play Welsh Legislation Bingo!' (*Institute of Welsh Affairs*, 31 March 2015) <www.iwa.wales/agenda/2015/03/lets-all-play-welsh-legislation-bingo/>
Xanthaki, H, 'Drafting Manuals and Quality in Legislation: Positive Contribution towards Certainty in the Law or Impediment to the Necessity for Dynamism of Rules?' (2010) 4 *Legisprudence* 111
—— 'Quality of Legislation: An Achievable Universal Concept or an Utopia Pursuit?' in L Mader and Marta Tavares de Almeida (eds), *Quality of Legislation: Principles and Instruments. Proceedings of the Ninth Congress of the International Association of Legislation in Lisbon, June 24–25, 2010* (Baden-Baden, Nomos, 2011)
—— 'Legislative Drafting: A New Sub-Discipline of Law Is Born' (2013) 1 *IALS Student Law Review* 57
—— *Drafting Legislation: Art and Technology of Rules for Regulation* 1st edn (Oxford, Hart Publishing, 2014)

Yeo, C, 'How Complex Are the UK Immigration Rules and Is This a Problem?' <www.freemovement.org.uk/how-complex-are-the-uk-immigration-rules-and-is-this-a-problem/?utm_source=rss&utm_medium=rss&utm_campaign=how-complex-are-the-uk-immigration-rules-and-is-this-a-problem&utm_source=FM+master+list&utm_campaign=f5aa408822-RSS_EMAIL_CAMPAIGN_DAILY&utm_medium=email&utm_term=0_792133aa40-f5aa408822-105097653&mc_cid=f5aa408822&mc_eid=bfe873d008>

Zamboni, M, 'Legislating Politics: An Introduction' (2008) 2 *Legisprudence* 155

—— 'Goals and Measures of Legislation', in *Legislation in Europe: A Comprehensive Guide for Scholars and Practitioners* (Oxford, Hart Publishing, 2017)

—— 'Legislative Policy and Effectiveness' (Conference: Effective Law and Regulation, Institute of Advanced Legal Studies, 7 July 2017)

Zander, M, *The Law-Making Process* 6th edn (Cambridge, Cambridge University Press, 2004)

INDEX

www.ingramcontent.com/pod-product-compliance
Ingram Content Group UK Ltd.
Pitfield, Milton Keynes, MK11 3LW, UK
UKHW020240290926
15470UKWH00002B/639

9 781509 938056